Mapping Borderless Higher Education
Policy, markets and competition

Brian Fleming Research & Learning Library
Ministry of Education
Ministry of Training, Colleges & Universities
900 Bay St. 13th Floor, Mowat Block
Toronto, ON M7A 1L2

Selected reports from
The Observatory on Borderless Higher Education

The Observatory on Borderless Higher Education
is a joint initiative of the
Association of Commonwealth Universities
and Universities UK

ASSOCIATION OF
COMMONWEALTH
UNIVERSITIES

Universities UK

'In the constantly changing world of global higher education, the Observatory provides critical analysis of policy and regulatory issues. Reports mapping trends and identifying key players in emerging markets provide unique insight for university leaders and government policy makers.'

> Sir Graeme Davies, Vice-Chancellor, University of London

'The Observatory provides a really important service to the busy and increasingly pressurised leaders in higher education. It targets the kind of information necessary to decision-making about the strategies fundamental to survival in a complex and fast changing HE landscape. Highly recommended.'

> Professor Brenda Gourley, Vice-Chancellor,
> The Open University, UK

'The Observatory provides some of the best in-depth analysis of key issues facing higher education worldwide - distance education, the for-profits, and marketization are all part of its purview.'

> Philip Altbach, Monan Professor of Higher Education,
> Boston College, USA

'I think the Observatory is an extremely interesting and helpful innovation in keeping one abreast of new developments in higher education around the world. I find it most helpful where there is clearly a lot happening, but not much up-to-date analysis, synthesis and reflection on its significance or implications for universities.'

> Lindsay Taiaroa, Executive Director, New Zealand
> Vice-Chancellors Committee

Mapping Borderless Higher Education
Policy, markets and competition

Selected reports from
The Observatory on Borderless Higher Education

The OBSERVATORY
on borderless higher education

www.obhe.ac.uk

© The Observatory on Borderless Higher Education

Published in 2004 by
The Association of Commonwealth Universities on behalf of
The Observatory on Borderless Higher Education

www.obhe.ac.uk

John Foster House
36 Gordon Square
London WC1H OPF

ISBN: 0 85143 187 9

All rights reserved.
No part of this publication may be reproduced, stored in a retrieval system, or transmitted, in any form or by any means, electronic, mechanical, photocopying, recording or otherwise, without the prior written permission of the Observatory.

Copies available from:
ACU Publication Sales
acusales@acu.ac.uk
Fax: +44 (0) 20 7387 2655

Price: £23

Discounted price for purchasers in developing contries: £18

Typeset and printed in Europe by the Alden Group, Oxford

Contents

About the Authors vii

Preface ix

Section I: Policy

Trade in Higher Education Services: the implications of GATS (March 2002*) 3
Jane Knight

GATS, Trade and Higher Education: perspective 2003 – where are we? (May 2003*) 39
Jane Knight

Quality Assurance and Borderless Higher Education: finding pathways through the maze (August 2003*) 89
Robin Middlehurst and Carolyn Campbell

The Rise and Regulation of For-Profit Higher Education (November 2003*) 154
Roger King

Section II: Competitors

Expanding Higher Education Capacity through Private Growth: contributions and challenges (January 2003*) 201
Daniel C. Levy

Corporate Universities: historical development, conceptual analysis and relations with public-sector higher education (July 2002*) 231
Scott Taylor and Rob Paton

Mapping the Education Industry, Part 1: public companies – share price and financial results (January 2003*) 271
Richard Garrett

Mapping the Education Industry, Part 2: public companies – relationships with higher education (February 2003*) 287
Richard Garrett

Section III: Market Analysis

Transnational Higher Education: major markets and emerging trends (November 2003*) 319
Richard Garrett and Line Verbik

Higher Education in China: context, scale and regulation of foreign activity (July 2003*) 372
Richard Garrett

*Indicates date reports were orginally published in electronic form on the OBHE website.

About the Authors

Svava Bjarnason is the Director of the Observatory on Borderless Higher Education and Head of Policy Research at the Association of Commonwealth Universities.

Carolyn Campbell is Assistant Director (International) at the UK Quality Assurance Agency for Higher Education.

Richard Garrett is Deputy Director of the Observatory.

Professor Roger King is Visiting Research Fellow at the Association of Commonwealth Universities in London and was previously Vice Chancellor of the University of Lincoln and Humberside, UK.

Dr Jane Knight is Adjunct Professor at the Ontario Institute for the Study of Education, University of Toronto, Canada.

Line Verbik is Research Officer at the Observatory.

Daniel C. Levy is Distinguished Professor at State University of New York, Department of Educational Administration and Policy Studies, University at Albany (SUNY), and Director of the Programme for Research into Private Higher Education (PROPHE), supported by the Ford Foundation.

Professor Robin Middlehurst is at the Centre for Policy and Change in Tertiary Education, University of Surrey, UK.

Dr Scott Taylor is a lecturer in organisational behaviour at Birmingham Business School, University of Birmingham.

Professor Rob Paton is Head of the Centre for Public Leadership and Social Enterprise at the Open University Business School, UK.

Acknowledgement

Commissioning and editing Observatory reports is the responsibility of the Director, Svava Bjarnason, and Deputy Director, Richard Garrett.

The Observatory would like to acknowledge the invaluable contribution of Sue Kirkland, from the Association of Commonwealth Universities, in providing technical and editorial expertise in publication of this book. Appreciation is also extended to Dugald MacLean and Line Verbik for their assistance.

Preface

This book contains a selection of reports that were originally published by the Observatory on Borderless Higher Education in 2002 and 2003. The reports were commissioned from acknowledged experts from the United States, the United Kingdom and Canada, to contribute to the understanding of the broad range of developments encompassed in 'borderless higher education'.

The reports selected for this volume represent only a fraction of the major Reports and Briefing Notes produced by the Observatory on Borderless Higher Education (OBHE) since its inception in 2001. Other Reports and Briefing Notes have examined a wide range of equally interesting and important issues, such as: the use of portals in universities; intellectual property rights; international branch campuses; institutional developments in e-learning; evolving relationships with the publishing sector and much more.

Background to the Observatory on Borderless Higher Education

The Observatory on Borderless Higher Education (OBHE) is an *international strategic information service*. It was initiated in 2001 by the Association of Commonwealth Universities (representing around 500 universities in 35 Commonwealth countries) and Universities UK, the representative body of the higher education sector in the United Kingdom. The Observatory was created following a recommendation from a landmark consulting report titled 'The Business of Borderless Education: UK Perspectives' (2000), commissioned by Universities UK (then the Committee of Vice Chancellors and Principals or CVCP) and the Higher Education Funding Council for England. The purpose of the consulting project was to review the scope and scale of what had been termed 'borderless' higher education (more on this later) and to endeavour to answer two questions: a) How significant and real are the challenges and opportunities for UK higher education institutions; and b) How might the sector and individual institutions respond?

The report concluded that:

"We consider that the drivers behind borderless developments are strong and will strengthen. As such the picture as it exists today is not a good predictor of the future. The opportunities are real and the threat, both direct and indirect, are already present." (Business of Borderless Education: UK Perspectives, 2000)

The authors of the report encouraged the CVCP (as was) to continue their leadership in tracking borderless higher education through the creation of an ongoing 'environmental scanning' mechanism that would provide regular intelligence and analyses. A 'scoping study' to determine how such a mechanism might be structured and whether the sector felt it would be of value, was undertaken in 2000. Following a positive response, the Observatory on Borderless Higher Education was established in 2001.

The term 'borderless higher education' was coined by a group of Australian academics in 1997 in a publication entitled *New Media and Borderless Higher Education: a review of the convergence between global media networks and higher education provision* (Cunningham et al.).[1] The Cunningham team used the term to describe a wide variety of educational provision that crossed what might be seen as 'traditional' boundaries. These included boundaries of:

- Time and space – enabling learners to study at a time and place convenient to them rather than in the traditional classroom;
- Level – the blurring of boundaries between higher, further and technical education, continuing professional development and lifelong learning.

---

[1] The Cunningham team was commissioned by the Australian government to undertake a second study exploring the developments of corporate universities in the United States at the same time as the UK team was researching the Business of Borderless Education. Their subsequent report helped to inform the findings of the UK report.

- Control – the growth of private (including for-profit higher education); corporate universities; public-private partnerships; and public universities operating private/for-profit entities.

The notion of 'borderless' is not just confined to time, space or level as there were further developments at play that served to blur boundaries that once might have been deemed 'traditional'. Growth in the use of new technologies in the education sphere heralded the potential for significant changes in the delivery of learning experiences. Increasing internationalization and globalisation, not only in education but in related sectors such as publishing and media companies and the corporate sector, were also creating new ways of understanding the boundaries between corporate education and more traditional education experiences. New providers were entering the fray, with considerable growth in private education providers – both for-profit and not-for-profit. All of these developments were implicated in the shift toward an increasingly 'borderless' terrain.

Along with these developments came the need for university leaders to have a clearer understanding of how such developments might impact the strategy, policy and provision of more traditionally bound institutions. National governments are actively changing their regulatory regimes to either attract or deter new providers, and encourage or constrain new modes of delivery; collaborative ventures amongst and between institutions and organisations are forming to provide a new global reach; students are increasingly liable to cover the costs of higher education and are becoming evermore concerned about the quality of their educational experience; and international organisations such as the World Trade Organisation are actively supporting trade in educational services. As the authors in the UK's *Business of Borderless Education* report argued, the pace of change was accelerating and the university sector could not afford to be complacent.

It was in this context that the Observatory was initiated. The purpose was to provide policy makers in institutions, government and other international bodies (e.g. UNESCO, World Bank, OECD) with regular strategic intelligence. The Observatory provides:

- *descriptive information* analysing news on the latest developments;
- *strategic information* attempting to explore rationales, decision-making processes and organisational change; and
- *reflection*, standing back from events to evaluate trends and implications.

In the early stages the Observatory focused on Commonwealth countries in acknowledgement of the support of the Association of Commonwealth Universities. However, this limitation very quickly became problematic and cumbersome as, by its nature, borderless higher education transcends such contexts. The research undertaken by the Observatory now embraces global developments with two major constraints – the language in which any research findings are published and the availability of data in the public domain. Constructive steps have been taken to address the issue of language with increased capability in-house as well as contracting with Associates covering most major geographical areas.

Following start-up funds from ACU, Universities UK and HEFCE, the Observatory moved to a subscription model in August 2002. The Observatory currently has over 120 institutional subscribers, including more than 80 universities, plus representative bodies, government departments and international NGOs. It is the OBHE's aim to continue to contribute to the research base and the ongoing conceptual understanding of borderless higher education as it evolves globally. This book is meant to contribute to that end, and to reach as wide an audience as possible.

Framework for the Publication

This book is the first hardcopy production from the Observatory on Borderless Higher Education. Its presence has been to date wholly web-based.[2] Access to Observatory material is, for the most part,

---

[2] See: Observatory on Borderless Higher Education, *Homepage*. Available at: www.obhe.ac.uk.

Preface

through a paid institutional subscription, with the website receiving some 6000 unique visits per month. It was felt appropriate and of value to put a selection of the reports into the public domain in book form. We do not wish to exacerbate the digital divide by denying access to our materials for those individuals without access to the internet. It was our belief that a hardcopy of the reports would be of interest to a significant number of individuals.

The framework for the book is set out in three main sections: the first explores the evolving regulatory and policy arena; the second examines the range of new providers operating in the broad area of higher education; and the final section looks at developments in selected transnational education markets.

The opening two chapters provide a framework for much of the discussion and debate on borderless education. The World Trade Organisation's attempt to liberalise global trade in services (including educational services), known as the General Agreement on Trade in Services (GATS) is a complex and potentially far-reaching regulatory mechanism. The author of the first two chapters, Jane Knight, is a leading international authority on the potential impact of the GATS on higher education. She has written two ground-breaking reports for the Observatory with a view to helping institutional leaders and government policy makers understand the complexity of the issues.

The first report was written in 2002 at a point when the GATS debate was only just beginning to surface in the higher education sector. The positions in the debate at that time were quite polarised. Some felt (and still do) that education is not a commodity that could or should be 'traded' in the same way as agricultural products or telecommunications; while others pointed to significant education-related trade and argued for the benefits of greater liberalisation. Dr Knight's first paper was written with a view to helping to 'unpack' the polarised debate from a relatively value-neutral position. Her second paper, written a year later, took our understanding further in examining different rationales for trade in education and exploring the potential impact this may have at national and international levels. The debate continues, and we believe that these two papers provide a sound grounding in understanding the issues at hand.

Growth in borderless higher education brings new challenges from a regulatory perspective. New providers and partnerships are entering the field and governments and consumers are becoming increasingly concerned about the quality of the educational experience and the potential reputational risk should due care and attention not be given in ensuring adequate provision. The co-authors of the third chapter, on quality assurance in this terrain, bring considerable experience in understanding the complexity and nuance of international quality assurance. Robin Middlehurst was formerly a Director of the UK's Higher Education Quality Assurance Agency and Carolyn Campbell is currently a Deputy Director of the UK Quality Assurance Agency with a remit for international activity.

As with the GATS debate, the use of language and terminology is crucial in discussing approaches to quality assurance. This third chapter clearly sets forth the differences between recognition of credit and qualifications, quality assurance of providers and accreditation of provision – three key elements of quality assurance that all too often are conflated or used interchangeably. There are numerous, and often overlapping, initiatives in place or under development to help consumers (students, parents, institutions) identify which institutions or providers of educational experiences are 'recognised', by who, in what way and on what authority. The authors explore in detail a number of trends and go on to outline some of the emerging tensions given the various vested interests.

The fourth and fifth chapters in this book concern the growth in private higher education providers – both for-profit and not-for-profit. The first of these two chapters is written by Roger King and examines the various approaches taken by governments to regulate for-profit providers. Too frequently the immediate connotation attributed to 'for-profit' is that the organisation exists simply to make money and that inherently this means a poorer quality learning experience. This is patently NOT the case, although sadly there are instances where it has been proven to be so, thus

Preface

perpetuating the myth. The argument is put forward that it is impossible to typify a for-profit provider and therefore what is required is a purposeful approach to policy making that addresses the heterogeneity of such providers.

Professor King articulates the various regulatory models that are currently in use internationally and identifies some of the tensions inherent in selecting any one approach over another. He argues for a "regulatory pluralism" that enables countries to experience the potential beneficial aspects of a healthy and vibrant for-profit sector while balancing the public good of maintaining an equally healthy and vibrant public not-for-profit sector.

The fifth chapter (the first in section two examining new providers and partnerships), follows logically from the previous chapter as it outlines the growth of private higher education globally. The chapter's author, Dan Levy leads the US-based Program for Research into Private Higher Education, which is supported by the Ford Foundation. Professor Levy's chapter exemplifies the heterogeneity of private providers with a particular perspective on how the enhancement of national higher education capacity. He characterises at least two types of expansion: more of the same (i.e. the introduction of institutions that 'look' much like existing public providers in shape and delivery) and differentiation (i.e. new modes of delivery that are often niche oriented).

The chapter also identifies particular challenges that arise from an exponential rise in private higher education. These challenges echo the issues addressed in our opening chapters, namely:

- competition to existing providers and the creation of an increasingly active 'market place' for higher education;
- consumer concerns about the quality of provision and the legitimacy of the providers;
- regulatory concerns to ensure adequate guidelines on recognition accreditation.

The chapter closes with the acknowledgement that private higher education is likely to increase in the coming decade and suggests that as the sector matures differentiation between public and private might begin to blur.

In the late 1990s there was considerable heralding of an explosion of so-called 'corporate universities' – particularly in the US. This was yet another example of what once were traditional boundaries (between corporate training and higher education) which were beginning to merge. The OBHE wanted to know whether this was the case – were corporate universities going to threaten the purview of traditional university business and management programmes, or was it yet more hype? The answer, provided by Scott Taylor and Rob Patton, from the UK's Open University Business School, was 'it depends'. The authors were undertaking a study tracing the historical development of the corporate university with a view to providing a conceptual map of the various types of provision prevalent in Europe. They also wanted to know what kinds of relationship were evolving between corporate universities and traditional universities.

The authors identified three possible types of relationships in which corporate universities and traditional universities might engage. They could be competitors for lucrative markets; they could be collaborators joining forces and resources; or a third, hybrid relationship could develop that allowed the two to co-exist in harmony.

One of the Observatory's primary aims is to undertake work in areas that are still emerging and have not, as yet, been thoroughly researched. The Observatory's Deputy Director, Richard Garrett leads the in-house research that underpins the writing of our regularly published 'Briefing Notes'. The remaining chapters reflect the range of research initiated by the Deputy Director.

'Mapping the Education Industry' is the theme of the next two chapters. The purpose of the research underpinning these reports was to begin to track publicly traded companies operating in the broad area of higher education and to assess their viability, business models and relationships with non-profit higher education. The first report focused on 50 publicly traded companies,

Preface

approximately half from the US and the balance from ten other countries. The companies represented a wide range of activities including e-learning firms, publishing houses and companies operating for-profit universities. Stock prices were tracked over a ten-year period and financial results over three years. The resulting analysis is now known as the 'Global Education Index'.[3]

The second chapter on this theme (Part II) focused on relationships between (largely) the same 50 companies and the traditional higher education sector. Was there evidence to suggest that these companies were posing a threat in terms of directly competing for students? Or was there a more collaborative relationship emerging? The findings suggest that the pattern of relationship is essentially collaborative or complementary – but how might this change over time? The 2004 analysis can be found on the Observatory website.

There is very little reliable data on the transnational activities of higher education institutions worldwide, even less that represents the activities of an entire national sector. The third and final section of this book provides an initial mapping of developments in transnational higher education; that is provision whereby the provider moves across borders either through setting up some form of branch campus or through a partnership with a local organisation.

The penultimate chapter explores transnational activities in two markets, namely Hong Kong and Singapore. There is also discussion of the activities of the transnational activities of Australian universities which are perhaps the most active in the world in this area. Line Verbik, Research Officer at the Observatory is the co-author of this chapter.

The final chapter brings together many of the threads interwoven throughout this book: education as a tradable commodity, regulation of private and foreign providers; quality assurance and new and emerging collaborations. Over the past five years, China has

---

[3] The Global Education Index has been updated in 2004 and can be found at www.obhe.ac.uk/products/reports/

surfaced as the target market for numerous national and institutionally driven transnational initiatives. The regulatory landscape has shifted dramatically in the recent past and it has become clear that China is open for (higher) education business.

There are two parts to this chapter as well. The first examines in some detail the regulatory situation with regard to foreign providers in China. Over the past ten years the Chinese government has welcomed foreign providers with a view to building capacity for mass higher education. While legislation exists to regulate foreign providers, legal authority is considerably devolved, leading to confusion over what is permitted and by whom.

The second half of the chapter goes on to provide working examples of institutions and institutional partnerships offering provision in China. Evidence shows that as the market matures there is a notable shift in the types of Sino-foreign partnerships from loose relatively unstructured alliances to more formal partnerships including the establishment of independent or semi-independent institutions. Findings suggest that current provision is still relatively limited in terms of the mix of courses on offer with business studies, accountancy, IT, English and law predominant.

In Conclusion

As the authors of the 'Business of Borderless Education' predicted, "*borderless developments are strong and will strengthen*". It is critically important that government and institutional leaders base higher education policy and strategy on sound empirical evidence. How might borderless development impact decision-making on behalf of their country through GATS negotiations or in instigating regulatory measures; or their institution in determining which markets or partnerships are potentially most viable? The Observatory on Borderless Higher Education provides an unrivalled service in its role as an 'international strategic information service', as this book exemplifies.

Svava Bjarnason
June 2004

Section I: Policy

Trade in Higher Education Services: *the implications of GATS*

Jane Knight

1 Introduction

This report is about the impact of trade liberalization on higher education services. Particular emphasis is placed on the implications of the General Agreement on Trade in Services (GATS) on borderless or transnational education. The paper focuses more on the education policy implications emanating from the GATS, than on the actual trade issues. The primary audience is higher education institutions in the Commonwealth.

The purpose of the report is to focus attention on GATS and higher education. The liberalization of trade in education services is high on the agenda of trade negotiators but is only just appearing on the radar screen of higher education managers and policy makers. This report aims to:

- to position trade in higher education services on the agenda of educators
- to provide information on the GATS and raise awareness about potential policy implications
- to stimulate debate and analysis of the risks and opportunities of increased trade in education services

There are definite limits to the scope and depth of analysis such a report can bring to the complex issue of trade in higher education services, especially given the diversity of countries in the Commonwealth. The objective for preparing such a report for the Observatory on Borderless Higher Education will be met if readers are stimulated to think about the potential positive and negative outcomes of increased trade in higher education services and enter informed debate on the policy implications for higher education.

1.1 Context

The demand for higher and adult education, especially professionally related courses and non-traditional delivery modes, is increasing in most countries. This is due to: the growth of the knowledge economy, movement to lifelong learning and changing demographics. While demand is growing, the capacity of the public sector to satisfy the demand is being challenged. This is due to budget limitations, the changing role of government, and increased emphasis on market economy and privatization.

At the same time, innovations in information and communication technologies are providing alternate and virtual ways to deliver higher education.[1] New types of providers such as corporate universities, for-profit institutions, media companies are emerging. This scenario is changing further by providers-public and private, new and traditional-delivering education services across national

---

[1] Cunningham, S. *et al.* (2000) *The Business of Borderless Education*, Department of Education, Training and Youth Affairs, Canberra, Australia.

borders to meet the need in other countries.[2] Alternative types of cross border program delivery such as branch campuses, franchise and twinning arrangements are being developed. As a result, an exciting, but rather complex, picture of higher education provision is emerging. So what?

It is important to ask 'so what'. Many educators would point out that demand for higher education has been steadily increasing for years and that academic mobility for students, scholars, teachers and knowledge has been an integral aspect of higher education for centuries. This is true. But the picture is changing. Now, not only are more people moving; academic programs and providers are also moving across borders. Economic rationales are increasingly driving a large part of the international or cross border supply of education. This commercial or profit motive is a reality today, and applies to both private providers and in some cases public institutions. In short, the business side of borderless education is growing and is a target of the GATS. It is therefore important that educators are cognizant of the impact of trade liberalization on higher education and are taking steps to maximize the benefits and minimize the threats to a robust and quality higher education system.

1.2 Terminology

Transnational[3] and borderless education are terms that are being used to describe real or virtual movement of students, teachers, knowledge and academic programs from one country to another. While there may be some conceptual differences between these terms, they are often used interchangeably. For the purposes of this discussion, borderless[4] education will be used in its broadest sense. The term cross border education is also used because in

---

[2] CVCP (2000). *The Business of Borderless Education: UK Perspectives.* Committee of Vice-Chancellors and Principles. London, United Kingdom.
[3] Davis, D. *et al.* (2000) *Transnational Education Providers, Partners and Policy.* IDP Education Australia. Brisbane, Australia.
[4] CVCP (2000). *The Business of Borderless Education: UK Perspectives.* Committee of Vice-Chancellors and Principles. London, United Kingdom.

many cases it is necessary to capture the importance and relevance of geographic and jurisdictional borders.

The term internationalization refers to the process of integrating an international dimension into the teaching, research and service functions of higher education institutions.[5] Its use has been more closely linked to the academic value of international activities than to the economic motive. In fact, recently the term 'non-profit' internationalization' has been coined to distinguish international education from trade in education services. The liberalization of trade is interpreted to mean the removal of barriers to promote increased cross border movement of educational services. Finally, in this report higher education refers to post secondary degree, certificate and diploma level of education.

1.3 About the Report

The report is intended for university managers, administrators and academics who want a shorthand version of what GATS is about and how it can affect higher education. The current debate on the impact of GATS is rather polarized. Critics focus on the threat to the government role, 'public good' and quality aspects of higher education. Supporters highlight the benefits that more trade can bring in terms of innovation through new delivery systems and providers, greater student access and economic value. This report tries to take a balanced approach by identifying both the risks and opportunities that GATS can bring to the higher education sector. The emphasis is on policy issues and implications rather than the size of the market, trade issues per se or the legal and technical aspects of the agreement itself. All members of the World Trade Organization (WTO) are involved which means that 144 countries are covered by the GATS. Clearly countries are affected differently.

---

[5] Knight, Jane (1999) *A Time of Turbulence and Transformation for Internationalization*. Research Monograph Canadian Bureau for International Education. Ottawa, Canada No. 14.

The report is divided into the following sections:

- Overview of GATS: This section gives a brief introduction to the structure, principles and purpose of GATS.
- Commitments to date: A review of the current commitments countries have made to liberalize trade in education services is presented in part two. A brief analysis of the negotiating proposals submitted by Australia, New Zealand and the United States is included.
- Trade barriers: The aim of the GATS is to promote trade. This involves eliminating or decreasing measures that inhibit the flow of services. Section three discusses some of the major barriers identified as impediments to trade in education services.
- Policy Implications: This section focuses on policy issues related to trade in higher education services. This includes – the role of government, student access, funding, regulation of providers, quality assurance and intellectual property.
- Moving forward: Several international governance bodies and non-governmental organizations (NGOs) are taking steps to deal with the implications of GATS. The last section highlights these actions, provides a summary of the significant dates and activities in the official GATS negotiations and urges educators to be better informed on the opportunities and risks associated with trade in higher education services.

2 Overview of GATS

It is easy to be overwhelmed with the legal and technical complexities of the GATS. The purpose of this section is to provide a clear and concise explanation of GATS and to review some of the key and more controversial articles of the agreement. Readers who are familiar with the basic structure and principles of GATS may want to skip the first four sections that provide background information and focus on section 2.5 that addresses the more controversial aspects of the agreement.

2.1 Structure and Purpose of GATS

The GATS is the first ever set of multilateral rules covering international trade in services. Previous international trade agreements covered trade in products, but never services. The GATS was negotiated in the Uruguay Round and came into effect in 1995. It is administered by the World Trade Organization (WTO) which is made up of 144 member countries. The World Trade Organization (WTO) is the only global international organization dealing with the rules of trade between nations. At its heart are the WTO agreements, negotiated and signed by the majority of the world's trading nations and ratified in their parliaments. The GATS is one of these key agreements and is a legally enforceable set of rules.[6]

The GATS has three parts. The first part is the framework that contains the general principles and rules. The second part consists of the national schedules that list a country's specific commitments on access to their domestic market by foreign providers. The third part consists of annexes which detail specific limitations for each sector can be attached to the schedule of commitments. This will be discussed in more detail later, but first it is essential to understand what kind of education services will be covered by GATS and what is meant by higher education services.

2.2 Modes of Trade in Services

The GATS defines four ways in which a service can be traded, known as 'modes of supply'.[7] These four modes of trade apply to all service sectors in GATS. Chart 1 provides a generic definition for each mode, applies them to the education sector and comments on the relative size of the market supply and demand. It is important to

---

[6] WTO (1999) *The WTO in Brief*. Prepared by the WTO Secretariat. Geneva Switzerland. Available at: www.wto.org/english/thewto_e/whatis_e/whatis_e.htm. Last Accessed 22 April 2004.
[7] WTO. *The General Agreement in Trade in Services – objectives, coverage and disciplines.* Prepared by the WTO Secretariat. Available at: www.wto.org/english/tratop_e/serv_e/gatsqa_e.htm. Last Accessed 22 April 2004.

Trade in Higher Education Services 9

note that the current use of the term 'borderless education' covers all four modes of supply.

Chart 1 Mode of Supply

Mode of Supply According to GATS	Explanation	Examples in Higher Education	Size /Potential of market
1. Cross Border Supply	–the provision of a service where the service crosses the border (does not require the physical movement of the consumer)	–distance education –e-learning –virtual universities	–currently a relatively small market –seen to have great potential through the use of new ICTs and especially the Internet
2. Consumption Abroad	–provision of the service involving the movement of the consumer to the country of the supplier	–students who go to another country to study	–currently represents the largest share of the global market for education services
3. Commercial Presence	–the service provider establishes or has presence of commercial facilities in another country in order to render service	–local branch or satellite campuses –twinning partnerships –franchising arrangements with local institutions	–growing interest and strong potential for future growth –most controversial as it appears to set international
4. Presence of Natural Persons	–persons travelling to another country on a temporary basis to provide service	–professors, teachers, researchers working abroad	–potentially a strong market given the emphasis on mobility of professionals

2.3 Categories of Education Services

Trade in education is organized into five categories or sub-sectors of service. These categories are based on the United Nations Provisional Central Product Classification (CPC)[8] and are described in Chart 2. The three categories that are most relevant to this report are 'higher', 'adult' and 'other'. The four modes of service described above apply to each of the categories.

---

[8] WTO The Services Sectoral Classification List, World Trade Organization. Prepared by WTO Secretariat. Document MTN.GNS/W/120. Available at: www.wto.org/english/tratop_e/serv_e/sanaly_e.htm. Last Accessed 22 April 2004.

Chart 2 Classification System for Education Services

Category of education service	Education activities included in each category	Notes
Primary Education (CPC 921)	–pre-school and other primary education services –does not cover child-care services	
Secondary Education (CPC 922)	–general higher secondary –technical and vocational secondary –also covers technical and vocational services for the disabled	
Higher Education (CPC 923)	–post secondary technical and vocational education services –other higher education services leading to university degree or equivalent	–types of education (i.e., business, liberalarts, science) are not specified –assumes that all post secondary training and education programs are covered
Adult Education (CPC 924)	–covers education for adults outside the regular education system	–further delineation is needed
Other Education (CPC 929)	–covers all other education services not elsewhere classified –excludes education services related to recreation matters	–needs clarification re coverage and differentiation from other categories –for example- are education and language testing services, student recruitment services, quality assessment covered?

Critics of this classification system believe that it does not reflect the reality of today where non-traditional and private providers exist and alternate forms of delivery using new technologies are being used. However, countries are able to add their own qualifications or supplements to the UN CPC classification scheme and therefore, in principle, should not be limited by the scheme.

2.4 Key Elements and Rules of the GATS

The overall framework contains a number of general obligations applicable to all trade in services regardless of whether a country has made a specific commitment to sectors or not. These are called unconditional obligations. Fundamental to this discussion is the Most Favoured Nation (MFN) rule.

Each WTO member lists in its national schedules those services for which it wishes to provide access to foreign providers. In addition to choosing which service sector/s will be committed, each country

Trade in Higher Education Services

determines the extent of commitment by specifying the level of market access and the degree of national treatment they are prepared to guarantee. Chart 3 lists the key elements[9] of the GATS and provides brief explanatory notes.

Chart 3 Key Elements and Rules

GATS Element or Rule	Explanation	Application	Issues
Coverage	All internationally traded services are covered in the 12 different service sectors. (e.g. education, transportation, financial, tourism, health, construction)	Applies to all services with two exceptions: i) services provided in the exercise of governmental authority ii) air traffic rights	Major debate on what the term "exercise of governmental authority" means.
Measures	All laws, regulations and practices from national, regional or local government that may affect trade	A generic term that applies to all sectors	
General or Unconditional obligations	Four unconditional obligations exist in GATS. • most favoured nation (mfn) • transparency • dispute settlement • monopolies	They apply to all service sectors regardless of whether it is a scheduled commitment or not	Attention needs to be given to "most favoured nation"
Most favoured nation (MFN) treatment	Requires equal and consistent treatment of all foreign trading partners MFN means treating one's trading partners equally. Under GATS, if a country allows foreign competition in a sector, equal opportunities in that sector should be given to service providers from all WTO members. This also applies to mutual exclusion treatment For instance, if a foreign provider establishes branch campus in Country A, then Country A must permit all WTO members the same opportunity/ treatment. Or if Country A chooses to exclude Country B from providing a specific service, then all WTO members are excluded.	May apply even if the country has made no specific commitment to provide foreign access to their markets. Exemptions, for a period of 10 years, are permissible	MFN has implications for those countries who already are engaged in trade in educational services and/or who provide access to foreign education providers MFN is not the same as national treatment

---

[9] WTO *The General Agreement in Trade in Services – objectives, coverage and disciplines.* Prepared by the WTO Secretariat. Available at: www.wto.org/english/tratop_e/serv_e/gatsqa_e.htm. Last Accessed 22 April 2004.

Chart 3 Continued

Conditional obligations	There are a number of conditional obligations attached to national schedules: -market access -national treatment	Only applies to commitments listed in national schedules Degree and extent of obligation is determined by country	GATS supporters believe that a country's national educational objectives are protected by these two obligations
National Treatment	Requires equal treatment for foreign and domestic providers Once a foreign supplier has been allowed to supply a service in one's country there should be no discrimination in treatment between the foreign and domestic providers.	Only applies where a country has made a specific commitment Exemptions are allowed	GATS critics believe that this can put education as a 'public good' at risk.
Market Access	Means the degree to which market access is granted to foreign providers in specified sectors Market access may be subject to one or more of six types of limitations defined by GATS agreement	Each country determines limitations on market access for each committed sector	
Progressive Liberalization	GATS has a built in agenda which means that with each round of negotiations there is further liberalization of trade in service. This means more sectors are covered and more trade limitations are removed.	Applies to all sectors and therefore includes education	
Bottom-up and Top-down approach	Bottom up approach refers to the fact that each country determines the type and extent of its commitments for each sector Top down approach refers to the main rules and obligations as well as the progressive liberalization agenda, there will be increasing pressure to remove trade barriers.		Sceptics maintain that the top down approach will have increasing importance and impact thereby increasing pressure to liberalize

2.5 Controversial Questions and Issues Related to Higher Education

The GATS is described as a voluntary agreement because countries can decide which sectors they will agree to cover under GATS rules. This is done through the preparation of their national schedules of commitments and through the 'request-offer' negotiation rounds. However, there are aspects of the agreement that question its voluntary nature, notably the built in progressive liberalization agenda and other elements described in this section.

Which education services are covered or exempted?
Probably, the most controversial and critical issue related to the agreement is the meaning of Article 1.3.[10] This article defines which services are covered or exempted.

According to the WTO, the agreement is deemed to apply to all measures affecting services *except* "those services supplied in the exercise of governmental authority". But what does 'exercise of governmental authority' mean? GATS supporters maintain that education provided and funded by the government is therefore exempted. Sceptics question the broad interpretation of the clause and ask for more a detailed analysis. The agreement states that "in the exercise of governmental authority" means the service is provided on a 'non-commercial basis' and 'not in competition' with other service suppliers. This begs the follow-up question-what is meant by non-commercial basis and not in competition? These issues are at the heart of much of the debate about which services are covered.

Education critics of the GATS maintain that due to the wide-open interpretation of 'non-commercial' and 'not in competition' terms, the public sector/government service providers may not in fact be exempt. The situation is especially complicated in those countries where there is a mixed public/private higher education system or

---

[10] WTO *The General Agreement in Trade in Services Text*. Available at: www.wto.org/english/tratop_e/serv_e/1-scdef_e.htm. Last Accessed 22 April 2004.

where a significant amount of funding for public institutions in fact comes from the private sector. Another complication is that a public education institution in an exporting country is often defined as private/commercial when it crosses the border and delivers in the importing country. Therefore, one needs to question what 'non-commercial' really means in terms of higher education trade.

The debate about what 'not in competition' means is fuelled by the fact that there does not appear to be any qualifications or limits on the term.[11] For instance, if non-government providers (private non-profit or commercial) are delivering services, are they deemed to be in competition with government providers? In this scenario, public providers may be defined as being 'in competition' by the mere existence of non-governmental providers. Does the method of delivery influence or limit the concept of 'in competition'? Does the term cover situations where there is a similar mode of delivery, or for instance, does this term mean that public providers using traditional face-to-face classroom methods could be seen to be competing with foreign for-profit e-learning providers?

There are many unanswered questions that need clarification. Supporters of the GATS emphasize that education is to a large extent a government function and that the agreement does not seek to displace the public education systems and the right of government to regulate and meet domestic policy objectives. Others express concern that the whole question of the protection of public services is very uncertain and potentially at risk in view of the narrow interpretation of what governmental authority means and a wide-open interpretation of what 'not in competition' and 'non-commercial basis' mean. Clearly, the question – which higher and adult education 'services exercised in governmental authority' are exempted from GATS – needs to be front and centre in the debate on the risks and opportunities associated with the agreement.

---

[11] Gottlieb and Pearson (2001) *GATS Impact on Education in Canada. Legal Opinion.* Prepared for the Canadian Association of University Teachers. Ottawa, Canada. Available at: www.caut.ca/english/issues/trade/gats-opinion.asp. Last Accessed 22 April 2004.

What does the principle of progressive liberalization mean?
GATS is not a neutral agreement. It aims to promote and enforce the liberalization of trade in services. The process of progressive liberalization involves two aspects – extending GATS coverage to more service sectors and decreasing the number and extent of measures that serve as impediments to increased trade. Therefore, in spite of the right of each country to determine the extent of its commitments, with each new round of negotiations, countries are expected to add sectors or sub-sectors to their national schedules of commitments and to negotiate the further removal of limitations on market access and national treatment.

The intention of GATS is to facilitate and promote ever-more opportunities for trade. Therefore, countries that are not interested in either the import or export of education services will most likely experience greater pressures to allow market access to foreign providers. GATS is a very new instrument and it is too soon to predict the reality or extent of these potential opportunities or risks.

What are the implications of negotiating across sectors?
At the 'request-offer' stage of the process, there are bilateral negotiations on market access and national treatment commitments. The key point at this step, is that sectors for which access is sought do not have to correspond to those for which requests are made. So country A may request of Country B greater access to transportation services. Country B can respond by requesting access to education services. It is up to each country as to where they are willing to make concessions on foreign access to domestic markets. This situation applies to all sectors and may be of greatest concern to countries, developing or developed, who have not made commitments to open up education services and might therefore consider their education service sector vulnerable to negotiating deals across sectors.

These issues relate to the mechanics and legalities of the agreement itself. Each one raises questions that need further clarification and analysis and collectively they serve to wave the red flag that more attention needs to be given to these matters.

There are other aspects of the GATS, such as the dispute mechanism, subsidies, treatment of monopolies which are controversial and apply to all sectors and which need further study. Article 6.4, which addresses measures relating to qualification requirements and procedures, technical standards and licensing requirements may have serious implications for education and requires further clarification. It must be remembered that GATS is still an untested agreement and a certain amount of confusion exists on how to interpret the major rules and obligations. It took many years to iron out the inconsistencies in the General Agreement on Tariffs and Trade (GATT) and the same will likely be true for GATS. While trade specialists and lawyers need to review the technical and legal aspects of the agreement, it is educators who need to study how the agreement applies to and impacts education services.

3 Commitments to Trade in Education Services

3.1 Extent of Country Commitments

The education sector is one of the least committed sectors. The reason is not clear, but perhaps it can be attributed to the need for countries to strike a balance between pursuing domestic education priorities and exploring ways in which trade in education services can be further liberalized. Or it could be linked to the fact that to date, education, in general, has taken a very low priority in the major bilateral agreements and rightly or wrongly, the same may be true for the GATS.

Only 44 of the 144 WTO Members have made commitments to education, and only 21 of these have included commitments to higher education.[12] It is interesting to note that Congo, Lesotho,

---

[12] WTO (1998). *Education Services. Background Note* by the Secretariat. Council for Trade in Services. Geneva, Switzerland. S/C/W/49, 98-3691. Available at: www.wto.org/english/tratop_e/serv_e/sanaly_e.htm. Last Accessed 22 April 2004.

Jamaica and Sierra Leone have made full unconditional commitments in higher education, perhaps with the intent of encouraging foreign providers to help develop their educational systems. Australia's commitment for higher education covers provision of private tertiary education services, including university level. The European Union has included higher education in their schedule with clear limitations on all modes of trade except 'consumption abroad', which generally means foreign tuition paying students. Only three (USA, New Zealand, Australia) of the 21 countries with higher education commitments have submitted a negotiating proposal outlining their interests and issues. The next section provides a brief summary of key elements of the three proposals.

3.2 Analysis of Negotiating Proposals

The purpose of Chart 4 is to provide a comparison of some of the key issues identified by the three countries. It is interesting to note that all three acknowledge the role of government as funder, regulator and provider of education services. A comparison of the rationales and benefits of freer trade in education services reveals different perspectives and raises key issues.

Role of government
It is clear that all three proposals acknowledge the central role government plays in higher education. Perhaps the controversy about which public services are exempted from the GATS has prompted this explicit recognition of the government role. Some are comforted and appeased by these statements. Others are even more concerned about the potential erosion of the role of government in higher education provision and the setting of domestic policy objectives.

In some countries, education is decentralized from national to provincial or state governmental bodies. Private education, though nominally under state authority, may not be primarily governed or regulated by a government. These situations further illustrate the complexities involved in determining which services are exempted from GATS coverage and the very different impact GATS will have on individual countries.

Chart 4 Highlights of Negotiation Proposals

	Australia[13]	New Zealand[14]	United States[15]
Role of Government	–government has a role in the financing, delivery and regulation of higher education – either alone or in partnership with individuals, NGOs and private education –governments must retain their sovereign right to determine own domestic funding and regulatory policies/measures	–international trade in education services can supplement and support national education policy objectives (i.e. reduce the infrastructure commitments required of governments and so free resources for other aspects of education policy) –the reduction of barriers does not equate to an erosion of core public education systems and standards	–the principle that governments should retain the right to regulate to meet domestic policy objectives should be respected –in education service sector, governments will continue to play important roles as suppliers of service –"education to a large extent is a government function and it does not seek to displace public education systems. It seeks to supplement public education systems"
Rationale/ Purpose of Trade Liberalization	–means of providing individuals in all countries with access to wide range of education options	–education as a role in economic and social development –in New Zealand, education exports are the fourth largest service sector export earner and fifteenth largest foreign exchange earner overall.	–help upgrade knowledge and skills through training and education, while respecting each country's role in prescribing and administering appropriate public education for its citizens.

---

[13] WTO (2001) *Communication from Australia. Negotiating Proposal for Education Services.* Council for Trade in Services. WTO. Document S/CSS/W/110. Available at: www.wto.org/english/tratop_e/serv_e/s_propnewnegs_e.htm. Last Accessed 22 April 2004.

[14] WTO (2001) *Communication from New Zealand. Negotiating Proposal for Education Services.* Council for Trade in Services. WTO. Document S/CSS/W/93. Available at: www.wto.org/english/tratop_e/serv_e/s_propnewnegs_e.htm. Last Accessed 22 April 2004.

[15] WTO (2000) *Communication from the United States. Higher (Tertiary) Education, Adult Education, and Training.* Council for Trade in Services. WTO. Document S/CSS/W/93. Available at: www.wto.org/english/tratop_e/serv_e/s_propnewnegs_e.htm. Last Accessed 22 April 2004.

Chart 4 Continued

Benefits of Trade Liberalization	–increased access to education in qualitative and quantitative terms that would otherwise not be available in country of origin –competitive stimulus with flow-on benefits to all students –effecient encouragment of internationalization and flow of students.	–in addition to generating revenue for private and state sector education institutions and Member economies, there are benefits at individual, institutional and societal level through: –academic exchange –increased cross-cultural linkages –technological transfer –increased access for members	–these services constitute a growing, international business, supplementing the public education system and contributing to global spread of the modern "knowledge economy" –benefits of this growth help to develop more efficient work force, leading countries to an improved competitive position in the world economy
Public/Private Mix		least committed service sectors due to recognition of its "public good" element and the high degree of government involvement in its provision	–private education co-exists with public domain –private education and training will continue to supplement, not displace public education systems

Rationales and benefits

The rationales that drive further liberalization differ from country to country. Australia stresses greater access for students, New Zealand points to economic and social benefits and the USA focuses on opportunities for new knowledge and skills. Benefits are closely linked to rationales. Australia believes that the competition inherent in more trade will have flow-on benefits to students. New Zealand emphasizes that in addition to revenue generation there are benefits at the individual, institutional and societal level through academic exchange, technological transfer and cross-cultural linkages. The USA highlights the contribution to global spread of the modern knowledge economy and improved competitiveness. It is not a surprise that the economic benefits are emphasized but it is noteworthy that social and academic value to individuals, institutions and society are not totally overlooked. More work is needed to understand and analyse the perceived rationale and benefits as this will lead to a clearer picture of what countries expect from increased import and export in education. Of course, expectations can be seen in terms of desirable or undesirable results. A better understanding of anticipated outcomes would assist in the development of policies to help achieve or prevent them. At the same time, it is equally important to be mindful of 'unintended consequences'.

Public/private mix
The public/private mix of higher and adult education provision is implicitly and explicitly recognized in the proposals. It is interesting to note that New Zealand suggests that education may be one of the least committed service sectors due to the recognition of its 'public good' element and the high degree of government involvement in its provision. The USA is more pointed when they state that private education co-exists with the public domain and will continue to supplement, not displace public education systems. There are mixed reactions to this statement and a great deal of uncertainty as to how the GATS will affect the balance of a mixed system, especially given the individualized nature of mixed systems.

Further analysis needed
Further analysis of the factors driving commitments or the lack of commitments in higher education is needed. There are diverse perspectives on the number and substance of commitments because countries have different national policy objectives and therefore different goals and expectations from trade in education services.

For example, a consumer oriented rationale can be interpreted as the need to provide a wider range of opportunities to consumers, or the need to protect consumers by assuring appropriate levels of access and quality. The economic rationale can be understood as a way to increase trade revenues for exporting countries or seen as a means to attract additional investment for education for importing countries. Others see the economic rationale as sabotaging the social development goals of education, or even scientific enquiry and scholarship. Any number of issues can be used to illustrate the debate and the dichotomy of opinions on the rationales and benefits of increased trade in education. Differences exist between and within countries and certainly among education groups as well. Further debate and analysis is necessary so that an informed position is taken on why or why not trade liberalization is attractive to an individual country and how trade agreements help or hinder achieving national goals and global interests.

Developing country interests
The voices of developing countries need to be heard so that the benefits and risks associated with increased trade are clear and do not undermine national efforts to develop and enhance domestic higher education. However, the voices and interests of the developing countries differ. The opportunity to have foreign suppliers provide increased access to higher and adult education programs or to invest in the infrastructure for education provision is attractive to some. The threat of foreign dominance or exploitation of a national system and culture is expressed by others. Trade liberalization for whose benefit or at what cost are key questions.

Quality and accreditation are at the heart of much debate. The importance of frameworks for licensing, accreditation, qualification recognition and quality assurance are important for all countries, whether they are importing and exporting education services. Developing countries have expressed concern about their capacity to have such frameworks in place in light of the push toward trade liberalization and increased cross border delivery of education.

The GATS is one of many factors and instruments encouraging greater mobility of professionals. Although the agreement focuses on temporary movement of the labour force, it may lead to and facilitate permanent migration as well. The implications of increased mobility of teachers and researchers are particularly relevant to developing countries. It will be a major challenge to improve education systems if well-qualified professionals and graduates are attracted to positions in other countries.

At the root of the impact of GATS on developing countries is the fundamental issue of capacity to participate effectively in the global trading system and to be equal members in the WTO. Strong feelings exist about the potential for trade rules to make poor countries poorer, instead of narrowing the gap between developed and developing countries. The perceived injustice that poor nations are expected to remove trade barriers while rich nations retain barriers on certain goods, contributes to the strong reactions of some developing countries about the impact of GATS in general.

4 Barriers

Identification of the barriers to trade in higher education services is fundamental because it is the elimination of these barriers which is the *raison d'être* of GATS. There are some barriers that are applicable to all sectors. There are other impediments that are specific to the education services sector. The following two sections list some of the generic barriers and also those most relevant to the four modes of trade in education. The sources used to identify these barriers are the three negotiating proposals described above, reports by non-governmental organizations[16] (NGOs) and intergovernmental bodies[17], and by the WTO itself. This is a comprehensive collection of perceived barriers, not a list of the most significant ones. There is no agreement or consensus on which barriers are the most critical as they are usually seen from a self-interest perspective. The list is for illustrative purposes only. Attention needs to be given to whether the barriers are seen from the perspective of an exporting or importing country. Finally, it is important to remember that what is perceived as a barrier by some countries is perceived as fundamental to the education system in another.

---

[16] NCITE (2001) *Barriers to Trade in Transnational Education*. National Committee for International Trade in Education. Washington, D.C, USA. Available at: www.tradeineducation.org/general_info/frames.html. Last Accessed 22 April 2004.
[17] APEC (2001) *Measures affecting trade and investment in education services in the Asia-Pacific region.*A report to the APEC group on Services 2000. Singapore. Available at: www.apecsec.org.sg. Last Accessed 22 April 2004.

4.1 Generic Barriers

The majority of these generic barriers are from an exporter country's point of view and focus on supply modes one and three.

- lack of transparency of government regulatory, policy and funding frameworks
- domestic laws and regulations are administered in an unfair manner
- subsidies are not made known in a clear and transparent manner
- when government approval is required long delays are encountered and when approval is denied, no reasons are given for the denial and no information is given on what must be done to obtain approval in the future
- tax treatment that discriminates against foreign suppliers
- foreign partners are treated less favourably than other organizations.

4.2 Barriers by Mode of Supply

Of course, many of these barriers are not new or specific to the GATS, as they already impact the flow of education services across borders. However, the barriers are significant as they are seen by some as key elements of a public education system that need to be maintained, and by others as impediments to trade.

Some of the barriers identified above affect internationalization initiatives, in other words, those activities that do not have an economic or for-profit motive. For instance, mobility of students and teachers for academic exchange or research purposes are affected by many of the barriers noted for supply modes two and four.

It is important to note that within a country's schedule of commitments, it is possible to list specific limitations to market access and national treatment. These are a type of barrier and must be honoured. For example, Mexico has telecom laws

Chart 5 Barriers to Trade by Mode of Supply

Modes of delivery	Barriers
1. Cross border supply Examples – distance delivery or e-education – virtual universities	– inappropriate restrictions on electronic transmission of course materials – economic needs test on suppliers of these services – lack of opportunity to qualify as degree granting institution – required to use local partners – denial of permission to enter into and exit from joint ventures with local or non-local partners on voluntary basis – excessive fees/ taxes imposed on licensing or royalty payments – new barriers, electronic or legal for use of Internet to deliver education services – restrictions on use/import of educational materials
2. Consumption abroad Example – students studying in another country	– visa requirements and costs – foreign currency and exchange requirements – recognition of prior qualifications from other countries – quotas on numbers of international students in total and at a particular institution – restrictions on employment while studying – recognition of new qualification by other countries
3. Commercial presence Examples – branch or satellite campus – franchises – twinning arrangements	– inability to obtain national licenses to grant a qualification – limit on direct investment by education providers (equity ceilings) – nationality requirements – restrictions on recruitment of foreign teachers – government monopolies – high subsidization of local institutions – difficulty in obtaining authorization to establish facilities – economic needs test on suppliers of these services – prohibition of higher education, adult education and training services offered by foreign entities – measures requiring the use of a local partner – difficulty to gain permission to enter into and exit from joint ventures with local or non-local partners on voluntary basis – tax treatment that discriminates against foreign suppliers – foreign partners are treated less favourably than other organizations – excessive fees/ taxes are imposed on licensing or royalty payments – rules for twinning arrangements
4. Presence of natural persons Examples – Teachers travelling to foreign country to teach	– immigration requirements – nationality or residence requirements – needs test – recognition of credentials – minimum requirements for local hiring are disproportionately high – personnel have difficulty obtaining authorization to enter and leave the country – quotas on number of temporary staff – repatriation of earnings is subject to excessively costly fees and/or taxes for currency conversion – employment rules – restrictions on use/import of educational materials to be used by foreign teacher/scholar

that restrict the use of national satellites and receiving dishes.[18] This has potential impact on cross border delivery of education services. It is hard to predict what future barriers, especially technological ones, could be applied in order to control the electronic movement of education services across borders. For instance, the capacity to install electronic fences may have major repercussions on cross border e-education.

Finally, it should be mentioned that countries that have not made any formal commitments to trade in higher education services are currently in the process of easing some of the identified barriers. A good example of this is the number of countries who are changing visa and employment requirements to attract more international students to study in their country. This is happening irrespective of the GATS.

5 Policy Issues and Questions

Given the current interest and pressure toward increasing trade liberalization, what are the policy implications that the higher education sector needs to look at?

It is a challenging task to examine policy implications as the impact of trade liberalization is firmly enmeshed with other issues and trends in higher education. These trends include:

- the increasing use of ICTs for domestic and cross border delivery of programs
- the growing number of private for-profit entities providing higher education domestically and internationally
- the increasing tuition fees and other costs faced by students of public (and private) institutions,
- the need for public providers to seek alternate sources of funding which sometimes means engaging in for-profit activities or seeking private sector sources of financial support.

---

[18] NCITE (2001) *Barriers to Trade in Transnational Education*. National Committee for International Trade in Education. Washington, D.C, USA. Available at: www.tradeineducation.org/general_info/frames.html. Last Accessed 22 April 2004.

- the ability of government to fund the increasing demand for higher and adult education

These trends are with us today in both developed and to some extent, developing countries. How does the existence of the GATS relate to these trends? While the GATS may lead to expanded use of electronic or distance education and may contribute to more commercial or market oriented approaches to education, it cannot be held responsible for the emergence or existence of these trends. Supporters of more trade in education services can celebrate the existence of the GATS to maximize the benefits of these trends and opportunities. Critics, on the other hand, can emphasize the risks associated with increased trade, believing that it leads to more for-profit providers, to programs of questionable quality, and to a market oriented approach – all of which are seen to challenge the traditional 'public good' approach to higher education. However, the impact of trade liberalization on education cannot be positioned as an 'either-or' question or answer; it is a multi-layered and complex set of issues.

5.1 Role of Government

The changing role of government is a contentious issues. First, let it be said that in general, globalization and the new public management are challenging and changing roles of government and nation state. The movement toward more trade liberalization is yet another factor. With respect to education, the government usually plays a role in the funding, regulation, monitoring and delivery of higher education or at least, designating bodies to do so. This is true in countries where a public system dominates or where a mixed public/private system exists. The advent of increased cross border delivery by foreign education providers raises the following issues all of which impact on the role of government:

- licensing and regulation procedures for foreign providers
- quality assurance and accreditation for imported and exported education services

- funding protocols including operating grants, loans, subsidies and scholarships
- qualification recognition and credit transfer systems

These issues will be discussed in more detail in other sections but the role of government as an education provider needs to be examined. A combination of increased demand for public services and limited financial capacity is forcing governments to examine their priorities and options for service delivery. In higher education, this has prompted a number of new developments. These include:

- developing funding formulas which are placing more of the financial burden on students
- forcing publicly funded institutions to seek alternate and additional sources of funds through entrepreneurial or commercial activities at home and abroad
- individual institutions wanting increased autonomy from government regulation
- permitting new private providers (non-profit and for-profit) to deliver specific education and training programs

These developments are further complicated if and when a) a foreign public or private education provider is interested in access to the domestic market; and b) if a domestic public provider is interested in seeking markets in other countries. Together these scenarios require the government to take a long term and macro perspective on the impact of increased foreign trade on their role in the provision of and regulation of higher education.

5.2 Student Access

Many governments and public education institutions have keenly felt the responsibility of ensuring broad access to higher education opportunities. In many, if not in most countries, this is a challenging issue as the demand for higher and adult education is steadily growing, often beyond the capacity of the country to provide it. This is one more reason why some students are interested in out-of-country education opportunities and providers are prepared to offer higher education services across borders.

When increased trade liberalization is factored into this scenario, the question of access becomes complicated. Advocates of liberalized trade maintain that consumers/students can have greater access to a wider range of education opportunities at home and abroad. Non-supporters of trade believe that access may in fact be more limited as trade will commercialize education, escalate costs and perhaps lead to a two-tiered system. Trade is therefore often perceived by critics as a threat to the 'public good' nature of education services.

This raises the question of the capacity and role of government with respect to providing access to higher education. For instance, if education is seen as a public function, can private providers or foreign providers help to fulfil this public function? If so, would foreign for-profit providers be eligible for the same grants, subsidies and tax incentives as public providers under the national treatment obligation of the GATS? Would this in turn decrease the amount of financial support available to public universities if funds were distributed across a larger number of institutions? Different education models exist and must exist in order to respond to the needs, resources and priorities of individual countries.

5.3 Funding

Many of the same issues and arguments regarding access can also apply to funding. Some governments have limited budget capacity or at least lack the political will to allocate funds to meet the needs of higher education. Can international trade provide alternate funding sources or new providers? Or, because of the GATS obligations such as most favoured nation treatment and national treatment obligations, does it mean that public funding will be spread too thinly across a broader set of domestic and foreign providers? Furthermore, does the presence of foreign providers signal to government that they can decrease public funding for higher and adult education, thereby jeopardizing domestic publicly funded institutions. Does international trade in education advantage some countries, such as those with well-developed capacity for export, and disadvantage others in terms of funding or access? Once again, the impact of more liberalized trade can be a double-edged sword with respect to funding, whether public or private, higher education teaching/learning and research activities.

5.4 Regulation of Foreign or Cross Border Providers

As already noted, a regulatory framework is needed to deal with the diversity of providers and new cross border delivery modes, and becomes more urgent as international trade increases. In some countries, this may mean a broader approach to policy which involves licensing, regulating and monitoring both private (profit and non-profit) and foreign providers to ensure that national policy objectives are met and public interests protected. It may also involve a shift in government and public thinking – while higher education remains a "public good", both public and private providers can fulfil this public function. This in turn may introduce greater competition among providers and general confusion for the consumer. Hence a coherent and comprehensive regulatory framework is called for – to serve national interests and protect the interests of different stakeholders, especially students.

More work is necessary to determine how national regulatory frameworks are compatible with, or part of, a larger international framework.[19] Increased connectivity and interdependence among nations, as well as liberalized trade, will urge greater coherence between national frameworks. How can coherence between a national framework and an international framework actually strengthen national regulatory and policy functions, not weaken them? Clearly there are risks and opportunities associated with this issue but doing nothing is a risk in itself.

---

[19] Van Damme, D. (2001) *Higher Education in the Age of Globalization: The need for a new regulatory framework for recognition, quality assurance and accreditation.* Working Paper. UNESCO. Paris, France.

5.5 Recognition and Transferability of Credits

New types of education providers, new delivery modes, new cross border education initiatives, new levels of student mobility, new opportunities for trade in higher education – all this can spell further confusion for the recognition of qualifications and transfer of academic credits. This is not a new issue. Trade agreements are not responsible for increased confusion, but they add to the complexity and also make resolution more urgent. National and international recognition of qualifications and the transfer of credits have already been the subject of a substantial amount of work. The 'Lisbon Convention on the Recognition of Qualifications of Higher Education in the Europe Region', the 'European Credit Transfer System', and 'University Mobility in Asia Pacific' are good examples of regional initiatives that could lead to a more international approach.

5.6 Quality Assurance and Accreditation

Increased cross border education delivery and a set of legal rules and obligations in trade agreements require that urgent attention be given to the question of quality assurance and accreditation of education providers. Not only is it important to have national mechanisms which have the capacity to address accreditation and quality assessment procedures for the academic programs of new private and foreign providers, it is equally important that attention be given to developing an international approach to quality assurance and accreditation.[20]

There is growing awareness that in the world of cross border education trade, national quality assurance schemes are becoming challenged by the complexities of the international education environment. While there may be growing awareness, there is no acceptance or agreement that harmonization of national policies

---

[20] Van Damme, D. (2001) *Higher Education in the Age of Globalization: The need for a new regulatory framework for recognition, quality assurance and accreditation. Working Paper.*UNESCO. Paris, France.

with an international approach to quality assessment and accreditation is needed. It is imperative that education specialists discuss and determine the appropriate regulating mechanisms at the national and international level and not leave these questions to the designers and arbitrators of trade agreements.

Another, potentially contentious issue is the application of quality assurance schemes to both domestic and foreign providers. It may well be that under certain conditions, the national treatment obligation requires that all providers, domestic and foreign, be subject to the same processes and criteria. In some countries this will not be a problem, in others it will be hotly debated.

Quality assurance of higher education in some countries is regulated by the sector, and in others by the government to a greater or lesser degree. The key point is that authority for quality assurance, regulation and accreditation of cross border delivery needs to be examined and guided by stakeholders and bodies related to the education sector and not left solely in the hands of the market.

5.7 Research and Intellectual Property Rights

In the new economy that emphasizes knowledge production and trade, there is increasingly more value attributed to the creative and intellectual content inherent in both products and services. The 'Trade-Related Aspects of Intellectual Property Rights' (TRIPS) is another trade agreement, completely separate from the GATS, but which also addresses trade liberalization.[21] TRIPS covers such things as patents, trademarks and copyright, all of which are salient to the research and teaching/learning functions of higher education. Careful monitoring of TRIPS is also necessary by the higher education sector.[22]

---

[21] WTO. *Frequently asked questions about TRIPS in the WTO*. Available at: www.wto.org/english/tratop_e/trips_e/tripfq_e.htm. Last Accessed 22 April 2004.
[22] OECD (2001) *Trade in Educational Services: Trends and Emerging Issues*. Working Paper. Organization for Economic Cooperation and Development. Paris, France.

A look at the potential implications of trade agreements on research and scholarly work reveals a number of issues. A consistent theme expressed by trade critics is a deep concern about the increased emphasis on commercialization and commodification of the production of knowledge. Sceptics believe that the highly valued trinity of teaching, research and service at traditional universities may be at risk. A more differentiated and niche oriented approach to higher education may be an unanticipated outcome of increased trade in education and the growing importance of agreements such as GATS and TRIPS.

5.8 Internationalization

Attention needs to be given to the impact of trade liberalization on non-profit internationalization activities. Will trade overshadow and dominate the international academic relations of countries and institutions, or enhance them? Many internationalization strategies might be jeopardized by a purely commercial approach. For example, participation in international development or technical assistance programs can lead to mutual benefits for all partners and important spin-off effects for research, curriculum development and teaching. Will these programs have less or more importance when there is increased pressure for trade? Will revenue raised from commercial education activities be used to subsidize internationalization activities? What might happen to student exchange, internships, and other forms of academic mobility that do not have an income generation or for-profit motive? Will limited financial resources be directed to trade initiatives that have an economic return instead of internationalization activities which stress added academic value? How can internationalization and trade activities complement each other? Will bilateral relationships and multilateral networks among institutions be shaped by trade opportunities at the expense of research, curriculum development and other academic endeavours? Effort is needed to profile the benefits and importance of non-profit internationalization and to direct resources to the implementation and sustainability of the international dimension of teaching, research and service.

5.9 Mobility of Professionals/Labour Force

It has already been noted that the GATS may address the widespread unmet demand for skilled workers by facilitating the mobility of professionals. This impacts many of the service sectors and has particular implications for higher education. Not only is higher and adult education providing education and training programs to meet economic needs, the sector itself is affected by the mobility of its teachers and researchers. In many countries, the increasing shortage of teachers is resulting in active recruitment campaigns across borders. Since many teachers and researchers want to move to countries with more favourable working conditions and salaries, there is a real concern that the most developed countries will benefit disproportionately.

5.10 Culture and Acculturation

Last, but certainly not least, is the issue of cultural and indigenous traditions. Education is a process through which cultural assimilation takes place. In fact education is a fundamental vehicle for acculturation. Concern about the homogenization of culture through cross border supply of higher and adult education is expressed by critics of GATS. Advocates maintain that a positive hybridization and fusion of culture will evolve through increasing mobility and the influence of ICTs. In fact, some argue that this has been happening for decades and is contributing to new cultural exchanges and richness. Once again, the divergence of opinion shows that there are potential opportunities and threats to consider.

5.11 Institutional Level Issues

The emphasis of this section has been on macro policy issues. But the effect on individual institutions, especially public higher education institutions, should not be ignored.[23] The foremost issues are institutional autonomy, academic freedom and conditions

---

[23] Nunn, Alex (2001) *The General Agreement on Trade in Services: An Impact Assessment for Higher Education in the UK*. Report. UK Association of University Teachers. London, United Kingdom.

of employment for academic staff. While these three issues are linked to trade liberalization, they are more closely associated with the larger issues of the commercialization and privatization of education in general, which many believe is advanced within as well as across borders.

5.12 Trade Dominates

Finally, it needs to be said that the question of trade liberalization, which most often is interpreted in economic terms, has the potential of dominating the agenda. There is a risk of 'trade creep' where education policy issues are increasingly framed in terms of trade.[24] Even though domestic challenges in education provision are currently front and centre on the radar screen of most countries, the issue of international trade in education services will most likely increase in importance. Supporters of freer trade applaud the fact that GATS is seen first and foremost as an economic agreement and that its purpose is to promote and expand free trade for economic reasons. Given that the market potential for trade in higher education is already significant and is predicted to increase, it is clear that GATS and other trade agreements will help to promote trade and further economic benefit. Critics of the trade agreements maintain that the domination of the trade agenda is at the expense of other key objectives and rationales for higher education such as social, cultural and scientific development and the role of education in promoting democracy and citizenship.

6 Moving Forward

6.1 Actions and Reactions of Stakeholders

One of the prime objectives of this report is to get the issue of trade liberalization in higher education services on the agenda of

---

[24] EI/PSI (2000) *Great Expectations. The Future of Trade in Services.* Joint paper by Education International (EI) and Public Services International (PSI). Brussels, Belgium. Available at: www.ei-ie.org/main/english/index.html. Last Accessed 22 April 2004.

university managers and higher education policy makers. Overall, there seems to have been little reaction to the issue. This does not dismiss, however, the work that has been done by some non-government organizations. One of the more interesting initiatives is the 'Joint Declaration on Higher Education and the General Agreement on Trade in Services'[25] developed and signed by four organizations: Association of Universities and Colleges of Canada (AUCC), American Council on Education (ACE), European University Association (EUA) and the Council for Higher Education Accreditation (CHEA).

This declaration encourages countries to not make commitments in 'Higher Education Services' or in the related categories of 'Adult Education' and 'Other Education Services' in the GATS. Instead it supports the notion of reducing obstacles to international trade in higher education using conventions and agreements outside of a trade policy regime. Clearly there are supporters of the principles of the declaration, but there are also critics who feel that the protectionist position is rather self-serving, especially given the degree of exporting activity already in existence. It is noteworthy that three of the signatories come from the USA and Europe, both of whom have made some commitments on education services in GATS. This is yet another sign of the heated debate, the complexities and the uncertainties related to GATS. The most important role of the declaration is that it is drawing more attention to the issue.

The declaration is the only internationally co-ordinated effort but there are many national level student, teacher and education organizations that are vocal in their questions and criticisms of the intent and impact of the agreement. There are similar groups such as the 'National Committee for International Trade in Education'

---

[25] AUCC (2001) *Joint Declaration on Higher Education and the General Agreement on Trade in Services*. 2001 Association of Universities and Colleges of Canada (AUCC), American Council on Education, European University Association, Council for Higher Education Accreditation. Available at: www.aucc.ca. Last Accessed 22 April 2004.

(NCITE) in the US and other business organizations which are expressing support for freer trade in education services. At the intergovernmental level there appears to be some level of interest in the issues – primarily from the economic organizations such as APEC or OECD. At the same time, there are international non-government organizations such as Association of Commonwealth Universities that are trying to raise awareness about the broad issue of trade liberalization and the specifics of the GATS. But, this is only a beginning. More work is needed to consult with the different education stakeholders so that their voices are heard in ongoing analysis and negotiations.

6.2 Important Dates for WTO Negotiations

The key dates to be aware of for the next phases of the GATS negotiations are:

June 30, 2002: Countries will file initial requests asking trading partners to open their markets in service areas.

March 31, 2003: Countries that were the subjects of requests will present offers to open their markets in service areas. Trading partners will hold meetings and discussions. Overall, if insufficient agreement is reached regarding higher education, the sector could be part of new round of global negotiations after talks conclude in January 2005.

January 2005: GATS negotiations will end.

This is a rather tight timetable and the next twelve months are key. By June 2002, the details of all education requests should be known. While it is important that the voice of the education sector is heard in the formulation of these requests, it may be even more important to influence the response to the requests. This involves working with the appropriate government officials and monitoring the offers made by one's own country in response to requests from other countries. The second part is monitoring the offers that are being received by one's own country in response to the requests originally made to other countries. This is an important, but a rather daunting task due to the reality that education stakeholders hold differing perspectives on the extent and nature of the limitations on national treatment and market access and may or may not speak with one voice to government trade officials.

6.3 Concluding Remarks

Complex and contentious. These two words sum up the current analysis and debate about the impact of GATS on higher education. Opinions on the risks and benefits are divided, if not polarized. They differ within and between countries. Each country must undertake the very serious challenge of balancing opportunities and commitments to liberalize trade for exporting higher education services, with the possible impact, related to the same commitments, of the import of education services. This is not an easy task. One can tend to be liberal while considering exporting opportunities and more protectionist when analysing the implications of importing.

At this stage, one is left with the impression that there are more questions than clear answers. The questions are complex as they deal with

- technical/legal issues of the agreement itself (see section 1.5)
- education policy issues such as funding, access, accreditation, quality and intellectual property (see section 5) and,
- the larger more political/moral issues for society, such as the role and purpose of higher education, and the 'public good' or 'market commodity' approach.

The one certainty in this picture is the need for the higher education sector to study these questions and to consult stakeholders. At the same time it is necessary to be proactive and strategic in monitoring and influencing government negotiating positions for the request/ offer stage of the GATS negotiations. This, of course, involves close communication with education departments and bodies in one's country. It is equally important not to lose sight of the need for international approaches and frameworks for the regulation of providers, quality assurance and qualification recognition. Finally, it is important not to overstate the impact of GATS. Trade in education was alive and well prior to and outside the purview of trade agreements. Yet, it is also critical not to understate the potential implications- risks and opportunities- of GATS.

The first aim of this paper is to highlight the potential impact of trade liberalization on higher education. The second aim is to raise questions and identify policy issues that require further attention and analysis. These will have been met if readers are better informed, and motivated to take appropriate action at institutional, regional, national or international level.

GATS, Trade and Higher Education: perspective 2003 – *where are we?*

Jane Knight

1 Introduction

...and the debate goes on. It is good news that discussions continue on the potential impact of new international trade regulations on higher education. During this past year, the education sector has become increasingly aware and involved in thinking about the General Agreement on Trade in Services (GATS), the emerging international trade agreement administered by the World Trade Organization (WTO). Stakeholder groups are talking about potential new opportunities, benefits and risks and are actively speculating on different countries' negotiating positions for increased liberalization of trade in education services. In short, GATS and trade are beginning to appear on the education agenda.

At the same time, many trade experts and educators note that international mobility of students, teachers, education and training programs has been happening for a very long time, and therefore question why there is such interest in the prospect of expanding import/export of education services. The answer partially lies in the fact that while cross-border education is an important aspect of the internationalization of higher education, it has not been subject to international trade rules and until recently, has not really been described as commercial trade. International trade agreements such as GATS, which clearly identifies education as a service sector to be liberalized, is relatively new territory for the education sector. This is why the debate within national and international education communities is necessary and welcomed. However, the discussions need to move from speculation towards informed analysis. The introduction of GATS serves as the catalyst for the education sector to move more deliberately into examining how trade rules may influence higher education policy, and determining whether the necessary national, regional and international education frameworks are in place to deal with the implications of increased cross-border education, including commercial trade.

1.1 Purpose of Report

This paper is a follow up to last year's Observatory report[1] which outlined the purpose and rules of GATS, explained the relevance of GATS to higher education and identified some key policy issues which neede to be addressed. The purpose of this paper is threefold: 1) to update on the current GATS negotiations, 2) elaborate on the implications of trade for the higher education sector, and 3) begin to situate trade of higher education services in the broader context of cross-border education.

1.2 Terminology

A few comments about the use and meaning of terms used in this paper may help to provide some context. When terms from the

---

[1] Knight, J. (2002) *Trade in Higher Education Services: The Implications of GATS.* The Observatory on Borderless Higher Education. London: United Kingdom.

trade sector migrate to the education sector and vice versa there is fertile ground for confusion and misunderstanding. This is to be expected. Therefore it is important to lay out how the principal concepts are interpreted and used by these two sectors. For example, 'trade in education services' is a key term for this paper. For the education sector, 'trade in education services' is a relatively new term and would probably be interpreted in a myriad of ways. For the trade sector, 'trade in education services' is understood to exclude any products such as text books but would include services such as education/training programs well as education support services such as testing.

The trade sector through GATS has developed four 'modes' to describe trade or supply of services. It is interesting that explicit definitions for the terms 'service' and 'trade' are not provided in the agreement. The four modes of trade in services are described as follows:

Mode 1 – Cross-border supply focuses on the service crossing the border, which does not require the consumer or the service provider to physically move. Examples in higher education include distance education and e-learning.

Mode 2 – Consumption Abroad refers to the consumer moving to the country of the supplier which in education means students taking all or part of their education in another country.

Mode 3 – Commercial Presence involves a service provider establishing a commercial facility in another country to provide a service. Examples in higher education include branch campuses or franchising arrangements.

Mode 4 – Presence of Natural Persons means people travelling to another country on a temporary basis to provide a service, which in education would include professors or researchers.

Three common terms used by the education sector to describe the international nature of education are internationalization, cross-border education and more recently trade in education. There is a hierarchy to these terms, with 'internationalization of education' being the most comprehensive, 'cross-border education' being one component of internationalization and then 'international trade in education' being used to characterize some cross-border activities. The last section of this paper elaborates on the issue of terminology and attempts to position trade in education services within a larger context of cross-border education but a few comments up front might help.

A review of reports and articles by trade experts reveals that often when they talk about internationalization of education they actually are referring to international trade in education services. When educators talk about internationalization they are talking about a broad range of activities some of which would have absolutely nothing to do with trade. More and more, internationalization is being seen to consist of two streams or components.[2] The first is 'internationalization at home'[3] which refers to the international and intercultural dimension of curricula, the teaching/learning process, research, extra-curricular activities, in fact a host of activities which help students develop international understanding and intercultural skills without ever leaving the campus. The second component is 'internationalization abroad' that is cross-border education (often referred to as transnational education) which involves students, teachers, scholars, programs, courses, curriculum, projects moving between countries and culture, in short, across borders.

So cross-border education is a term that educators are using to capture a wide range of education activities that are part of international academic linkages and agreements, international development/aid projects and international commercial trade initiatives. Therefore, 'trade in education services' is usually interpreted by educators as a subset of cross-border education, and for the most part is described as those activities that have a commercial or for-profit nature or purpose to them. This interpretation is much narrower than one used by economists or the trade sector. From

---

[2] Knight J. (2003) *Internationalization Remodelled: Responding to New Realities and Challenges.* In publication.
[3] Nilsson, B. (1999) *Internationalization at home – Theory and Praxis.* European Association for International Education Forum, 12.

their perspective, even if a cross-border education activity is seen to be non-commercial in purpose – for instance the exchange of students or professors for a semester – there is still export value in a country's balance of payments from accommodation, living, travel expenses, and therefore there are commercial implications.[4]

It is not an easy task to have a clear and shared interpretation of what trade in education services really means across the two sectors. It may be dangerous to oversimplify how the different sectors perceive and use the term 'trade in education services' but the clear message is that more effort is needed to help the two sectors understand the different approaches to using and defining trade in education services. It is equally important to have clarity and assurance as to which international cross-border education activities would fall under the purview of international/regional trade agreements and be labelled as trade. As will be noted later, there is ambiguity in GATS on this point.

For the purposes of this paper, the term 'trade in educational services' is primarily used in the trade and GATS 'four mode' sense, and the term 'cross-border education' is used to depict a broad range of activities, some of which are commercial in nature and some of which are not, which move across borders.

1.3 Assumptions

This paper assumes that readers have a rudimentary understanding of GATS. The basic information on the structure and disciplines of the trade agreement is not repeated in this paper.[5] There are a number of other assumptions that are worth noting. This paper is written from an educator's point of view, not from an economic or trade perspective. An international approach is

---

[4] Larsen, K. and Vincent-Lancrin, S. (2002) 'International trade in Education Services: Good or Bad?' in *Higher Education and Management Policy*, 14 (3).
[5] See Knight, J. (2002) *Trade in Higher Education Services: The Implications of GATS*. The Observatory on Borderless Higher Education. London: United Kingdom.

emphasized meaning that implications for both developed and developing countries are noted. It is recognized that trade issues are closely related to the larger issues of commercialization and commodification of education but the focus remains on the potential impact of trade rules on cross-border education. More attention is given to the delivery of education/training courses and programs across borders (modes 1 and 3) than to the movement of students to study in foreign countries (mode 2). Again, the intention is to take a balanced approach in discussing the implications of new trade rules and increased trade in education services. Potential benefits and risks are identified.

1.4 Outline of Paper

There are six major sections to the paper. The first constitutes the introduction. The second provides information on the current status of the GATS negotiation process. A brief update on the number and nature of requests and offers is given. Several of the barriers that the United States has requested other countries to remove are listed to give a concrete idea of what liberalizing trade in education can involve. The third section includes a brief discussion on the rationales driving countries to increase trade in education services through import or export. The fourth part identifies key higher education policy issues related to the potential impact of increased trade and new trade regulations. The issues addressed include the following: the role of government, student access, registration and licensing of education providers, quality assurance and accreditation, recognition of academic and professional qualifications, and funding among others. The fifth section of the paper recognizes the four trade modes outlined by GATS but suggests that they need to be situated in the larger arena of cross-border education. In the last section, the actions and interests of different stakeholders are described to illustrate the breadth of the debate. The conclusions reiterate that there are still more questions than answers. GATS is a new and untested agreement and we simply do not know what some of the intended and unintended consequences will be.

2 Update on GATS and the Negotiation Process

The purpose of this section is to give an update on the key dates and expected outcomes of the current round of negotiations and to provide a cursory review of some of the requests/offers and identified barriers.

2.1 Facts and Realities about GATS

- GATS has existed since 1995. It will not go away.
- The purpose of GATS is to reduce or eliminate barriers to trade.
- GATS is a worldwide agreement covering all 145 member countries of WTO.
- GATS is the first multi-lateral agreement on trade in services. GATT covers trade in products.
- Education is one of the 12 primary service sectors. This will not change.
- There are five subsectors in education – primary, secondary, higher, adult and other. The descriptions of these need to be reviewed and updated.
- GATS is a new and untested agreement. Key articles/ disciplines are still being developed. For example, the disciplines dealing with subsidies, domestic regulation and government procurement are still under negotiation.
- Individual countries have the power to determine the degree of market access to each of the subsectors. This can include no access at all. However, due to the most favored nation principle all countries must be treated equally in terms of market access and national treatment for services covered in the scope of the agreement.
- National treatment requires equal treatment for foreign and domestic providers where a country has made a specific commitment. Exemptions are allowed.
- Due to the principle of progressive liberalization, there will be increased pressure for further liberalization of trade barriers with each round of negotiations.

2.2 Key Dates and Actions

Table 1 Key Dates and Actions of GATS

Date	Action	Notes for Education Sector
1995	GATS founded; initial commitments	44 countries (if you count the EU as one country) made commitments to Education. Of these 44 countries, 21 included commitments to higher education[6]
End of 2001	Negotiating proposals due	Four countries- USA, Australia, New Zealand and Japan submitted a proposal outlining their general positions related to commitments in the education sector. Japan's proposal was remarkably different as their statement highlighted quality assurance, recognition of credentials and distance education as key issues that required further consideration.
June 2002	All requests for access to foreign markets due	To date, only 34 out of the 145 WTO members have tabled their requests. It is not mandatory for a country to publish their tabled requests for market access in other countries. However, there were leaks and it is known that the USA made substantial requests of other countries to remove barriers to enable greater access to higher, adult and other education services.
March 2003	Offers from each country to provide access to their domestic market due	As of the end of April 2003, only 20 countries had submitted their offers. Argentina, Australia, Bahrain, Canada, European Union, Hong Kong, Iceland, Israel, Japan, Liechtenstein, New Zealand, Norway, Panama, Poland, Paraguay, South Korea, Switzerland, Taiwan, the United States and Uruguay. It is not necessary for a country to publish their offers and only 8 of the 20 countries have done so to date. These countries are Australia, Canada, European Union, Japan, Liechtenstein, New Zealand, Norway and the United States.

(Continued)

---

[6] See Knight, J. (2002) *Trade in Higher Education Services: The Implications of GATS.* The Observatory on Borderless Higher Education. London: United Kingdom.

GATS, Trade and Higher Education

Table 1 (Continued)

Date	Action	Notes for Education Sector
Up to January 1, 2005	Countries can submit offers and requests until end of Doha round	The end date of this round may be extended given the significant delays in the tabling of both requests and offers. Further rounds will occur. It is important to note that offers made during the negotiation phase of the Doha round are conditional up to the conclusion of the negotiating round and at that time, final offers are included in a country's schedule of commitments.

2.3 Status of Requests/Offers to Date

All in all, Table 1 shows that education has not been a priority sector for the GATS negotiations. Secondly, only a handful of countries have tabled their requests or offers by the targeted dates; and thirdly, there is very little concrete information on access to education markets. The targeted end date for this round of negotiations is January 1, 2005. This will give the education sector more time to become better informed and prepared for the potential implications of increased trade, including countries taking whatever steps are considered necessary to ensure that trade in higher, adult and other services is undertaken in accordance with national/ educational priorities.

While the low and slow response rate is providing time to become better informed and prepared, it can also be troublesome. It should be noted that there are very few developing countries that have submitted either their requests or offers. There are several possible reasons for this. First, is the question of capacity. All in all, there are 160 subsectors covered by GATS and it takes both time and expertise to be informed on all of them. Some technical assistance is available to developing countries through multi-lateral agencies and bi-lateral donors but the commitment should not be underestimated. Secondly, there is an element of 'wait and see' in many national trade negotiating strategies. Given that commitments on market access made for one country are automatically applied to all WTO members (due to the most favored nation obligation), it is not necessary for all countries to make official requests. It is also true that requests and offers can be made at any time during this present round – that is until January 1, 2005. It is clear that the majority of WTO members are not ready or are hesitant to table their offers. This means that to date, it is the quad (four of the most influential countries – USA, Japan, EU and Canada) plus several other OECD member countries, who are taking the lead and shaping the negotiation process. This may not be a surprise but it may have some unintended consequences.

2.4 Brief Analysis of Leaked Requests and Published Offers

An analysis of the requests provides some insight into the extent and type of trade one can expect in educational services. As already mentioned, only 34 countries have tabled their requests to date and because it is not necessary to publicize them, there is a great deal of speculation as to their contents. Speculation is inevitable but it is important to be cautious about the veracity or completeness of the leaked requests. Unofficial versions of the requests from the United States and from the European Union are available and while one is not certain whether they are completely accurate it is interesting and informative to review them.[7]

The US request for market access and national treatment in education has been described as maximalist or 'go for the moon and see what you get' approach. The US has asked that all 145 WTO members "undertake full commitments for market access and national treatment in modes 1, 2, and 3 for higher education and training services, for adult education, and for 'other' education.

---

[7] See news groups GATSWATCH and GATS education for information on requests/offers www.gatswatch.org/requestsoffers.html; GATSeducation@yahoo groups.com

Consistent with the commitments, countries remain free to review and assess higher education and training, by governmental or non-governmental means, and to co-operate with other countries, for purposes of assuring quality education." In other words, the United States is asking for extensive liberalization of the higher and adult education markets in all WTO member countries. It is interesting that the US has added that governments should be able to assure quality. Quality was not mentioned in the US negotiating proposal,[8] but it is one of the most critical issues in the debate and will be discussed later in the paper. In addition to this generic request to all countries, the US makes more specific requests of particular countries. Some of these are listed in Table 2. Finally, the question must be asked whether the US is willing to offer the same degree of access to its domestic higher education markets as it has requested of other countries. This is not anticipated but is not yet confirmed. By contrast, and contrary to some expectations, the EU request barely mentions education at all.

To date, only eight countries have made their total GATS offer public. In the Canadian offer, no offers were made in any of the education subsectors. Canada did not make any education requests either. Australia has not tabled any new offers. This means that Australia's commitments remain for private tertiary level education only. New Zealand has also not made any further offers beyond its original commitments. Japan only published an offer summary and have made offers on adult and other education services but none on higher education.

The offer tabled by the United States[9] included offers on "Higher Education Services (including training services and educational testing services, but excluding flying instruction)." The most

---

[8] World Trade Organisation, *Proposals for the New Negotiations*. Available at: www.wto.org/english/tratop_e/serv_e/s_propnewnegs_e.htm#education. Last Accessed 22 April 2004.
[9] See full text of US offer at: Office of the United States Trade Representative, *The United States of America Initial Offer*. Available at: www.ustr.gov/sectors/services/20030331consolidated_offer.pdf. Last Accessed 22 April 2004.

Table 2 Examples of US Requests to Remove Barriers to Trade in Education Sector

Request to remove barrier	Targeted Country
Remove nationality requirements for certain executives and directors of educational institutions	Taiwan
Remove ownership limitations on joint ventures with local partners	Egypt, India, Mexico, Philippines, Thailand
Remove prohibition on joint ventures with local partners	El Salvador
Remove requirement that foreign entities teach only non-national students	Turkey
Remove ban on education services provided by foreign companies and organizations via satellite networks	China
Remove requirements for foreign educational institutions to partner with Chinese universities	
Remove ban on for-profit operations in education and training services	
Relax other operational limits and restriction on geographic scope of activities	
Recognize degrees issued by accredited institutions of higher education (including those issued by branch campuses of accredited institutions)	Israel, Japan
Adopt a policy of transparency in government licensing and accrediting policy with respect to higher education and training	
Remove burdensome requirements, including non-transparent needs tests, applicable to foreign universities operating, or seeking to operate in South Africa	South Africa
Remove restrictions that the granting of degrees is limited to Greek institutions only	Greece
Remove requirement that foreign entities teach only non-national students	Italy
Remove quantitative limitation on education institutions	Ireland
Adopt a policy of transparency in government licensing and accreditation with respect to higher education and training	Spain, Sweden

interesting part of the US offer is the 'limitations' that were noted in text format. (The word 'limitations' is used here to mean national stipulations that limit an offer). These limitations are evidence of a conditional approach to access to domestic markets, and an attempt to assuage concerns of domestic higher education institutions and groups. Examples of limitations include the following:

> *'Nothing in this agreement will interfere with the ability of individual U.S. institutions to maintain autonomy in admission's policies, in setting tuition rates, and in the development of curricula or course content. Educational and training entities must comply with requirements of the jurisdiction in which the facility is established'*, and secondly *'the granting of U.S. federal or state government funding or subsidies may be limited to U.S. schools. Scholarships and grants may be limited to U.S. citizens and/or U.S. residents of particular states. Tuition rates may vary for instate and out-of-state residents.'*

Additionally, the US offer addresses the issues of admission policies and accreditation by indicating that 'Admission policies include considerations of equal opportunity for students (regardless of race, ethnicity or gender), as well as recognition of credits and degrees; state regulations apply to the establishment and operation of a facility in the state; and accreditation of the institution and its programs may be required by regional and/or specialty organizations; required standards must be met to obtain and maintain accreditation; foreign-owned entities may be ineligible for federal or state funding or subsidies, including land grants, preferential tax treatment, and any other public benefits; and to participate in the U.S. student loan program, foreign institutions established in the United States would need to meet the same requirements as U.S. institutions.'

These stated limitations are evidence of how a country can determine the degree and conditions of access to its domestic market. However, it is revealing and intriguing when one compares the 'limitations' imposed by the US on access to their own market to the requests they make of other countries to remove the kinds of barriers noted in the next section. It will be interesting to see whether in future requests, countries will perceive the above 'limitations' as barriers and ask the US to remove them – see below.

2.5 Removal of Barriers

The purpose of GATS, as stated by the WTO, is to reduce or eliminate barriers to trade. In order to give concrete examples of barriers in the education sector, Table 2 lists a sample of the US requests to targeted countries to remove specific barriers. It is interesting to note the range of barriers different countries have established to regulate the import of education services. Of major importance are matters of quality assurance, accreditation and recognition of credentials. One of the GATS principles is that countries can determine the degree of market access they will give to foreign providers (e.g. the 'limitations' imposed by the US above). This is seen as a certain kind of safeguard. However, safeguards can be interpreted as barriers. Therefore, when one considers the GATS principle of progressive liberalization, one questions whether these so called safeguards will in fact be able to withstand the pressure of liberalization in future rounds of negotiations. It should also be noted that barriers to trade seen from the exporting country's point of view, may be seen by the importing country as fundamental aspects of domestic higher education policy.

3 Rationales and Benefits of Increased Trade in Higher Education

It is somewhat surprising and perhaps worrisome that very little has been written by educators or trade specialists on rationales for and benefits from the import/export of education services. Besides the four negotiating proposals (USA, Australia, New Zealand, Japan) there are few statements which have championed the benefits, other than the obvious ones by the WTO[10] and other trade

---

[10] See WTO (1998) *Education Services. Background Note* by the Secretariat. Council for Trade in Services. Geneva, Switzerland. S/C/W/49, 98-3691.

secretariats. It appears that rationales and benefits specific to education are taken for granted in the overall assumption that liberalized trade will increase a nation's economic prosperity. The analysis provided by Larsen and Vincent-Lancrin[11] (2002) is one of the few comprehensive studies on the implications of trade in education services. They conclude that due to the complexity of the factors involved and because the issues vary substantially with the country, mode of delivery and sector of education, it is difficult to draw a definitive conclusion on whether trade in education services is 'good or bad'. They suggest that there will be a deeper impact on the lifelong learning market than on the traditional higher education.

3.1 Overview of Rationales for Import/Export

Unfortunately, there are few statements or policy papers which specifically discuss the different rationales and anticipated impact of trade in higher education. Therefore it is only possible to provide a general overview of possible motivations. Reasons for importing higher education services include:

- limited domestic capacity to meet growing demand for higher education
- provide greater access to specific knowledge or skilled-based education and training
- improve the quality of higher education provision by allowing market access to prestigious/reputable foreign providers
- create cultural or political alliances
- secure trade tied aid development projects and funds
- develop human capital and stem 'brain drain'
- foreign competition may improve cost effectiveness in domestic institutions
- imported programs may offer better value than studying abroad.

---

[11] Larsen, K. and Vincent-Lancrin, S. (2002) 'International trade in Education Services: Good or Bad?' in *Higher Education and Management Policy*, 14 (3).

Reasons for exporting higher education services include:

- excess national capacity in higher education
- income generation
- international recognition and branding
- strategic cultural, political, economic and education alliances
- institutional strengthening and innovation
- a tool for further internationalization of domestic institutions
- education as a conduit to access trade in other service sectors.

This overview of rationales illustrates the range of motivations that different countries, actors and education institutions bring to the dialogue on trade in education. Despite this diversity, the common factor underlying them all is 'self-interest'. Self-interest appears to be the strongest motivator for trade, even if there are seen to be benefits for all parties involved. A former secretary-general of the Association of Indian Universities clearly articulates this view. "Commitments will be made in the best interests of the country. They have to be in the areas of the country's strengths and where there are strategic opportunities for exploitation through trade" (Powar, 2002, p18). Other concrete examples of 'self-interest' being the fundamental driver are those countries who are requesting more liberalization of the education market in other countries than they themselves are willing to offer.

3.2 View from Developing Countries

There is definitely more written on why countries are cautious and guarded about the impact of trade, than on the benefits of trade. This is especially true for developing countries. For instance, the Minister of Education in South Africa states very clearly that "it is important that we remain vigilant to ensure that increased trade in education does not undermine our national efforts to transform higher education and in particular to strengthen the public sector so that it can effectively participate in an increasingly globalizing environment. Trade considerations cannot be allowed to erode the public good agenda for higher education." On the other hand, he warned against parochialism and stressed the need for genuine international collaboration in education.[12] It will not be a surprise if South Africa does not respond positively to the requests by Kenya, New Zealand, Norway and the US for unlimited access to its domestic education market.

Mohamedbhai, Vice Chancellor of the University of Mauritius (2002/ 2003) notes when considering the WTO proposal to liberalize trade in education services through GATS that "while there is no doubt globalisation may have some positive effects from the point of view of increasing access in higher education and reducing the knowledge gap in developing countries, it equally has negative aspects which can seriously threaten universities in those countries." He believes that foreign providers have helped to provide courses locally and at a significantly lower cost than travelling abroad but they do not share the same national values and priorities. Their purpose is to provide education in the most cost-effective way for them. He worries that developing countries may be "flooded with foreign and private providers delivering essentially profitable subjects... and in these areas they will pose as serious competitors to local universities, leaving the latter to deal with non-profitable subjects in arts, humanities, science and technology, so vital for a country's development."[13]

India is a good case study of diverse motivations for increased trade. India is interested in new opportunities for import and export of higher education and sees benefits as well as potential risks.[14] Powar, cited above, believes "that because India has a large higher education system with many institutions that provide a good quality

---

[12] See full article in *Linda Ensor Business Day*, 1st Edition, March 06, 2003.
[13] Mohamedbhai, G. (2002) *Globalisation & Its Implications on Universities in Developing Countries,* presentation at the conference 'Globalisation: what issues are at stake for universities?', Université Laval, Quebec, Canada, 19 September.
[14] For a discussion on issues for India's response to GATS see Deodhar S. (2002) *Managing Trade in Educational Services: Issues for India's Response in WTO Negotiations.* India Institute of Management Working Paper No. 20001-20-01. Ahmedabad, India.

education... it can benefit both economically and politically by exporting education, especially to the developing countries that have a substantial Indian Diaspora." In terms of importing higher education services, Powar recognizes that "the effect on quality can be both beneficial and detrimental." He sees the potential for quality to be "improved from interaction and competition with reputable international institutions and decreased if low quality providers offer 'canned degrees'." Powar maintains that "quality education provided by reputed international providers will be accessible only to the privileged few that can pay for it. Access to education that can lead to decent employment will probably be limited to those with more-than-adequate financial resources. This is likely to create, in the long run, three classes of graduates. The resultant inequity will be the cause for economic disparity and possibly for social tension." In terms of the impact on both the public and private education subsystems he comments that "GATS will affect the two sub-systems differently but it is difficult to precisely foresee the effects on either of them. The greater impact will be on the public sub-system as the private sub-system, by its very nature, will be in a better position to absorb the effects. There is a possibility of the government slowly withdrawing from its commitments to higher education, seeing that the alternate mechanism of funding is gaining support from international sources. We may end up with an inefficient and languishing public sector and a dominant private sector." He adds "from the point of view of the academics, the most serious consequence of GATS is that it has led to the 'commodification' of education... In the case of the Indian higher education system, commodification is bound to affect access and equity, funding and quality." Finally, he notes that "with the infrastructure for quality education being deficient in most developing and underdeveloped countries, the potential of higher education services as a trade is large. This has been realized by the developed countries and for many of them the rationale for internationalization of higher education has shifted from cultural and political to economic" and furthermore "in a WTO controlled regime there is a real danger of the universities in the developing world being swamped by overseas institutions intent on earning a profit but not concerned about contributing to national development".[15]

Patil, President of the Association of Indian Universities and Vice-Chancellor of Indira Ghandi Agricultural University, makes an additional point on the economic benefits. He states that "the efforts of WTO to include education in the GATS agreement should be seen as a significant contribution to enhance further total factor productivity leading to a higher growth-rate in GDP. Therefore, India has to pay serious attention to the GATS agreement as applicable to educational services, identify opportunities and competitiveness in various sub sectors, and negotiate WTO commitments accordingly." He believes that "while India seeks to liberalize trade in education services and offer specific commitments in its proposal for negotiations, Indians must understand that they are not trading off their rights and controls on issues that are integral to their nationhood, cultural ethos and security. There are many exemptions and safeguards allowed in GATS which can be effectively utilized to protect Indian interests."[16]

These comments from Indian academics are a good illustration of the analysis of opportunities and risks associated with increased trade in higher education. The strong link between commercialization, commodification and trade is noted and underlines the point that it is often difficult to separate the challenges related to trade from these two other issues.

The following section moves away from the requests/offers and rationales, and concentrates on policy issues and implications that new trade rules and the advent of increased trade liberalization may have for the higher education sector.

---

[15] Powar, K.B. (2002) *WTO, GATS and Higher Education: An Indian Perspective*. Paper prepared for meeting convened by the Association of Commonwealth Universities. Perth, Australia, pp 11–18.
[16] Patil, V.K. (2002) *Higher Education in India under GATS*. Paper prepared for meeting convened by the Association of Commonwealth Universities. Perth, Australia, p8.

4 Policy Issues

In the past year, limited progress has been made in studying the implications of new trade policy and regulations on higher education. More attention has been focused on interpreting the rules and articles of the GATS agreement and speculating on the requests and offers made. Given that this is the second and more public round of GATS negotiations, it is understandable that more effort has been directed to studying the actual education requests and offers than to thinking about some of the larger policy issues. However, it is timely and important that more attention be devoted to examining the aspects of higher education policy which may be affected by or need to be developed because of the existence of trade agreements and new regulations.

4.1 Role of Government

In most, if not all countries of the world, the government plays a critical role in regulating, funding, and monitoring the provision of higher education. This applies where education is more or less publicly funded and also where there is a mixed public/private system. Will trade liberalization affect a mixed system differently than a public system, and how might the role of government change in particular cases? Inherent in these questions is the issue of just what services are covered or exempted from GATS. There is an implicit understanding that public services will be exempted, but close scrutiny of article 1.3 raises several related questions and concerns.

Article 1.3 states that "those services supplied in the exercise of governmental authority", are "not in competition" with other service providers and operate on a "non-commercial basis" are exempted. So, if one takes the first condition, "supplied in the exercise of governmental authority", one would believe that education supported by government funding and regulation would not be covered by GATS. However, the two additional conditions raise concerns. What does "not in competition" mean? In a mixed public/private education system there is implicit and explicit competition and therefore one could interpret the article to mean that public institutions could therefore not be exempted. The second condition ensures that the services are provided on a "non-commercial basis". Again, one asks what does this mean and again there is no stated definition. Given that public institutions are increasingly dependent on non-governmental sources of income, including research contracts or fee-based training, the term 'non-commercial' may not apply to all public institutions. Secondly, if tuition fees are charged, is that a commercial transaction? Legal opinion[17] and the general consensus in the higher education sector is that there is so much 'wiggle room' in the definition that one should not count on government funded and mandated institutions being exempted from GATS rules unless a country stipulates this in their commitments.

The second point relates to GATS Article 6.4 that addresses domestic regulations and a country's ability to set qualifications, quality standards and licences. The articles reads that "qualifications, requirements and procedures, technical standards and licensing are not more burdensome than necessary to ensure the quality of the service." The language is purposely vague and there are no definitions for terms such as "more burdensome than necessary" or for "quality of services". This leaves the higher education sector troubled about the potential impact of this statement on quality assurance and accreditation procedures. There is also concern about the implications of this article for the regulation of the professions given the increasing mobility of skilled and professional workers across borders. This is one of the articles which is "still under development". Direct questions to trade specialists do not yield any concrete answers other than "it is still being developed" and it is a wait and see situation. However, they state strongly that it is certainly not the intention of GATS to limit governments' role in the regulation of quality assurance of education or the professions. Clearly this article, part of which is often referred to as the 'necessity test', merits close monitoring by the education sector given that a country's ability to establish

---

[17] Gottlieb and Pearson (2001) *GATS Impact on Education in Canada*. Legal Opinion. Ottawa, Canada.

quality assurance and accreditation policy for domestic and foreign providers is central to the role of government.

Much discussion about the impact of globalization on governance has focussed on the 'push up' factor from national to international levels and the 'push down' factor from national to sub-regional to local, thereby leaving the scope of national governance in question and perhaps diminished. Trade analysts and WTO staff are quick to alleviate any concern that the role of national government will change in terms of policy objectives and regulation, but the 'jury is still out' on this issue until there is further clarification and development of Articles 1.3 and 6.4.

4.2   Student Access

Demographic changes, lifelong learning, and developing human resource needs created by the knowledge economy are increasing the unmet demand for post-secondary education and training worldwide. GATS supporters maintain that increased international trade will help countries satisfy this growing demand. Public and private higher education institutions also recognize this need and are increasingly involved in cross-border education through development projects, linkages and commercial ventures. Private commercial providers who are primarily concerned with teaching (meaning limited attention is given to research and service) are targeting niche markets. GATS supporters believe that increased student access to education and training is one of the strong rationales and articulated benefits linked to trade liberalization. GATS critics question the need for trade rules when much trade (and national regulation) is already underway. So while there is general agreement on the need for greater student access, questions of affordability and the impact of trade rules on providers and governments remain.

4.3   Registration and Licensing of Foreign Providers

Many educators believe that one of the negative consequences of market driven for-profit education is that the number of 'diploma mills', 'canned degrees' and 'accreditation mills' will increase. This worry applies to both domestic and cross-border provision and can potentially be exacerbated with increased trade. New types of commercial providers such as private education, media and information technology companies, and new forms of program delivery such as branch campuses, franchises and distance education, introduce new challenges for national regulation. Some countries have established new regulations for registering and licensing foreign/private providers, but many have not, and some may not have the ability to implement policy. There is also apprehension that some of the requirements established for licensing will be perceived as potential barriers to trade and will therefore be targeted for liberalization during future rounds of GATS negotiations.

While these may still be 'what if' scenarios, it is important to discuss the role and capacity of national governments, especially from the developing world, to establish and monitor systems for registering new private international providers. It should be noted that the term 'private provider' is used because in most cases, public institutions are classified as private entities as soon as they cross the border and deliver in a foreign country. There are of course exceptions to this trend. Partly for tax reasons, some public institutions setting up branch campuses abroad are trying to get classified as non-governmental organizations or foundations instead of private commercial enterprises. All and all, the issue of regulating and licensing providers delivering education across borders needs further attention. Consideration of what national policies and frameworks are necessary and feasible in light of new trade regulations merits study by the education sector at both national and international levels. This is a complex and increasingly urgent issue to address.

4.4 Accreditation and Quality Assurance

If we thought the questions related to registration and licensing were complex, it becomes even more complicated when one looks at accreditation and quality assurance. The terms accreditation and quality assurance have different meaning and significance depending on the country, actor or stakeholder using the term. Terminology related to quality is a minefield and the cause of much debate and confusion at the international level. For the purposes of this paper, 'quality assurance' is used in a general sense and includes audit, evaluation, accreditation and other review processes and elements. This generic approach is not meant to diminish the differences in meaning and approach used by various countries. However, a macro interpretation of quality recognition and assurance of cross-border education is needed to attract the attention that this issue deserves.

Increased importance has been given to quality assurance at the institutional and national level in the past decade. Over that period, new quality assurance mechanisms and national organizations have been developed in over sixty countries.[18] Regional quality networks have also been established. Most effort has been targeted at quality assurance of domestic higher education provision by public and/or private higher education institutions. However, the increase in cross-border education by such institutions and commercial providers has raised new challenges.

Generic international quality standards might be applied to education in this territory. ISO standards, or other industry – based mechanisms such as the Baldridge Awards, are examples of quality systems that might be applied or modelled for cross-border education. ISO 9001 is already popular among many private education providers, particularly in Asia. Of course, the education sector has mixed views on the appropriateness of quality standards being established for education by those outside the sector. There is also the matter of whether international standards or criteria for quality assurance might jeopardize the sovereignty of national systems, and whether such an approach would lead to unhealthy standardization. The issue is complex and there are many different

---

[18] See the website of the International Network of Quality Assurance Agencies in Higher Education for a database on quality assurance and accreditation bodies. Available at: www.inqaahe.nl. Last Accessed 22 April 2004.

actors and stakeholders involved. However, given the growth in the number and type of cross-border education providers, the prospect of increased trade and new trade rules, there is again a sense of urgency.

The credibility of higher education programs and qualifications is extremely important for students, employers, the public at large and the academic community itself. Thus the question of quality for all forms of cross-border education needs to taken very seriously. Of current interest and debate, is whether national level accreditation and quality assurance systems (where they exist) are able to attend to the complicating factors of education mobility across countries, cultures and jurisdictional systems. A fundamental question is whether countries have the capacity and political will to establish and monitor quality systems for both incoming and outgoing education programs given the diversity of providers and delivery methods. Should national quality/accreditation systems be complemented and augmented by regional or international frameworks? Is it advisable and feasible to develop mutual recognition systems between and among countries? Would an 'International Code of Good Practice' be appropriate or strong enough to monitor quality? These are key questions for the education sector to address and of course, in the exploration of these issues it is imperative that trade rules are given due consideration.

It is also important to acknowledge that there is a great deal of cross-border mobility of students, teachers and programs through non-commercial initiatives. Education activities that are part of development aid projects and international academic linkages and networks are good examples. Therefore, international trade of education services is not the only factor driving the urgency of addressing international quality recognition and assurance. However, it is the idea and prospect of using trade-based rules to govern the quality assurance and recognition of cross-border education that is troublesome to certain segments of the education sector. At this point, it must be clarified that GATS and other bilateral trade agreements do not claim to be establishing rules for quality assurance and recognition of education, but they are important catalysts for more urgent attention being given to these issues.

As the discussion moves forward it will be of strategic and substantive importance to recognize the roles and responsibilities of all the players involved in quality assurance, including individual institutions/providers, national quality assurance systems, non-government accreditation bodies, and regional/international organizations, all of which contribute to ensuring the quality of cross-border education. It will be important to work in a collaborative and complementary fashion to build a system that ensures the quality and integrity of cross-border education and maintains the confidence of society in higher education. It is timely that this question is currently being addressed by UNESCO through the Global Forum, OECD, several international/regional NGOs, and that different approaches to developing national, regional and international frameworks are being discussed.[19]

4.5 Recognition of Qualifications

The need to have mechanisms which recognize academic and professional qualifications gained through domestic or international delivery of education is another important consequence of increased cross-border activity. Even if the education program does not move, the student or the prospective employee can move and therefore credentials need to be recognized if further study or employment is desired. Once again, this issue is relevant to all forms of cross-border education, not just commercial trade initiatives, but the existence of international/bilateral trade agreements is pushing the education sector to give more priority to this issue.

UNESCO has long acknowledged the need for an international system to facilitate recognition of academic and professional

---

[19] Van Damme, D. (2002) 'Trends and Models in International Quality Assurance in Higher Education in Relation to Trade in Education', *Higher Education Management and Policy*, 2002, vol.14, no.3.

qualifications. Regional UNESCO conventions on the 'Recognition of Qualifications' were established more than twenty-five years ago and have been ratified by over 100 Member States in Africa, Asia and the Pacific, the Arab States, Europe and Latin America. They are unique legally binding instruments dealing with crossborder mutual recognition of qualifications. There is limited general awareness of these instruments except for the European regional convention that was jointly updated in 1997 by UNESCO and the Council of Europe in the form of the Lisbon Convention. In 2001, the same two organizations established a 'Code of Good Practice for Transnational Education' which is now a recognized part of the Lisbon Convention. At the present time, there is discussion on how these UNESCO conventions can be used as instruments to complement trade agreements and assure students, employers and the public that there are systems in place to recognize academic and professional qualifications. Given the growth in academic mobility, the increased mobility of the labour force and the fact that GATS is encouraging greater professional mobility, there is a clear and urgent need to address this issue. Questions are also being raised whether these UNESCO conventions could also be used to help address the quality assurance and accreditation issues as well. This idea will be certain to stir up increased interest in the subject and hopefully give the issues the attention they deserve.

4.6 Funding

A discernible trend in many developed and developing countries is that the growth in public funding of higher education is not keeping pace with the accelerated levels of private investment in the sector.[20] This trend, plus the pervasive climate of stricter accountability for public support, is creating a more receptive environment for private and commercial providers of post-secondary education.

---

[20] Levy, D. (2003) *Expanding Higher Education Capacity Through Private Growth: contributions & challenges.* The Observatory on Borderless Higher Education. London, UK.

As already noted, private provision of education in niche markets is increasing. These three factors are contributing to an expectation that there will be more private investment in education in the future. When forces for increased liberalization of trade are added to this scenario, there is an expectation that private and commercial providers will be very active in the international education markets. The Global Education Index, recently developed by the Observatory on Borderless Higher Education,[21] tracks the progress of 50 such companies in ten countries.[22] Many of the firms operate on an international scale.

The greatest fear among many education leaders is that while private investment in education rises, the public support will fall even more steeply. The role that trade plays in this scenario is that countries without the capacity or political will to invest in the physical and soft infrastructure for higher education will begin to rely more and more on foreign investors and providers. This will give trade rules a heavy influence on the terms and use of the private investment and thereby national policy for education. A review of the barriers to trade in education services show that measures relating to commercial presence/foreign investment (mode 3) are being targeted for removal. Of course, a huge proviso in this scenario is that the private and commercial education providers will find it economically viable to deliver internationally, and if this is not the case then new questions will arise.

4.7 Internationalization of Academic Relations

In the last section, emphasis was placed on private and commercial education providers with a strong orientation to for-profit delivery. There are many public and private non-profit institutions committed to an international dimension of education that goes beyond the

---

[21] Garrett, R. (2003) *Mapping the Education Industry – Part Two: Public Companies – relationships with higher education*. Observatory on Borderless Higher Education. London, UK.
[22] Examples of GEI companies include Apollo (USA), Aptech (India), Informatics (Singapore), Sylvan (USA) all of whom work internationally.

delivery of education across national boundaries. Higher education institutions are actively expanding the international dimension of their research, teaching and service functions. This collaborative research and scholarly activity is a necessity given the increasing interdependency among nations to address global issues such as climate change, crime, terrorism and health. The international and intercultural aspects of the curriculum and the teaching/learning process are important contributions to the quality and relevance of higher education. One of the leading rationales at the institutional level for internationalization is the preparation of graduates to live and work in more culturally diverse communities at home and abroad (Knight, 1999). An important question is how an increased emphasis on international trade in education and new trade regulations will affect the nature and priority given to non-commercial international education activities.

4.8 Cultural Diversity and Acculturation

The influence of trade and new trade regulations on the recognition and promotion of indigenous and diverse cultures is a subject that evokes strong positions and sentiments. One camp believes that new technology and movement of people, ideas and culture across borders presents fresh opportunities to promote one's culture and furthers chances for fusion and hybridization of culture. This position rests on the assumption that this flow of culture across borders is not new at all, it is just the accelerated speed which has changed. Others contend that these same forces are eroding national cultural identities and instead of forming new forms of cultures through hybridization, cultures are being homogenized (in most cases interpreted to mean westernized). Given that education has traditionally been seen as a vehicle of acculturation, these arguments are played out in terms of curriculum content and the teaching/learning process of exported/imported programs. Both perspectives have strengths but the real question is whether trade agreements will have an impact. This is still an unanswered question. Does the fact that commercial exports are often based on surplus capacity suggest that efforts are made, or are not made, to customize programs to local needs and to make programs culturally sensitive? This too merits further investigation before conclusions are drawn.

Will commercially traded education programs be any more or less culturally imperialistic or diversified than programs or curriculum which cross borders as part of development projects or academic exchange programs? Many would want to argue that for-profit private providers will not be willing to invest the time and resources to ensure that courses respect cultural traditions and include relevant local content. Given that private providers are market driven there may be a demand from the students and employers for what is perceived to be modern (read western) education. The question of the impact of commercial trade (as well as non-commercial cross-border delivery) of education on cultural diversity requires significant study.

4.9 Higher Education Role and Values

At the heart of the debate for many educators is what impact will increased trade and new trade policy have on the purpose, role and values of higher education. The discussion on GATS has, to date, focused more on the technical, legal, and economic aspects of the movement of students, programs and providers/institutions across borders. But, the growth in new commercial and private providers, the commodification of education, and the prospect of new trade policy frameworks are catalysts for stimulating serious reflection on the role and funding of public higher education institutions in society. The trinity of teaching/learning, research and service to society has traditionally guided the evolution of universities. Is the combination of these roles still valid or can they be disaggregated and rendered by different providers? Values that have traditionally underpinned public education, such as academic freedom and institutional autonomy, are under scrutiny in many countries. Is education still considered to be a public good[23] in the sense of

---

[23] See Singh, M. (2001) 'Re-inserting the 'Public Good' into Higher Education Transformation', *Kagisano.* Council on Higher Education, South Africa. Issue No 1.

contributing to the development of society or is it now perceived as more of a private good for consumption by individuals? Some believe that these traditional values are even more relevant and important in today's environment, others argue for a shift away from these traditional values in light of globalization. And still others argue that if higher education is to fulfil its role as a 'public good' then it will need to move away from its traditional public funding sources in favor of more market-based approaches. Once again, the new emphasis on trade and the introduction of trade rules, demand a rigorous review of the values of higher education. Perhaps the issues of trade and the commercialization of higher education will eventually be critical elements that define and contrast national approaches to the role and purpose of higher education.

4.10 Trade Creep

The term trade creep refers to the quietly pervasive introduction of trade concepts, language and policy into the education sector. The nuance behind trade creep is an unconscious adoption of trade jargon and its underlying values. In some countries there is a deliberate positioning of education as an export industry, accompanied by considerable investment of resources. One would not characterize this approach as trade creep but as trade choice. For other countries and education actors there is a less visible and perhaps unwitting tendency to frame education in trade terms. Language is often the first sign of a shift and this is evident in trade creep. For many years, the education sector referred to incoming and outgoing students or programs. Now we talk about the import and export of education services. The education sector has become the education industry in some countries. The student or learner is the consumer. Students travelling abroad to study is now referred to as mode two or 'consumption abroad'. Reference to the four modes of trade is being used to describe internationalization in general and cross-border education in particular. The next section focuses on this last point and aims to acknowledge the existence and importance of trade in education services but suggests that it needs to be understood and placed in the larger context of international academic mobility and cross-border education.

5 Trade as a Subset of Cross Border Education Activities

The first task is to clarify the meaning of the terms central to the discussion. As outlined in the introduction, the phrase ' trade in education services' and the four mode classification system- cross-border trade, consumption abroad, commercial presence, movement of natural persons – have been especially developed by trade experts to categorize trade in services. The education sector also has its own lexicon of terms to describe education programs and services delivered internationally. These terms include transnational, offshore, cross-border, borderless and the more generic term internationalization. The use of these terms across sectors is inevitable and misunderstanding about their meanings is predictable. The purpose of this section is to provide some clarity on what terms are used by the trade and education sectors and to ensure that 'cross-border education' as interpreted by educators is much broader than 'cross border supply' as used in the trade sector.

5.1 Trade Talk – Education Speak

First the education sector. In the past decade, the interest and growth in international academic mobility has exploded. It involves students, teachers, institution/provider, program and/or curriculum moving across a border. This increased mobility is reflected in the introduction of new terminology to describe or characterize these phenomena. Transnational education is a term used by UNESCO and the Council of Europe in their 'Code of Practice on Transnational Education'. The term is used to mean all types of higher education study where the learners are located in a country different from the one where the awarding institution is based.[24]

The term 'borderless education' first appeared in an Australian report by Cunningham et al.[25] Basically the term refers to the blurring of conceptual, disciplinary and geographic borders traditionally inherent to higher education.[26] It is interesting to juxtapose the terms borderless education and cross-border education. The former acknowledges the disappearance of borders while the latter term emphasizes the existence of borders. Both approaches reflect the reality of today. In this period of unprecedented growth in distance and e-learning, geographic borders seem to be of little consequence. Yet, on the other hand, we can detect a growing importance of borders when the focus turns to regulatory responsibility, especially related to quality assurance, funding and accreditation. Off-shore education is a term used to denote education delivered abroad, but its use is arguably decreasing due to the more recent introduction and popularity of the term cross-border. Cross-border seems to be emerging as the more widely used phrase and refers to the movement of education across a jurisdictional or national border.

The trade sector when referring to GATS uses the term services in order to differentiate from products which are covered by GATT (General Agreement on Trade and Tariffs). In terms of education services, GATS covers primary, secondary, higher and adult education and training programs as well as various 'other' education services such as language testing. Within GATS, the services are supplied through four modes. In short, Mode 1 deals with the service moving, Mode 2 deals with the consumer moving, Mode 3 deals with the provider and investment moving and Mode 4 deals with the human resources or human capital moving. It must

---

[24] UNESCO and Council of Europe (2001) *The UNESCO-CEPES/Council of Europe Code of Good Practice for the Provision of Transnational Education.* UNESCO, Paris, France.
[25] Cunningham, S. et al. (2000) *New Media & Borderless Education*, Department of Education, Training and Youth Affairs, Canberra, Australia.
[26] CVCP (2000) *The Business of Borderless Education: UK Perspectives.* Committee of Vice-Chancellors and Principles. London, United Kingdom.

be said that it is quite an accomplishment to have a generic framework applicable to the supply of commercial services for the 12 major service sectors and 160 subsectors included in GATS. But this framework does not capture or reflect the full range of international cross-border education activity. As more attention is given to the analysis of major actors, stakeholders, rationales, benefits and delivery of cross-border education activity, and as one examines the implications for quality assurance, credential recognition, accreditation, funding and access, it is important that these matters are addressed in terms of the larger picture of cross-border education, not just the four trade modes.

5.2 An Education Framework for Cross-Border Education

The growth and changes in cross-border education are staggering.[27] There are now new types of providers, new methods of delivery, new learners, new partnerships, new financial arrangements, new types of awards, new policies and new regulatory frameworks. All this presents new challenges for how cross-border education is conceptualized (and regulated). Using a trade framework to categorize cross-border activity is one approach, but given these new developments, it is argued that a trade framework is too limited. Cross-border education occurs for a variety of reasons and under a diversity of arrangements – for example, through academic linkages and exchange programs, through development/aid projects and through commercial trade. The GATS trade mode framework only covers commercial trade. Therefore it is proposed that the education sector begin to develop its own classification system to categorize cross-border education in a manner which includes all types of activities not just commercial ventures.

Table 3 presents four education categories for cross-border education based on two elements – what moves (people, providers,

---

[27] For further information especially on international student mobility see OECD 2002. 'The Growth of Cross-border Education' in *Educational Policy Analysis*, Organization for Economic and Community Development. Paris, France.

Table 3 Education Framework for Cross-border Education

Category/Model	Description	Arrangements	Notes
1. People Students/ Learners Trainees	– full academic program – semester or year abroad – internship program – research/field work	– exchange agreements – scholarship/ bursaries – govt/public/ private sponsored – self-funded	– involves credit-based educational activities and programs
Professors Instructors Scholars Experts	– teaching and/or research purposes – technical assistance/ consulting – sabbaticals/professional development	– self or institution funded – govt/public/ private sponsored – contract/fee for service	
2. Providers Institutions, providers, organizations, companies	– foreign provider has academic responsibility for programs – foreign award granted – provider secures physical or virtual presence in receiving country	– academic/ financial partner/s in receiving country possible but not required. – includes private, public, commercial & non-commercial providers	– branch campuses – franchises – stand alone foreign providers – some twinning arrangements
3. Programs Credit/award based academic partnership programs	– involves domestic qualification awarded by receiving country or double/joint award – courses and programs move, not the student	– based on academic linkages between sending and receiving institutions – can be commercial or non-commercial	– primarily involves institutional linkages – some twinning and franchise arrangements

(Continued)

Table 3 (*Continued*)

Category/Model	Description	Arrangements	Notes
4. Projects & Services Wide range of education related projects and services	– no award based program involved. – examples of projects include: research; curriculum design; professional development; capacity building, technical assistance and services	– includes development/ aid projects, partnership programs and commercial contracts	– involves all types of HEI institutions, providers and educational organizations/ companies

programs and projects) and where the qualification is awarded – not on whether the initiative is public, private or commercially oriented.

This framework is a 'work in progress'.[28] It is purposely generic in order to be relevant to many different countries, jurisdictions, cultures and education systems and to include the diversity of cross-border activities and providers. The categories will have to be porous as not all new developments fit neatly into four conceptual groups. Ideally the framework will be used as an alternative to the trade modes and will help the education sector to 1) analyze policy implications for issues such as quality assurance, funding, equity of access, accreditation, recognition of credentials at the national and international levels; 2) study the relationship of cross-border education with trade agreements and trade policy; 3) examine the different and common trends and issues within and among categories; 4) determine the major actors and stakeholders and level of provision within each category; and 5) help to ensure that the international dimension of post-secondary education, specifically cross-border, is not conceptualized only as a commercial activity.

---

[28] Knight J. (2003) 'Trade Talk – the four modes', *International Higher Education*, Spring, Boston, USA.

6 Update on Stakeholder Interests and Actions

There is no doubt that certain education stakeholder groups are clearly and loudly expressing their views about potential risks associated with GATS and further trade in higher education services. There seems to be more debate within countries than between countries. Larsen and Vincent-Lancrin[29] note that at the 'Washington Forum on Trade in Educational Services', the debate was less about conflicting country positions than about conflicting professional groups, each with their own culture and interests. Furthermore, there is little discussion as to whether the anticipated economic and supply benefits to education are reasonable and probable. One reason for this is the lack of hard data on forecasted growth in each of the four supply modes and in-country impact. The movement of students to study in other countries (Mode 2- Consumption abroad) is the only mode where there is good information available.[30]

6.1 Examples of Involved Stakeholder Groups

During the last year, there has been a surge in the attention given to the impact of GATS and trade policy on post-secondary education. Intergovernmental bodies such as UNESCO, OECD, and the World Bank have given prominence to the issue. International and regional non-governmental organizations such as Education International, International Association of Universities, Association of Commonwealth Universities and European Universities Association are taking concrete steps to inform the education community and engage their members. At the national level, associations of universities, student groups and university teacher organizations have been active in expressing their opinions to their respective

---

[29] Larsen, K. and Vincent-Lancrin, S. (2002) 'International trade in Education Services: Good or Bad?' in *Higher* Education and Management Policy, 14 (3).
[30] OECD (2002) *Indicators on Internationalisation and Trade of Post-secondary Education*. OECD/CERI. Paper prepared for the OECD/US Forum on Trade in Education Services. Washington, D.C., USA.

governments. In fact, it is probably the teachers' unions around the world that have been most engaged in speaking out about the potential impact of trade and the commercialization of education. There are also, of course, democracy, civil society and development groups who have been very vocal about their concerns regarding the impact of GATS on public services, including education. On the supportive side, the International Chamber of Commerce, the European Services Forum, and the Coalition of Service Industries in the United States are examples of three powerful and active organizations promoting increased trade liberalization of services; but these organizations have shown limited, if any, interest in the education sector.

It is both informative and revealing to see the variety of declarations, meetings, newsgroups, and campaigns mobilized around the issue of GATS and education. To maintain a balanced approach in this paper, substantial efforts were made to locate education groups actively campaigning in favour of increased trade in education. This search only identified the US based National Committee for International Trade in Education (NCITE) and an organization in New Zealand called Education Forum which is linked to the New Zealand Business Round Table. This does not necessarily mean other groups do not exist. It may mean that they are not as visible to the public or to the education community.

To illustrate the diversity of groups and actions engaged with the issue of GATS and higher education, a sample of declarations, meetings and organizations are listed in Appendix A. This is not a comprehensive list, it is for illustrative purposes only. Unfortunately the list is very oriented to Europe and North America, and does not include sufficient examples from Africa, Asia and Latin America.

6.2 Issues being Discussed by Stakeholders

It is important to recognize the range of issues different stakeholder groups are raising. Those aspects which relate to the technical and legal issues of GATS are not included in the list below as they have already been addressed in the previous paper[31] and by different authors.[32] Prominent issues and arguments include:

- Of common concern is the fear that public domestic provision of higher education may be undermined by foreign competition and national education policy objectives may be at risk.
- It is believed that trade, coupled with commercialization and commodification of higher education, will put more importance on economic benefits than on the academic, social, scientific and cultural contributions of higher education to society.
- It is suggested that increased trade by for-profit providers using new delivery methods may jeopardize consumer confidence and public trust in the quality of higher education. It is also important to be alert to public opinion and confidence in public/private higher education institutions who are active in trade of education services.
- Higher education is seen to be different from other service sectors due to the public mandate and the role of government.
- Even though in some countries the demand for higher education surpasses the capacity of the domestic system, the introduction of foreign commercial providers and public/private institutions requires close monitoring in terms of equitable access for students.
- Many of the barriers identified for Mode 2 (study abroad) and Mode 4 (movement of people) do not fall within the GATS framework. These include aspects such as visas, work permits, immigration status as well as those barriers put into place by a country wanting to prevent consumption abroad. It is Mode 3 (commercial presence) that merits the closest scrutiny. It is pointed out that what may be seen as barriers by exporting countries are in fact, fundamental aspects of the regulatory system in the importing country.

---

[31] Knight, J. (2002) *Trade in Higher Education Services: The Implications of GATS*. The Observatory on Borderless Higher Education. London: United Kingdom.
[32] See Sauvé, P. (2002) Trade, Education and the GATS: 'What's in, What's Out, What's All the Fuss About?', *Higher Education Management and Policy*, 2002, vol.14, no. 3.

- The impact of trade in education services on institutional autonomy, academic freedom, brain drain and academic employment requires further investigation.
- One of the most critical implications is the impact of increased trade on the quality of higher education provision and the recognition of qualifications and accreditation. Quality standards and mutual recognition issues should be addressed by the education sector, and outside the purview of trade agreements.
- There is significant concern that increased trade in education will characterize and promote higher education as a 'private good' rather than a 'public good'.

6.3   What is Not Being Addressed by Stakeholders?

It is equally interesting to note which actors/stakeholders are not involved and what issues have not been addressed.

- There has been very little discussion on the benefits of increased trade in education. Most of the concern is on the respective roles of the government and the market in the regulation of higher education. It would be useful to have further analysis on the contributions of more liberalized trade in higher education to the international demand post-secondary education.
- The primary and secondary education sectors have been almost silent on the implications of GATS. There seems to be an implicit understanding or assumption that public compulsory education will not be covered by GATS. This may or may not be the case. Time will tell, especially for those countries that have liberalized access to compulsory education.
- It is the university sector within the post-secondary education category that has been most involved in discussing GATS. The professional, technical and vocational providers have not been very vocal. It would be useful to have more information and discussion with the non-university sector.
- The impact of trade rules on the regulations of the professions needs further attention, especially in relation to domestic regulation and the 'necessity test'.

- To date there has been little discussion of issues related to the 'other services' category. Increased trade in education services such as language testing or quality assessment and evaluation services may have implications for higher education. The category of adult education has also not been fully addressed even though commitments have been made in this category.
- TRIPS is another WTO agreement. TRIPS stands for 'Trade Related Aspects of Intellectual Property Rights'. Of particular interest to the higher education community are issues related to whether intellectual property rights will encourage or inhibit innovation and research, who owns copyright of materials used in e-education, and protection of indigenous knowledge.
- The focus thus far has been almost entirely on the teaching side of education and has not addressed implications for research. Research is an integral part of the university role and further investigation is needed into the potential impact on applied research and especially privately contracted or funded research. Do public education institutions that undertake research and development activities have unfair advantage over private organizations who do not usually receive public support for their activities? Could public subsidies be construed as a barrier to fair trade or under the national treatment condition be applicable to private providers?
- Attention needs to be given to potential public backlash to the efforts of public higher education institutions efforts to recruit large numbers of international students (even if they are paying differential fees) and invest public funds in overseas commercial ventures that may or may not be profitable.
- Commercial trade is only one aspect of cross-border education. Analysis of the implications of new trade rules and increased trade on non-commercial cross-border education is required.

Individually, the issues outlined above merit further investigation and rigorous analysis. Collectively, they demonstrate the breadth of interest and concern. They also point to the need for further consultation within the higher education sector, with other service sectors, and certainly with trade officials.

6.4 Ongoing Questions

At this stage of exploring the implications of GATS on the provision of higher education, there are still many more questions than answers. The questions, not all of which are new but most of which are still not answered, deal with a broad range of issues:

- Technical issues related to the continuing development of specific articles/rules in the GATS agreements – subsidies, domestic regulation, dispute resolution.
- Clarification issues regarding the implications of which services are covered by GATS and how to distinguish between commercial and non-commercial cross-border education.
- Policy issues related to fundamental aspects of higher education – access, funding, quality, both for domestic and cross-border delivery.
- Philosophical issues dealing with the core values of higher education (domestic and international provision) and its role and purpose in society.
- Negotiation issues related to the current requests and offers and identified barriers.
- Market issues as to actual size of trade forecasted growth and where it will occur.
- Data collection issues so that reliable information exists on the size and scope of commercial trade in education by all types of institutions, providers, companies.
- Education stakeholder issues related to increased awareness, understanding and action.
- Consultation issues within and among the education community, government and trade actors and sectors.

7 Concluding Comments

As has been repeated many times, GATS is a new, untested and evolving agreement. The interpretations of existing articles and obligations can change and new disciplines can be developed. There continue to be more questions than answers. To date, there have been fewer commitments to trade in education than expected.

This means that there is time for the higher education sector to become better informed about how best to move forward to maximize the benefits and minimize the risks of commercial trade. Working in a trade policy environment is relatively new territory for the education sector. It will take further work and analysis for the various education sectors to be confident and credible actors in shaping and reacting to new trade policy developments. However, the education sector as a whole has considerable experience in other policy arenas – immigration, foreign relations, culture, science and technology to name a few. It will require that the higher education community at the national level be vigilant in monitoring new developments and work collaboratively with government and non-government representatives from education, trade, industry and commerce and foreign affairs.

While it is true that both the benefits and risks of increased international trade in education will be felt most keenly at the national level, it also important that the wider international higher education community continues to work together on these issues so that 1) educators' views and expertise come to bear on developments in trade in education services; 2) the higher education sector continues to work towards national/regional and international education frameworks that addresses the quality assurance, accreditation and recognition of qualifications for cross-border education; 3) further work is done on investigating the implications of trade agreements on scholarly pursuits, research and intellectual property; 4) trade is seen as one subset of the larger phenomenon of cross-border education; and 5) that the impact of trade on the larger more philosophical questions related to the purpose, values and role of higher education continue to be explored.

Further details on selected stakeholder organisations and activities associated with GATS

1 Declarations

Joint Declaration on Higher Education and the General Agreement on Trade in Services – September 2001. Developed and signed by the European Universities Association, the Canadian Association of Universities and Colleges, the American Council for Education and the Council for Higher Education Accreditation. The declaration states that "our institutions are committed to reducing obstacles to international trade in higher education using conventions and agreements outside of a trade policy regime. This commitment includes, but is not limited, to improving communications, expanding information exchanges, and developing agreements concerning higher education institutions, programs, degrees or qualifications and quality review practices." It is expected that the signatories to this declaration will be issuing a second one in mid 2003 that will address the need for a new international policy framework for cross-border education.

Brixen/Bressanone Declaration on Cultural Diversity and GATS (2002). The European Regional Ministers for Culture and Education adopted this declaration which focussed on the protection of diversity in education, culture and media. The declaration states that we "believe that GATS carries the tendency of the precedence of commercial priority over democratically agreed quality", and calls for "democratically supported services in education, culture and media [to be] excluded from further GATS involvement".

Port Alegre Charter (2002) The participating rectors at the 'Iberoamerican Summit of Rectors of Public Universities' signed this charter and requested "the governments of their respective countries not to become engaged in any commitment concerning higher education". This Charter in turn stimulated other Brazilian organizations such as the 'National Association of Leaders of Federal Institutions of Higher Education' to send the Port Alegre Charter to the president of Brazil, asking for an explicit statement of the government's position on GATS and higher education services.

Education Group Charter (2002) The European Social Forum established a number of principles to guide the actions and construction of the 'Europe of Education'. Examples of these principles include: "Education is a right, not a commodity. Education must be a public service, free and secular. Its financing must be public. The mission of education is to educate, form and qualify workers, citizens and humans. Economic profits must not guide its objectives. Education also has a role of fostering social change." The Charter concludes with a rejection of the integration of education into trade liberalization and advocates a 'no' position to GATS.

2 Intergovernmental Organizations' Meetings

UNESCO Global Forum on International Quality Assurance, Accreditation and the Recognition of Qualifications (2002) was convened by UNESCO to bring together governments, institutions, policy makers, educators and students to look at the impact of globalization on quality assurance and accreditation. In light of increased cross border education delivery and new trade agreements, the topic of international recognition of qualifications was also addressed. There was an urgent call to move forward on looking at the relationship between trade agreements and the 6 Regional UNESCO Conventions on Recognition of Qualifications, including the Lisbon Europe Region Convention.

OECD/US Forum on Trade in Educational Services (May 2002), in co-operation with the World Bank, brought together a broad range of stakeholders with an interest in cross-border trade in higher education services. Perspectives on the benefits, risks and issues on trade in educational services were heard from representatives from different regions of the world, from private/public, for-profit/non-profit education providers, trade experts, students, non-government organizations, sceptics and supporters. This was a first opportunity for education and trade policy makers and other stakeholders at an international level to address this issue. There was a broad consensus and acknowledgement by the higher education sector and governments that among the key issues needing further and immediate attention are quality assurance, accreditation and recognition of qualifications. http://www.oecd.org/EN/document/0,,EN-document-4-nodirectorate-no-20-25748-4,00.html

3   International non-governmental Associations

Education International is a worldwide confederation of education trade unions and was one of the first groups to address the issue of GATS and trade in education. This group has prepared several reports cautioning against the potential risks and threats of including education services in GATS. EI's central objective is to have education excluded from the scope of GATS. The EI documents address the technical and legal aspects of GATS as well as some anticipated implications for higher education. These documents are available on their website. http://www.ei-ie.org/action/english/Globalisation/e%20wto_gats%20index.htm.

International Association of Universities is a signatory to the 'Joint Declaration on Higher Education and the General Agreement on Trade in Services' mentioned above. IAU links trade liberalization of education with globalization and commodification and provides a website with information and links to organizations dealing with these issues. http://www.unesco.org/iau/globalization/wto-gats.html

4   National/Regional Associations

National Committee for International Trade in Education is a US group whose mission is to be "an organized voice for United States education, training and testing institutions, corporations and organizations which provide services internationally". One of its stated purposes is to "provide accurate, current and organized information related to US education and training interests to the proper US government agencies, and particularly the Office of the US Trade Representative, as well as keeping NCITE members informed of governmental and other related activity." The organisation serves as an active advocate/lobby group to the government on the matters relating to access to foreign education markets. http://www.tradeineducation.org/general_info/frames.htm

People and Planet is an example of one of the most active student groups. It is a UK-wide student network organizing campaigns on a number of international issues, one of which is GATS. This organization has produced a major report entitled 'Trading it away: How GATS threatens UK education' which is examines in detail the rules and disciplines of GATS and speculates on potential impact on the quality, funding and role of UK higher education. http://www.peopleandplanet.org/tradejustice/

Education Forum is an association of individuals who have a common concern for the future direction of New Zealand education. The membership is drawn from the primary, secondary and tertiary sectors, together with leaders of industry and commerce. They take the position that GATS and education is a 'win/win' situation for New Zealand and actively support the Government's position on gaining greater access to foreign education markets. http://www.educationforum.org.nz/

5 National Associations of Students, Teachers, Universities

There are numerous other student groups, teachers' associations, and university organizations at the national/regional which have prepared informative reports, briefing papers, and press releases on the implications of GATS for higher education. These groups are especially active in Europe, Australia, New Zealand, Canada, South Korea, USA, India, South Africa.

Selected Sources of Further Information on GATS and Higher Education

Altbach, P. (2003) 'The United States and International Education Trade', *International Higher Education*, Spring, Boston, USA.
APEC (2001) *Measures affecting trade and investment in education services in the Asia-Pacific region*. A report to the APEC group on Services 2000, Singapore.
Ascher, B. (2001) *Education and Training Services in International Trade Agreements*. Paper presented to Conference on 'Higher Education and Training in the Global Marketplace: Exporting Issues and Trade Agreements'. Washington, D.C.
AUCC (2001) *Canadian Higher Education and the GATS: AUCC Background Paper*. Association of Universities and Colleges of Canada. Ottawa, Canada.

AUCC et al. (2001) *Joint Declaration on Higher Education and the General Agreement on Trade in Services.* Association of Universities and Colleges of Canada, American Council on Education, European University Association, Council for Higher Education Accreditation. Ottawa, Canada.

Canadian Federation of Students (2002) *Friend or Foe: Trade Agreements and their Impact on Post-secondary Education.* Ottawa, Canada.

Cohen, M. G. (2000) *The World Trade Organization and post-secondary education: Implications for the public system in Australia.* Hawke Institute, University of South Australia. Adelaide, Australia. Working Paper Series No. 1.

Corporate University Xchange (1999) *Annual Survey of Corporate University Future Directions.* Corporate University Xchange. New York, USA.

Cunningham, S. et al. (2000) *New Media & Borderless Education*, Department of Education, Training and Youth Affairs, Canberra, Australia.

CVCP (2000) *The Business of Borderless Education: UK Perspectives.* Committee of Vice-Chancellors and Principles. London, United Kingdom.

Deodhar S. (2002) *Managing Trade in Educational Services: Issues for India's Response in WTO Negotiations.* India Institute of Management Working Paper No. 20001-20-01. Ahmedabad, India.

EI/PSI (2000) *Great Expectations: The Future of Trade in Services.* Joint paper by Education International and Public Services International. Brussels, Belgium.

EI/PSI (1999) *The WTO and the Millennium Round. What is at stake for Public Education?* Joint paper by Education International and Public Services International. Brussels, Belgium.

European University Association (2002) *The Bologna Process and the GATS Negotiations.* Geneva, Switzerland.

Garrett, R. (2003*) Mapping the Education Industry – Part Two: Public Companies-relationships with higher education.* Observatory on Borderless Higher Education. London, UK.

Gottlieb and Pearson (2001) *GATS Impact on Education in Canada.* Legal Opinion. Ottawa, Canada.

Knight, J. (1999) 'Issues and Trends in Internationalization: A Comparative Perspective' in S. Bond and J.P. Lemasson (Eds) *A New World of Knowledge: Canadian Universities and Globalization.* Ottawa: International Development Research Centre (IDRC). pp. 201–239.

Knight, J. (2002) *Trade in Higher Education Services: The Implications of GATS.* The Observatory on Borderless Higher Education. London: United Kingdom.

Knight J. (2003a) *Internationalization Remodelled: Responding to New Realities and Challenges.* In publication.

Knight J. (2003b) 'Trade Talk – the four modes', *International Higher Education*, Spring, Boston, USA

Knight, J. (2003c) *A Wake up Call – Trade Talk and Higher Education.* Paper presented at CHEA Conference, Phoenix, USA.

Larsen, K., Morris, R. & Martin, J. (2002) 'Trade in education services: trends and issues', *World Economy*, Vol. 25, No 6.

Larsen, K. and Vincent-Lancrin, S. (2002) 'International trade in Education Services: Good or Bad?' in *Higher Education and Management Policy*, 14 (3).

Levy, D. (2003) *Expanding Higher Education Capacity Through Private Growth: contributions & challenges*. The Observatory on Borderless Higher Education. London, UK.

Mohemedbhai, G. (2003) 'Globalization and Its Implications on Universities in Developing Countries' in G. Breton and M. Lambert (eds) *Universities and Globalization: Private Linkages, Public Trust*, UNESCO/Université Laval/ Economica. Paris, France.

Mundy, K. & Ika, M. (2003) *Hegemonic Exceptionalism and Legitimating Bet-Hedging: Paradoxes and Lessons from the US and Japanese Approaches to Education Services under the GATS*. Paper prepared for 'Comparative International Education Society' Conference, New Orleans, USA.

National Unions of Students in Europe (2000) *Information Sheet/CoCo/BM41 Commodification of Education Introductory Information*. Brussels, Belgium.

Nilsson, B. (1999) *Internationalization at home – Theory and Praxis*. European Association for International Education Forum, 12.

NCITE (2001) *Barriers to Trade in Transnational Education*. National Committee for International Trade in Education. Washington, D.C. USA.

Newman, K. & Couturier, L. (2002) *Trading Public Good in the Higher Education Market*. The Observatory on Borderless Higher Education. London, United Kingdom.

OECD (2002) *Current Commitments under the GATS in Educational Services*. OECD/CERI Paper prepared for the OECD/US Forum on Trade in Education Services. Washington, D.C., USA.

OECD (2002) *Indicators on Internationalisation and Trade of Post-secondary Education*. OECD/CERI. Paper prepared for the OECD/US Forum on Trade in Education Services. Washington, D.C., USA.

OECD (2002) 'The Growth of Cross-border Education' in *Educational Policy Analysis*, Organization for Economic and Community Development. Paris, France.

Patil, V.K. (2002) *Higher Education in India under GATS*. Paper prepared for meeting convened by the Association of Commonwealth Universities. Perth, Australia.

Peace Lenn, M., Deupree, J. & Johnson, M. (eds) (2002) *OECD/US Forum on Trade in Educational Services: Conference Proceedings*. Centre for Quality Assurance in International Education. Washington, D.C.

Powar, K.B. (ed) (2002) *Internationalization of Higher Education*. Association of Indian Universities. New Delhi, India.

Powar, K.B. (2002) *WTO, GATS and Higher Education: An Indian Perspective*. Paper prepared for meeting convened by the Association of Commonwealth Universities. Perth, Australia.

Sauvé, P. (2002) Trade, Education and the GATS: 'What's in, What's Out, What's All the Fuss About?', *Higher Education Management and Policy*, 2002, vol.14, no3.

SAUVCA (2002) *Briefing Document on WTO, GATS and Higher Education.* South African Universities Vice-Chancellors Association. Pretoria, South Africa.

Scott, P. (2000) 'Globalisation and higher education: Challenges for the 21st century' in *Journal Of Studies in International Education,* vol. 4, no.1.

Singh, M. (2001) 'Re-inserting the 'Public Good' into Higher Education Transformation', *Kagisano.* Council on Higher Education, South Africa. Issue No 1.

UNESCO and Council of Europe (2001) *The UNESCO-CEPES/Council of Europe Code of Good Practice for the Provision of Transnational Education.* UNESCO, Paris, France.

Van Dalen & Dorrit (ed) (2002) *The global market for higher education.* Netherlands Organization for International Co-operation in Higher Education (NUFFIC). The Hague. The Netherlands.

Van Damme, D. (2001) *Higher Education in the Age of Globalization: The need for a new regulatory framework for recognition, quality assurance and accreditation. Working Paper.* UNESCO. Paris, France.

Van Damme, D. (2002) 'Trends and models in international quality assurance in higher education in relation to trade in Education', *Higher Education Management and Policy,* 2002, vol.14, no.3.

WTO (1998) *Education Services. Background Note* by the Secretariat. Council for Trade in Services. Geneva, Switzerland. S/C/W/49, 98–3691.

WTO (1999a) *An Introduction to the GATS.* World Trade Organization. Geneva, Switzerland.

WTO (1999c) *The General Agreement in Trade in Services – objectives, coverage, and disciplines.* Prepared by the WTO Secretariat. Geneva, Switzerland.

WTO (2001) *GATS – Fact and Fiction.* World Trade Organization. Geneva, Switzerland.

Quality Assurance and Borderless Higher Education: *finding pathways through the maze*

Robin Middlehurst and Carolyn Campbell

1 Introduction

Through its role as an international strategic information service, the Observatory is tracking specific aspects of borderless higher education to identify the potential impact of these developments for higher education systems, institutions and agencies. In this paper we focus on quality assurance, a policy area that is not only deeply affected by borderless developments, but also heavily implicated in the task of addressing the dilemmas and consequences arising from them.

Quality assurance is an important part of academic professionalism. It is also a key mechanism for building institutional reputation or brand in a competitive local and global arena and a necessary foundation for consumer protection. Across the world, it is part of the armoury used by governments to increase, widen or control participation in the face of rising demand for higher education and it is central to current debates about higher education as a public good or tradable commodity. Quality assurance is also fundamental to the security of qualifications and the mobility of professionals. Without effective and appropriate quality assurance policies and practices, aspirations towards knowledge economies, lifelong learning, community development and social inclusion cannot be fully realised. It is for these reasons that quality assurance is receiving increasing attention at all levels.

In part two of our paper, we highlight the context and some of the 'problems and issues' to which borderless developments have given rise. In the third part, we map developments in quality assurance policies and practice, illustrating the ways in which quality assurance is being harnessed to provide 'solutions'. We draw attention to issues that are being addressed or remain unresolved. In the fourth part, we summarise trends, speculate on future directions and provide some conclusions about the interplay between borderless developments and quality assurance. In providing this overview of the quality assurance territory, our purpose is to alert readers to ongoing initiatives and concerns that have consequences for institutions, agencies, countries and regions.

PART TWO

2.1 Context

Borderless higher education is driven by factors that reflect wider economic, social and political trends. These include developments in information and communications technologies (ICT), the growth of knowledge-driven economies, globalisation trends and requirements for lifelong learning. Such developments affect all sectors and countries, albeit in different ways. In addition, Newman and Couturier[1]

---

[1] Newman F & Couturier L (2002) *Trading Public Good in the Higher Education Market*, London, Observatory on Borderless Higher Education.

note four trends that appear to be affecting higher education across the world:

- Expanding enrolments (accompanied by shifts in student needs and expectations);
- The growth of new competitors, virtual education and consortia within the operating spheres of 'traditional' higher education providers and provision;
- The global activity of many institutions; and
- The tendency for policy makers to use market forces as levers for change in higher education.

Both the fundamental socio-economic drivers and these specific trends have their consequences for quality assurance, practically and politically. In essence, quality assurance has moved to centre stage for all the actors in higher education. At a national level, for institutions, quality assurance is usually key to accessing public funds and at an international level, it is also key to accessing new markets. For professions and disciplines, it ensures continuing student enrolments and the promise of employment as licensed practitioners. Governments seek to use quality assurance regulations to promote their national agendas or to counteract aspects of globalisation that may interfere with these agendas. As the learning landscape changes and becomes more complex, participants and purchasers of higher education depend on quality assurance arrangements to provide information and guidance about their educational choices. Quality assurance arrangements must also act as insurance, if not a guarantee, of the present and continuing value of educational investments.

2.2 Borderless Higher Education and Quality Assurance Issues

The term 'borderless education' was originally coined by an Australian research team.[2] It was subsequently adopted and

---

[2] Cunningham S, Tapsall S, Ryan Y, Stedman L, Bagdon K, Flew T (1998) *New Media and Borderless Education: A Review of the Convergence between Global Media Networks and Higher Education Provision*, Canberra, DETYA.

amplified by British researchers[3] working in association with the Australians.[4] The researchers describe the territory of borderless education as encompassing educational providers, provision and services that cut across conventional boundaries, both geographical and conceptual. The boundaries include:

- levels and types of education, such as further and higher education, vocational and academic, adult and continuing education; in some cases, this represents a genuine effort to create seamless life-long learning opportunities;
- private and public, for-profit and not-for profit education: combining 'public good' and 'private gain' organisational structures and forms of provision;
- state and country boundaries as in the many forms of transnational education;
- sector boundaries, for example, between business or the public sectors and higher education, creating new consortia, joint ventures and strategic alliances;
- boundaries of time and space that are crossed in the creation of virtual universities and online learning programmes.

The crossing or blurring of boundaries and borders is producing new educational forms and new educational opportunities, both positive and negative. On the positive side, new opportunities include corporate universities, blended learning, educational brokerage, international consortia, educational partnerships, joint degrees and e-universities.[5] On the negative side there is evidence

---

[3] CVCP (2000) *The Business of Borderless Education: UK Perspectives*, vols 1–3, London, Universities UK.
[4] Cunningham S, Ryan Y, Stedman L, Tapsall S, Bagdon K, Flew T, Coaldrake P (2000) *The Business of Borderless Education*, Canberra, DETYA.
[5] Middlehurst R (2003) 'The Developing World of Borderless Education: Impact and Implications' in D'Antoni, S (ed) (2003), *The Virtual University: Models and Messages, Lessons from Case Studies*, Paris UNESCO. Available at: www.unesco.org/iiep. Last Accessed 22 April 2004.

of duplicity and fraud[6] in the form of so-called diploma mills, accreditation factories, bogus degrees and fraudulent visa operators. There are also concerns about higher education as a tradable 'commodity'.[7] The net effect of these developments and their perceived impact, individually and collectively, is to increase competition and collaboration in higher education and to multiply existing complexities and concerns.

Borderless developments have other consequences that are less tangible and more profound since they challenge existing *conceptual* boundaries. The rise of corporate universities and expansion of for-profit education businesses, for example, has prompted questions about the nature and definition of 'universities' since the new entities do not always possess the same features as traditional institutions. Developments in work-based learning and the accreditation of experiential learning raise issues about the comparability and portability of credit and degrees, and the expansion of international trade in education is sharpening debates about the role and purposes of higher education and its relations with the state. These issues have practical consequences for quality assurance since existing definitions, standards, policies, processes, criteria, evidence and measurements are at one and the same time challenged by new developments *and* used to defend traditional boundaries.

Some specific examples may help to illustrate the quality assurance issues that can arise from borderless developments:[8]

- Trade in higher education is growing, with different countries involved as exporters and importers of educational provision and

---

[6] CHEA (2003) "Important Questions about 'Diploma Mills' and 'Accreditation Mills'", Fact Sheet #6, May 2003 and Observatory on Borderless Higher Education (2003a), *Breaking News Articles* (13 February 2003 and 20 February 2003) on fraud and deception.

[7] See National Unions of Students in Europe, *Policy Paper on the Commodification of Education*. Available at: www.esib.org/policies/CommodificationEducation.pdf. Last Accessed 22 April 2004.

[8] For further detail see Middlehurst R (2003) 'The Developing World of Borderless Education: Impact and Implications' in D'Antoni, S (ed) (2003), *The Virtual University: Models and Messages, Lessons from Case Studies*, Paris UNESCO. Available at: www.unesco.org/iiep. Last Accessed 22 April 2004.

services. Regulatory environments differ and institutions have to deal with a range of quality assurance requirements in different countries. From the perspective of governments, some countries are establishing sound regulatory regimes to guide and control local and non-national providers, others lack the resources or the mechanisms to differentiate between legitimate and fraudulent providers and provision;
- ICT developments are making virtual learning a growing reality and have increased the amount of distance learning provision available from a variety of providers. Some countries have quality assurance arrangements for these modes of learning, others do not;
- Collaboration between institutions to create new programmes and degrees requires at least 'mutual recognition' of quality and standards, if not directly comparable criteria and assessment practices to allow for credit accumulation and transfer. Guidelines, benchmarks and reference points do not exist in many countries at a national level and are still embryonic at an international level;
- Partnerships (and competition) between sectors and countries has given access to a range of new quality assurance mechanisms (such as industry standards and methodologies) and has increased the market for new accreditation arrangements and kite-marks; this is also increasing levels of competition between 'accreditors';
- The 'unbundling' of educational processes in ways that allow delivery by different providers, perhaps in different countries, is creating the need for quality assurance arrangements for each process (e.g. for learning centres, learning resources, educational guidance, assessment, teaching, etc) as well as a need for quality assurance arrangements for whole new entities to assure the quality and standards of the qualifications awarded;
- New categories of provider, provision and service have given rise to problems of terminology and definition and these in turn affect understandings of criteria and quality assurance arrangements.

The dependence on quality assurance for different reasons by each of the key actors described above can be a source of tension as each player seeks to have their requirements and purposes reflected in regulatory frameworks and quality assurance arrangements. The dimensions of borderless higher education clearly add further layers of complexity and potential for confusion. As a result, the domain of quality assurance is fluid, contested and volatile, with an array of overlapping initiatives in train. Within this domain one can distinguish between 'doers' (the institutions and providers, professional associations, agencies and governments), the 'thinkers' (researchers and analysts) and the 'talkers' (networks of various kinds). Each of these players is making a contribution to the debates about quality assurance arrangements for the future, resulting in a great deal of activity, but also 'noise' in the system. In the end, it is only the 'doers' that can decide and implement appropriate arrangements. In mapping the territory we will try to distinguish between the different voices and the varied political stances involved.

2.3 Problems of Terminology: Dealing with Complexity, Confusion and Change

Borderless education and quality assurance are both plagued by problems of terminology. For borderless education, the difficulties are associated with convergence of categories, overlaps between categories and the emergence of new categories. Official statistics often lag behind developments, and data that are necessary for quality assurance and other purposes may prove difficult to identify and collect. For example, an institution that is categorised as 'public' in one country (De Montfort University in the UK) may be designated as 'private' in another jurisdiction (De Montfort University Business School in South Africa). An institution may embrace both public and private entities (Tsinghua University and Tsinghua Tongfang, its private online venture, in China). And a 'provider of higher education' may include a bundle of provision and services each supplied by different providers (UNext and Cardean University in the US).

With quality assurance, the issues are different. They include the use of similar terms in different countries to cover rather different processes or the use of technically different terms to mean the same thing (for example, quality assurance, accreditation or recognition). The interrelationship of the two fields-borderless education and quality assurance-merely adds complications. As a consequence, most national agencies and international networks are seeking to create agreed glossaries of terms to facilitate dialogue and mutual understanding. Without a common 'language', shared and acceptable judgements and standards are difficult to reach.

In the following section we touch on the four domains that are relevant to this paper: Higher Education; Distance Learning; Quality Assurance and Trade in Educational Services. In each domain, there are few internationally agreed definitions, and where these do exist, ongoing developments are likely to require their amendment.

Higher education
The term 'higher education' is often used synonymously with other terms – tertiary education, post-secondary education or universities – but also has specific meaning in different contexts. In different countries:

- Timing (post 16 or 18), level (third stage or foundation), type of learning (education versus training, academic versus vocational), and range of study-fields differ;
- Differentiation may be institutional (polytechnics, community colleges, universities); elsewhere, such distinctions have gone (Australia and the UK, for example, have abolished their 'binary line'); Alternatively, boundaries exist at the *programme and degree level*, rather than between institutions (as in the reforms proposed in the Netherlands);
- Functions may be differentiated – research or teaching institutions – or combined, and the qualifications awarded may or may not lead directly into employment (or may give access or not to particular employment sectors);

Quality Assurance and Borderless Higher Education

- Higher education includes study on programmes leading to degrees and a narrower definition linked to the award of a degree or diploma (the London University External Programme is solely an examination system that leads to a degree);
- Increasingly, 'higher education' includes education provided at recognised universities and colleges that does not lead to a degree (such as adult education and continuing professional development, often labelled 'lifelong learning');
- Higher education also includes education and training offered by other providers (such as educational businesses) that leads to diplomas, degrees and other kinds of qualifications or credit.

The implication of many aspects of borderless developments is that definitions need to be both broader and more clearly articulated. The World Bank's[9] and OECD's[10] use of the term 'tertiary education' is arguably more appropriate and more accurate. Regulatory regimes will also need to create new and broader definitions since these are necessary foundations for quality assurance.

Distance learning, distance education and e-learning
As John Daniel, currently Assistant Secretary General for Education at UNESCO has stated, "distance education has evolved as a function of time, place and technology, so it now means different things in different countries".[11] Across countries, the terminology used to describe 'distance education' or 'distance learning' often reflects Daniel's three variables:

- In the US, distance education was often understood as the linking of students in remote classrooms by simultaneous video-conferencing (synchronous communication); in South

---

[9] World Bank (2002) *Constructing Knowledge Societies: New Challenges for Higher Education*, Washington DC, World Bank.
[10] OECD (1998) 'Redefining Higher Education', Wagner, A. OECD Directorate for Education, Employment, Labour and Social Affairs, in *The OECD Observer*, No. 213, October 1998.
[11] Daniel J (1996) *Mega-Universities and Knowledge Media: Technology Strategies for Higher Education*, London, Kogan.

Africa, distance learning describes educational programmes that provide interactive study materials and de-centralised learning facilities that students can access according to need, (i.e. asynchronously).[12]

- In Australia and New Zealand, terms like 'external', 'extra-mural' or 'off-campus study' reflect the fact that places of study are 'at a distance from a formally recognised educational establishment'. In several countries there is now increasing diversity in study locations, from formally accredited learning centres to homes, offices, public libraries, museums, shopping centres and recreational spaces.
- In France, the technology of instruction is reflected in the terminology: distance learning is called 'tele-enseignement'.

ICT developments are bringing convergence in the two traditions of remote-classroom and correspondence education and are also breaking down the boundaries between distance and on-campus learning. Convergence is happening both at the institutional and programme level such that 'dual mode' or 'mixed mode' provision (and providers) are becoming commonplace.[13] The term 'distance learning' is now often used interchangeably with 'open' or 'flexible learning'. The convergence of face-to-face and distance learning modes is also reflected in the term 'blended learning' which is widely used in the field of corporate education. Terms such as 'virtual learning' and 'e-learning' reflect the interaction of the variables of time, place and technology to create innovative educational opportunities that can be created and delivered by a wide variety of providers.

Developments in distance learning impact on quality assurance in that understandings of 'the quality of the student's experience' will differ in relation to the context of learning, and the 'quality of student learning' itself may differ in relation to number of hours of study and

---

[12] National Commission on Higher Education as quoted in Daniel J (1996) *Mega-Universities and Knowledge Media: Technology Strategies for Higher Education*, London, Kogan.

[13] Tait A and Mills R (ed) (1999) *The Convergence of Distance and Conventional Education*, London, Routledge.

'time on task'. Online learning providers seeking accreditation may not conform to standard accreditation criteria such as 'numbers of PhDs among staff', 'residence qualifications for students' or 'quantity of books in the library'. In transnational contexts, there may be different understandings of the appropriate levels of attainment for particular awards and the assessment practices that underpin them. The quality assurance initiatives that we discuss in this paper are seeking to address such issues.

Quality assurance and regulatory frameworks

Quality assurance and accreditation arrangements in different countries need to be understood in the wider context of each country's legislative and regulatory framework. In conceptual terms, approaches to quality assurance are part of a hierarchy of mechanisms used by the state (or states) both to grant powers to institutions and agencies and to exercise control (or seek accountability) for the ways in which these powers are used to deliver educational products and services and realise social and political objectives. Different arrangements across countries are linked to particular 'quality policies' that represent differing levels of devolution of authority from the state (or states) to agencies and institutions and with different histories of voluntarism and compliance to state expectations.

Legal and regulatory frameworks: national and international levels

At the top of the hierarchy, statutes and laws provide a general direction for quality assurance, in terms of legislation on human rights, discrimination, employment practices or health and safety. Legislation will also, in most countries and states, set out the formal powers of institutions and the regulatory framework which guides their governance and operations. Charters are another formal mechanism through which these powers are granted. Academic freedom and institutional autonomy as well as the awarding of degrees are often key aspects of legislation and charters. The legal framework may also establish the role and powers of those agencies charged with monitoring the exercise of institutions' powers (such as accreditation or quality assurance agencies). The awarding of degrees and diplomas, the use of public funds and increasingly, consumer protection and information, are central concerns in most regulatory frameworks. In many countries, the development of intellectual, economic, social and cultural capital is also formally addressed. The legal position and powers of institutions differ across countries, as do regulatory frameworks.

Recognition and approval: institution and agency levels
There is considerable ambiguity in the terms: 'recognition', 'approval', 'licensing', 'registration' and 'accreditation' across countries. Formal 'recognition' is usually linked both to charters and statutes and to particular regulatory mechanisms such as 'accreditation' or to other processes associated with the granting of 'degree-awarding powers'. In the UK, for example, such processes lead to becoming a formally 'recognised' or 'listed body' on a list maintained by the relevant government department.[14] The regulatory framework may also provide formal 'approval' of those agencies charged with monitoring the framework and delivering its associated regulatory processes. It is clearly important in each country to know the official sources of 'recognition' and 'approval' and their practical manifestation in authoritative lists, databases and agencies.

Recognition and approval status may apply separately to national and non-national institutions, to institutions of different types (for example public, private and for-profit) and may also, in some countries, be linked to modes of instruction such as distance learning. It may also apply to the awarding of degrees or to the offering of programmes of study.

Other terms that are used – and either confused with or used synonymously with recognition and approval – include 'licensing' or

---

[14] Department for Education and Skills, *Degrees from Recognised Universities and Colleges Webpage*. Available at: www.dfes.gov.uk/recognisedukdegrees/bdw.shtml. Last Accessed 22 April 2004.

'registration'. These terms can refer to permission for an institution or organisation to operate as a business in a city or country and need not imply approval of the quality of its degrees. In other cases, licensing is a pre-requisite for accreditation, and is the authority for degree-granting status, but standards and criteria may vary (as is the case in different states in the US). 'Licensing' may also be used at degree-level as an outcome of the qualification that grants the graduate a 'license to practice', as in the field of nursing or midwifery (although arrangements again differ across and within countries).

In the international context, another form of 'recognition' is particularly important: the recognition of qualifications earned in one country for use (for academic, professional or employment purposes) in another country. In some countries, there are national centres that provide advice or have the power to decide on the comparability of qualifications. Within the European Union, all countries have National Academic Recognition Centres (NARICs) although the status and competence of the centres vary across member states with some having legal competence to make decisions and others having an advisory capacity only. A wider network, the European National Information Centres (ENICs), operates under the auspices of the Council of Europe and the UNESCO-CEPES Europe region.

Accreditation: institution and professional levels
Accreditation can apply at institutional, programme or degree level. It is typically a formal process of enquiry against a set of agreed criteria (or standards). However, in many countries it is possible to award degrees without accreditation (e.g. through the granting of licenses) while elsewhere, as in many parts of Central & Eastern Europe public institutions may not even offer a programme unless it has been accredited. The process of enquiry is undertaken by a formally constituted body and will lead, if successful, to a formal status (as an accredited institution or accredited programme/degree). There may be different stages en route to full accreditation, for example, provisional or candidate,

and the process may be voluntary or compulsory with a fee charged for the process.

Accreditation has a long history at institution and specialised programme level in the US and at programme/degree level in other countries (e.g. the UK, Australia). In the light of developments in borderless education, the concept of accreditation is gaining ground. Recent converts exist in continental Europe and in South Africa where a new accreditation process has been launched for private and for-profit providers. The outcomes of accreditation differ and include permission to run a programme, access to funding for institutions, programmes or students and license to graduates to practise as a professional.

Validation: agency or programme/degree level
Validation has much in common with programme accreditation. Typically, it describes an approval or authorisation process at programme level. In the UK, universities validate their own degrees (i.e. approve the curriculum design and content, learning resources and assessment methods). Another confusion is that in Australia the term 'self-accrediting' is used instead of 'validation'. In many professional areas such as engineering, law or medicine, validation and accreditation go hand-in-hand at the programme level to ensure appropriate academic and professional standards.

In addition to universities, authorised validating agencies may exist to approve particular types of programmes and awards. The UK's Open University operates a Validation Service (OUVS) that validates programmes from a variety of providers. Provision often incorporates elements of distance learning and transnational arrangements. A further complication is that the power to validate degrees may also include the power to authorise others to teach all or parts of the programme leading to the award. This 'authorisation' leads to arrangements such as twinning or franchising where the educational process is shared between providers in different countries or is delegated to another institution (while the awarding function is typically retained by the home institution).

Quality assurance policies and arrangements: various levels

The term, 'quality assurance' may include:

- All the arrangements made at any of several levels (national, international, supranational, regional) to assure the reliability and quality of institutions, consortia, other providers, programmes, qualifications and other educational services. Thus recognition, accreditation and validation may be parts of a national, regional, or state-level quality assurance system.
- A narrower definition that refers to the monitoring and review of institutional activity from an internal or external perspective (or both) and refers to similar arrangements at the level of disciplines, programmes and awards.

Institutions will (usually) have their own internal quality assurance systems; professional bodies may monitor institutions' programmes through an external review process and governments may also prescribe an external quality assurance process to review institutions, programmes, disciplines or wider educational activities. 'Accreditation' may be the term used to describe an external review process that is undertaken every five years or so. In other cases, an external quality assurance process follows accreditation (i.e. the latter provides initial approval, while the former offers a regular review mechanism). In several countries, the arrangements are different depending on the ownership, governance or economic status of institutions (i.e. public, private, for-profit or not-for-profit).

A 'quality assurance system' may (and arguably, should) include:

- Definitions and criteria that explain the scope and 'confidence levels' that the system is designed to achieve in relation to academic quality and standards. These two terms are often used interchangeably, but this may blur or obscure important distinctions. 'Academic quality' typically refers to the educational process, learning experience and resources for learning; 'academic standards' refer to outcomes such as student achievements and capabilities that are reflected in the qualifications awarded.

- A range of external reference points such as qualification frameworks and level descriptors, quality standards, benchmarks, codes of practice and guidelines. These reference points are designed to provide greater clarity and transparency about the meaning of 'academic quality' and 'academic standards' and to act as a basis for judgements. They are also potentially important components in developing mutual understandings, interpretations and comparisons across countries.
- Review mechanisms such as self-assessment frameworks and review visits (assessments, audits or inspections). Different countries are increasingly using similar mechanisms, but it is still dangerous to assume that such mechanisms alone will provide common understandings of quality and standards and an adequate basis for mutual recognition across countries (as we discuss further below).
- Outputs from the system may include reports, gradings, published statistics, performance indicators, league tables and kite-marks and may lead to different outcomes (e.g. access to funding).
- Independent or integrated arrangements to promote and support quality improvement. These arrangements may produce best practice guidance, or develop support networks for practitioners and other interested parties. An example of the latter is the International Council for Open and Distance Education, officially recognised by the United Nations as the global non-governmental organisation responsible for the field of open and distance learning.

Trade in educational services
The import and export of higher education from one country or region to another is not new. What is changing is the volume of activity across the world and the range of types of 'trade' involved, both official and unofficial, linked both to profit-making and non-profit educational activities.

Since the World Trade Organisation decided in 1995 to include education within the scope of its General Agreement on Trade in Services (GATS), importing and exporting issues have entered a new arena. Leaving aside the political impact of these developments,[15] the GATS has provided us with some definitions that can be applied in relation to the import, export and 'exchange' of higher education in a variety of forms.

The 'modes of supply' within GATS are:

- *Cross-border supply:* where the service and not the individual cross a border (e.g. education and training offered via distance learning)
- *Consumption abroad:* where the individual travels across Member country borders to consume the service (e.g. individual students studying abroad)
- *Commercial presence:* where a service supplier (institution or other provider) establishes a physical presence in a second country to provide services (e.g. franchise or twinning arrangements, off-shore campus)
- *Presence of natural persons:* where an individual from one Member country supplies a service in another Member country (e.g. faculty exchange or visiting lecturers).

While these definitions of modes of supply are useful, the five sub-categories of education services used within the GATS framework are more problematic (i.e. primary, secondary, higher, adult and other). For reasons discussed earlier, definitions of higher education are widening to include adult (lifelong learning) and other forms of education (such as continuing professional development). It is not in practice easy to distinguish between 'higher, adult and other' since much convergence is taking place. There are also specific problems related to transnational distance learning in that many types of provision do not fall neatly into just one category of the GATS terminology.

---

[15] Which are covered in detail in Knight J (2002) *Trade in Higher Education Services: the implications of GATS*, London, Observatory on Borderless Higher Education and Knight J (2003) *GATS, Trade and Higher Education: Perspective 2003 – Where are we?* London, Observatory on Borderless Higher Education.

2.4 Beyond Terminology: Quality Assurance, Reputation and Educational Misconduct

Beyond terminology, there are some other issues that are relevant to quality assurance and borderless education. They shed further light on the rationale behind current developments at different levels and in different parts of the world.

Quality assurance and reputation: providers and provision
In many cases, the reputation (for quality) of providers and particular forms of provision does not appear to be directly linked to the forms of quality assurance in use. For example, in some countries, degrees gained by distance learning have lower status than those acquired through face-to-face contact, despite the operation of relevant quality assurance; this may be manifested by governments barring access to certain public employment for distance learning graduates (e.g. in Indonesia). In other cases, public higher education providers may enjoy higher status than private or for-profit institutions, despite the latter being subject to stringent quality assurance arrangements while the former are not. In addition, the opposite situation may be true: particular forms of quality assurance (such as accreditation by international agencies) may significantly enhance the reputation of domestic private or public providers. Alternatively, acceptable quality assurance in one country may not be sufficient to assure quality within the regulations of another country.

Perceptions of what counts as 'quality higher education' and 'effective quality assurance' are often culturally and socially determined and may take a long time to build and change. Innovative developments such as transnational higher education or blended learning may take time to become accepted and valued − or conversely may be valued (for example by governments or students) for the new opportunities they offer beyond or in contrast to traditional forms of higher education. Formal quality assurance processes may be necessary − but not sufficient − to the building of a reputation for quality educational processes and outcomes. In addition, innovative forms of provider and provision may challenge traditional conceptions of 'quality' and associated quality assurance arrangements, producing the need for adaptations or totally new arrangements. ICT developments and the growth of transnational higher education are fostering calls for new arrangements at supranational level while at the same time, a wide range of regional, disciplinary and consortia arrangements are emerging.

Stages of development and quality assurance
The variety and complexity of developments in borderless higher education are creating increasing pressure on quality assurance agencies and their mechanisms. In some countries, it is difficult to respond since arrangements are at a rudimentary stage of development or are limited in scope. The present global diversity in quality assurance regimes makes the idea of mutual recognition of agencies and arrangements a formidable proposition to agree and undertake in practice. It also leads to other significant difficulties, for example, with the mutual recognition of qualifications. Many institutional, national and regional initiatives are seeking to build capacity by sharing information, practice and experience. However, given the social and cultural dimensions of 'quality frameworks and reference points' there is a danger of exporting or importing inappropriate models. Also, some models are expensive and may impose economic burdens and other regulatory constraints on countries or institutions. This is where notions of 'trade liberalisation' under the auspices of GATS intersect with developments in quality assurance.

Quality assurance and educational misconduct
Quality assurance arrangements are designed to ensure that provision and providers meet certain expectations (often in the form of formal criteria and standards) and that there are levels of comparability and degrees of consistency in educational processes. Rules and procedures form part of the system; these may (or should) aim to control, *inter alia*, forms of misconduct that can

occur within the educational process, for example, plagiarism or patronage, or more seriously, bribery and corruption in assessment and grading.

The drivers behind borderless developments (such as the expansion in demand for higher education, the growth in income-generating activities, globalisation and ICT developments) have created a climate in which there appears to be more – and a darker side to – educational misconduct. Anecdotally, the situation appears to be significantly worse in some countries than others (although hard data is not easily available). 'Misconduct' involves misrepresentation and fraud of various kinds, for example: false promises of enrolment by fraudulent providers, false claims of accreditation or licensing of providers and provision, the sale of educational materials to support plagiarism, fake attendance records, and the sale of false degree certificates, transcripts, diplomas and visas. Individuals use fake certificates and other documentation to gain access to recognised programmes, financial aid and employment. These fraudulent activities are supported by supply and demand and represent a 'black market' in educational services and qualifications.

Providers that operate legally are seeking to protect students, their own reputations, professions and employers from such misconduct. In many cases, they are seeking 'quality assurance solutions' to these problems from governments, agencies and international bodies, for example by creating guidelines, codes of practice or kitemarks. However, quality assurance arrangements by themselves are unlikely to solve the problem as they are not strong enough without the force of law and law enforcement agents to support implementation. Recent examples indicate this to be the case[16] and we pick up this issue again in our discussion of current quality assurance initiatives.

---

[16] Greek D (2003) "Where is the University of Palmers Green?" Available at: www.vnunet.com/News/1139348. Last Accessed 22 April 2004.

PART THREE

3.1 Development and Change in National Quality Assurance Systems

Expanding numbers of evaluation agencies

Recent publications by quality assurance membership organisations – the International Network of Quality Assurance Agencies in Higher Education (INQAAHE) and the European Network for Quality Assurance (ENQA) – reveal that quality assurance is a growing activity. There are more quality assurance agencies throughout the world than five years ago and the scope and focus of their activities are being extended. The longest established external quality evaluation system, which is in essence neither national nor one system, is the accreditation of institutions and programmes in the US. This initiative was, and still is, controlled by the higher education community, in contrast with the establishment of national agencies and external quality evaluation systems elsewhere in recent times where the initiative has mainly come from governments.

The INQAAHE Directory[17] lists forty-seven countries from Albania to Vietnam with quality assurance agencies and provides details of more than seventy agencies in membership of the network. The ENQA report,[18] which overlaps significantly with INQAAHE, covers twenty-three countries and describes thirty-four agencies in the European Higher Education Area.[19] But, the picture from these surveys is incomplete. As membership of INQAAHE is voluntary, less than 10% of the ninety or more recognised US accreditation agencies are listed in the INQAAHE Directory. There is no mention of the Central American Accreditation Council (CSUCA), an organisation operating across six countries in the region with a base in Guatemala. There is also little or no mention of existing agencies in the former Soviet republics such as the Ukraine or

---
[17] INQAAHE and IAUP (2003) *Quality Assurance Agencies*, Dublin, HETAC.
[18] ENQA (2003) *Quality Procedures in European Higher Education*, ENQA Occasional Papers 5, Helsinki.
[19] For details see *Berlin Summit 2003* Website. Available at: www.bologna-berlin2003.de. Last Accessed 22 April 2004.

those in the South East Europe region. Therefore, the directories cannot as yet be relied upon as the definitive source on formal quality assurance arrangements in different countries.

What these publications do usefully demonstrate, however, is that it is not uncommon for there to be more than one agency operating at national level within a country and institutions, other providers and learners need to be aware of this. Further information on the development of quality assurance systems at national and regional level has recently been gathered within the UNESCO regional framework as part of the preparatory work for the 'World Conference plus 5' and for the meeting of the Global Forum on International Quality Assurance, Accreditation and the Recognition of Qualifications.[20]

The drivers for the introduction of external evaluation (beyond satisfying the 'traditional' purposes of accountability and improvement) vary and depend on local, national and regional circumstances. The impact of borderless developments – as well as localised change – can be seen in these examples:

- a need to control the rapid growth of higher education provision which in many countries has, for lack of public funds, had to come from private providers (e.g. in Jordan, Poland and Malaysia);
- to support or legitimise new types of provision such as polytechnic type institutions and applied higher education studies (e.g. the Fachhochschulen in Austria) or new academic structures and qualifications (e.g. the introduction of two-cycle higher education studies in Germany);
- to contribute to the regulation and management of imported higher education services (e.g. the activities of the Hong Kong Council for Academic Awards in relation to advising on the registration of non-local higher and professional education provision).

It could also be argued that the existence of a national quality assurance agency is being seen as 'a badge of maturity' of a higher

---

[20] UNESCO, *Study Abroad Webpage*. Available at: www.unesco.org/education/studyingabroad. Last Accessed 22 April 2004.

education system. Every government appears to want one even if there is barely sufficient critical mass in terms of the size of the national higher education sector to support a quality assurance system that is independent of an individual university.

Diversity of scope, focus and authority
Within countries, evaluation agencies operate at national and/or regional level: there are centralised, national systems and decentralised regional agency systems, depending on national political and legal structures. Often the 'regions' do not match or cover all political regions.

Some national agencies:

- cover all tertiary education providers (e.g. the QAA in the UK, the AUQA in Australia which also reviews state accreditation agencies);
- deal exclusively with either universities (e.g. ANECA in Spain) or non-university higher education institutions (e.g. HETAC in Ireland);
- deal only with private higher education provision (LAN in Malaysia);
- cover public institutions and programmes (NIAD Japan which works with national and local universities
- only cover a single discipline or regulated profession, such as teacher training (e.g. INAFOP in Portugal);
- have compulsory external evaluation, often linked to funding and the formal recognition of qualifications for employment in the public sector;
- use accreditation or equivalent processes that are voluntary, but also have links to, or implications for funding. An example is the US recognition system where *accreditation* brings the possibility of accessing Federal Title IV funds for student loans, but where institutions are *licensed* by individual states, all of which have different criteria for *granting authority* to award degrees.

The size of the country and higher education system provides no common rationale for the nature of the quality assurance arrangements. The US has more than ninety autonomous accreditation agencies recognised by the US Department of Education and/or the Council for Higher Education Accreditation (CHEA). The new German system of accreditation appears on the surface to emulate the US model with an overarching body (Akk – the Akkreditierunsgrat) that recognises individual accreditation agencies, but there are significant differences. In Germany, accreditation covers only the new two-cycle undergraduate programmes and is compulsory. In the US, accreditation may cover institutions and/or programmes, (but only a range of programmes such as engineering), and is voluntary. While in many large countries and/or higher education systems, the institution tends to be the main focus for evaluation (e.g. the US, India, UK); in Germany it is currently only the programme of study.

Even when countries have similar social, economic and political backgrounds, such as the Nordic countries, there is little apparent convergence in quality assurance systems.[21] A recent project[22] between the agencies of Denmark (EVA) and Finland (FINHEEC) has however, explored the possibility of a mutual recognition process for agencies and set out a series of recommendations for a method of mutual recognition.[23] In other cases such as the Central American Agency, differences have been set aside as countries with a shared language have come together to establish a regional agency (CSUCA).

Responding to borderless developments and wider changes in higher education
Where national agencies have not previously existed, there are many developments in motion. Five years ago, Jordan was the only

---

[21] Smeby J C and Stensaker B (1999) "National Quality Assessment Systems in the Nordic Countries: developing a Balance between External and Internal Needs", *Higher Education Policy*, vol 12: 3–14.
[22] ENQA (2002) *A Method for Mutual Recognition*, ENQA Occasional Papers X, Helsinki.
[23] ENQA (2003) *Quality Procedures in European Higher Education*, ENQA Occasional Papers 5, Helsinki.

Arab state with an accreditation body dealing with new private institutions. In 2001, the Association of Arab Universities set up a Regional Committee for Assessment and Accreditation.

One of the aims of the Committee was to create a culture in which assessment and evaluation were seen as necessities by higher education institutions. The committee has produced guidelines for the licensing and establishment of private higher education institutions and mechanisms for self-assessment and accreditation.[24]

At national level, countries including Algeria, Egypt, Lebanon, Morocco, Oman, Saudi Arabia, the United Arab Emirates, Yemen and the Palestinian Authority have established or are planning to establish accreditation and quality evaluation systems. What is interesting about some of these developments is that they include in the normal evaluation process aspects that are yet to be captured in many other countries with longer established systems. For example, the new licensing and accreditation guidelines for the United Arab Emirates incorporate a policy statement on, and standards for, distance learning. The draft guidelines for a new quality assurance system in Oman (with processes for both institutional and programme accreditation) incorporate a national qualifications' framework describing qualifications not only in terms of credit points and years, but also in terms of learning outcomes. Emerging evaluation systems may be quicker than more established ones to address 'borderless' developments.

Where national quality assurance systems are not new, there is still change and innovation: new processes, standards and activities. Countries with well developed higher education systems such as Australia, the UK, Korea, India, New Zealand and Malaysia (for private education) continue to make changes or are undertaking major new initiatives, especially in relation to the quality assurance of transnational education. In Australia, the Australian Universities Quality Agency (AUQA) was established as a joint federal-state

---

[24] UNESCO (2003b) *Higher education in the Arab Region 1998–2003*, Paris. Available at: www.unesco.org/education/wche. Last Accessed 22 April 2004.

government initiative to undertake academic audits of universities and also to audit the state agencies that are responsible for the accreditation of private providers. In Thailand, the National Education Act of 1999, set in train an ambitious initiative intended to cover both the public and private higher education sectors with a requirement that all higher education institutions be evaluated every five years through the newly established Office of Education, Standards and Evaluation.[25]

No two national agencies are the same in terms of purpose, scope, focus, criteria or standards used. This diversity reflects the different national and regional contexts in which agencies operate and the constituencies they serve. Within the emerging European Higher Education Area, there have been several initiatives to try to negotiate and develop common terminology and criteria as external (and international) reference points for academic quality and academic standards. Outcomes to date include the development of 'generic' descriptors for qualifications at Bachelor and Masters' degree level (the 'Dublin' descriptors[26]) and subject specific competencies at Bachelors' level for a range of disciplines (the Tuning project[27]). It appears that the Dublin descriptors, with some customisation, have been incorporated into the standards of some of the agencies in Germany and the Netherlands.

Within the ENQA, there have been several projects to explore the utility of such shared standards and tools (an example of which is the Transnational European Evaluation Project[28]) and to explore methods for mutual recognition of agencies. A planned initiative for 2004 will be an exploration of the circumstances and context within which agencies operate to explore barriers to convergence.

---

[25] UNESCO (2003) *Synthesis Report on Trends and Developments in Higher Education since the World Conference on Higher Education (1998–2003)*, Paris.
[26] Joint Quality Initiative, *Homepage*. Available at: www.jointquality.org. Last Accessed 22 April 2004.
[27] Tuning Educational Structures in Europe, *Homepage*. Available at: www.relint.deusto.es/TUNINGProject/index.htm. Last Accessed 22 April 2004.
[28] European Network for Quality Assurance in Higher Education, *Homepage*. Available at: www.enqa.net. Last Accessed 22 April 2004.

The project will be managed by the Comité National d'Evaluation (France) and the QAA (UK).

Towards criteria and standards: from input to outputs
As discussed earlier, definitions of 'quality' in higher education have tended either to be elusive or relative but this position is changing. For example, a survey of quality assurance in Europe suggested that quality was "as a rule interpreted in terms of the extent to which the individual programmes achieve their own goals and the legal provisions under which they operate".[29] This contrasted with the accreditation approach that determines whether or not the object of accreditation meets some external criteria and/or standards. In some agencies, there are attempts to shift accreditation criteria and standards from a focus on traditional 'input' standards to a focus on outcomes of student learning and achievement (completion rates, graduate first destinations and employment). A focus on outcomes will make it easier to accredit different kinds of providers and forms of provision, however and wherever delivered.

The development and use of explicit criteria, standards and external reference points is slowly emerging in other types of evaluation activities. The drivers for these changes include a need to address the quality assurance of new modes of learning and delivery such as distance learning, or transnational education and the need to provide clearer information about quality to a wide range of external stakeholders. The internationalisation of higher education is also a driver to move notions of standards and quality from opinions or assessment on an intuitive basis to a more transparent and consistent basis.

3.2 International Developments in Quality Assurance

As noted earlier, one of the trends in higher education is the increasing global activity of many higher education institutions. New kinds of provision also often include transnational elements and

---
[29] ENQA (2003) *Quality Procedures in European Higher Education*, ENQA Occasional Papers 5, Helsinki.

through collaborative arrangements, institutions are seeking to create joint degrees and international programmes. Quality assurance arrangements are responding in different ways to these international dimensions of higher education.

International members in governance and review processes
Some quality assurance agencies in smaller countries include members from outside the country on their Executive Board or Committees (e.g. HETAC and HKCAA), or have separate advisory committees with international members (e.g. HAC in Hungary). These members are asked to provide either a sounding board for new ideas or some kind of monitoring of comparability of standards and quality.

Other agencies, not necessarily in small countries, include non-national members in their evaluation or accreditation teams. There are many examples of this practice as a routine activity, for example, AUQA, the agencies in the Nordic region and in the Netherlands. However, these 'international' experts are not always included in the Agency's regular training programmes and often appear to be used on a one off or ad hoc basis rather than being appointed for a fixed period or number of engagements. It is difficult, therefore, to conceive that international members can undertake benchmarking of an explicit nature between one system and another. Rather it increases the 'pool' of independent experts and may provide different (individual) perspectives on quality and standards. Other agencies have no *specific* requirement for 'international' experts to be included in their review teams. This tends to be the case in larger higher education systems such as the UK where the QAA publicly invites applications from individuals to participate in the selection, appointment and training process for membership of the pool of auditors and reviewers. There is no bar to international applications, but all reviewers have to undertake the training process.

Common processes and mechanisms?
Much of the interest in examining 'convergence' between national QA systems or in creating new international quality assurance

systems is focusing on 'methodology'. A growing (but potentially flawed) consensus seems to be that if the same process is followed, then the quality of higher education systems will also become comparable. Increasingly, the four-stage model of evaluation is promoted as good practice: establishing external criteria, self-evaluation of the object of assessment, a peer or expert review visit to the institution, programme or subject and production of a public report on the outcomes of the review.

Assuming comparability through common processes and mechanisms appears to ignore differences in criteria and standards, in expectations as to appropriate levels of student attainment and learning outcomes, definitions about what is (or is not) higher education, and differences in assessment regulations and practice. Also, a single model of good practice is unlikely to encompass the diversity of requirements and may also constrain necessary change and innovation. More seriously, emphasis is likely to be placed on the inappropriate things: structures rather than outcomes and the mechanics of processes rather than underlying principles for quality assurance practice such as transparency, consistency, fairness, equity and integrity.

The search for international standards
While the definition of standards, criteria and external quality reference points for education and qualifications is becoming a stronger focus at national level, there are also examples of the emergence of 'international' standards. This is particularly the case within the professions. National standards are also being used in the international domain. Such standards apply variously to programmes, qualifications, modes of study and to the activities of quality assurance and evaluation agencies themselves. The globalisation of business and industry has been a driving force for international standards such as the International Accounting Standards (IAS) and these standards will in turn have an impact on education and training (or re-training) in that subject area.

The search for international standards (and comparability across national standards) has brought in actors who are new to the higher education sector. These include the International Organisation for Standardisation (ISO) and the European Foundation for Quality Management (EFQM). An interesting aspect of these developments is that higher education institutions themselves have chosen to pursue international certification of their quality management systems such as ISO 9001 certification (e.g. institutions in Turkey and Singapore) and the EFQM excellence model (e.g. institutions in Germany and the UK). They may also choose to look for cross-sector certification in relation to their e-learning operations.[30]

Some commentators may question the appropriateness of 'industry' standards for higher education. However, the certifying organisations have themselves demonstrated an interest in accommodating their standards for the public sector (as in the case of the EFQM communities of practice) or extending them to encompass new modes of learning. To date, no government or national agency has required higher education institutions to seek this type of external certification. However, growing interest from governments and institutions prompted ISO to convene an international workshop in Mexico in 2002 to begin the process of formulating 'guidelines for the application of ISO 9001 to education'.[31]

Quality assurance agencies have shown some interest in external certification for their own activities with the AQU of Catalunya having achieved ISO 9001 certification, and others such as the QAA in the UK and HAC in Hungary exploring the applicability of aspects of the EFQM model. As e-learning and blended learning become more prevalent we are also likely to see an increase in the demands from providers of qualifications that suppliers of associated services such as student support, admissions, etc are 'industry certified' as is common in industry supply chains.

---

[30] Observatory on Borderless Higher Education (2003) "Quality Assurance in Borderless Higher Education: six initiatives", *Briefing Note*, No. 11, May, 2003.
[31] Ibid.

Quality Assurance and Borderless Higher Education 119

The British Association of Open Learning (BAOL) already supplies some such services to a small number of accredited institutions.[32] Meanwhile, the debate as to the quality assurance of the quality assurance agencies themselves has grown. Concerns that agencies are not accountable for their actions or activities and not subject to scrutiny has led to initiatives promoting the 'meta-accreditation' of quality assurance and accreditation agencies. The idea of 'World Quality Labels and Registers' has been floated, for example, by the International Association of University Presidents.[33] The most recent initiative comes from INQAAHE where a working party is developing 'Principles for Quality Assurance Agencies' along the lines of a code of good practice. These principles are currently subject to public comment[34].

Networking and benchmarking
There are a variety of examples of international co-operation in cross-border networks. Some of these are formalised and have been in existence for many years, for example, the ICDE, mentioned above, which publishes extensive guidelines for the quality assurance of distance and e-learning, and has recently established an International Standards Agency. Another, the European University Association's (formerly the Conference of European Rectors) Institutional Evaluation Programme provides a training programme for reviewers and undertakes institutional reviews for a number of European institutions, on the invitation of the Rector. An independent evaluation of this programme has recently been undertaken.[35] These networks are designed to share good practice and, in the words of the EUA, to

---

[32] Observatory on Borderless Higher Education (2003) "Quality Assurance in Borderless Higher Education: six initiatives", *Briefing Note*, No. 11, May, 2003.
[33] INQAAHE and IAUP (2003) *Quality Assurance Agencies*, Dublin, HETAC.
[34] International Network for Quality Assurance Agencies in Higher Education, *Homepage*. Available at: www.inqaahe.nl. Last Accessed August 2003.
[35] But they have made it very hard to find-need to go to press releases and click on link to institutional evaluation alumni report. European University Association, *Homepage*. Available at: www.unige.ch/eua. Last Accessed 22 April 2004.

'develop and spread a quality culture' among institutions. Some recent examples go further still, for example, Universitas21 Global, a consortium of 16 universities from 10 countries has set up an independently operated body, U21 Pedagogica to 'accredit' all U21 global awards and may also market its quality assurance services more widely.[36]

While the trend appears to be towards more and more varied forms of networks, we lack data on the impact of these arrangements on the quality of programmes and how they do, or do not, affect student choice. The extent of external stakeholder involvement is also unclear; and tensions may exist between the requirements of national systems and such international arrangements. Nonetheless, institutions are likely to reap benefits from staff mobility and the building of shared understandings of quality and standards.

National systems go international: following cross-border developments
As the delivery of national education across international borders becomes more common through distance learning, the establishment of branch campuses and partnerships, national quality assurance agencies using either standard or adapted processes have started to follow the trails of their domestic providers to destinations around the world. The major visible 'exporters' of education are the US, the UK and Australia. In the case of the two former countries, the quality assurance of several forms of transnational provision has for some time been subsumed within the processes of the regular quality assurance and accreditation agencies (rather than being part of a separate agency).

In the case of the US, CHEA carried out a survey of the 78 CHEA and USDE recognised institutional and programmatic accreditors to

---

[36] Observatory on Borderless Higher Education (2003) "Quality Assurance in Borderless Higher Education: six initiatives", *Briefing Note*, No. 11, May, 2003.

establish the extent of their international activity.[37] Of the 53 responding organisations, some 29 indicated that they were operating internationally, accrediting 461 institutions and programs in 65 countries outside the US. Most of this activity by regional accreditors involved the review of US institutions operating abroad, whereas the specialised accreditors were more active in accrediting non-US programmes (see below for examples). The regional accreditation commissions tackle the quality review of international branch campus activity by their members in different ways. While all of them include such activity in their accreditation processes and standards, some visit all branch campus operations overseas as part of the re-accreditation of the 'mother' campus, others do not visit all overseas operations. In 2001, CHEA developed International Principles as a framework for US accreditors working internationally which invite accrediting organisations, amongst other matters, to communicate with the quality assurance agencies in countries in which they are working.

The Quality Assurance Agency for Higher Education in the UK has continued the practice of predecessor organisations of carrying out the quality audit of the overseas partnership links of UK higher education institutions through which UK degrees are awarded. The expectations concerning the standards of these qualifications are no different from national ones and the academic infrastructure of UK qualifications' frameworks, subject benchmark statements and the Code of Practice for Quality Assurance apply equally to provision delivered outside the UK. More than 100 such audit visits have been made since 1997, and the reports of all of them are published.[38] Section 2: Collaborative Provision, of the Agency's Code of Practice[39] focuses specifically on collaborative links,

---

[37] CHEA (2002) *The Role of Accreditation and Assuring Quality in Electronically Delivered Distance Learning*, Fact Sheet #2.
[38] Quality Assurance Agency, *Homepage*. Available at: www.qaa.ac.uk. Last Accessed 22 April 2004.
[39] QAA (1999b) *Code of Practice for the assurance of academic quality and standards-Section 2: Collaborative Provision*.

(whether national or international) and institutions' adherence to the precepts in the Code is a focus of the overseas audit activity. It is a measure of how fast the international environment is changing that this section of the Code (approved in 1999) is currently under review and that this review is being carried out in parallel with that of the Guidelines for the Quality Assurance of Distance Learning.

Australia, the third major provider of 'offshore' education, is now moving towards introducing external quality assurance processes for its exported education through audits of provision on a country basis. These processes will be managed by the AUQA. Australia is the first of the major exporting nations to include 'off-shore' students in the number of registered international students, and recent figures indicate that a significant number of its international students are studying outside Australia.[40]

Information on the quality assurance of exported education from other countries such as Russia, Spain, Portugal and India in terms of standards, processes and outcomes, is less accessible at present. However, the pressure from international agencies, regional networks and governments for greater transparency, information and consumer protection in transnational education may encourage all exporting nations to monitor this type of provision.

Responses to importing transnational provision
The quality assurance of transnational provision is not simply an issue for exporting nations and institutions; it is also of interest and importance to importing countries. Transnational provision is therefore increasingly being regulated at the point of delivery by national authorities. Attitudes to the import of transnational education vary from cautious welcome for an increase in capacity, innovation and quality enhancement, to serious concerns about the

---

[40] AVCC (2001) *Practice and Guidelines for Australian Universities*, Australian Vice Chancellors' Committee, Canberra, Available at: www.avcc.edu.au. Last Accessed 22 April 2004.

undermining of national strategies and imperatives for higher education and about the quality of imported provision.

Many states have found that it is impossible to stop transnational education provision even where the qualifications are unrecognised by the legal authorities and where the students are well aware of this situation before undertaking the degree. For example, in Greece – for more than twenty years-there has been substantial imported education provision from other European countries and beyond. This is delivered mainly through partnerships with local private providers that cannot be recognised as part of the higher education community (as they charge fees). There are, however, countries (such as Malaysia) which have developed national strategies to use local private and imported higher education to increase the size of the local higher education sector and expand access to higher education within the context of constrained public funding. This has been matched by the introduction of enabling legislation and procedures for the licensing and accreditation of private providers by the National Accreditation Board (LAN).

In Singapore, there is a mixture of entrepreneurial and individual initiatives (either local or foreign) and some specific import invited by the Government. The government's strategy is to encourage prestigious universities from the United States and Europe to establish branch campuses and create partnership links with local universities.[41] Within the last year, both China and India have announced decisions to encourage more private and imported transnational provision, in part to enhance national capacity.[42] It is interesting to note that while the largest, 'public' market for transnational education is Asia Pacific, the strongest critics of transnational education are elsewhere, for example, in Europe and Latin America.

Transnational education in Europe has been the focus of three recent studies funded by the European Commission looking at

---

[41] Observatory on Borderless Education (2003) – *Breaking News Articles*.
[42] Ibid.

provision in Western Europe, Central and Eastern Europe and in lifelong learning.[43] The results of the first two studies produced an interesting contrast in attitudes and findings in relation to transnational education. Western European institutions in France, Spain, Portugal and the UK were more likely to be exporters than their counterparts in Central and Eastern Europe where the import of education, primarily, though not exclusively, from the UK and US was common. However, in many of the countries in Central and Eastern Europe there was less 'fear' of transnational education than is evidenced in Western Europe where there is, as yet, less 'visible' import.

Other major importing countries include SAR Hong Kong where there are Ordinances for the registration of non-local provision. Different standards of recognition can apply: where foreign programmes are registered the qualification must be comparable in standards to the country of origin; for accreditation, the standards of non-local provision must be comparable to those of SAR Hong Kong qualifications. This process is managed by the local quality assurance agency, the HKCAA, and lists of recognised and exempted programmes (those which are offered in partnership with a local provider) are published by the Ministry.[44] HKCAA publishes list of accredited postsecondary courses.[45] This approach illustrates a solution to one of the dilemmas about transnational education – is it a part of the local higher education provision or should it be recognised as something foreign and different and offering an opportunity for a different kind of

---

[43] Adam S (2001) *Transnational Education Project Report and Recommendations (Western Europe)* Confederation of European Rectors' Conference, Brussels. Available at: www.eua.be/eua. Last Accessed 22 April 2004, and Adam S, (2003) *The Recognition, Treatment, Experience and Implications of Transnational Education in Central and Eastern Europe 2002–2003*, Stockholm, Högskoleverket.
[44] Education and Manpower Bureau, Government of the Hong Kong Special Administrative Region, *Non-local Higher and Professional Courses*. Available at: www.emb.gov.hk/index.aspx?nodeID=226&langno=1. Last Accessed 22 April 2004.
[45] Hong Kong Council for Academic Accreditation, *Homepage*. Available at: www.hkcaa.edu.hk. Last Accessed 22 April 2004.

experience? However, the approach does not address the apparent contradiction about valuing the standards of foreign qualifications gained abroad over foreign ones gained at home, particularly where they are meant to be comparable.

Concerns and complaints
Serious concerns have been expressed about the nature and impact of transnational education in several countries and regions, notably parts of Africa and Central and Eastern Europe (CEE).[46] The reasons underlying expressed concerns differ, for example:

- There is a lack of capacity and resources in many countries for strategic planning and the implementation of legislation to regulate imported educational provision.
- There has been an explosive growth of indigenous private provision and this may be associated or confused with foreign provision.[47]
- Fragmented national regulatory frameworks may inhibit local capacity to regulate transnational provision.
- Bureaucratic, state-led programme accreditation systems may not be capable of adapting to more flexible delivery methods in either national or transnational education.[48]
- Quality and standards are often perceived to be lower in transnational or for-profit provision than in public, national provision.
- Imported transnational education provision may focus on a relatively narrow range of subject areas which are 'cheap' and profitable to offer such as information sciences and technologies or business and management; this may lead

---

[46] HEQC (2000) *Founding Document for the Higher Education Quality Committee*, Pretoria, South Africa, Available at: www.che.org.za./publications/heqc_documents.php. Last Accessed 22 April 2004, and Adam S, (2003) *The Recognition, Treatment, Experience and Implications of Transnational Education in Central and Eastern Europe 2002–2003*, Stockholm, Högskoleverket.
[47] Adam S, (2003) *The Recognition, Treatment, Experience and Implications of Transnational Education in Central and Eastern Europe 2002–2003*, Stockholm, Högskoleverket.
[48] Ibid.

to over-provision in certain fields at the expense of others. In South Africa, this prompted the Minister of Education to request the national quality assurance agency, the HEQC, to undertake an exercise to accredit all MBA programmes operating in the country, foreign and local, public and private.
- The subject material delivered in transnational education programmes is not always pertinent to national needs or contexts.

In relation to many of these concerns and complaints, there is an urgent need for empirical data to understand more fully the nature of the concerns, to explore the reality on the ground in different countries and to examine the issue from the perspective of different stakeholders. For example, the popularity of certain subjects (such as business studies) is not unique to imported transnational education. Such popularity is reflected in similar patterns of demand in many exporting countries since learners are deciding for themselves what is relevant in terms of subjects and qualifications for their personal development and career. Also, the lack of tailoring of subject material to the local context may indeed reflect cultural insensitivity on the part of the provider or a lack of attention to curriculum relevance. However, it may also reflect a deliberate aim to offer an international programme, or a deliberate choice on the part of students (or parents or employers) to choose an international programme that is more market-oriented, with a potential for enhanced employment opportunities. In particular, we need to examine the motives and experience of learners who are engaged with a variety of borderless provision so that we can understand better the value and quality of such provision. At present, these 'new learners' have no unified voice or representation, in comparison with traditional students and their unions, and although some individual providers are tracking alumni, there do not appear to be many comprehensive studies available.

Finally, a new but increasing dimension to the import of education is 'import for export'. For example, countries such as Singapore and Malaysia import education and encourage the recruitment of international students to such provision. This leads to interesting challenges around responsibility for, and ownership of, standards and quality and a need to revise understandings about who are the exporters, who are the importers, who are the students and what does 'relevance' of studies mean in such contexts?

Status and recognition of transnational education

Accessing reliable and easily understood information about the recognition and status of transnational education providers and the qualifications they offer is a growing problem. This is both a case of needing more information and better access to existing information. The major exporters have lists of their recognised higher education institutions available either through government websites (DfES, UK and CRICOS, Australia) or in the case of the US of accredited institutions and programmes through the directories of members of USDE and CHEA recognised accreditation commissions. These lists are in the public domain, but it is not clear that the public necessarily knows how to access them or can understand the consequences and implications of 'recognition and approval' (or lack of either).

In many importing countries, the regulations for licensing and recognition are complex, subject to interpretation and change, and although some lists of approved transnational education providers are available, they are not always easily accessible. At present, because of the complexities involved, quality assurance arrangements by themselves offer insufficient insight and protection and because of this, interested parties also fall back on 'reputation' or other familiar sign-posting. In practice, 'assurance of quality' often rests on a mix of formal and informal processes. One may either be 'a reputable foreign provider with internationally recognised (marketable) degrees and qualifications' or a provider of degrees that are recognised or accredited as part of the national host system. There are providers, legitimate and otherwise, that do not fall into these categories and this remains a challenge for the quality assurance of transnational education.

Attempts have been made to develop international codes for assuring the quality of transnational education. An example is the Code of Good Practice in the Provision of Transnational Education, developed by the Council of Europe and UNESCO-CEPES, and approved within the framework of the Lisbon Convention on the recognition of qualifications.[49] However, as with many international initiatives, without any monitoring of its implementation and use, it remains a series of good intentions and exhortations with no indication as to its effectiveness – as was found in the recent survey of transnational education in Central and Eastern Europe.[50] Also, the pace of change and the blurring between imported and exported education in some systems makes it more challenging to define import and export and potentially reduces the 'shelf-life' of codes unless they are regularly reviewed and updated.

Other initiatives to secure good practice and exchange information on matters of mutual interest in transnational education include the emergence of bilateral co-operation agreements between quality assurance agencies. Examples include an agreement between the QAA (UK) and the LAN (Malaysia) and emerging co-operation between quality assurance agencies and authorities with responsibilities for the recognition of foreign qualifications.

At a distance – old challenges and new applications
The activities of national quality assurance agencies also increasingly cover distance learning, the delivery of which may cross national borders. National debates on the extent to which this activity requires specialist quality assurance agencies and separate standards and criteria remain unresolved. This may in part reflect the degree of integration – or not – of distance learning activity in traditional institutions and quality assurance processes and the changing nature of distance learning itself. In some

---
[49] European Centre for Higher Education, *Homepage*. Available at: www.cepes.ro. Last Accessed 22 April 2004.
[50] Adam S, (2003) *The Recognition, Treatment, Experience and Implications of Transnational Education in Central and Eastern Europe 2002–2003*, Stockholm, Högskoleverket.

countries, separate distance learning universities were never created since traditional institutions offered their programmes in dual-mode (e.g. Australia, Sweden and Finland). In other countries separate (often very large) open or distance learning universities were created as an integrated part of the national higher education sector (e.g. Open University in the UK, UNED in Spain). These institutions are subject to the same quality assurance processes as 'traditional' institutions. However, this fact has often not been enough to convince authorities abroad, where distance learning was either non-existent or at a low level, to recognise qualifications gained through distance learning, whether within their territories or not.

A recent report on the implications of transnational education in Central and Eastern Europe observed that, 'there is evidence that some CEE states maintain a strong distrust of open and distance education as a matter of principle'.[51] This has also been the case in other regions of the world such as the Arab states where until recently there has been no indigenous distance learning provision. As the use of flexible patterns of learning in transnational education has become more common, particularly where such provision is targeted at working adults and professionals, these attitudes create problems and concerns about quality and standards which are difficult to resolve through reassurances about quality assurance processes. However, the development of indigenous distance learning provision (such as the establishment of the Arab Open University) may do more to foster a climate of confidence in open and distance learning in general by offering concrete standards and criteria against which the quality of imported transnational provision can be compared, rather than being rejected out of hand.

Distance education is a mode of provision where there appears to be increasing competition between quality assurance providers, national, international and industry-based, to develop standards

---

[51] Adam S, (2003) *The Recognition, Treatment, Experience and Implications of Transnational Education in Central and Eastern Europe 2002–2003*, Stockholm, Högskoleverket.

and processes. This may reflect expansion in this kind of provision across sectors and countries. The US, for example, has over the past three years seen huge growth in the number of distance learning programmes and student enrolments on them. The recent report of the National Centre for Education Statistics (2000/01) noted that there had been a 110% increase in the number of students enrolled on US distance learning programmes and distance education students in the US now represent 19% of all enrolled students.

The growth of distance learning has had an impact on domestic quality assurance standards and criteria and has in some instances been a catalyst for co-operation between agencies. For example, in 2001 the regional accrediting commissions in the US published a 'Statement of Commitment for the Evaluation of Electronically Offered Degree and Certificate Programs' and 'Best Practices for Electronically Offered Degree and Certificate Programs'. They were seeking to adopt a common platform for the review of distance learning.[52] Despite such moves towards consistency of principles and practice, the nine national US accreditors have independently developed standards for distance learning which in some cases make additional requirements. Some of these standards are new, others are supplemental. Other accreditors use the same standards for review of distance learning as for site-based education.

In the UK, a range of organisations have emerged to promulgate standards and criteria in respect of Open and Distance Learning, but none has to date had statutory recognition or regulatory authority. This may change in the future; for example, the British Standards Institute has recently published a British Standard for the use of information technology in the delivery of assessments (BS7988) and has released for comment a draft code of practice for e-support in e-learning systems (BS8426).[53] In higher education,

---
[52] CHEA (2002) *The Role of Accreditation and Assuring Quality in Electronically Delivered Distance Learning, Fact Sheet #2.*
[53] BSI EDD System. Available at: http://edd.bsi.org.uk. Last Accessed 22 April 2004.

the Quality Assurance Agency has reviewed distance learning provision by UK higher education institutions within the UK at institutional and subject level as part of its regular activities. It has also undertaken a specific overseas audit to look at UK distance learning provision in Hong Kong. In 1999, the QAA issued Guidelines on the Quality Assurance of Distance Learning. These are now under review with the intention that they become incorporated into the Code of Practice on Quality Assurance.

As we have seen above, it is often the case that novel forms of provision (such as e-learning) are initially deemed to be specialist, requiring separate standards, criteria and regulators. Subsequently, as they become subsumed within traditional higher education provision, they are included in 'normal' quality assurance processes whose standards and criteria are adapted accordingly. Additionally, where common ground is found across sectors, institutions may choose to 'double badge' or there may be convergence between 'industry-based' and 'higher education-based' standards. We remain at the stage where there is a diversity of approaches and agencies.

International accreditation by national agencies

As mentioned above, some of the regional US accreditation commissions operate outside the US and accredit non-US institutions. Most of these institutions are 'international' or effectively stateless as they are not part of the higher education system where they are located (e.g. Deree College in Greece or the American University in Bulgaria). Such institutions often, but not always, recruit a majority of international rather than local students. For many of these institutions this is the only opportunity available to them for recognition. Some could not be accredited or recognised locally because they are private, or because they wish to offer different educational experiences from the local pattern. Others consider themselves international, so local accreditation would not be appropriate. These institutions have few opportunities open to them for international benchmarking and potentially wider recognition.

To date only three of the six regional commissions in the US undertake such transnational activities. Activities are demand-led and there has been debate amongst the regional commissions as to whether individual commissions should be thus engaged, or whether there should be a joint initiative in the international review of institutions whereby the regional commissions would work together to review 'American-style' institutions outside the US. The aim would be to achieve a consistency of approach and to remove the possibility of commissions being played off against each other.

The Department for Education and Skills in the UK does not give advice on overseas institutions operating outside the UK. The department states that overseas higher education institutions operating in the UK are subject to the quality assurance mechanisms of their own country as well as the provisions of the Education Reform Act (1988) concerning UK university title and degree awarding powers.[54] The Further and Higher Education Act (1992) established four funding bodies in England, Scotland, Wales and Northern Ireland. These Funding Councils have statutory responsibility for ensuring the quality of education is assessed in the institutions they fund. Since 1997, the QAA (UK) has through contracts with the Funding Councils carried out the external evaluation of this funded provision and also of other institutions with UK degree awarding powers. The Agency is constrained by its current Articles from operating outside the UK except for carrying out the audit of UK higher education institutions' overseas links and partnerships through which UK higher education qualifications are awarded. However, many UK professional and regulatory bodies are very active in validating and accrediting programmes around the world.

At programme level there is extensive cross-border accreditation and recognition, carried out mainly by US specialist accreditors and by UK professional and regulatory bodies such as the Royal

---

[54] Department of Education and Skills, *Studying for a UK Degree*. Available at: www.dfes.gov.uk/recognisedukdegrees. Last Accessed 22 April 2004.

Institute of British Architects and the Royal Institute of Chartered Surveyors. This international activity represents a significant proportion of the work of some of these organisations as they may be recognising more programmes outside their national border than within. Typically, they are invited to accredit programmes in countries where local provision in the subject/profession is relatively limited, thus creating difficulties for independent external evaluation or benchmarking. Several of the programmes recognised by the UK organisations are in Latin America.

Co-operation and competition in internationalising professional accreditation
At professional or subject level, international co-operation (particularly in research) is long standing. Emerging co-operation in the accreditation and quality assurance of higher education programmes in subjects such as engineering has supported the mobility of students and qualified professionals and offered opportunities for the benchmarking of programmes and institutions. But professions or disciplines appear to be taking different approaches to the internationalisation of quality assurance.

The cooperative engineers?
An oft-quoted example of co-operation in international quality assurance and the mutual recognition of qualifications is the Washington Accord.[55] The Accord was established in 1989 and is an agreement between the engineering quality assurance organisations of several nations. It recognises the substantial equivalency of programmes accredited by those organisations and recommends that the graduates of accredited (undergraduate) programmes in any of the signatory countries be recognised by the other countries as having met the academic requirements for entry into the practice of engineering. The current signatories are from Australia, Canada, Hong Kong, Ireland, New Zealand, South Africa, the United Kingdom

---

[55] Washington Accord, *Homepage*. Available at: www.washingtonaccord.org. Last Accessed August 2003.

and the US, with Japan as a provisional member. The agreement applies only to accreditation conducted by the signatories within their respective national or territorial boundaries. The signatories are not bound to recognise programmes accredited or recognised as substantially equivalent by other signatories outside their national boundaries, so some types of transnational education appear to be excluded from the process. While individual universities are not signatories to the Accord, their graduates may benefit from it.

A provisional member of the Accord must demonstrate that the accreditation system for which it has responsibility 'appears to be conceptually similar to those of the other signatories'. By conferring provisional status, the signatories indicate that they consider the provisional signatory has the potential capability to reach a full signatory status, but there is no guarantee that this will be granted. All members have to undergo a review process. In June 2003, provisional membership status was granted to Germany, Malaysia and Singapore through three organisations: the Accreditation Agency for Study Programs in Engineering, Informatics, Natural Sciences and Mathematics, Germany; the Engineering Accreditation Council of Malaysia; and the Institution of Engineers, Singapore.

The Accord does not appear to prevent signatory organisations from offering separate 'benchmarking' type activities such as 'substantial equivalency' by ABET and programme accreditation by the Engineering Council in the UK. These opportunities are most frequently taken up either by institutions in small countries with few or no national comparators and no national external quality assurance or occasionally, it would appear, by institutions seeking an 'international' label for their programmes.

The competitive (and overlapping) world of accreditation in business and management
In contrast to the engineers, the accreditation activity in the domain of business and management appears to be a more competitive

phenomenon with AACSB International, AMBA, FIBAA (which competes in Germany with three regional agencies) and EQUIS (EFMD) emerging as contenders for the title 'international accreditors'.

- AACSB International – the Association to Advance Collegiate Schools of Business[56] – is a US-based accrediting agency for bachelors, masters and doctoral degree programs in business administration and accounting which is recognised by the USDE and CHEA. The Association accredits 406 institutions in the United States. Since 2001 it has 'eagerly sought outreach activities to globalise the Association and its services' and now accredits more than forty institutions in 19 countries outside the US.
- AMBA – the Association of MBAs – is an independent accreditation body based in the UK that assesses the quality of MBA programmes. It is also a membership organisation for students and graduates of accredited programmes around the world. The Association currently accredits programmes in 18 countries outside the UK.
- FIBAA – the Foundation for International Business Administration Accreditation – is based in Germany and is accredited by the AKK. It accredits programmes delivered in institutions in Austria, Germany and Switzerland. In common with the other accreditors, it has tackled the accreditation of new providers such as international institutions. It is not competing in the wider market place, but has 'competition' within Germany as some of the regional German agencies (ZevA, ACQUAS, AQUIN) are also accrediting MBA programmes. This may account for the small representation of German institutions in the lists of the other international accreditors.
- EQUIS – the European Quality Improvement System-was launched in 1997 by the European Foundation for Management

---

[56] Association to Advance Collegiate Schools of Business, *Website*. Available at: www.aacsb.edu. Last Accessed 22 April 2004.

Development (EFMD), based in Brussels. EQUIS accredits globally, with 65 Business Schools now accredited in five continents. It has no 'national' base, does not seek to replace national quality assurance systems and is not based on any particular educational model. It could be argued that this is the most international of all these organisations.

The origins of the organisations are different and indeed they have different focuses, some accrediting institutions and others programmes. In addition, some have formal recognition within national systems of higher education whereas others have 'practitioner' recognition within their community. All appear to be comfortable with accrediting and recognising new modes of provision, distance learning, transnational delivery, branch campuses and partnership arrangements, and new providers. EFMD has recently established a pilot project, 'CLIP', to evaluate the provision offered by 'corporate' universities with Allianz being the first to undergo the process, which closely mirrors the EQUIS procedures. In this subject area, innovation and difference appear not to be feared as threats to quality and standards.

While these approaches to internationalisation have obvious benefits, there are also some potential concerns. Is such an approach becoming a club for the wealthy? In 2002, AACSB International and EFMD signed a Strategic Relations agreement, but this did not appear to have any bearing on the 'competition' – real or unintended – between the organisations. The phenomenon of 'multiple accreditation' is becoming a reality in this world, with several institutions either double or triple 'badged'. Canadian, Dutch, French, Spanish and UK Business Schools are the most prevalent holders of multiple accreditation. In some countries this would be in addition to the usual national quality assurance and recognition processes.

The cost of undertaking such international accreditation is beyond the reach of institutions in many parts of the world, thus excluding them from the perceived competitive advantage of international labels. In addition, other institutions who see their mission as being more to serve local, regional or national communities may miss out on the 'perceived' excellence attributed to the possession of an international label because the focus of their activities may not meet the requirements and criteria of these international accreditors. And finally, there is a potential for confusion as incorrect inferences are drawn from the labels. Accreditation by the AACSB International, for example, gives an assurance of having met a 'threshold standard' as defined in the US context but in the international market the label appears to be taken as a badge of excellence.

Quality assurance information and sources: ranking and labels
The introduction of performance indicators in many national systems of education throughout the world has provided opportunities for new commentators to enter the arena, notably the media. They provide additional information for consumers in the form of increasing numbers of surveys, rankings and 'guides' to higher education and qualifications. These commentators include local and national press, such as The Times in the UK, Die Stern in Germany and McLean's Magazine in Canada. Such commentaries and rankings have in some cases gone international, especially in relation to business schools, with The Economist, Business Week and the Financial Times all publishing their rankings of 'the 100 best'. These rankings appear to be taken very seriously by institutions and students alike and often feature in recruitment literature along with accreditation and other quality assurance findings. As observed in the report of an UNESCO-CEPES roundtable, "the proliferation of ranking systems is not surprising. With the massification of higher education round the globe, there is an increasing appetite for this kind of independent information. The private sector has responded to this demand appetite, with apparent commercial success, since, without a consumer market, the rankings could not be published".

In Germany, a variation on the hard copy publications is a web-based 'ranking' based on the experiences of students which is intended to inform the decisions of students intending to study in Germany. It covers 242 German higher education institutions and the 34 most popular subject areas and represents a co-operation between the DAAD/CHE and Stern.[57]

There is also a proliferation of 'directories' and international guides which provide information variously on international study, distance learning etc. It is sometimes necessary to be cautious about the information contained in these publications since their independence is not always apparent. Some are financed by the institutions featured in them-so are in fact 'promotional' – and several appear not to be very clear as to the criteria for inclusion of material.

Trade in education services

The current debate on trade in education services within the current (Doha) round of negotiations in the WTO's General Agreement on Trade in Services (GATS) is contentious and polarised. But one issue common to all parties, whether for or against liberalising trade in education services, is interest in and concern about the quality of education. A consequence of this has been to bring even more actors into the already crowded arena of quality assurance in higher education. A range of inter-governmental and non-governmental organisations, some of which have no legal competence in, or experience of, managing quality assurance in higher education have entered the field. Their activities range from commenting on quality assurance to potentially regulating aspects of it through international conventions and codes of practice.

Different organisations play different roles:

- UNESCO, through its Global Forum on International Quality Assurance, Accreditation and the Recognition of Qualifications, is promoting the development of principles of good practice in cross-border education, national capacity building in quality assurance and the modernising of regional conventions on the recognition of qualifications. UNESCO has therefore both a formal, quasi-regulatory role (through its international

---

[57] German Academic Exchange Service. *Website*. Available at: www.university-ranking.de. Last Accessed 22 April 2004.

scope and its governmental membership) and a less formal, guidance, capacity-building and information role.

- The OECD is aiming to be the 'bridge' between the world of trade and education, improving communication and understanding and providing data about trends in trade in education and new forms of learning.
- The WTO has an interest in the role of quality assurance as a support or an impediment to trade in educational services.

None of these organisations actually has responsibility for or carries out quality assurance activities. Nonetheless they provide international forums for the variety of stakeholders to raise and debate concerns about trade in educational services, the impact of new forms of provision and the activities of providers, legitimate or fraudulent. While the debates and the sharing of information and practice are valuable, there is also considerable potential for duplication of activities and for the promulgation of contradictory findings by the 'talkers' and 'thinkers' as to the right direction to take in international quality assurance. Establishing appropriate action for the future requires parallel and linked co-operation between the players and must ensure that the 'doers' are firmly on-board.

Within the separate arena of regional and bilateral free trade agreements, arrangements are increasingly being made concerning the mutual recognition of qualifications and for co-operation in accreditation. An example of this is within MERCOSUR, created by the Treaty of Asuncion in 1991, a grouping comprising Argentina, Brazil, Paraguay, Chile and Uruguay. A regional technical committee is to be created to serve as a forum to resolve differences between member states about accreditation and recognition and to establish equivalence of degrees and certificates between educational systems. Given such developments, it is increasingly important for close co-operation to occur between quality assurance agencies and those with a remit to recognise qualifications. It is also essential to ensure the exchange of information between Ministries of trade and education. In due course, just as 'borderless education' is witness to convergence across educational boundaries, so these same developments may drive convergence across agencies and government departments.

Tackling deception and fraud in higher education – whose responsibility is it?
There are many calls for the international regulation of higher education – especially transnational education – by a supra-national body. But no matter what quality assurance systems are introduced at national or international level, they alone cannot tackle issues of fraud, corruption and deception which are becoming an increasing problem, especially in relation to the proliferation of Internet based institutions and accreditation bodies. The difficulty of tackling these issues is compounded by the fact that it is not always the case that 'consumers' (learners) are the victims of such diploma and accreditation mills. For example, earlier this year, the BBC reported on the culmination of four years co-operation between trade officials in the UK and the US that led to the demise of a chain of diploma mills operating on the Internet with activities from Israel to Romania to the UK and the US. It was observed that "the people sending out the e-mails were not conning anyone. These people who bought the degrees knew exactly what they were doing. The complaints received were actually from colleagues of those who got jobs by lying".[58] By moving from jurisdiction to jurisdiction, obeying the letter of the law but denying the spirit of the law, clever operators can, as in the reported case, make millions of dollars and by all accounts have 'satisfied' customers. The 'trade in qualifications' as opposed to education is a booming one as is the emergence of the academic flags of convenience in the form of governments who are apparently willing to lend credibility to sundry dubious diploma mills.[59]

National authorities and quality assurance and accreditation agencies can contribute to consumer protection by publishing

---
[58] 'Bogus Degree Sites Shut Down'. *BBC News*, (7 March, 2003). Available at: http://news.bbc.co.uk/go/em/fr/-/1/hi/education/2829237.stm. Last Accessed 22 April 2004.
[59] Contreras, A. L. (2003) *A Case Study in Foreign Degree (Dis)approval*, *International Higher Education*, Number 32 Summer 2003.

easily accessible lists of recognised institutions and/or programmes and by providing advice to would-be learners. Examples include the CHEA Facts sheets containing '12 Important Questions About External Quality Review' and 'Important Questions about 'Diploma Mills and Accreditation Mills'. Another example, recently published by OECD, is the 'Guidelines for Protecting Consumers from Fraudulent and Deceptive Commercial Practices Across Borders'. Such guidance is useful and necessary, but there is a limit to what can be achieved through information alone or through the awarding of 'quality labels' for quality assurance and accreditation agencies, as advocated in some circles. Legal instruments and legal powers to implement them are required, with common interpretations of the law. It may be that the WTO will in due course provide a route to stronger consumer and stakeholder confidence and protection, if supported by revised national regulatory frameworks, new quality assurance arrangements and international agreements and conventions.

PART FOUR

4.1 Trends and Issues

It is not straightforward to establish clear trends in a field where much is changing or under development and where developments vary by country, region and sector. Nonetheless, we offer a provisional summary of trends and issues, based on the overview of debate and activity described above.

At national level, there is growth in the number of agencies, networks and initiatives focused on quality assurance and much of this growth is linked to developments in borderless higher education. The scope and focus of the work undertaken by evaluation agencies are expanding and diversifying, albeit at different paces in different countries and regions. In relation to new agencies, it is noteworthy that some have been established with a comprehensive range of functions in relation to quality assurance *and* the recognition of qualifications (e.g. Sweden's Högskoleveret and the Centre for Quality Assessment in Higher Education Lithuania).

Others are comprehensive in dealing with the evaluation of all levels of education from kindergarten to university (e.g. the EVA in Denmark) or all types of provider and provision. In addition, as examples from the Arab region illustrate, new agencies may be quicker or better able to respond to new developments than existing agencies.

The purposes and agendas of existing national agencies are also evolving from traditional emphases on quality improvement and accountability to wider responsibilities for the provision and dissemination of information on programmes and institutions to the wider public and to government. The provision of expert opinions and advice to governments and institutions is increasingly significant; in some cases this also involves investigating and even deciding on legal matters relating to higher education institutions (e.g. ENQA and INQAAHE publications). Given some of the concerns raised in relation to transnational and for-profit education and the growing problem of fraud and deception, one can expect this trend to continue. National agencies are also, of course, refining their quality assurance approaches in the light of their experiences of evaluation and as a result of the sharing of practice across agencies, as well as in response to wider changes in higher education and society. The growth in popularity of 'accreditation', especially in Europe, may be part of such evolutionary change.

There is increasing pressure (in countries and regions) for 'convergence' of quality assurance systems, criteria and approaches. A number of different types of initiatives are in train to promote convergence, mutual co-operation and understanding. These include the development of similar or common external reference points such as qualification frameworks; work on glossaries and typologies that address problems of terminology; attempts at convergence of methodologies and efforts to bring quality assurance and the recognition of qualifications closer together, at national and international levels. Several of these initiatives are visible in the emerging European Higher Education Area.

Two common approaches to the fostering of mutual understanding and exchange of information that provide a potential for convergence are networking and benchmarking, both of which are much in evidence.

Networking
There is an apparent increase in networking and co-operation in quality assurance and enhancement activities:

- between governments through free trade agreements and agreements on the mutual recognition of qualifications;
- between quality assurance agencies at international level (INQAAHE) and through bilateral mutual recognition and co-operation agreements;
- between universities through associations such as EUA and its institutional review process and other thematic networks;
- by the professions (e.g. the Washington Accord);
- by agencies such as UNESCO that aim to create a forum for dialogue both across countries and between the variety of stakeholders concerned with quality in education.

Benchmarking
Benchmarking is increasingly referred to as a purpose of evaluation, and some agencies in smaller countries or regions in Europe have tended to mention this as a core activity (e.g. FINHEEC). It is being used as a tool for self-evaluation and improvement, helping institutions and/or systems to monitor performance on a range of dimensions, and to compare performance either with the past or with that of others with similar characteristics. An example of benchmarking in a large system is its use by the NAAC in India where a five-stage process has been developed at institutional level. This involves: setting the platform; choosing the appropriate benchmarking activity; identifying the aspects to be benchmarked; fixing the norms and indicators; and, applying the benchmarks. Consortia of institutions such as Universitas21 are also using benchmarking as an instrument for quality assurance, and individual institutions, particularly from smaller countries or those with less mature national quality

assurance systems, are using accreditation and validation services from other countries to benchmark their quality and standards.

It is clear that the international dimensions of higher education are creating a need for international initiatives and action. Once again, a diversity of approaches is in train. For example:

- National agencies are going international and 'international' agencies are emerging in accreditation, if only, as yet, in certain fields;
- The development of regional and international subject or profession-based quality assurance and accreditation organisations;
- The use of international industry standards;
- Exporting and importing countries are both developing regulations and quality assurance arrangements;
- Some regions are actively seeking mutual co-operation or convergence in quality assurance arrangements.

The growth of new forms of learning and the emergence of new providers are prompting a range of work on developing instruments to assure and evaluate the quality of different modes of provision such as 'e-learning' and 'blended learning' and to monitor the activities of new providers. But what is 'new' varies from country to country and over time. Novelty and innovation also provoke a range of reactions – initially a call for increased and new regulation – and over time, often, the absorption of innovative practice into existing regulations and quality assurance practice. As discussed, there are also a variety of concerns being raised about borderless developments. There is a potential here for both legitimate and fraudulent developments to be tarred by the same brush. In order to take appropriate action, national and international agencies and governments require good data on which to base their decisions and target their actions.

Expansion and change in higher education and the associated complexities involved (including those associated with the quality assurance world) are prompting calls for more and better information for all stakeholders. There appears to be growth in the range and sources of information about quality and standards (such as the media) and the use of such data as well as other 'labels' for promotional and branding purposes by institutions. Also, the provision of more and better information about judgements made by agencies is prompting debates about changes to the nature of judgements, questions about rankings, pressure for routine publication of evaluation reports and efforts to improve the language of quality.

4.2 Conclusion

Our review of the domain of quality assurance in this increasingly borderless terrain leads us to some conclusions both about future directions and some unresolved issues.

First, there is no apparent steady state in quality assurance at national level. This may mitigate against any comprehensive international agreement on quality and standards beyond necessary agreements on general principles or values and standards that should be applied to the activity of quality assurance. The focus on convergence of methodology or processes as an indicator of comparability of quality and standards can be misleading.

Second, both the frameworks and outcomes from quality assurance appear to be strengthening through the development of new performance indicators, benchmarking processes and agreed reference points for quality and standards such as frameworks of qualifications, output standards and criteria that focus on students' learning attainments. Progress is very uneven, but such instruments may provide greater transparency at national level which in turn may facilitate international understanding, mobility and the recognition of qualifications.

Third, the development of 'international accreditation' has brought about a new 'access' issue. The cost of seeking recognition by non-national accreditation and 'international quality labels' may exclude institutions in developing countries from achieving international recognition. Also, a lack of national accreditation agencies especially at subject level may preclude involvement in international systems such as the Washington Accord. International agreement on quality and standards may be easier to achieve when the focus is narrower, the constituents fewer, and the common interest greater (e.g. in certain professions where mobility is common). This is potentially more likely to lead to co-operation and collaboration. However, where there is no shared professional corpus, the incentive for co-operation may be less and the scope for competition greater.

Fourth, inter-institutional benchmarking and quality assurance arrangements may be valuable for the institutions involved, but it is unclear how the wider interests of students, potential students and external stakeholders are met. Given the ever-increasing demand for information about quality and standards, such arrangements are not likely to be regarded as sufficient to meet requirements for accessible public information.

Fifth, universities and other individual providers of transnational education do not and cannot know what is the cumulative or aggregated impact of their individual actions and presence in another higher education system. This does not, of course, exonerate them from doing their own 'triple bottom-line' impact assessment and reporting in relation to the social, economic and environmental impact of their actions wherever they operate. However, it is only the importing country that can make an overall assessment and judgement on the impact and relevance of transnational provision for meeting national needs. Where regulations for imported education are being developed, there needs to be clearer information as to what these are, how they apply, what the outcomes are and what levels of confidence can be assumed by their enactment.

Sixth, the quality assurance of transnational education may in certain circumstances be less of a pressing issue than the control of indigenous private provision. Indeed the two are often confused, especially where local institutions are operating with foreign sounding names. There are promising signs that some of the providers of transnational education are increasingly aware of their responsibilities and that competition between them and indigenous providers will increase, not diminish, their national quality assurance efforts in relation to exported education. While international codes have their place, without some kind of monitoring of adherence and implementation, they will not be as effective instruments of quality assurance as the review and evaluation activities carried out by national agencies.

Seventh, quality assurance agencies and recognition authorities cannot be the 'Academic Interpol' when it comes to matters of international fraud, corruption and deception. There are two aspects to this. As discussed earlier, 'quality and standards' are at least in part, socially and culturally constructed and politically framed. Through regulatory arrangements, the activities of formal agencies and the actions of institutions, they tend to reflect the presence or absence of wider standards of integrity and probity in public life. Quality assurance arrangements can therefore be weak or strong, depending on context and more or less able to cope with fraud, deception or corruption. The second point is that new forms of fraud and deception go beyond the academic quality and standards remit of most agencies and institutions into arenas of trade, crime, immigration and employment. These are not areas that academic quality assurance alone can address or resolve, whether national, regional or international.

References

ACA (2002) *Borderless education: lifelong learning knows no borders*, Academic Cooperation Association, www.aca-secretariat.be

Adam S (2001) *Transnational Education Project Report and Recommendations (Western Europe)* Confederation of European Rectors' Conference, Brussels, www.unige.ch/eua

Adam S (2003) *The Recognition, Treatment, Experience and Implications of Transnational Education in Central and Eastern Europe 2002–2003*, Stockholm, Högskoleverket.

AVCC (2001) *Practice and Guidelines for Australian Universities*, Australian Vice Chancellors' Committee, Canberra, www.avcc.edu.au.

Campbell C & van der Wende (2000) *International Initiatives and Trends in Quality Assurance for European Higher Education*, ENQA Occasional Papers 1, Helsinki.

Campbell C & Roysnyai, C (2002) *Quality Assurance and the Development of Course Programmes*, _Papers on Higher Education, UNESCO-CEPES, Bucharest.

CHEA (2001) *Principles for United States Accreditors Working Internationally: Accreditation of Non-United States Institutions and Programs.* CHEA.

CHEA (2002a) *The Role of Accreditation and Assuring Quality in Electronically Delivered Distance Learning*, Fact Sheet #2.

CHEA (2002b) *International Quality Review and Accreditation: The Role of US Recognized Accrediting Organizations, Letter from the President.*

CHEA (2003) "Important Questions about 'Diploma Mills' and 'Accreditation Mills", Fact Sheet #6, May 2003

Commission for Academic Accreditation (2003) *The Standards for Licensure and Accreditation*, Second Edition, United Arab Emirates.

Contreras A L (2003) *A Case Study in Foreign Degree (Dis)approval, International Higher Education*, Number 32 Summer 2003, pp 7–9.

Cunningham S, Tapsall S, Ryan Y, Stedman L, Bagdon K, Flew T (1998) *New Media and Borderless Education: A Review of the Convergence between Global Media Networks and Higher Education Provision*, Canberra, DETYA.

Cunningham S, Ryan Y, Stedman L, Tapsall S, Bagdon K, Flew T, Coaldrake P (2000) *The Business of Borderless Education*, Canberra, DETYA.

CVCP (2000) *The Business of Borderless Education: UK Perspectives*, vols 1–3, London, Universities UK

Daniel J (1996) *Mega-Universities and Knowledge Media: Technology Strategies for Higher Education*, London, Kogan.

DICES (2003) *International Guide to Postgraduate Programmes*, Madrid, Circulo de Progresso.

ESIB (2003) *Policy paper on Commodification of Education.*

ENQA (2002) *A Method for Mutual Recognition*, ENQA Occasional Papers X, Helsinki

ENQA (2003) *Quality Procedures in European Higher Education*, ENQA Occasional Papers 5, Helsinki

Greek D (2003) "Where is the University of Palmers Green?" Available at: www.vunet.com/News/1139348.

HEQC (2000) *Founding Document for the Higher Education Quality Committee*, Pretoria, South Africa, Available at: www.che.org.za./publications/heqc_documents.php.

Habrinska, M (2000) *Transnational Education in the Slovak Republic: Threat or Challenge?* Higher Education in Europe, Vol XXV, No 3

INQAAHE and IAUP (2003) *Quality Assurance Agencies*, Dublin, HETAC.

Knight J (2002) *Trade in Higher Education Services: the implications of GATS*, London, Observatory on Borderless Higher Education.

Knight J (2003) *GATS, Trade and Higher Education: Perspective 2003 – Where are we?* London, Observatory on Borderless Higher Education.

Middlehurst R (2001) *Quality Assurance Implications of New Forms of Higher Education*, Helsinki, ENQA Occasional Paper.

Middlehurst R (2003) 'The Developing World of Borderless Education: Impact and Implications' in D'Antoni, S (ed) (2003), *The Virtual University: Models and Messages, Lessons from Case Studies*, Paris UNESCO (available at www.unesco.org/iiep/).

Newman F & Couturier L (2002) *Trading Public Good in the Higher Education Market*, London, Observatory on Borderless Higher Education.

Observatory on Borderless Higher Education (2003a), *Breaking News Articles* (13 February 2003 and 20 February 2003) on fraud and deception.

Observatory on Borderless Education (2003b) – *Breaking News Articles* (15 January 2003, 30 January 2003, 12 February, 24 February, 6 March, 11 March, 2 April, 9 April and 11 April 2003) about private and transnational education.

Observatory on Borderless Higher Education (2003c) "Quality Assurance in Borderless Higher Education: six initiatives", *Briefing Note*, No. 11, May, 2003.

OECD (1998) 'Redefining Higher Education', Wagner, A. OECD Directorate for Education, Employment, Labour and Social Affairs, in *The OECD Observer*, No. 213, October 1998.

OECD (2003) *Guidelines for Protecting Consumers from Fraudulent and Deceptive Commercial Practices Across Borders*, Paris.

QAA (1999a) *Guidelines for the Quality Assurance of Distance Leaning*. Available at: http://www.qaa.ac.uk.

QAA (1999b) *Code of Practice for the assurance of academic quality and standards – Section 2: Collaborative Provision*.

Smeby J C and Stensaker B (1999) "National Quality Assessment Systems in the Nordic Countries: developing a Balance between External and Internal Needs", *Higher Education Policy*, vol 12: 3–14.

Stella A (2001) Quality Assurance in Indian Higher Education: lessons learnt (sic) on benchmarking, in Harman G (ed) *International Conference on Quality Assurance in higher Education: standards, mechanisms and mutual recognition*, Ministry of University Affairs of Thailand and UNESCO Principal Regional Office for Asia and the Pacific, Bangkok.

Tait A and Mills R (ed) (1999) *The Convergence of Distance and Conventional Education*, London, Routledge.

UNESCO (2003a) *Synthesis Report on Trends and Developments in Higher Education since the World Conference on Higher Education* (1998–2003), Paris.

UNESCO (2003b) *Higher education in the Arab Region 1998–2003*, Paris. Available at: www.unesco.org/education/wche.

World Bank (2002) *Constructing Knowledge Societies: New Challenges for Higher Education*, Washington DC, World Bank.

Yonezawa A and Kaiser F (eds) (2003) *Sysytem-Level and Strategic Indicators for Monitoring Higher Education in the Twenty-First Century*, Studies on Higher Education, UNESCO-CEPES, Bucharest.

Glossary of Acronyms and Web Resources

AACSB – Association to Advance Collegiate Schools of Business

ABET – Accreditation Board for Engineering and Technology – www.abet.org

ACA – Academic Cooperation Association – www.aca-secretariat.be

ACQUAS – FIBAA's Agentur für Qualitätssicherung durch Gessche Akkreditierung von Studiengängen

ACQUIN/AQUIN – Accreditation, Certification and Quality Assurance Institute – www.acquin.org

AKK – Akkreditierungsrat-Germany

AMBA – Association of MBAs

ANECA – National Agency for Quality Assurance and Accreditation of Spain – www.aneca.es

AOU – Arab Open University – www.unu.edu/api

AQU – Agencia per a la Qualitat del Sistema Universitari a Catalunya – www.aqucatalunya.org

AVCC – Australian Vice Chancellors Committee

AUQ – Agency for Quality Assurance in the Catalan University System – www.agenqua.es

AUQA – Australian Universities Quality Agency – www.auqa.edu.au

BAOL – British Association of Open Learning – www.baol.co.uk

BMBK – Austrian Accreditation Council – www.akkreditierungsrat.at

CHE – Centrum für Hochschulentwicklung – www.che.de

CHEA – Council for Higher Education Accreditation – http://www.chea.org

CRICOS – Commonwealth Register of Institutions and Courses for Overseas Students – www.dest.gov.au/esos

CSUCA – Consejo Superior Universitario Centroamericano

DAAD – Deutscher Akademischer Austausch Dienst – www.daad.de

DICES – Directorio de Centros de Formación – www.infoformacion.com

EFMD – European Foundation for Management Development – http://www.efmd.be

EFQM – European Foundation for Quality Management – http://www.efqm.org

ENQA – European Network for Quality Assurance – www.enqa.net

ENIC/NARIC – the European recognition networks – http://enic-naric.net

EQUIS – European Quality Improvement System

ESIB – The National Union of Students in Europe – www.esib.org

EUA – European University Association – www.unige.ch/eua

EVA – Danmarks Evalueringsinstitut – www.eva.dk

FIBAA – Foundation for International Business Administration – http://www.fibaa.de

FINHEEC – The Finnish Higher Education Evaluation Council – www.finheec.fi

HETAC – Higher Education and Training Awards Council – www.hetac.ie

HKCAA – Hong Kong Council for Academic Accreditation – www.hkcaa.edu.hk

HSV – Högskoleverket, National Agency for Higher Education, Sweden – www.hsv.se

HAC – Hungarian Accreditation Committee – www.mab.hu

IAUP – International Association of University Presidents – www.ia-up.org

ICDE – International Council for Open and Distance Education – www.icde.org

INAFOP – Instituto Nacional de Accreditacao de Professores-Portugal

ISO – International Organisation for Standardisation – www.iso.ch

LAN – Lembaga Akreditasi Negara, the National Accreditation Board of Malaysia

INQAAHE – International Network for Quality Assurance in Higher Education – www.inqaahe.nl

NAAC – National Assessment and Accreditation Council – www.naac-india.com

NIAD – National Institution for Academic degrees and University Evaluation, Japan – www.niad.ac.jp

OECD – Organisation for Economic Co-operation and Development – www.oecd.org

– Open University (UK) – www.open.ac.uk

QAA – Quality Assurance Agency for Higher Education (UK) – www.qaa.ac.uk

SKVC – Centre for Quality Assessment in Higher Education, Lithuania – www.skvc.lt

UNED – Universidad Nacional de Educación a Distancia – www. uned.es

UNESCO – CEPES – www.cepes.ro
  – UNESCO – http://www.unesco.org/education/studyingabroad

USDE – United States Department of Education – www.ed.gov

The Washington Accord – http://www.washingtonaccord.org

ZevA – Zentrale Evaluations – und Akkreditierungsagentur Hannover – www.zeva.uni-hannover.de/

The Rise and Regulation of For-Profit Higher Education

Roger King

1 Introduction

It is now commonplace to observe that governments around the world regard a substantial, or growing, higher education system as essential for economic development. Despite some sceptics who argue that the causal connection between the two has yet to be demonstrated, there is widespread acceptance that a nation's human capital, and the new ideas and innovations generated by that human capital, are the major drivers of economic growth. This is regarded as especially true for the often fastest-growing parts of economies, the knowledge sectors of the service industries, where investments in people through higher education are particularly productive.

The problem that governments face, however, is paying for this investment. In poorer countries the funding is simply not available. In most advanced countries the growth of higher education traditionally has been largely publicly funded. Even in countries with established private sectors of higher education, such as the USA, state aid in the form of student grants, loans (on favourable terms), and tax breaks (including for endowments) has been larger than is generally appreciated. But alternative claims on public expenditure (such as health) and relatively low direct personal taxation have reduced units of state funding for university systems.

Unsurprisingly perhaps, in many countries the part of the higher education sector growing fastest is the private segment. As yet, there is little focused work on the regulatory models available for governments as they formulate policies for this growth area, although it is possible to glimpse interesting new regulatory developments in a number of countries. Here we speculate on the options open to policy-makers and examine the advantages and disadvantages of particular regulatory instruments. Particularly there is discussion of the policy dilemmas facing governments as they seek both to encourage and to control private higher education, especially as the for-profit mode becomes more predominant (including for-profit universities), and go on to examine whether regulatory models generally seek an essential similarity for universities of all types.

2 The Expansion of Private Higher Education

Although countries such as the USA, Chile, and Japan possess established private sectors of higher education, in many developing and transitional societies a host of new private providers has arisen – many for-profit. UNESCO indicates, for the 2000/1 academic year, that such institutions educate up to 30 per cent of the higher education student population in eastern and central Europe. The Czech Republic, Hungary, Poland and Romania have a private market share of around 22 per cent (the same as the USA) after large recent growth rates.[1] In South America, over half university enrolments are in private universities, with higher numbers if non-university post-secondary institutions are counted.

---

[1] Geisecke, H. (1999) 'Expansion and the Development of Private Higher Education in East Central Europe', *International Higher Education*, Summer.

Private higher education institutions are growing faster than the public sector in many nations, such as South Korea, Japan, Taiwan and the Philippines, where they enrol around 80 per cent of those going on to post-secondary education.[2] Tan describes private higher education in Malaysia in the late 1990's as having become "a fully-fledged industry" with 10 private universities and over 600 private colleges.[3] In sub-Saharan Africa, the World Bank estimates that the number of private sector institutions grew from around 30 in 1990 to over 85 in 1999.[4] In the USA the number of degree-granting, for-profit higher education institutions increased by over 300 per cent between 1981–99, rising from 165 to 721. Although for-profit institutions still enrol fewer than 5 per cent of all college students (1.3 million), their enrolment rate is growing at least three times faster than at traditional colleges. Perhaps a little surprisingly, in the Islamic republic of Iran, which has had a private tertiary sector since 1983, private institutions now enrol more than 30 per cent of the student population. Similar pictures of private growth are found elsewhere in the world.

At this point we need to offer a few clarifications. First, private institutions of higher education are not new. In the USA, for example, they include some of the longest-established and most prestigious organisations, such as Harvard, Stanford and Yale; something that also applies in Chile and Japan. These institutions possess large research and endowment funds and are not reliant on tuition fees as their only or primary source of funds. Such established private universities rarely have been 'for-profit', at least in a formal sense. Usually they have adopted a charitable 'non-profit' structure, sometimes for tax advantage, even if business-like and quite commercial in their operations. Typically, they have pursued, not least in South America, what we might describe as

---

[2] Altbach, P. (1998) 'The Anatomy of Private Higher Education', *International Higher Education*, Summer.
[3] Tan, Ai Mei (2002) *Malaysian Private Higher Education*, (London: Asean Academic Press).
[4] World Bank (2002) *Constructing Knowledge Societies: New Challenges for Tertiary Education*, (Washington DC: World Bank).

'civil society' purposes. These include providing 'something better' as a result of dissatisfaction by the socio-economically privileged with mass public higher education, and providing 'something different' as a result of religious aims (to maintain and promote particular faiths), or ethnic or nationalist goals (aimed at protecting social groups often perceived to be potentially 'at risk' in some way). In mainly historically Catholic parts of Europe we find that universities have the principle of 'freedom of action' written in their constitutions, which permits the Church and other religious or philosophical bodies to set up universities, although these days they are little different to the public institutions.

In contrast, as Levy has noted, the recent private providers usually are demand-absorbers, setting up shop where there is a demand not met by conventional providers.[5] The University of Phoenix, part of the Apollo Group in the USA, is a well-known example of a successful private (for-profit) university that caters for the demands of the working adult in ways generally not employed by more traditional providers – such as tying provision to employability, standardising curricula, instituting rapid credit accumulation, and providing convenient class times and locations. Elsewhere, in eastern and central Europe, for example, many private higher education bodies are quite small, sometimes little more than 'shop fronts' run by one individual, with few resources and highly reliant on tuition fees.

Second, the fastest-growing form of private higher education is for-profit. That is, education is regarded as a commodity for which individuals are prepared to pay a price that enables a profit to be made by investors. Although this may include the small operator of the kind referred to in eastern and central Europe, increasingly for-profit organisations are publicly-listed corporations. In Malaysia, there has been growing corporate presence since the early 1980's, and this has accelerated with the passing of the Private Higher Educational Institutions Act in 1996. This Act stipulates (Section 12)

---

[5] Levy, D. (2003) 'Expanding Higher Education Capacity Through Private Growth', *Observatory on Borderless Higher Education Report*, January.

that each private higher education institution is to be managed by a locally incorporated company, a provision that has markedly influenced the form of corporate governance and has served as an incentive to private corporations to become heavily involved in offering higher education. Tan notes, too, that the Act requires that private higher education institutions have a minimum working capital of RM250,000 (US$65,000), reflecting governmental beliefs that corporate backing is likely to ensure better facilities, finance and quality than purely small scale entrepreneurial outfits.[6] Remarkably, by 1999, three of the (then) six new private universities were being run by governmental utility corporations. In contrast, non-profit private organisations have usually been established by foundations, charitable organisations, and through community support.[7]

These corporations believe that higher education can be organised to produce a profit in its own right, and with year-long cash flow. Moreover, a number of property developers have seen successful private colleges as a vital component of the development of new precincts and townships that they own, and as contributing to the capital appreciation of their real estate. It is not surprising that Malaysian private higher education (much of it for-profit), with student numbers exceeding those in the public institutions, has now achieved a mass and stratified form of the kind usually associated with the more traditional sector in other countries.

For-profit private higher education that involves sizeable corporate ownership and management groupings can be found elsewhere. In Australia, the Queensland city of Cairns has sought to gain permission from the state authorities to host Australia's fourth private university, and the first to seek approval under national guidelines on standards agreed to by all state and federal ministers three years ago. Initiated by a development consortium under the

---

[6] Tan, Ai Mei (2002) *Malaysian Private Higher Education*, (London: Asean Academic Press).

[7] Lee, M. (1998) 'Corporatization and Privatization of Malaysian Higher Education', *International Higher Education*, Winter.

title of Cairns International University Limited, it features local and foreign investors, and the backers have a site for the campus on a prime piece of real estate in central Cairns. The application was recently rejected but with the possibility of re-submission.

In South Africa some private colleges are part of larger business groups, generally quoted on the stock exchange, such as Adcorp.[8] However, it is in the USA where for-profit national corporations and groups have forged ahead in recent years. The for-profit sector is large and diverse in the USA, but it is possible to identify a band of the largest companies, what are sometimes termed 'super-system' corporations. These include the 10 or so for-profit higher education specialists listed on the NASDAQ and New York Stock Exchange (consolidation here too is reducing the number of these players), and most have accreditation from one of the seven mainstream regional higher education accreditation bodies in the US. Many of the bigger for-profits, as a consequence of their national, multi-divisional corporate form, lack a sense of the geographical place that tends to characterise more conventional colleges and universities, and this is reinforced by their demand-absorbing functions. Generally they target states with the fastest-growing populations and economies, typically attracting working students who have neither the time, freedom or desire to enrol at traditional campuses. The University of Phoenix, the largest and best-known to use a corporate business model, seeks to ensure consistency in its delivery in a range of localities by unbundling the various academic teaching functions found in the conventional university, including course design, content production, and delivery, which become subject to a more specialised division of labour. Inconsistency in teaching performance (claimed to be characteristic of the conventional university) is said to be reduced, enabling a form of national (and increasingly international) 'branding' to be realised whatever the geographical location for course delivery. Moreover, as a for-profit organisation, the University of Phoenix argues that

---

[8] Levy, D. (2002) 'South Africa and the for-profit/Public Institutional Interface', *International Higher Education*, Fall.

Figure 1 Leading For-Profits Quoted on NASDAQ/ New York Stock Exchange
Number of Degree Programs Offered (as at 18/09/03)

Institution	Associate	Bachelors	Masters	Doctorate	Total
Apollo* Group	1	12	27	4	44
Career Education**	86	29	9	2	126
Corinthian Colleges	23	10	2	0	35
DeVry	2	7	7	2	18
Education Management	25	21	23	13	82
ITT	6	8	1	0	15
Strayer	10	8	6	0	24
Sylvan***	0	2	23	12	37

*   includes University of Phoenix
** includes Whitman Education Group
*** does not include the 50 plus undergraduate and graduate degrees offered at Sylvan's ten overseas institutions
Source: Chronicle of Higher Education 18/09/03

it offers the state a particular advantage – it is primarily a taxpayer rather than a tax-spender, unlike conventional universities (both non-profit private and public). These companies have been remarkably expansionary in recent years and their stock prices have performed well above the norm in a flat-line market.

In a number of countries it is becoming difficult to distinguish between higher and other forms of post-secondary education as the boundaries seem increasingly blurred and permeable. Many so-called higher education for-profits operate closer to further education, while their subject range is often quite limited compared to a conventional university. In a study of South Africa, Levy found that most private higher education occurs at fairly low levels, at what he describes as the 'level 5' interface between further and higher education, and he suggests that this is the situation in other countries too.[9] Nonetheless, there is little doubt that, in the USA and Malaysia, for example, not only is the number of advanced

---

[9] Levy, D. (2002) 'South Africa and the for-profit/Public Institutional Interface', *International Higher Education*, Fall.

Figure 2 Enrolments and Revenue for Institutions in Figure 1 (ordered by annual enrolment growth)

Institution	Annual Enrolment +/-	Annual Revenue 2002 (US$m)	% +/- over 2001	Locations
University of Phoenix Online	68%	Included in Apollo	Included in Apollo	N/A
Corinthian Colleges	38%	338m	38.5%	21 states
Education Management	36%	500m	35%	18 states and international
Career Education	21%	529m	63%	17 states and international
Sylvan	18%	484m*	54%	Strong international presence (8 countries)
Strayer	18%	93m	18.7%	3 states
Apollo Group	14%	1 billion	31.2%	25 states and international
ITT	8%	410m	18.1%	28 states
Whitman**	7%	92m	18.7%	13 states
DeVry	–6%	648m	14.1%	18 states and international

*   62% attributed to higher education division
** Whitman is being taken-over by Career Education (see Figure 1)
Source: Chronicle of Higher Education 18/09/03

degree programs increasing but subject coverage is also extending outside business and information technology. Teacher education appears to be an increasingly lucrative area for for-profit provision in the USA, with the introduction of masters and doctoral degrees for existing teachers who already possess an undergraduate degree, and where professional accreditation requirements are less strict in comparison with other subjects, such as law and medicine. Considerable regulation occurs at the professional subject level in the USA and offers opportunities in niche markets, such as health assistant programmes, for the for-profits.

3   Government Views

For developing countries especially, private institutions, including for-profit examples, are often welcome to both governments and the wider population. As demand for higher education increases, fuelled by population growth and expanding access and qualifications at lower educational levels, and with inadequate public funding to satisfy it, private and foreign provision may be the only means for some countries of building national capacity. Governments may also view a growing private sector as a useful spur for what some may regard as complacent state-funded domestic institutions, and as a source of innovative and international good practice.

What factors are likely to underpin the growth of for-profit, demand-absorbing higher education, and which factors are likely to act as inhibitors?

First, for-profit higher education is becoming increasingly recognised by governments where previously they had suffered constraints or ambiguity. China, Malaysia and South Africa are among those who, in the last six years or so, have formally recognised private providers by law so that public sector employment and access to the public universities, for example, are not denied its students. As we shall see, formal recognition and regulation generally go hand-in-hand.

Second, for-profit higher education is likely to continue to grow because governments are increasingly recognising its role in meeting domestic needs and also in attracting export earnings. In Singapore, for example, private higher education is set to expand much faster than public provision over the next decade or so, while, as we have seen, in Malaysia its size has already surpassed that of the public sector. For-profit higher education (including the overseas operations of foreign universities, which are usually classified as such) is seen as helping to attract students from the rest of Asia, assisting the goal of both countries to become regional 'hubs' with expanding earnings from higher education as a service industry. In countries such as India and China, too, there is awareness that the top elite and research-focused public (and some private) universities will only succeed if they are left out of 'access' or 'demand-absorption' goals, which, in part at least, can be picked up by the private sector.

A third reason why private higher education is likely to grow is that public and non-profit universities are either having to introduce more user-pays fees, or to raise considerably those charges that already operate, which reduces a major market barrier for the for-profits. In the USA, the 2003 student intake at public universities have found strikingly higher tuition costs and fees, and reduced services, after budget cuts by states experiencing stagnant economies, large budget deficits and mushrooming enrolments. These are estimated to be the largest enrolment increases of any in the last three decades. California, with the largest public-college system in the country, is experiencing particular difficulty, forcing a 30 per cent tuition fee increase. Rising charges appear to mark a significant shift of funding from the state to the student or family in the USA. The extent of state involvement in the setting of fees varies from state to state, but many are refusing to budget for enrolment growth. Under these conditions, community colleges and the for-profits will pick up the demand either immediately, or down the track when working students seek to reclaim their lost education at the University of Phoenix and other similar providers.

Fourth, a range of political, technological and trade factors are also likely to increase the scope of for-profit higher education, not least across borders. The General Agreement on Trade in Services (GATS) process at some point, (whatever the snail-like progress currently), is designed to reduce regulatory and other barriers to commercial educational operations between countries, which will benefit particularly the larger for-profits in the USA. Sylvan and Apollo are two organisations with a growing international presence, plus, particularly in the case of Apollo, a firm grasp of online delivery. The increase in bi-lateral and regional trade deals (where the USA is able to use the size of its domestic economy, and access to it, as a major lever in negotiations, persuading countries to 'free up' their higher education sectors to for-profit organisations), is also likely to stimulate cross-border commercial educational activity.

Finally, national governments are increasing public grants and loans available to students in for-profit higher education. Australia's 'fee-help scheme' and the USA's forthcoming re-authorisation of the Higher Education Act (where Republicans control both Congress and the White House and have close links with the major for-profit corporations) are two examples of such reforms. Public funds seem increasingly likely to be tied to performance criteria that may benefit the for-profits, such as on retention and employability.

However, there are factors that militate against the growth of private provision, such as the constant possibility of a sudden media 'scare' about 'diploma mills' and dubious quality (as occurred in the USA with private higher education in the early 1990s). Also, transforming or nation-building states, such as South Africa, view private and foreign providers with a much more sceptical eye, as essentially seeking commercial advantage, but without providing the public goods (that the traditional universities are seen to provide) which are deemed essential for national development. As we have noted, the for-profits often provide a kind of 'stripped down' version of a university, with a restricted subject range, no real sense of community or place, and little, if any, research. Governments, in these circumstances, look to conventional universities to deliver both the innovative economic payoffs necessary in knowledge-based societies (such as commercialisation of research), and to provide wider public goods, such as the formation of national and cultural identity, enhanced individual opportunity, and democratic commitment. Moreover, governments may regard traditional institutions as being more amenable to national objectives and policies than foreign or for-profit entities.

It is important to recognise that governments are often in a dilemma when it comes to policy-making for the conventional universities. Currently ministers in some administrations are more inclined than previously to view them as rather costly, inefficient, poorly managed, unaccountable and slow in responding to external change. They also know that they need the traditional universities for economic development, and are reliant on their scientific and academic judgements, not least in various state-imposed peer assessments and evaluations. Consequently, when such institutions use all the means and connections at their disposal, notably in accreditation and other 'gate-keeping' bodies, to resist the competition from the for-profits, then governments, whatever their feelings, are not always in a position to resist. Moreover, traditional universities may have a point when they regard the for-profits as unfairly competitive – such institutions are not mandated to provide public goods, and frequently the for-profits use academics from the conventional universities on a part-time basis, usually with no compensation to the main employer.

One consequence is that, in quality assurance, accreditation and other regulatory processes, the for-profits come under constraints to act more like a traditional university. In a recent collection of essays on private higher education in South Africa, it is argued that, just as traditional universities face government demands that they raise their private profile, the for-profit organisations should be required to exercise public purposes, such as equity or controls on fee levels.[10] In these circumstances the consequence is likely to produce a convergence around a particular university model – a kind of 'third way, public/private' one – rather than, if not full-blown diversity, then at least functional differentiation.

An issue for political leaders, especially as prestigious institutions increasingly set up abroad, is the extent to which higher education is provided by a range of institutions/corporations from around the world, rather than by a domestically-owned sector. In some countries, such as Japan, there is a long industrial and regulatory history in protecting home producers even in more international, liberalising times. In places such as the UK and the USA, however, there is a stronger tradition of encouraging wider competition in sectors. This may be attributed, in part, to the perceived benefits of a globally-valued 'centre' for a service or industry with high export earning capabilities (such as the City of London in UK financial services), almost irrespective of the domestic ownership

---

[10] Kruss, G. and Kraak, A. (2003) (eds) *A Contested Good?: Understanding Private Higher Education in South Africa*, (Boston, USA: Boston College Center for International Higher Education and 'Perspectives in Education', South Africa).

contribution to such centres. Will some governments come to feel that consumers are likely to benefit more from lower costs, and perhaps better services, from importers than from what they may regard as expensive, protected and less efficient domestic suppliers? On the other hand, in the case of the for-profits especially, outside institutions do not usually provide the range of economic services or public goods that national states require, including applied research.

These issues take us to the matter of regulation and how governments face up to the dilemma of both encouraging and controlling for-profit providers.

4 Regulation

As Levy has observed, the growth of private higher education in many countries has, for the most part, not been planned; it has been unexpected or a 'surprise' to most politicians.[11] It has occurred, if not within a policy vacuum, at least within an ill-sketched regulatory environment. In the member states of the European Union, for example, generally no specific regulations exist for controlling transnational education. The usual method is to completely ignore non-national providers unless they set out to become officially recognised institutions within a national system.[12] Undoubtedly, as a consequence, some private providers have been bogus and of questionable probity.

As might be expected of market-based provision, where the policy framework often lags, there is opportunity for both the respectable and the 'fly-by-night' to establish businesses relatively unhindered by governmental restrictions. This has made some governments wary of private providers, particularly the for-profit kind. Such institutions often lack track records and many are small and medium-sized

---

[11] Levy, D. (2002) 'Private Higher Education's Surprise Roles', *International Higher Education*, Spring.
[12] Dos Santos, S. (2002) 'Regulation and Quality Assurance in Transnational Education', *Tertiary Education and Management*, 8, 97–112.

enterprises, strongly dependent on tuition fees, and vulnerable to sudden changes in market demand and to the potential loss and drive of founding owners. They are also functioning in an environment where public doubts on the quality of their provision are frequently reinforced by the state universities.

Two key policy issues are generated by these developments. First, how is private higher education to be best regulated so that it is encouraged, but within a framework that establishes good practice, quality assurance, resourcing confidence, consumer protection, and avoidance of unfair competition for a domestic public university sector undertaking wider national purposes? Identifying the right regulatory model, and understanding the advantages and drawbacks of particular regulatory instruments, is vital. But rarely, if ever, do we come across such evaluations, and we attempt an initial consideration here.

Most regulatory approaches to for-profit higher education exhibit many of the features of what is termed 'command-and-control', with the emphasis on negative containment. But might other regulatory models, perhaps based more on self-regulation, work better? Given the declining trust by governments, businesses and the professions in conventional 'command-and-control' regulatory environments (which are usually backed up by statutory or other legal codes, penalties and independent agencies, particularly as found in the USA) it would seem appropriate to consider alternatives, including the use of voluntarism, the media and other public performance outlets, and economic incentives, such as tax breaks. Each of these regulatory models has its merits and its disadvantages, and these will be explored shortly.

Second, should regulatory policy aim to ensure that for-profit private higher education is similar in character to public and conventional higher education, or should it be regarded as providing essential diversity to the overall system through its distinctiveness? That is, should regulatory models and processes recognise this distinctiveness and set standards for such organisations that reflect their relative novelty and which differ in marked ways to those for the conventional institutions? Or should they, in the pursuit of a goal of quality, extinguish variation through institutional homogeneity and convergence, on the grounds that all higher education institutions should operate under the same rules, thus reducing overall systemic diversity? Governments are often under considerable pressure to pursue homogeneity and they can face major difficulties in handling the objections of the traditional universities in matters of academic judgement. Yet it is a common complaint from private institutions that conventional quality assurance methods focus too strongly on traditional resource inputs and take little account of new technology and student outcomes such as 'real world' capability.

A key issue here is the extent to which for-profit institutions are offering something distinctive and valuable that contributes to the innovation and diversity of the system. If they are largely offering more of the same, then arguments that they be regulated differently are weakened. As demand-absorbers covering a limited range of subjects, it would appear that they have much to prove if their case that they are truly innovative and distinct is to be persuasive. However, it is clearly true that *something* must be different if only for them increasingly to be so much in demand. From what we know it would seem that organisations such as Apollo offer a convenience – a range of 'just-in-time', or directly and immediately career-relevant programmes. These are marketed towards mature and working professionals who are highly instrumental and have no need of the traditional campus services offered to school-leavers, and are attracted by the quick pace of credit accumulation and the ability to earn a quick employment return for their expenditure. As such, most classes involve a mix of theory and practice and make considerable use of practitioners from relevant fields. Moreover, as we have noted, the various teaching functions become more specialised. For-profit organisations are frequently reported in the USA as claiming, in contrast to many conventional universities, much higher expenditure on marketing, student placements, and the employment and training of career counsellors.

In these circumstances it is difficult to argue that the for-profits should be treated exactly the same as conventional universities. In Malaysia, the initial growth of private higher education reflected a wish, by the Chinese population particularly, for instruction in the English language following its elimination in all public universities. Other drivers were the introduction of racial quota systems and nationalist curricula studies that both restricted access for non-Malays, such as the Chinese, and limited the range of more 'modern' subjects for business and employment that could be offered. The growing private colleges also began to link with major universities abroad, paving the way for the development of credit transfer and twinning programs, and the introduction of subjects, such as management, tourism and information technology, that better suited the human resource needs of private sector employers.[13]

More generally we should consider a range of environmental pressures – not just regulatory but also cultural – on the for-profits, especially on the larger companies, that may drive in the direction of homogeneity. At the same time it is recognised that those organisations based on the private corporate enterprise model have an alternative source of legitimacy, as found in the business sector, to that offered by more conventional universities. Business norms of order, planning, centralism, functional training for just-in-time relevance, and customer focus may provide sufficient alternative magnetism for the for-profits. Traditional university cultures – more disorderly, decentralist and loosely-coupled, even chaotic, with the professional rather than the customer being privileged – are resisted, and for wider systemic diversity based on distinctive approaches to be promoted.

In these circumstances, national states face dilemmas in the extent of the homogeneity or diversity to be allowed in their regulatory approaches to for-profit higher education. Some countries, such as Hungary, appear resolved to impose regulatory uniformity on

---

[13] Tan, Ai Mei (2002) *Malaysian Private Higher Education*, (London: Asean Academic Press).

private and public higher education institutions, and they expect the former to comply with established 'ideas' of a university, in part with governments under considerable pressure from existing public university interests.[14] Elsewhere, such as Malaysia, there is greater recognition of the value of a 'mixed economy' of public and private universities, with each regarded as offering something distinctive to both the system and the consumer. Governments are becoming increasingly confident in asserting the benefits of such an approach. Of course, private higher education is rarely entirely private. Such institutions are normally dependent on government-acceptable accreditation, licensing, quality assurance and, in some cases, public funding. This public funding, if not provided directly to institutions takes the form of grants, loans, and other types of financial assistance to students.

However, we lack research on how distinctive for-profit higher education is and whether, for example, public-private alliances or partnerships have any influence of homogenising or diversifying tendencies. Is for-profit higher education novel in some respects but not others? And do governments vary in the intensity of regulatory controls for different aspects of for-profit provision, such as for quality and for governance? That is, what are the limits on diversity and distinctiveness that for-profit higher education potentially offers? And to what extent do for-profit institutions vary among themselves? These are important questions that need further investigation, and they impinge greatly on the right regulatory approaches to for-profit provision, if the purpose is for wider choice to be offered.

The regulatory issue lies less in the rather abstract claims that the for-profits should be treated differently than in knowing in what areas and circumstances they should be so. For some, it would appear that the primary regulatory issues thrown up by the for-profits lie in the areas of finance and governance, rather than

---

[14] Nagy-Darvas, J. and Darvas, P. 'Private Higher Education in Hungary: The Market Influences the University', in Altbach, P. (ed) (1999) *Private Prometheus: Private Higher Education and Development in the Twenty-First Century* (Westport, Connecticut: Greenwood Press).

in the nature of the academic product as such. A review of perceptions held by regional accreditors in the USA supports this observation.[15] Among the findings it was reported that while most accreditors do not have separate standards for proprietary institutions, most apply their existing standards differently to for-profits, especially when it concerns governance and finance. Governance issues focus on public representation on boards and the independence of boards from the CEO or stockholders. This includes collegiality matters the independence of academic governance, the issue of who appoints the Principal and CEO, and whether this occurs locally or in a far-away corporate headquarters. Finance issues involve reinvesting profits into the education infrastructure and reporting the distribution of profits to shareholders, and the assurance that profits derived from educational activities will not be siphoned away for other corporate purposes.

In turn, however, it is clear that the major for-profit institutions in the USA value regional accreditation highly and they are prepared to go the extra mile to secure it. Accreditation is regarded as important for student, employer and market confidence and in accessing public funds, particularly financial support for students. (Conversely, as the University of Phoenix once discovered, any hint of an adverse report can be detrimental to stock prices; as reported in The Chronicle of Higher Education of 2 October 1998, its stock temporary lost 21 per cent of its value after news reports of possible regulatory difficulties). While states often include the for-profits in student financial aid programs, which is essential for their business models, this tends to bring increased levels of regulation. The for-profits operate in different states and consequently they often have to deal with multiple levels of regulation when these respective jurisdictions are taken together. Each operation in a new state requires addressing a fresh regulatory process. It is clear that the 'placeless' for-profit institution poses particular problems for regional accreditation

---

[15] Education Commission of the States (2000) *Report from the Regions: Accreditors' Perceptions of the Role and Impact of For-profit Institutions in Higher Education*, (Denver: USA).

and state approval procedures, which were not established with the multi-state, multi-national institution in mind.

We need to be clear that state approval and regional accrediting frameworks in the USA contain groups with often-contrasting perspectives and interests. State legislatures, for example, can often be highly supportive of the for-profits but on party political or ideological grounds. Conversely state licensors can also give the for-profit newcomers a hard time. The University of Phoenix has recently concluded an agreement with the New Jersey Commission on Higher Education after five years of tough negotiations. Opposition came from local academics such as the Rutgers University Chapter of the American Association of University Professors who, along with others, objected in particular to the lack of library facilities. The more peer-driven regional regulators can also prove difficult, although here again the appearance is that regional regulatory officials may be more sympathetic than the regional association's members.

For obvious reasons, the for-profits champion the need for national accreditation standards with the emphasis on desired functions or outcomes (such as academic program consistency) rather than on specified numbers of resources, (such as the number of books in a library), or the proportion of full-time faculty. National standards would also enable all the sites of a for-profit institution within the various states to be treated uniformly and consistently. Such developments would start to ease regulation more generally away from the intimate, insider, 'professional' and trusting processes that traditionally have characterised regional regulatory modes of operation in US higher education, toward ones based more formally on codified, transparent and juridical approaches.

5 Regulatory Models

In this section we will focus on national or within-country regulation for the for-profit sector, noting that in higher education there are no official international regulatory bodies. (Of course, as business corporations, the for-profits are increasingly subject to a range of international rules, including on accounting and governance). It is useful to start by recalling that the most important resource disposed by governmental bodies in the increasingly competitive international economic order is the system of regulation – the ability to set rules and to which providers must comply. The private sector economy is composed of markets and products that are constituted and maintained by state-backed institutions and instruments of various kinds. Generally the largest and most powerful organisations seek constantly to have governments change regulatory policies to allow them greater market opportunities. The for-profit higher education sector is not likely to be different.

For-profit institutions are particularly concerned with regulation by governments for several reasons. First, what they desire to sell in the form of prestigious certification and awards, and what they sometimes aspire to in the form of university title, is usually heavily regulated by states or by state-licensed private regulatory bodies. Second, for-profit economic operations may be fragile and potentially vulnerable to the high costs and bureaucratic hurdles that regulation can impose. A major feature of growing regulation for the for-profits is forms of accreditation, the processes of which may be slow, opaque, conservative and uncertain, and which are not generally required of long-standing public institutions. Third, their markets depend on regulation and trust, and punitive regulatory measures that appear to impugn for-profit behaviour, perhaps because of the activities of bogus operators or at the insistence of existing higher education interests, can be highly damaging.

There are a number of different models or instruments available to governments for regulating the for-profits. It will be useful to outline their respective strengths and weaknesses. In doing so we draw particularly on socio-legal studies and the work of regulatory theorists such as Braithwaite, Gunningham and Grabosky which, for the most part, has been concerned with the regulation of the business sector. We shall be concerned with the relevance of such models for higher education, and particularly for-profit higher education.

5.1 Command and Control

The command-and-control regulatory model has been associated especially with the USA, although it is widespread in many countries and policy areas. Broadly such models are formal and usually juridical. Command-and-control refers to the prescriptive nature of the regulation – the command – supported by the imposition of some negative sanction – the control.[16] Rules are passed that ban certain activities and governments generally establish a regulatory agency to monitor and police compliance with statutory standards. Command-and-control regulation in areas such as environmental policy usually sets targets (on toxic emission or the use of clean technology, for example) and then imposes sanctions if the standards are not achieved.

A major advantage of command-and-control regulation is its reliability, providing that there is sufficient monitoring and enforcement. Specific and clear rules tend to be its characteristic, which enables breaches to be readily identifiable and allows organisations to know exactly where they stand. Such frameworks also have the merit of transparency, which can reduce opportunities for rent-seeking, corruption and generally manipulative and empire-building behaviour, by regulatory officials.

A problem, however, is that command-and-control can be rather inflexible and, in the wrong hands, its applications can become overly hostile to those being regulated. This in turn provokes resistance and proves generally unproductive. Moreover, especially with the fast-moving world of for-profit and borderless education in mind, command-and-control can become rigid and slow to change or take account of new circumstances and players. In such instances it may lead to companies leaving the market and prevent

---

[16] Gunningham, N., Grabosky, P. and Sinclair, D. (1998) *Smart Regulation*, (New York: Oxford University Press).

new ones from entering. Furthermore, once the easy targets for compliance have been met by organisations, incremental progress is often slow and not always cost effective.

As yet, most approaches to the regulation of for-profit higher education are of the command-and-control type, although this is beginning to change. South Africa appears to be developing a detailed and explicit system of regulation along command-and-control lines. Recent legislation allows private providers of higher education (which includes both local and foreign providers outside the South African public education sector) to apply for registration in order to operate. Although the criteria are still developing, registration involves submitting an annual audit to a Registrar, reporting on staff and student numbers, and providing full details of qualifications and programs offered, and on student attainment. All private providers must have all qualifications accredited against the detailed standards developed by the South Africa Qualifications Authority. The Registrar must also be satisfied that, in the words of the legislation, the private institution "will maintain acceptable standards that are not inferior to standards at a comparable public higher education institution".[17]

Private institutions must "conspicuously display" (the words in the 1997 Higher Education Act) a 'Certificate of Registration', and the use of the term 'university' is strictly regulated. Foreign providers must establish a legal presence in South Africa, registering as a company. They must submit five-year business plans and financial forecasts and, to repeat the legislation, like all private institutions, they must "maintain acceptable standards that are not inferior to standards at a comparable public higher education institution". Franchising provision to a local institution – without separate registration of the foreign provider – is ruled out. Consequently, franchising models as commonly practiced by many Australian and UK universities in places such as Singapore and Malaysia effectively

---

[17] South African Department of Education, (2002), 'Instructions from the Registrar to private providers who wish to register'; and the South Africa 'Higher Education Act', 1997, Chapter 7, Pretoria.

have been made illegal. A more preferred model for the South African government is that of the branch campus, which requires a greater commitment and resourcing on the part of the incoming provider. The purpose is to ensure that genuine capacity building in the country occurs rather than a narrowly focused commercial exploitation.

The result is that from a total of at least 202 private providers known to be operating in South Africa in January 2000, by July 2002 the total number of registered providers had dropped to less than 100 (the figure has since risen somewhat – see below). The number of foreign university-level providers had fallen from 38 to 4 – representing less than 4 per cent of all registered providers, compared to almost 20 per cent prior to the introduction of the new registration regulations in 1999. This is not to imply criticism of South African regulations; rather, the important question here is to enquire whether the regulations fulfilled the policy purposes asked of them. In the circumstances, is command-and-control the right regulatory approach? Certainly it can be argued that while commercial institutions from abroad are not prepared to meet the stiff regulatory conditions that have been imposed, the local private institutions appear to have been encouraged to seek their own degree-awarding powers rather than use those of external universities.

In the light of the desire of the South African government to build wider university capacity, including research, and the public goods associated with this, then it could be argued that the relative regulatory strictness towards for-profit providers is justified. Different policies – such as encouraging the establishment of more foreign and for-profit providers – would require a different regulatory approach. The problem would arise if South Africa changes policies but does not reconsider its regulatory framework. Moreover, criticism and relative hostility to commercial higher education appears to continue at a high level in South Africa. The Council on Higher Education recently issued a report based on a survey of the re-accreditation by the Higher Education Quality Council of programmes offered by 58 of the 117 private providers in

South Africa.[18] It outlines a fairly negative scene, with inadequate quality management, a lack of well-qualified staff, and poor learning support and library resources.

Apart from the issue of 'fit' between policy and regulatory framework, in considering for-profit higher education particularly, we should note that command-and-control regulation works better in some circumstances than in others. The application of clear and specific standards are easier to apply to larger, more identifiable and accessible companies, than to the faster-moving and more remote smaller sectors that predominate in some countries. But command-and-control is not especially workable when technologies and economic circumstances are changing quickly, as in virtual education across borders. Regulators have great difficulty in such circumstances in keeping apace or in marshalling the resources to track change and its implications regularly. The minimum and common standards found in command-and-control systems may also militate against the institutional differentiation that may be regarded as one of the strengths of the for-profit sector, and they may not incentivise institutions to strive for a higher level of performance rather than merely complying with minimum requirements.

Command-and-control regulation is often the first port of call when a sector has been hitherto virtually unregulated. In China, where the political system is inclined towards this form of regulatory intervention, a private education law has recently been introduced. It provides an example of seeking to remove the disadvantages of a more arbitrary and legally indistinct system in favour of at least formal transparency. The new law seeks to provide a legal framework in a situation where one hardly or only dimly existed previously. Yan and Levy indicate that although the 1982 Constitution in China allowed private higher education for the first time in 30 years, its ambiguities resulted in unpredictable and unfair conduct and taxes by state officials at all levels, leaving both private

---

[18] Council on Higher Education (2003) *The State of Private Higher Education in South Africa: CHE Monitoring Report No. 1*, Pretoria.

institutions and their students seeking greater legal clarity and protection.[19]

China offers an example of how command-and-control re-regulation may accompany increased market liberalisation. Frequently there is confusion in higher education generally between the terms 'liberalisation' and 'de-regulation'. There is an assumption that both refer to essentially similar processes: that liberalisation and de-regulation are interchangeable terms, and that stronger markets (liberalisation) equal fewer rules and weaker governments (de-regulation). But they do not. Rather, with more markets, competition and choice we are more likely to find re-regulation. Governments of the advanced industrial nations have reorganised their control of private sector behaviour, but not substantially reduced the level of regulation.[20] Maintaining 'fair' market competition generally entails more rules, as does the necessity for greater consumer protection and public accountability. Moreover, countries tend to achieve different degrees of liberalisation and types and styles of regulation.

In China, more market competition, greater respect for private property rights, increased private capital formation, and enhanced conditions for trading and profit-making (in large part required by China's recent entry into the World Trade Organisation) can also be linked strongly to more formal and codified regulation. This regulation is aimed at fair competition for providers, customer protection and retention of at least some socialist principles. It is an example of how regulatory changes in the for-profit education sector may be a consequence more of wider societal changes than of specific educational dynamics.

Thus, although private institutions will be formally allowed, under the new dispensation, to make profits in China, this is subject to it being a "reasonable return". This latter proviso has yet to be officially

---

[19] Yan, F. and Levy, G. (2003) 'China's New Private Education Law', *International Higher Education*, Spring.
[20] Vogel, S. (1996) *Freer Markets, More Rules: Regulatory Reform in Advanced Industrial Societies*, (Ithaca and London: Cornell University Press).

elaborated although it has been mooted that a 10 per cent return may fit the bill. The regulations also aim to protect the legal rights, not only of private owners, but also students, and the welfare rights and interests of the teachers working in the for-profit institutions. Moreover, military, policing and political education are excluded as potential markets for for-profit higher education. The issue in China, however, is perhaps less the type of regulatory framework but rather the securing of widespread compliance with the rules. The jury is out on whether the clearer rules in China will help to introduce orderliness, as opposed to more sophisticated evasion.

Unsurprisingly, critics of command-and-control regulation tend to look for less law-like methods and seek to locate the secret of 'smart regulation' in understanding the wider behavioural context of the sectors or industries being regulated, and in comprehending the motivations of individuals and their professional cultures. The outcome with these approaches is to stress that regulation works better when those being regulated have the chance, at least initially, to either construct a form of self-regulation, or perhaps to operate a system of co-regulation, where the self-regulatory system is generated with state agreement.

5.2 Self-regulation

Whatever its form there is little doubt that the 'self-regulatory' approach is generally lauded, at least in rhetoric, by both regulators and regulatees. Virtually every regulatory system, irrespective of levels of overbearing intrusiveness, likes to describe itself as 'self-regulatory'. The warm glow associated with the notion of self-regulation reflects the fact that every system of regulation requires at least some element of compliance from those being regulated in order to succeed. A problem is distinguishing between models that are self-regulatory and those that merely profess to be.

Broadly, self-regulation refers either to an organisation, or more frequently, an industry or sector body, regulating the actions of its members, usually by formulating and setting rules and standards. This process may be relatively free of state intervention (although the state usually has to recognise legally or 'license' the ensuing arrangement in some form), with the sector association voluntarily establishing codes, standards and processes for compliance, and exacting sanctions. The attractions of such an approach are that the standards are likely to be better and more knowledgeably informed and enforced than in more directly state command-and-control systems. Additionally, the speed and flexibility in changing the regulatory environment in the light of, say, technological advances, are more likely, and there is an increased possibilitiy of those being regulated to accept and internalise the standards involved.

However, self-regulation rarely works out so clearly. Self-regulation can be used to serve the private interests of the sector rather than the public interest, and is easily subject to atrophy. Without a strong external hand, it could be argued that standards will be weak, un-policed, and rarely sanctioned. Moreover, such processes are not particularly open or transparent and may involve 'insider' or secretive judgements out of the public gaze, with little public accountability.

As with command-and-control systems, there are circumstances when self-regulation works well, such as when the public and private interest are broadly convergent. In the chemical industry, for example, Gunnigham *et al.* indicate that often it is in the interests of both the producer and the general public for the producer to adopt new process technology which uses less raw materials and generates less waste.[21] Self-regulation can work well when this situation exists. However, whether we are referring to the desire of businesses to maximise profits, or to that of university academics to reduce their teaching time in favour of their private research, there are circumstances when private and public interests more clearly diverge. In such cases, self-regulation may be insufficient without some stronger form of state intervention to secure the wider interest or specifically that of the consumer.

---

[21] Gunningham, N., Grabosky, P. and Sinclair, D. (1998) *Smart Regulation*, (New York: Oxford University Press).

There are other circumstances than simply the convergence of public and private interests when self-regulation may still work quite effectively. For example, when industry organisations are reliant on the good behaviour of all their members for 'not letting the side down', because reputation is a major survival or promotion variable for the sector overall, then self-regulation can work quite well. No-one wishes to have the whole industry jeopardised by the actions of a few rogues. This is particularly likely when the sector has a sufficient number of large firms to act as 'ethical leaders', and when these have the time and the resources to take on such a role. They may be able to insist on 'moral' behaviour by smaller companies, including through exercising power in supplier or customer relationships when these opportunities occur.

For-profit institutions already labour under the negative reputational perception in many places that they are providers 'on the fly'. Generally they have to work assiduously to demonstrate their worth and market attractiveness in order to survive. The larger, ambitious and better-resourced for-profits do not want too many 'cowboys' to spoil the patch and may be attracted by self-regulatory forms that clearly demonstrate their commitment not only to customer satisfaction but also to the wider public interest. At this stage in the worldwide development of for-profit higher education, an open question is whether firms can put aside their inevitable competitiveness to associate and regulate in this way. In some countries, as we have seen, the still small and largely fragmentary nature of the for-profit sector may militate against sector-wide self-regulation. Nonetheless, many forms of industry self-regulation are generated by worries that, without it, governments will regulate more directly and less satisfactorily. This may, in time, prove a powerful motivator for many for-profit organisations to establish sector-wide associations capable of fulfilling a self-regulatory role, especially when they are able to point to a long self-regulatory tradition, for the most part, in the conventional university sector.

In the USA, for example, much of the growth in enrolment by the for-profits is due to expansion by long-established institutions through mergers and acquisitions, new campuses, and the implementation of Internet-based programmes. Moreover, concentration at the apex of the for-profit sector, where the publicly-listed 'super-systems' congregate, continues, with, for example, the recent acquisition of Whitman by Career Education. A number of these large for-profits are acquiring greater respectability through the recruitment of well-known politicians and academics as lobbyists or executives. In some cases, the smaller for-profits complain that it is increasingly difficult to distinguish the large for-profits from more conventional universities, as these large for-profits seek accreditation, better support from the federal government, and a reputation 'for doing the right thing' as they turn their attentions to overseas markets.

It is not clear whether the increased visibility and respectability of the large for-profits is leading to the cohesive field or organisational association that could be a precursor for self-regulatory functions. Moreover, it would appear that collective association is aimed more at increasing lobbying effectiveness rather than any yearnings to function as regulators. As yet, we have little research available on these issues. We also need to be careful about the use of terms such as 'sector' or even 'field'. In the case of conventional higher education, it is becoming less clear whether a 'higher education sector' actually exists in this way or not. Processes of both formal and informal stratification between institutions, even between all those entitled universities, often militates against 'shared communities of fate' and this becomes reflected in the formation of representative bodies for different status groups of universities. Do universities in one status group feel any responsibility towards the 'roguish' activities of universities in other status groups, on the grounds that all universities are likely to suffer a more negative image from such behaviour? Or, do they regard these other institutions with indifference, as belonging to a different community of fate, or even (with a secret smile) as competitors that have got it terribly wrong? In the for-profit 'sector' it is not at all clear that the leading for-profits necessarily feel responsible for the actions of smaller such organisations. On the other hand, especially given the broad judgements levelled at all for-profit activity, they may increasingly feel that it is unavoidable that they undertake some form of regulatory responsibility for those organisations who it is felt are letting down the whole of the for-profit industry.

As we have noted above, Malaysia offers another case to that of the USA of a mature private higher education sector. If self-regulation by an industry association emerges, we would expect it to occur here. Tan, in her account of Malaysian private higher education, points to the increasing significance since the mid-1990's of the MAPCO group of leading private higher education institutions (in contrast to the two associations representing smaller players and the Malay colleges respectively).[22] She uses the notion of "a path of dependency", particularly noticeable during the period of the Malaysian currency downturn in the late 1990's, in which a path within a network is generally shaped by the bigger, more powerful organisations.

To join MAPCO requires a minimum capital of half a million Ringgit Malaysian, and as a result it is the large corporations who dominate the grouping. MAPCO is regarded by the Malaysian government as more dependable than other groups and private organisations. Its members are deemed better able to fill the gap locally for students unable to study abroad, more likely to deliver on the prospect of Malaysia becoming a regional exporter, and capable of strengthening the sector as a marketplace overall. Most of the MAPCO members have expressed their interest in becoming universities or university colleges and appear to have strongly influenced the government in holding out such prospects. On the matter of self-regulation, it is not clear that MAPCO feels any broader responsibility for private higher education institutions, including the much smaller organisations, or that the Malaysian government envisages that they undertake any wider responsibility.

The related question is whether MAPCO members feel any regulatory responsibility to each other, if not to the industry overall.

---

[22] Tan, Ai Mei (2002) *Malaysian Private Higher Education*, (London: Asean Academic Press).

That is, is MAPCO likely to adopt a self-regulatory role, but only in respect to its members? An emerging issue with self-regulatory models is accounting for the 'self' involved. With the increasing stratification and competitiveness of higher education in both its public and private modes, this question is not easily answered without considerably more investigation.

5.3 Voluntarism

As Gunningham *et al.* point out, as well as self-regulation through social control by an industry association, there is regulation of a more voluntary kind in which the company commits 'to doing the right thing' unilaterally, without being coerced. Usually such an approach is triggered by the state and it may act as a facilitator or co-ordinator. It generally takes the form of voluntary or non-mandatory agreements between a government and individual businesses as equal partners, in which incentives based on mutual interest rather than on sanctions are its key features.

It might be thought that such a regulatory approach to for-profit higher education would be attractive to those countries where there is a strong desire to encourage its development, and a recognition that students, employers, the wider public, and the traditional universities require at least a minimum of regulatory assurance. Voluntarism may provide this but within a regulatory regime where the presumption is based on incentive rather than control, where not all for-profit institutions may be regarded as deserving of such arrangements, but where the 'best' are clearly legitimated on a selective basis. In these circumstances, as with other forms of self-regulation, it is a model that works best when there is official agreement that the public and private interest is largely convergent in the circumstances and for the organisations under review.

Singapore offers an indication of how a voluntary form of regulation could operate. The Singapore approach is to encourage greater institutional diversity through the expansion of private higher education (so that it becomes twice the size of the public sector by 2012) within a more de-regulated operating environment. Individual for-profit providers are *invited* to apply for a 'quality mark' in which their processes and procedures are tested against good practice. This form of government-approval provides firms with a useful marketing resource, plus tax breaks and access to fast-tracked student visa authorisations.

Such moves indicate growing governmental recognition, in Asia but also elsewhere such as Argentina, that for-profit providers may benefit from national accreditation and other regulatory rules, provided that the approach combines incentives as well as control. Malaysia, too, is dropping existing moral, language and cultural curriculum requirements for for-profit organisations, but in exchange for the shared recognition that strengthened quality assurance benefits all parties.

A problem with the voluntary regulatory instrument, however, is that high monitoring and administrative costs may be incurred, which would be particularly difficult for smaller countries. Moreover, there is heavy reliance on the organisation's senior managers to ensure compliance throughout the organisation and this may not always be sustained, especially in difficult trading conditions. Finally, there is still the issue of the best regulatory model for those for-profit providers outside such arrangements.

5.4 Media and Performance Publications

A form of regulation may be achieved through publicity on institutional performance that can have an impact on institutional reputation and markets. However, such an approach requires adequate and well-founded information against a coherent cluster of indices, usually from the organisations themselves, in order to carry weight, and this may not always be forthcoming. It also depends on company behaviour being sufficiently influenced by the outcomes, (as opposed to temporary exhortations to staff from top managers, who are temporarily embarrassed by public rankings), but which are not carried through the organisation. Recipients of official awards for good practice may also serve as role models, but again widespread scepticism may result and be counterproductive if the outcomes are not widely and readily believed. As the for-profit sector matures, the industry, the media or governments, or probably a combination of all three, may find that such methods may have beneficial outcomes for both the encouragement and public accountability of the sector, especially as the costs involved tend to be relatively low.

5.5 Economic and Related Instruments

In recent years economic instruments have been widely adopted as a means of regulation by a number of governments, not least reflecting the increasing popularity of liberalism as the predominant form of macro-economic policy, and increasing criticism of direct state interventionism and command-and-control forms of regulatory modelling. For example, tax breaks and other incentives for good practice can be used (including in the context of voluntary agreements, as outlined above), although it is difficult to set these at the right levels. Tax concessions in return for compliance with a government-backed regulatory framework may be a crucial factor in the willingness of commercial banks, for example, to establish private student loan schemes, perhaps underpinned by government guarantees and interest subsidies.

In a number of countries, corporate governance and other statutory provisions enacted by governments have sought to increase the motivation and opportunities for shareholders and other investors to take account of wider public concerns and standards of expected behaviour, even though governments themselves are reluctant to intervene more directly. In the case of the for-profits, it is possible that increased shareholder influence on corporate behaviour may also be a consequence both of governmental and other regulatory reforms, and wider exposure of for-profit practices. By influencing market forces and other less obvious forms of activity, governments can influence public interest groups, commercial third parties, and the sector itself to act as quasi-regulators, thus facilitating more innovative, flexible and multi-centred forms of regulation than found in traditional command-and-control systems.[23]

6 For-Profit Higher Education and Environmental Constraints for Diversity and Homogeneity

To answer the question of whether the for-profit sector will mature sufficiently for regulatory instruments such as co- or self-regulation, and voluntarism, to be effective, we must examine those external factors that influence especially the larger for-profit organisations to seek respectability and acceptance in the eyes of government and regulators. Associated with this is the extent to which this involves emulating the characteristics of the conventional universities, or whether the corporate business model is likely to become an alternative source of legitimacy for the for-profits, and increasingly influence conventional universities also.

6.1 Organisational Analysis

The notion of 'sector' or 'regime' is used to indicate that organisations in similar lines of business do not operate in isolation but interact and constitute particular 'orders'. In turn these 'orders', broadly constituted of cultures, practices, power relationships, and so on, act back on organisations and often shape their key aspirations. They build upon, homogenise, and reproduce standard expectations and, in doing so, help to stabilise a field or sector.

Thus, a key factor in understanding for-profit higher education organisations is how, if at all, they are constituted as a sector and how the external environment influences the organisations in a broadly convergent manner. More especially, are there environmental constraints that eventually lead them to seek respectability and wider acceptance, and to become more like conventional universities, thus, potentially at least, reducing diversity in the system

---

[23] Gunningham, N., Grabosky, P. and Sinclair, D. (1998) *Smart Regulation*, (New York: Oxford University Press).

overall? That is, do initial goals of efficiency and profit-maximisation become overtaken by more political objectives, such as status and acceptability, once certain levels of organisational development have occurred? Or is the attraction of homogeneity with the established university order reduced by the compelling nature of the business models they employ and the markets that they service, and which constitute an alternative and equally authoritative cultural order, thus helping to maintain systemic diversity?

There is a taken-for-granted quality in much organisational practice in higher education that helps to reproduce structures that are to some extent self-sustaining. These also influence governmental policy-makers and are reinforced by the modelling and 'epistemic community' policy processes of private-public networks of the 'expert' and the 'insider', as found in bodies such as the OECD or the World Bank. Nonetheless, it is not impossible for challengers and entrepreneurs to refashion existing rules or create new institutional orders. In normal times, cultural frames establish approved means and define desired outcomes, leading business people to pursue profits, bureaucrats to seek effective policy steerage, and academics to aim for publication and scholarly recognition. But when sectors or industries are subject to more rapid change, such as with the 'privatisation' of higher education, clashes occur between institutional orders, such as academia and business. An example would be the debate concerning whether intellectual property falls under the rules of the marketplace, or under the rules of science and a worldwide common intellectual heritage.[24]

Meyer and Rowan suggest that organisational isomorphism or homogeneity in a sector proceeds along two dimensions.[25] First,

---

[24] DiMaggio, P. and Powell, W. (1991) 'Introduction', in *The New Institutionalism in Organisational Analysis* (Chicago and London: University of Chicago Press).
[25] Meyer, J. and Rowan, B. (1977) 'Institutionalized Organisations: Formal Structure as Myth and Ceremony', in Powell, W. and DiMaggio (eds) (1991) *The New Institutionalism in Organisational Analysis* (Chicago and London: University of Chicago Press), (original in *American Journal of Sociology*, 83, 2, 340–63).

powerful organisations force their immediate relational networks to adapt to their structures and relations. Second, powerful organisations attempt to build their goals and procedures directly into society as institutional rules. If successful, isomorphism with environmental rules and practices has major consequences for organisations as (a) increasingly they incorporate elements which are legitimated externally, rather than in terms of efficiency; (b) they employ external or ceremonial evaluation in judging the value of structural elements; and, (c) rising dependence on externally fixed institutions helps to maintain stability and avoid shocks. Consequently, institutional isomorphism and systemic homogeneity promotes the success and survival of organisations.

In following prescribed ways of doing things, organisations demonstrate that they are acting in accordance with widely held values (for example, by setting up welfare employment schemes, or establishing human resources departments), irrespective of whether this actually aids efficiency or not. It defends the organisation from outside questioning (responding to which, of course, can also consume funds). The organisation thus becomes legitimate, a crucial resource in surviving and prospering. Alternatively, organisations that innovate and take risks may incur extensive diminutions in (or rising barriers to) legitimacy.

In the case of for-profit higher education, conflicting business and academic models show that pluralistic societies can make available distinct and sometimes quite contradictory forms of legitimacy, leading to potentially ambiguous or conflicting organisational purposes. One way that this can be handled is to loosely couple the organisation – so that, for example, the business management of the organisation is distinguished from the processes of academic judgement. However, as we have seen in the instance of regional accreditation of the for-profits in the USA, regulators are often concerned at the impact of one sphere on the other. The challenge by regulators in the 'separation of the spheres' in for-profit organisations – one of the keys to the successful straddling of the corporate business and the conventional academic environments as they seek to reassure different audiences – can generate some of the most difficult and often embarrassing of issues for for-profit leaders.

In a famous article on organisations, DiMaggio and Powell suggest that in the initial stages of their life cycle, organisational fields display considerable diversity.[26] But once a field becomes well-established there is a relentless push toward homogenisation. This process of 'structuration' consists of four parts: an increase in the extent of interaction among organisations in the field; the emergence of sharply defined inter-organisational structures of domination and patterns of coalition; an increase in the information load with which organisations in a field must contend; and the development of a mutual awareness among participants that they are involved essentially in the same enterprise. Once initially disparate organisations in the same line of business become structured into an actual field (by the state, by competition, or by the professions), powerful forces emerge that influence them to become more similar to one another. Organisations compete not just for markets, but also for political power and institutional legitimacy.

DiMaggio and Powell identify three isomorphic mechanisms at work. First, there is the coercive, resulting from formal and informal pressures exerted on organisations by other organisations upon which they are dependent, including government, the law, or the group company. Second, there are mimetic processes, such as modelling or copying of what are perceived to be successful others, which are often found in situations of uncertainty. Finally, normative pressures, such as professionalisation, may lead to isomorphism. Professional managers and networks, based on formal education and specialist training, and on personnel recruitment practices and career mobility, help promulgate common normative rules about organisational behaviour. Moreover, organisational prestige is a key element in attracting professionals, such as academics, and this process encourages homogenisation as organisations seek to

---

[26] DiMaggio, P. and Powell, W. (1983) 'The Iron Cage Revisited: Institutional Isomorphism and Collective Rationality in Organisational Fields', *American Sociological Review*, 48, April, 147–60.

ensure that they can provide the same benefits and services as their competitors.

An analysis of for-profit higher education, not least for the purpose of evaluating regulatory instruments, needs to examine the extent to which it is possible to describe for-profit higher education as a 'field'. As organisations grow in size and become involved in sector activities, as well as in dense networks of exchange, the institutionalised expectations of other firms, consumers and the government exert greater influence on their behaviour. Is for-profit higher education sufficiently mature, at least in some countries, to be described as a 'field', or is it still at the 'pre-field' stage? How does the increasing stratification that we observe in maturing for-profit higher education, such as in Malaysia and the USA, fragment or hinder some sense of 'field' or 'sector'? Is it just as possible that 'sector' maturity produces not so much a 'field' as an increasing crystallisation of small 'allotments'?

Additionally, for-profit organisations face the strategic choice between potentially competing environmental models of 'respectability'-particularly the larger companies. Do they identify with private corporations, or with conventional universities, or with post-secondary education and training providers more generally? Depending on these decisions, for-profit higher education organisations will be located within varying regulatory environments. Their reliance on at least some academic staff with a primary background in conventional universities (in their employment as teachers, or on those facing them in regulatory agencies) may lead to pressures for normative convergence between the public and the for-profit institutions. Similarly, the more for-profit institutions compete with traditional universities for staff, funds, and students within common policy environments, the more emulation of older models may increase. The proposed higher education reforms in Australia appear to be moving in this direction, with additional funded places and government-supported student loans for 'eligible' private institutions. The Higher Education Act Re-Authorization process in the USA may also take such developments further, not least in extending student loans and grants to those in the for-profit sector.

An alternative scenario would see both the for-profits and the older universities converging around some 'third way' model, in which both academic and corporate business values are to be found. This might include clear 'walls' between the organisational elements where each model is supreme (although regulators may not accept such distinctions).

6.2 Regulatory Pluralism

It is likely that these organisational scenarios will underline the need for governments to take a pluralistic approach to regulating private higher education, in which combinations of instruments may serve the best outcome. In this way, what may be appropriate for one set of, say, large companies in selected countries, may be inappropriate for smaller companies elsewhere. Governments may also want to experiment with 'responsive' regulatory modes by starting with forms of self- or co-regulation and being prepared to move to more interventionist and punitive methods if recalcitrants persist,[27] or to focus regulatory attention on persistent or the most blatant offenders.[28]

Systems-based approaches based on benchmarking and continuous improvement (such as ISO 9001 and other standards under the International Organisation for Standardisation) may also help to reduce the regulatory burdens on governments and companies alike, although such approaches, like all regulatory methods, have their own drawbacks, including costs and credibility. It is likely that the for-profit sector, in countries where it is looked upon most favourably, may be in a position to negotiate forms of co-regulation with government. Under these conditions, companies, or associations of companies, may establish the details of a regulatory scheme, but subject to wider governmental approval on the approach and the willingness of the state to act as a back-stop.

---

[27] Braithwaite, J. and Ayres, I. (1992) *Responsive Regulation* (Oxford: Oxford University Press).
[28] Braithwaite, J. (2002) *Restorative Justice and Responsive Regulation* (New York: Oxford University Press).

7 Conclusion

Some additional final points need to be made.

First, regulatory models adopted by governments are likely to reflect patterns of overarching institutional structures and cultures in countries. For example, in coordinated market societies such as Germany and Japan, we are more likely to find forms of regulation that are 'self-regulatory corporatist', in the sense that traditionally organisations are incorporated into governance arrangements by ministries, and the system relies on high levels of informal and networking knowledge.[29] Japanese officials, for example, use licenses to tame competition, to expand ministerial control, to reward compliance, and to protect domestic companies.[30] In Britain, however, there is a longstanding political tradition of liberalism and market competition; independent regulators traditionally have not sought to integrate regulatory policy within wider industrial policies and protection for home-based firms.

In the case of for-profit regulation, McBurnie and Ziguras point to institutional and cultural differences (in Hong Kong, Malaysia and Australia, for example), as influencing its form.[31] In broadly free-market Hong Kong, the key goal has been customer protection, with an element of *caveat emptor* ('buyer beware'), whereas in Malaysia the advancement of specific nationalist goals until recently has been primary, and government legislation has specified aspects of curriculum content. In Australia, on the other hand, protecting the local system and the reputation of Australian higher education generally (including as an exporter) has been the main objective, and this has led to a greater formal transparency of regulations.

---

[29] Hall, P. and Soskice, D. (eds) (2001) *Varieties of Capitalism*, (Oxford: Oxford University Press).
[30] Vogel, S. (1996) *Freer Markets, More Rules: Regulatory Reform in Advanced Industrial Societies*, (Ithaca and London: Cornell University Press).
[31] McBurnie, G. and Ziguras, C. (2001) 'The Regulation of Transnational Higher Education in Southeast Asia', *Higher Education*, 42, 85–105.

Second, it may be a mistake to regard any one regulatory model as more efficient, effective or modern than another. As we have highlighted, all regulatory systems have strengths and weaknesses. All are essentially contestable.[32] As we are dealing with predominantly soft human systems, most policy instruments have unintended consequences that generate reactions, including opposition. Consequently, it would not be surprising to find considerable regulatory oscillation characterising for-profit higher education within countries.

Third, so far we have examined the rise of for-profit higher education within the context of predominantly national policies. We have not examined the prospect for its regulation at regional or international level, even though increasingly much for-profit higher education crosses borders and utilises virtual delivery. This omission is almost unavoidable as there is no real international system of accreditation or quality assurance yet established. However, the World Bank has sought to encourage international collaboration between national regulators based on simple licensing procedures with minimum thresholds, and where the emphasis is on learning outcomes rather than a host of input and process variables.[33] UNESCO, too, has established a Global Forum to see how an international system of degree recognition could be progressed, as well as linking existing national frameworks of quality assurance and accreditation. Existing national and subject associations are also undertaking more out-of-country recognition. Around 60 per cent of officially recognised accrediting bodies in the USA operate internationally, covering over 65 countries.[34] In business studies (a major element of for-profit provision) accreditation has become more internationalised with three main associations allowing both private and public sector business schools to be recognised over many countries, thus avoiding

---

[32] Hood, C. (1998) *The Art of the State*, (Oxford: Clarendon Press).
[33] World Bank (2002) *Constructing Knowledge Societies: New Challenges for Tertiary Education*, (Washington DC: World Bank).
[34] Eaton, J. (2003) 'The International Role of US-Recognized Accrediting Organisations, *International Higher Education*, Spring.

engagement with a range of specific country processes. The GATS process may also lead to gradual regulatory standardisation internationally.

Fourth, it is not always conventional university interests that are the main barrier to the effective regulation of the for-profits. Melbourne University Private (MUP), for example, was created in 1998 as one of the first private universities in the world by an existing public university. The most severe criticisms of it appear to have come from elected politicians who may have been even more committed to conventional university criteria than the universities themselves. The Review Panel established by the State of Victoria, and composed of representatives from the existing university sector, appears to have gone out of its way to give MUP a fair hearing in the light of the controversy surrounding it.

The MUP episode indicates that private universities can face considerable difficulties in obtaining and keeping the university title in some domains, while at the same time also seeking to be responsive, culturally and organisationally, to the needs of the so-called 'real world'. Balancing academic and commercial objectives and criteria within one institution is not easy, but seeking to resolve such issues through separate and distinctive public and private entities in the same ownership, and both with the university title, could run into greater regulatory difficulties. Yet not having the university title for the private body risks severe market negativity.

Finally, in many countries, when it comes to the regulation of universities, including the for-profit sector, the idea of the 'laid back' state engaged in 'light-touch enabling mode' may be wide of the mark. Rather, governments remain as interventionist and as ambitious in a regulatory sense as they ever were, and possibly more so. It is increasingly important, therefore, that we understand the advantages and disadvantages of varying regulatory models better than we do now.

References

Altbach, P. (1998) 'The Anatomy of Private Higher Education', *International Higher Education*, Summer.
Braithwaite, J. and Ayres, I. (1992) *Responsive Regulation* (Oxford: Oxford University Press).
Braithwaite, J. (2002) *Restorative Justice and Responsive Regulation* (New York: Oxford University Press).
Council on Higher Education (2003) *The State of Private Higher Education in South Africa: CHE Monitoring Report No. 1*, Pretoria.
DiMaggio, P. and Powell, W. (1983) 'The Iron Cage Revisited: Institutional Isomorphism and Collective Rationality in Organisational Fields', *American Sociological Review*, 48, April, 147–60.
DiMaggio, P. and Powell, W. (1991) 'Introduction', in *The New Institutionalism in Organisational Analysis* (Chicago and London: University of Chicago Press).
Dos Santos, S. (2002) 'Regulation and Quality Assurance in Transnational Education', *Tertiary Education and Management*, 8, 97–112.
Eaton, J. (2003) 'The International Role of US-Recognized Accrediting Organisations, *International Higher Education*, Spring.
Education Commission of the States (2000) *Report from the Regions: Accreditors' Perceptions of the Role and Impact of For-profit Institutions in Higher Education*, (Denver: USA).
Geisecke, H. (1999) 'Expansion and the Development of Private Higher Education in East Central Europe', *International Higher Education*, Summer.
Gunningham, N., Grabosky, P. and Sinclair, D. (1998) *Smart Regulation*, (New York: Oxford University Press).
Hall, P. and Soskice, D. (eds) (2001) *Varieties of Capitalism*, (Oxford: Oxford University Press).
Hood, C. (1998) *The Art of the State*, (Oxford: Clarendon Press).
Kruss, G. and Kraak, A. (2003) (eds) *A Contested Good?: Understanding Private Higher Education in South Africa*, (Boston, USA: Boston College Center for International Higher Education and 'Perspectives in Education', South Africa).
Lee, M. (1998) 'Corporatization and Privatization of Malaysian Higher Education', *International Higher Education*, Winter.
Levy, D. (2002, a) 'Private Higher Education's Surprise Roles', *International Higher Education*, Spring.
Levy, D. (2002, b) 'South Africa and the for-profit/Public Institutional Interface', *International Higher Education*, Fall.
Levy, D. (2003) 'Expanding Higher Education Capacity Through Private Growth', *Observatory on Borderless Higher Education Report*, January.
McBurnie, G. and Ziguras, C. (2001) 'The Regulation of Transnational Higher Education in Southeast Asia', *Higher Education*, 42, 85–105.

Meyer, J. and Rowan, B. (1977) 'Institutionalized Organisations: Formal Structure as Myth and Ceremony', in Powell, W. and DiMaggio (eds) (1991) *The New Institutionalism in Organisational Analysis* (Chicago and London: University of Chicago Press), (original in *American Journal of Sociology*, 83, 2, 340–63).

Nagy-Darvas, J. and Darvas, P. 'Private Higher Education in Hungary: The Market Influences the University', in Altbach, P. (ed) (1999) *Private Prometheus: Private Higher Education and Development in the Twenty-First Century* (Westport, Connecticut: Greenwood Press).

South African Department of Education, (2002), 'Instructions from the Registrar to private providers who wish to register'; and the South Africa 'Higher Education Act', 1997, Chapter 7, Pretoria.

Tan, Ai Mei (2002) *Malaysian Private Higher Education*, (London: Asean Academic Press).

UNESCO (figures derived by Levy, 2003).

Vogel, S. (1996) *Freer Markets, More Rules: Regulatory Reform in Advanced Industrial Societies*, (Ithaca and London: Cornell University Press).

World Bank (2002) *Constructing Knowledge Societies: New Challenges for Tertiary Education*, (Washington DC: World Bank).

Yan, F. and Levy, G. (2003) 'China's New Private Education Law', *International Higher Education*, Spring.

Section II : Competitors

Expanding Higher Education Capacity through Private Growth: *contributions and challenges*

Daniel C. Levy

1 Introduction

One of the most pressing concerns for higher education policy and study is capacity. One of the most dramatic developments in higher education in the last few decades has been the growth of private institutions. The concern about capacity and the growth of private institutions are keenly related, and this relationship is the focus of this report. The theme is that private higher education enhances enrolment capacity through multiple dynamics and forms, each bringing a set of contributions and challenges.

The major route for expanding capacity in the worldwide higher education boom of the mid-twentieth century was public growth. This occurred through both the enlargement of existing institutions and the proliferation of new ones. Nearly all industrialized countries moved to mass public higher education, and public expansion is how many developing countries expanded their cohort enrolment rate from a few percent to ten, twenty, and even thirty percent. In the third quarter of the century, the U.S. public to total enrollment ratio increased from half to roughly four-fifths. Europe and indeed most of the developed world outside the U.S. and Japan remained almost fully public, as did Africa and some other parts of the developing world. Latin America started significant private growth but, outside Brazil, until the 1970s or later this was mostly not about large capacity, but rather Catholic alternatives to public secularism or elite alternatives to the expanding public sector, perceived to be deteriorating. Enrollments in Spanish-speaking Latin America were still nearly four-fifths public as late as 1980.[1] Asia was the major exception. Certain countries expanded mostly through the private sector (e.g., India, Thailand), but even in Asia others (e.g., China, Malaysia) followed the more common pattern of building capacity on the public side.

Capacity building through public institutions continues but has run into serious problems. On the one hand, near consensus remains that higher education should and will keep enlarging. Demand will continue expanding for several inter-related reasons: belief in favorable individual rates of return and social mobility, belief in higher education as a key to the 'knowledge society', lifelong education, demographics, political pressures, mimicking of industrialized countries, and so forth.[2] On the other hand, traditional

---

[1] For background data, see Background Paper, developing working paper list, and emerging sub-site on Data and Laws from Program for Research on Private Higher Education (PROPHE), *Homepage*, available at: www.albany.edu/~prophe. Last Accessed 22 April 2004. Also see Altbach, Philip. G. (ed.). 1999. *Private Prometheus: Private Higher Education and Development in the 21st Century*. Westport, CT.: Greenwood Press. On Latin America, for historical data and other references in this paper, see Levy, Daniel C. 1986. *Higher Education and the State in Latin America: Private Challenges to Public Dominance*. Chicago, Illinois: University of Chicago Press.
[2] World Bank. 2000. *Task Force on Higher Education and Society*. World Bank: Washington DC.

public supply is ill-suited to meeting this expanding demand. This supply has been publicly funded, sometimes exclusively so. Yet now the dominant political-economic reality or at least the perception in ruling circles is that the state must trim its costs and insist that beneficiaries assume more of the financial burden. One way this is being accomplished is through a partial privatization of public institutions, as the percentage of costs covered by the state shrinks and 'private' management forms increase.[3] The other way, the subject of this paper, is the growth of private institutions, with mostly or fully private funds.

Aside from representatives of private higher education institutions and government representatives seeking to influence the growth of private provision, this paper will also be of interest to members of public higher education institutions in places where private provision is strong or may grow in the future, and where public-private partnerships may prove mutually beneficial.

The paper consecutively considers three overlapping concerns:

- *how* private higher education enhances capacity;
- the main *types* of private expansion;
- *challenges* to this expansion.

Obviously, the paper can only sketch key trends and how they may be understood. It cannot explore the enormous variation across regions, within countries, and even within private sectors. Its country examples illustrate more than prove. Often they are typical examples of a phenomenon that could easily be illustrated with different examples; in other instances, the chosen examples are poignant. Also, several countries that represent broad patterns are drawn on repeatedly.[4] These countries are mostly developing or

---

[3] See the website and working papers of the project on International Comparative Higher Education, available at: www.gse.buffalo.edu/org/inthigheredfinance. Last Accessed 22 April 2004.
[4] Among the countries are Bulgaria, China, Kenya, Malaysia, Russia, and South Africa, as well as the United States. Each of these countries is among those under active study by PROPHE's Collaborating Scholars or PROPHE Affiliates, and on each more definitive papers should be produced in the near future.

transitional (away from statist economies). The reason is simple: these countries exhibit private growth as a major route, often the principal one, to capacity building, whereas industrialized countries continue to rely primarily on public institutions (though often with increased private funding). An additional qualification to terminology is that by capacity is meant enrollment capacity. Private higher education generally makes a lesser contribution to other types of capacity, such as research.

A further qualification is that major global research on the growth of private higher education is in the early stages. PROPHE, the Program for Research on Private Higher Education (funded principally by the Ford Foundation and based at the University of Albany, New York), aims to build the knowledge base. The PROPHE website lays out PROPHE's mission, substantive and geographical foci, production to date and work in progress. The website now shows detailed statistical data on two countries, Chile and Russia, giving the viewer an idea of the extent and organization of data that PROPHE is building for many other countries across the world.

Aside from the United States, only two regions can be significantly documented from existing sources, and even then the data cover only the bare outlines on enrollment and institutional numbers. On Eastern and Central Europe, UNESCO[5] shows a private share of enrollments ranging from 1 to 30 percent in academic year 2000–2001 and an institutional share ranging from 10 to 82 percent. For Latin America, also from UNESCO, but for 1994 and earlier, only five countries had private enrollments under 20 percent, eight had between 20 and 40 percent, and six had between 40 and 65 percent.[6] See Annex A for further details on Eastern and Central Europe.

---

[5] See European Centre for Higher Education, *Statistical Information on Higher Education in Central and Eastern Europe*. Available at: www.cepes.ro/ information_services/statistics.htm. Last Accessed 22 April 2004.
[6] See García Guadilla, Carmen. 1996. *Situación y principales dinámicas de transformación de la educación superior en América latina*. Caracas: UNESCO p40; The region's private percentage moved to 34% by 1975 and 1980 and now

The qualification about being in the early stages of research applies also to the typologies presently available for the study of private higher education. The typology best developed in the international literature and most relevant for the topic of capacity building is identified in this paper's section on types of private expansion. It focuses on different forms of private growth and how they condition the size and behavior of different private subsectors. These growth forms include religious and other cultural, elite, and a kind of demand-absorption. The last category makes the largest claim on our attention, with a need to distinguish different sub-types, and leading us to related types and potential typologies involving for-profit versus nonprofit, private higher education institutions in partnership with public higher education institutions, and private higher education institutions tied to foreign public universities or international business chains. Other typologies (on the relative size of the private and public sectors and/or on how they are financed) are less relevant to this paper.[7] There is no firm line between what is integral to a typology and what simply marks a significant distinction among institutions, as in dimensions of size, prestige, seriousness, accreditation, and so forth.

2 How Private Higher Education Enhances Capacity

2.1 Finance

We can identify two basic ways in which the financial dynamics of private institutions enhance capacity. The first is mostly

---

there is evidence being accumulated in other countries showing increases, e.g., Chile at 71%. For more information see Levy, Daniel C. 1986. *Higher Education and the State in Latin America: Private Challenges to Public Dominance*. Chicago, Illinois: University of Chicago Press, p4–5.

[7] It has proven useful to distinguish institutions by their private or public juridical status and then to explore empirically how they in fact exhibit private or public characteristics in practice along dimensions of finance, governance, and function or mission. See Levy, Daniel C. 1986. *Higher Education and the State in Latin America: Private Challenges to Public Dominance*. Chicago, Illinois: University of Chicago Press.

straightforward, by providing private income for private institutions. The second is more complex and uncertain, concerning impact on public institutions.

Private higher education adds enrollment capacity to the higher education system, mostly escaping the constraints about public expenditures that now restrict public expansion. Most private institutions get virtually no public funds. Exceptions include the U.S., with sector-blind federal research funds and with student aid, and some emulation of such funding in other countries (e.g., student aid in Kenya) as well as isolated special funds or even subsidies.

Most private higher education institutions depend on tuition and fees. This is particularly true of the least prestigious institutions, which are the majority. Yet tuition is generally higher in more prestigious institutions (than in public institutions), where it may be mixed with other private funds. In Kenya, even the most elite private institution depends fully on tuition and fees. So capacity expands as clients pay for it.

Other sources of private income are more sporadic but nonetheless important and have potential to increase, especially where significant tuition increases are not feasible. Where and when business thrives, corporations or groups of financiers or industrialists have launched efforts to provide for major and well-endowed private universities. The Aga Khan University in Pakistan, now twenty years old, is a large and much-cited example, capturing the attention of the World Bank and others. Success in such endeavors may stimulate alumni and other philanthropic contributions. Of course, the global economic crises of the last few years have dampened such developments. Charitable foundations have not thus far been a prominent option. Contributions from churches have been common for 'their' institutions. Fast-growing financial sources include contracts and entrepreneurial units that generate funds through consultancies and services. Any of these funding sources can increase higher education capacity.

To the extent private institutions spend funds efficiently, capacity increases even more than income. The World Bank and others typically criticise developing countries' public universities as highly inefficient. There is ongoing debate as to the extent to which private institutions engender viable efficiency or merely low quality. However, there is little question that private higher education operates with much lower costs per student than public higher education. For example, there are fewer staff, usually part time.[8] Students move through more quickly, including through more flexible provision of courses and tighter institutional controls. Costly fields of study and other undertakings, such as conventional academic research, are usually bypassed. Commercially oriented private institutions, whether formally for-profit or not, epitomize these tendencies.

Private income generation and efficiency sometimes contributes, through example or competition, to public reform in finance and management. A dramatic illustration is the admission into public institutions of tuition-paying students, alongside subsidized students. For example, at Australian universities, full-fee paying students may constitute up to 25% of total student numbers per programme. This phenomenon is also prominent in Russia and other post-communist countries where tradition, political conviction and self-interest continue to favor a basic policy of free or low tuition charges. Revenue is generated by imposing charges on students admitted beyond the basic, subsidized, quota. A different reform within public institutions that also can be attributed to private example and competition is movement into fields of study pioneered in private institutions, as in Kenya. In Bulgaria some private institutions appear to drive some of the public ones to increase efficiency. China appears to be unusual for the degree to which government and public university presidents speak openly and explicitly about how public universities can learn from private institutions regarding entrepreneurship, including the creation of revenue-generating offshoots.

---

[8] To draw on PROPHE's extensive data on Russia, for example, 34% of private institutions' faculty are full time, versus 74% for public institutions; the parallel figures for students are 39% and 57% respectively.

But the net impact on public entities is difficult to gauge and depends greatly on what change one postulates for these entities were there not the private competition. How stagnant would they be versus how much would they be trying to generate more capacity through private revenues and efficiency? If the latter, then arguably they are hampered in those respects by the private 'skimming off' of lucrative fields, donors, and so forth.[9]

In any event, such public reform is only part of the public story for there is also considerable public resistance to reform as either not needed or even pernicious. The Left mostly holds that the state should expand public provision, with public money. With a combination of conviction and self-interest, many in and around public universities resist most forms of privatization.

How and how much private institutional growth has affected public capacity is thus unclear. Perhaps the simplest point, which itself can be oversimplified, is that pulling some students into the privately funded private sector allows public institutions to open additional spaces for other students. But even this point is less clear or potent than the main effect of privately funded private institutions – taking in students who would not otherwise be in higher education and would not be covered through public funds.

2.2 Capacity Through Institutional Differentiation

Private sectors hold a significant share of enrollments and especially of new enrollments in many countries. Whereas only one industrialized country has the majority of its higher education enrollments in the private sector (Japan), this is the situation in many developing countries in Asia and Latin America. Moreover, many others countries have moved from small private sectors to sectors with anywhere from 10–40 percent of

---

[9] The 'Challenges' section of this paper indicates, however, that where public institutions do compete along these lines they can pose dangers for private institutions.

enrollments; post-communist countries have moved up usually from zero. But whatever the enrollment percentage, the percentage of institutions is generally higher. For Eastern and Central Europe this holds for twelve of the thirteen countries for which UNESCO reports data on both enrollment and institutions, and the institutional ratio is often twice or more the enrollment ratio. (See Tables 1–2 for details). In other words, the private sector supplies capacity for higher education through institutional proliferation. Commonly there are many small private institutions, sometimes alongside a few medium or large ones.

Private growth is often about creating institutions not meant to be much different from public ones with the exception of operating on private money. This is capacity building largely through 'more of the same.' But private growth is also often about creating institutions notably different from public ones; capacity building largely through differentiation. This differentiation often means the kind of institutions that are less costly to operate, even apart from considerations of efficiency. So private proliferation contributes to higher education capacity by relying upon institutional forms with high ratios of enrollment to cost.

Accordingly, as a rule private institutions more than public are 'non-universities.' These may be colleges or institutes and the spectrum trails off into a variety of forms that make for ambiguity in what is 'higher education' or what is an 'institution.' In China's private sector, colleges by far outweigh universities but the bulk of enrollments are 'self-study' as students prepare for examinations. South Africa's private sector has strong roots in 'correspondence courses' and now has a blurred line with 'further education.' An increasing number of countries have privately operated distance education, and many have various forms of part-time study. Even a country like Bulgaria, 10 percent private (the same as Russia), which has had much less private proliferation than regional counterparts such as Rumania (30 percent private), has a variety of private options alongside the colleges and universities. Whether officially counted as higher education or not, such institutions broaden capacity.

The private institutions tend to be much narrower than public ones in what they do. The capacity of an average individual private institution is less than that of the average public institution. This is a reflection of smaller size and a different and more restrictive number of activities. The concentration is greatest in what students demand. Again much of this is traditional demand in excess of public capacity, while much is demand for something different. That something different is usually job-related, through fields and processes that can move the student quickly toward employment. What is striking is job-oriented capacity building by institutions that lack official recognition for degrees. Greece and Malaysia are good examples. Many of these institutions partner with foreign universities in order to offer degree programmes. Barriers to state employment may not faze students looking toward private or international employment. Whether through such intriguing forms or through degree-granting nonprofit institutions, when private institutions build novel areas or otherwise attract students who would not attend higher education, they build capacity.

The 'new people' private higher education helps accommodate are varied. Probably the most common are those academically unable to gain admission to the limited public sector. This then is private 'demand-absorption.' It involves a large proportion of students from socioeconomic backgrounds lower than that in public institutions, notwithstanding tuition charges. The point is crucial for capacity building if we consider that the main obstacle to access for those from poor backgrounds is not higher education tuition but rather a variety of factors that limit their chances to perform well through schooling and thus to be qualified for selective public higher education. Accommodating delivery modes, including class times, help enable working and other non-traditional students to enroll. In South Africa, the percentage of black students in private institutions is estimated to match that in the public sector.[10] Often the private sector (including a religious or other socially

---

[10] Subotzky, G. (2002) "The Nature of the Private Higher Education Sector in South Africa: Further Quantitative Glimpses," *Perspectives in Education*, December.

conservative subsector) is especially attractive for women, avoiding the social permissiveness and political protests, strikes, and other turmoil more common – and commonly permitted – in public institutions. Also, private institutions often provide capacity for those who aspire in vain to enter the top public institutions, even though they could win a place at less prestigious public equivalents. Other clientele, whether socio-economically more modest or not, may include working adults.

In considering the reasons and dynamics of how private higher education increases capacity, we must note that what is unfolding is not simply a natural process or a pure marketplace phenomenon. Real actors are crucial. These include clearly self-interested actors, principally students and institutional leaders and backers, and also promoters from 'outside' the higher education system. Among these are international businesses (e.g. the SungeiWay Group and Boustead Holdings, backers of a number of private higher education initiatives in Malaysia), and the World Bank. The Bank's spin-off, EdInvest,[11] at the International Finance Corporation, has a pointed and active mission to build capacity through various forms of higher education privatization, including the creation and growth of private institutions. Regarding government, there is great variation. Private growth often arises quite outside government planning, even catching government and others by surprise.[12] Yet, compared to Latin America a generation and more ago where private provision grew up outside state directive, it appears increasingly common for governments today in Asia, Eastern Europe, and now even Africa and the Middle East to articulate a rationale for private provision of capacity beyond what the

---

[11] For an introduction to EdInvest see International Finance Commission, *Facilitating Investment in the Global Education Market*. Available at: www2.ifc.org/edinvest. Last Accessed 22 April 2004.

[12] Levy, Daniel C. (2002) 'Unanticipated Development: Perspectives on Private Higher Education's Emerging Roles'. *PROPHE Working Paper #1*, Program for Research on Private Higher Education (PROPHE), State University of New York at Albany, April 2002. Available at: www.albany.edu/~prophe/publication/paper.html. Last Accessed 22 April 2004.

public can provide. Great debate surrounds this tendency, as the paper notes again later regarding the challenges of quality and regulation.

3 The Main Types of Private Institutional Expansion

3.1 Demand-Absorbers and Related Blends

Up until the 1970s or 1980s, the main institutional forms of private higher education could be described as religious or other cultural, elite, and demand-absorbing.[13] Since that time, it is the third category that has exhibited most significant growth. Moreover, it is obviously the category that is crucial when the concern is enrollment capacity. Thus a major concern of PROPHE is to analyze the demand-absorbers more closely, to determine the varied forms they take.

Until the middle of the twentieth century, the public higher education sector of developing countries and even of Europe could be considered rather elite. As demand grew and was increasingly accommodated, either the sector became less elite or a private sector emerged to handle the newcomers; usually it was a combination but with great variation as to whether public or private managed the bulk. In recent years, the private share of such enrollments has clearly grown, whether private institutions become the 'mass' (majority) sector or not.

Where religious private higher education has recently expanded it may be more closely aligned with demand-absorbers, compared to a past where it often was closer to elite private institutions. This is the case where Catholic universities proliferate in Latin America, where the oldest Catholic universities remain among the most selective institutions, as in Chile. In the U.S., the younger Catholic

---

[13] See Levy, Daniel C. (1986) *Higher Education and the State in Latin America: Private Challenges to Public Dominance*. Chicago, Illinois: University of Chicago Press; Geiger, Roger. (1986) *Private Higher Education in Eight Countries*. Ann Arbor: University of Michigan.

colleges, created in the middle of the twentieth century, are becoming more like private secular colleges scampering to maintain or build their market share in an increasingly competitive setting. Worldwide, existing Catholic colleges and universities struggle to maintain some religious essence.

Meanwhile, there is a sharp proliferation of other religious institutions, including Moslem and Protestant of various denominations. Kenya has both as well as Catholic private higher education and, though some of the institutions are for the fairly well-to-do, the main selective institutions are still the top public universities, and so the religious institutions play a major role in private capacity building. Also on a cultural front, whether religious or not, many institutions grow to provide places for a cultural minority, as for Russians in Ukraine.

More research is needed to map the proliferating private institutions that are neither elite nor the opposite. As in the U.S. and now many developing countries, some provide capacity for well-to-do youth who cannot get into selective institutions and are disinclined to mix into unselective public ones. Common too are institutions that approach neither the academic top nor bottom. Instead, they may perform very well in a chosen specialty, reflecting the point about narrow private institutions. The specializations typically relate to commercial fields of study, such as business administration, tourism, information technology, or English. Racing into such fields ahead of public institutions, the private sector adds capacity through institutional proliferation. But there is also evidence of subsequent enhancement of capacity through institutional broadening. As in China, many narrow institutions pursue aspirations to grow, often using revenues generated from their lead commercial fields to finance the opening of new fields or new campuses.

3.2 New Forms: For-profits

Many of the tendencies thus far identified are epitomized in a growing for-profit sector. Until recently, capacity in higher education had little to do with this sector. Private growth was basically nonprofit. Even countries that permitted private higher education sometimes prohibited for-profits, though sometimes there was just an assumption against for-profits, without specific legal proscription. The U.S. has long had a for-profit sector but its role in capacity has increased in recent years. Several other countries now have formal for-profit sectors. We know that cases include South Africa (where the for-profits are much more extensive than the private nonprofits), Brazil, Peru, Jordan, Ukraine, and the Philippines, and fresh Chinese legislation now allows such a sector there.[14] Further research is needed to see how far this listing might be extended. But even these examples already provide evidence for the proposition that capacity building through novel forms (whether judged good or bad) is more common in developing and transitional than in developed countries outside the U.S.

Furthermore, consistent with points above about definitional ambiguities in private higher education, much formally nonprofit higher education is functionally for-profit. Increasingly, private colleges are largely or even essentially commercial institutions. The line is blurred between formally distributing profits to shareholders and distributing benefits in the form of perks, inflated salaries, and the construction of non-educational facilities. Often legitimately, the line is also blurred between institutions that reap profit and those (including public ones) that build capital in certain endeavors and use that capital to fund non-profitable activities. Scattered international evidence seems to suggest core similarities with U.S. for-profits in the pride displayed in taking the for-profit form. Sympathizers cite Milton Friedman in asserting that the key difference between for-profit and nonprofit institutions is that the former are tax-paying and the latter are tax-evading.[15]

---

[14] For example, Jordan's for-profit growth in its eight year life is 26-fold, to 35,000, or one-third of Jordan's total enrollments in 1999. The private institutions include seven universities and ten community colleges. See World Bank.(2000) *Jordan-Higher Education Development Project*. World Bank: Washington DC, p2.
[15] Ruch, Richard. S. 2001. *Higher Ed, Inc.: The Rise of the For-Profit University*. Baltimore, MD: John Hopkins University Press, p92.

Thus many of the capacity arguments for the private over the public sector are sharpened when it comes to for-profits. The main one is that capacity expands without drawing on public money; this for-profit versus nonprofit distinction is relevant where nonprofits receive tax breaks, as in the U.S., but information is lacking on how widespread such breaks are internationally. A corollary argument is that capacity building produces great benefits to the economy because the training is practical, and accumulating evidence on the U.S. is that job placement appears impressive.[16] Elsewhere, we usually lack evidence beyond limited data on student and employer satisfaction. For example, recent surveying in South Africa suggests such satisfaction but there is still intense national debate over whether the private higher education sector makes a solid contribution on balance. Of course, the main economic argument related to capacity remains that individuals benefit from good private rates of return on their investment, without forcing the public to invest. Thus, a market justification of for-profit capacity building is that students and employers are rendering positive evaluations by their choices in attendance and hiring. By contrast, evaluation of the performance of nonprofit and public institutions that expand capacity is notoriously complex.[17]

Related to the economically oriented capacity claims of for-profits are socioeconomic claims about who is added to the system. The examples cited above about novel delivery modes and about black enrollments in South Africa come largely from the for-profit sector. Again, extensive evidence is available only for the U.S., where it shows socioeconomic background for students at for-profits to be

---

[16] Brimah, Tunde. 1999. *Literature Review: For Profit Degree-Granting Institutions Within Higher Education*. Education Commission of the States, November. Available at: www.ecs.org/clearinghouse/14/47/1447.htm. Last Accessed 22 April 2004.

[17] Such claims also apply to functional for-profits unless their formal nonprofit status gives them public money and other protection from market challenges in building capacity. For a helpful overview on the U.S. for-profit surge, see Brimah, Tunde. 1999. *Literature Review: For Profit Degree-Granting Institutions Within Higher Education*. Education Commission of the States, November. Available at: www.ecs.org/clearinghouse/14/47/1447.htm. Last Accessed 22 April 2004.

more like that of public community colleges than of either public or nonprofit four-year institutions.[18] Yet there is little doubt that for-profits and their formally nonprofit commercial brethren are opening places for groups that have difficulty making it into selective public or nonprofit higher education. The greater flexibility for simultaneous study and work is particularly attractive for both youths and older adults who do not see full-time study as a viable economic choice.

For-profits also illustrate in sharp terms the tendency for private higher education to build capacity through the proliferation of institutions, generally quite different from the classic university model. Sometimes the for-profits are not allowed to be 'universities,' instead functioning as colleges and institutes and, increasingly, they go under the name of the owning business that opens a higher education enterprise.

Capacity building through for-profits and related commercial nonprofits bring opposition, often heated opposition. As we will see in the 'Challenges' section of the paper, the concerns turn on issues of quality and deceit: how much do these institutions provide capacity on narrow economic over real educational grounds, through weak and even dubious types of institutions, and through taking advantage of groups desperate for higher education but unable to secure a place in serious, honorable institutions?

3.3 New Forms: Beyond Freestanding Institutions

Although both for-profits and nonprofits still arise and grow mostly as freestanding institutions, sometimes novel, sometimes not, both also build capacity through various sorts of inter-institutional linkages. After identifying a few forms briefly, we concentrate on one: partnerships between private and public higher education institutions.

---

[18] Kelly, Kathleen F. 2001. *Meeting Needs and Making Profits: The Rise of For-Profit Degree-Granting Institutions.* Education Commission of the States. www.ecs.org/clearinghouse/27/33/2733.htm.

Corporate universities and other formal links between businesses and higher education fit our list of expanding options beyond freestanding higher education institutions. Perhaps the capacity role is greatest here when it involves offering higher education to employees who otherwise would not receive it. A parallel point holds for graduate training.

A dramatic development is the rise of 'chains.' Until recently, for-profit higher education institutions tended to be quite small. Now, alongside such institutions are multi-site campuses. The University of Phoenix is among the leading examples in the U.S. – and is one of a number of chains now operating internationally (e.g. Career Education Corporation and Sylvan Learning Systems), whether through buying existing institutions or creating new ones. Whether strictly within one country or across countries, all operations are put under one brand name. This is not just a marketing ploy. It is also a pointed strategy that declares: our product is working well in its pioneer places and now we can offer it, through institutional cloning, to populations that cannot reach the initial places. Though the multiple sites may have some autonomy, the core idea is a rather standard package for curriculum, pedagogy, hiring, and admissions. The potential exists for huge capacity building, with profits, through such chains.

Again, a for-profit trend is also a trend for commercial nonprofits and even broader nonprofits. For decades, Mexico's individual private higher education institutions were concentrated into one site or only a very few sites. In recent decades, leading institutions have opened multiple sites. Monterrey Tec has been a pioneer in taking its product throughout the nation, and other private institutions have followed suit. The Tec itself has gone abroad as well, into other parts of Latin America and even into the U.S.[19]

---

[19] It has long been common in some countries for established public universities to open campuses elsewhere in the country, arguing the virtues of building capacity outside the capital city while at least ostensibly including a means of quality control beyond that accompanying the proliferation of freestanding public institutions – or private ones.

In most countries, strong linkages between private and public higher education institutions remain rare. But a powerful exception, which PROPHE aims to study extensively, and which goes beyond ad hoc cooperative ventures or projects, concerns formal partnerships between private and public higher education institutions. Much of the rationale for this development involves capacity building. It is capacity building that offers something for both the private and the public partner. Prominent examples of private-public partnerships include China, Malaysia, Russia, and South Africa.

The South African case illustrates the capacity-related motivations for the partnerships and the possibilities of partnership as a vehicle of private growth. Perhaps half the country's private enrollments are in the private partners of public institutions, though in 1999 the government slapped a moratorium on new partnerships. The private partner allows expanded capacity and reach for the public sector in several ways. This reach may have a geographic aspect but it is mostly again about groups that do not gain significant access to selective public universities. Fearing political fall out from impending majority rule, Afrikaans public universities developed the idea of joining with private colleges that attracted black students; seeing the success, English-speaking public universities have partly followed suit. Whether or not they provide formal transfer paths, public universities may use the private partners as screeners; they then take in a share of those who prove themselves at the private partners but who might not have gained direct admission to the public universities. Sometimes the expanded capacity comes also from the fact that the private partner specializes in fields that are in great demand, usually job relevant. These may be fields that the public university considers low status, or itself moves into belatedly. Or the private institutions may merely offer extra places for students to enter the same programs as at public institutions.

Enrollment capacity building is also financial capacity building. The private partner always charges tuition. Public partners often have no tuition or low tuition, and changes to this policy often entail great political cost, so partnership offers a partial escape. The particulars of what share of private tuition gets transferred to the public institution vary. Moreover, the private partners may also provide opportunities for entrepreneurial activity difficult at the public universities, including beachheads for foreign investment.

The reciprocity comes from the value private entities get from their ties with public entities. In the end this too is about capacity building since they are able to attract and administer to more students than they otherwise could. Part of the story relates to their right to use the much more established facilities of public universities, including campuses, libraries, laboratories, and even personnel. This may help fend off student reluctance to attend narrow and relatively poorly funded private institutions. But beyond the facilities per se, the benefits of partnership lie largely in quality assurance – or at least the appearance thereof. Where curriculum from public institutions is employed, private institutions save the cost of curriculum development and they offer what people typically accept as educationally sound and proven. Examination control by the public partner can provide further assurance. In different ways, then, private institutions eager to attract students boost what otherwise is a weak point in their pursuit: their legitimacy in the eyes of the citizenry. It is no surprise that the public partner is usually a university, often prestigious, while the private partner is usually a college. In turn, this helps explain why such partnerships appear to be more common in regions where the public sector has been academically selective, as in Africa and much of Asia and certainly Eastern Europe, more than in Latin America.

Partnership between private and public higher education institutions thus provides new forms in which to play out the basic logic of increasing capacity. Compared to other modes of increasing capacity, this one brings the private and public together. It prioritizes cooperation over competition but does so in ways that tend to make mutual use of private-public distinctiveness rather than to minimize it.

The private-public partnerships treated thus far are for the most part indigenous, but overlapping dynamics also appear on the international front. Of course, foreign providers can sometimes simply offer their product inside another country; where the providers are private, this is an additional private capacity builder. But even public universities may function abroad like private entities. Best fitting our discussion here, however, is where foreign universities join up with local private providers. The mutual benefits between foreign university and local college may be much like that of the domestic partners just discussed. The foreign institution expands its reach geographically and often socioeconomically, and garners tuition. The local private college gains a legitimizing link, curriculum, and the ability to offer a diploma or degree that may lack state recognition but can have job-market or international value. Malaysia has been the leading example of a country where the government has actively encouraged such arrangements.[20]

4 Challenges to Private Higher Education Expansion

4.1 Quality and Legitimacy

It is easy to understand why quality is a major concern. Most of the world's contemporary private higher education expansion comes outside well-established institutions, including outside the gold standard of 'universities'. It reaches students unable to access the selective public institutions (or the selective private ones). It often reaches them through unconventional modes. Common is a pointed emphasis on practicality over intellectual pursuits. Capacity building is fundamentally about enrollments. Indeed it is about enrollments at rather low cost, thus minimizing other forms of capacity.

By standard measures of academic quality, the bulk of fresh capacity is clearly low. Faculty tend to be part time, often without advanced academic credentials. Research is rare, especially basic research. Scholarly cross-fertilization across the sciences and humanities is likewise rare. Libraries and laboratories are meager.

---

[20] Lee, Molly N.N. 2002. International Linkages In Malaysian Private Higher Education, *International Higher Education*, Number 30.

But beyond these rather obvious points, the picture is more complex. First, we have seen that not all of the private growth occurs in demand-absorbing institutions, as there are mixes with elite and religious orientations. Second, and sadly a heftier qualifier, is that poor undertakings and performance do not necessarily mean contrast with the expanding portions of the public sector. Third, and more upbeat, is consideration of multiple types of quality. How much does the expanding private sector provide useful forms of 'value added' for clients, society, and the economy? Positive answers may be linked to matters of innovation and efficiency, even as they move far from the academic gold standard. Among the major concerns of PROPHE research is to shed light on the frequency and dynamics of such value-adding private institutions versus counterparts that fit critics' views of 'garage' institutions offering little of value. A major reason to shed such light is to be able to assess what is going on but one can also ponder the matter with a focused concern on whether concerns over quality will lead to a curbing of capacity.

The mix of concerns over quality, whether valid or invalid, objective or subjective, then overlaps very much with questions of legitimacy. By legitimacy we have in mind mostly citizens' views of the private institutions, though this can affect and be affected by official policy in regulation and accreditation. At an extreme, illegitimacy can lead to forcible closings. In the 1990s, after quite unregulated and troublesome proliferation in El Salvador, the government reviewed and shut down many of the institutions. Short of that come various forms of restrictive regulation or simply a dwindling desire by students to entrust themselves to the private providers. Legitimacy is a strong challenge where private institutions undertake, with perceived lower quality, similar tasks to public counterparts. But legitimacy is an especially striking challenge where fresh private capacity emerges in modes unknown in the established public sector. Thus, distinctiveness is often a double-edged sword, bolstering claims of innovation but inviting doubt about the worth and appropriateness of the new. This point holds powerfully for the mass of commercial private higher education, epitomized by the for-profits. Legitimacy tends to be especially problematic where statist traditions are strong, broader market activity has been weak or itself problematic, and public universities have strong and selective academic traditions. Russia is an excellent example.[21]

On the other hand, it would be misleading to think of widespread legitimacy as a condition of continued private expansion. Such a thought is more suited to the public sector of higher education. In contrast, our analysis of private growth to date shows how it depends on a match between seekers and suppliers, particularly around individual aspirations for higher education and then jobs. Where all this is built upon client money, and other private decisions, it need not matter if the majority of public opinion is opposed or even angry, regarding the private sector as largely illegitimate.

4.2 Regulation and Competition

The negative views of majority public opinion or of a powerful minority can cripple private growth if they lead to regulations to restrict the choices many private interests would like to continue to make. Even in the broad political economy of countries with high legitimacy for markets, regulation is common. In some sense, it is a friendly alternative allowing private provision rather than forcing public provision. So the twin question for private capacity becomes how much regulation and how much it is onerously restrictive or enabling? Regulation may confer much needed review and a stamp of approval that then leads to greater legitimacy among the citizenry.

---

[21] The following source analyzes the legitimacy question in Russia in empirical and conceptual detail that goes beyond that available on any other country. Suspitsin, Dmitry. 2002. Exploring the Complexity of Organizational Legitimacy in the Context of Russian Private Higher Education. Paper presented at the conference *Advancing the Institutional Research Agenda in Education*. Albany, NY: University at Albany, SUNY. September 20–22.

The determinants of the answers to the twin question are at least three fold. One concerns honest assessments made of the private providers, including not only objective analysis but also subjective analysis and strong normative elements about what is appropriately higher education. All this is often quite hard to separate in practice from a second concern: raw self-interest. Suppliers and stakeholders in public higher education often have much at risk in private growth. A third matter is of course the policymaking influence of those who would like to restrict or revamp private developments.

The extreme in coercive limitation is of course the proscription of private higher education (or the closing of existing institutions). Once common, proscription has usually yielded either to permissiveness or to more open debate about the degree and shape of regulation. Regulations often have the intent and/or effect, in the name of quality assurance, of limiting distinctiveness. Paradoxically, as many regulations mandate increased capacity at individual institutions, they may render it impossible for those institutions to make ends meet, thus reducing the higher education supply and capacity. Examples include required proportions of full-time staff, minimum infrastructure, number of books, number of fields of study, and so forth. Or in other ways regulations insist on certain modes or measures of quality that many private institutions cannot meet.[22]

The most significant form of expanding regulation is accreditation. Accreditation is one of many developments often particularly problematic in the private sector. In fact, public universities are sometimes free from some of the accrediting requirements due to their pre-existence, stature, tradition, or political strength. Public

---

[22] Another pursuit in regulation is equity and it too can have paradoxical effects. For example, private institutions that must receive government permission to raise tuition may not be able to offer the capacity they otherwise would – even perhaps then denying space to relatively less privileged candidates for higher education. This point must be balanced against the real concern that privates of even modest academic levels often get priced beyond what aspiring groups can manage; for the Mexican case see Post, David. 2000. 'Student Movements, User Fees, and Access to Mexican Higher Education: Trends in the Effect of Social Background and Family Income, 1984–1996'. *Mexican Studies/Estudios Mexicanos* 16:141–163.

institutions may be considered to have their right to exist noted by their very creation while private institutions need to prove themselves. Where accreditation exists for all higher education there may be one system or there may be separate systems for public and private institutions.

From South Africa to Hungary and beyond one of the common cries of private higher education is that they are crippled in their ability to offer opportunities for students not only by the content of the regulations but by the uncertainty and time lags often involved. It is often difficult to know when one can safely proceed with a novel field of study or with curriculum or instructional forms unknown in the public sector. Private officials claim they are often confronted suddenly with regulations that are costly and allow little time for compliance. Problems are exacerbated when private institutions attempt to offer studies in fast changing fields.[23]

Accreditation can have especially retarding effects on private growth where public university representatives are prominent in making or enforcing public policy provisions. This point goes back to the dual motivations of public higher education restraining private growth: conviction and self-interest. Conviction often argues against novel things private higher education attempts; so does a defensive form of self-interest.

At the same time, however, public sector self-interest in thwarting private institutions appears increasingly to have to do with competition, indeed competition focused on the novel endeavors. This public higher education reaction contrasts with several earlier and still pertinent ones. One reaction was rejection of private initiatives largely on ideological grounds. Another was indifference,

---

[23] But, consistent with the comment that regulation can help through legitimizing, so accreditation has sometimes helped particular institutions gain acceptance, as in Bulgaria according to Slantcheva, Snejana. 2000. *Public And Private Initiatives in Higher Education: The Case of Bulgaria*. PHARE-ACE Report. By the same token, privates gaining accreditation may join forces with interests opposing accreditation for 'lower-level' privates whose presence competes for enrollment or undermines public impressions about the quality of the private sector.

stemming from a sense of only minimal threat. The private sector's surprising surge often meant a delayed public policy reaction. Sometimes the public sector reaction, as in many post-communist settings, was to see the new private capacity as 'complementary' more than competitive. It could even allow public universities to focus on high status academic activities rather than to get 'watered down' providing the system's expanded capacity for less-prepared students or in academically non-prestigious endeavors.

Examples where public institutions increasingly operate where only private institution once did include the charging of tuition, the opening of job-related commercial fields of study, flexible delivery modes, and money-making units. All this may in a sense be flattering for the pioneering private providers and may in turn bolster their attractiveness by bolstering the legitimacy of their activities. Or it may be that the effects on private growth are neutral, as the public sector's entrepreneurial steps allow it to maintain or increase its capacity, with reduced public funding. But the prospect also exists for the public and private sectors to compete for the same students.

Sharpening competition is seen in Russia, much of Eastern Europe and elsewhere as public universities either institute tuition across the board or, more so, where they take in 'extra' students, fee-paying, alongside the subsidized students.[24] Whereas public universities once might have had a more detached view about private growth, they themselves now want the profits reaped through lucrative fields and activities, which can then cross-subsidize their more academic fields and endeavors. China is a dramatic example of fresh public entrepreneurial endeavors. Yet it might be other transitional countries that see greater public higher education efforts to slow the private sector, if the state can be pressured, and especially if demography suggests a stagnant

---

[24] In Argentina and other countries where first-degree public education remains tuition-free, enterprising public universities have nonetheless raised funds by charging tuition at the graduate level, in fields with high individual rates of return; counterpart public universities also want to take advantage of that market of paying students.

or even shrinking pool of candidates for higher education overall. At least one analyst has thus speculated on a relative fall in private provision in Eastern Europe after its meteoric rise following the end of European communism in 1989.[25]

It remains unclear how private higher education will fare in this building competition with public institutions. It enjoys advantages at times in governance and financial flexibility or in having moved first into novel activities, gaining experience and credibility. But its public competitors have increasing incentives to act and they enjoy certain competitive benefits springing from remaining public funding. Many retain natural advantages through their prestige; if a degree counts for more from a public than from a private competitor, then students may head there even for a field of study first or more competently offered at the private institution. Perhaps most of all, the public institutions take advantage of their privileged position to influence the regulatory framework in ways that inhibit private growth.

5 Conclusion

How much to care about the private sector's share of future enrollment depends on many facts and values. It is possible to care about the system's capacity without preferring either public over private expansion or private over public expansion. But it is impossible to understand contemporary expansion, including its size and contours and policy dimensions, without knowledge about both sectors.

Even when one's interest is largely the private sector, it is reasonable to analyze intersectoral dynamics. Thus, the private sector may play a major role in system capacity where it ultimately

---

[25] Tomusk, Voldemar. 2002. 'The War of Institutions, Episode I: Rise and Fall of Private Universities in Eastern Europe'. Paper presented at the conference *Advancing the Institutional Research Agenda in Education*. Albany, NY: University at Albany, SUNY, September 20–22.

spurs diversifying and expanding public sector capacity. Also common, where private higher education has existed for some time, is private-public blurring. Nonetheless, blurring rarely comes to mean the absence of significant private-public differences. Thus, private sectors will likely continue to provide capacity in ways importantly different (though not totally different) from how public higher education provides capacity.

Whatever the future brings, this paper has attempted to improve understanding of how capacity building occurs within the private sector. Globally, higher education continues to grow and a rising share of that growth is private. Private higher education provides stark solutions to the dilemma of how to keep expanding enrollments while not expanding public budgets. This has much to do with private payments, efficiency and low-cost, market-oriented endeavors, concentrated in an array of proliferating institutions distinct from traditional universities.

Annex A – Data from Central and Eastern Europe

Table 1 Private Higher Education Enrollment, Central and Eastern Europe (academic year 2000–2001)

Country	Number of Students	
	Private	% of total enrollment
Albania	–	–
Belarus	35,900	13.0
Bulgaria	27,916	11.5
Croatia	1,646	1.4
Czech Republic	2,000	1.0
Estonia	12,963	25.2
Hungary	42,561	14.3
Latvia	11,353	12.7
Lithuania	–	–
The FYR of Macedonia	–	–
Moldova	23,210	22,6
Poland	471,443	29.9
Romania	130,492	28.9

(*Continued*)

Table 1 (Continued)

Country	Number of Students	
	Private	% of total enrollment
Russian Federation	470,600	10.0
Slovak Republic	842	0.7
Slovenia	2,900	4.3
Ukraine	–	–

Source: Derived from UNESCO European Centre for Higher Education, www.cepes.ro/information_services/statistics.htm

Table 2 Private Institutions of Higher Education, Central and Eastern Europe (2000–2001 academic year)

Country	Number of Institutions	
	Private	% of total institutions
Albania	3	27.3
Belarus	15	26.3
Bulgaria	9	10.3
Croatia	9	9.5
Czech Republic	14	33.3
Estonia	21	60
Hungary	32	51.6
Latvia	13	39.4
Lithuania	4	9.6
The FYR of Macedonia	–	–
Moldova	57	50
Poland	195	62.9
Romania	83	59.3
Russian Federation	358	37.1
Slovak Republic	2	10
Slovenia	9	81.9
Ukraine	163	16.4

Source: Derived from UNESCO European Centre for Higher Education, www.cepes.ro/information_services/statistics.htm

References

Altbach, Philip. G. (ed.). 1999. *Private Prometheus: Private Higher Education and Development in the 21st Century.* Westport, CT.: Greenwood Press.
Brimah, Tunde. 1999. *Literature Review: For Profit Degree-Granting Institutions Within Higher Education.* Education Commission of the States, November. www.ecs.org/clearinghouse/14/47/1447.htm.
García Guadilla, Carmen. 1996. *Situación y principales dinámicas de transformación de la educación superior en América latina.* Caracas: UNESCO.
Geiger, Roger. 1986. *Private Higher Education in Eight Countries.* Ann Arbor: University of Michigan.
Kelly, Kathleen F. 2001. *Meeting Needs and Making Profits: The Rise of For-Profit Degree-Granting Institutions.* Education Commission of the States. http://www.ecs.org/clearinghouse/27/33/2733.htm.
Lee, Molly N. N. 2001. Private Higher Education in Malaysia: Expansion, Diversification and Consolidation. In *Second Regional Seminar on Private Higher Education: Its Role in Human Resource Development in a Globalised Knowledge Society.* Bangkok, Thailand: Organized by UNESCO PROAP and SEAMEO RIHED, June 20–22.
Lee, Molly N.N. 2002. 'International Linkages In Malaysian Private Higher Education', *International Higher Education,* Number 30.
Levy, Daniel C. 1986. *Higher Education and the State in Latin America: Private Challenges to Public Dominance.* Chicago, Illinois: University of Chicago Press.
Levy, Daniel C. 2002. The Emergence of Private Higher Education's Roles: International Tendencies Relevant to Recent Chinese Reality. Peking University, *Higher Education Forum,* no. 1, 2002, pp 89–96; Xiamen University, *International Higher Education,* no. 2, 2002:1–8.
Levy, Daniel C. 2002. Unanticipated Development: Perspectives on Private Higher Education's Emerging Roles. PROPHE Working Paper #1, Program for Research on Private Higher Education (PROPHE), State University of New York at Albany. http://www.albany.edu/~prophe/publication/paper.html. April 2002.
Levy, Daniel C. 2002. Profits and Practicality: How South Africa Epitomizes the Global Surge in Commercial Private Higher Education. PROPHE Working Paper #2, SUNY at Albany, December.
Otieno, Wycliffe. 2002. In Between the Master and the Mammon? Privatizing Trends and Challenges in Kenyan Higher Education. Paper prepared for discussion at PROPHE, University at Albany, SUNY, Albany NY, November 7.
Post, David. 2000. Student Movements, User Fees, and Access to Mexican Higher Education: Trends in the Effect of Social Background and Family Income, 1984–1996. *Mexican Studies/Estudios Mexicanos* 16:141–163.
Ruch, Richard. S. 2001. *Higher Ed, Inc.: The Rise of the For-Profit University.* Baltimore, MD: John Hopkins University Press.

Slantcheva, Snejana. 2000. Public And Private Initiatives in Higher Education: The Case of Bulgaria. PHARE-ACE Report. (This research was undertaken with support from the European Community's Phare-ACE Programme 1998. The content of the report is the sole responsibility of the author and it in no way represents the views of the Commission or its services.)

Suspitsin, Dmitry. 2002. Exploring the Complexity of Organizational Legitimacy in the Context of Russian Private Higher Education. Paper presented at the conference *Advancing the Institutional Research Agenda in Education*. Albany, NY: University at Albany, SUNY. September 20–22.

Tan, Ai Mei. 2002. *Malaysian Private Higher Education: Globalisation, Privatisation, Transformation and Marketplaces*. Singapore: Asean Academic Press.

Task Force on Higher Education and Society. 2000. *Higher Education in Developing Countries: Peril and Promise*. Washington DC: World Bank.

Tomusk, Voldemar. 2002. The War of Institutions, Episode I: Rise and Fall of Private Universities in Eastern Europe. Paper presented at the conference *Advancing the Institutional Research Agenda in Education*. Albany, NY: University at Albany, SUNY. September 20–22.

World Bank. 2000. Jordan-Higher Education Development Project. World Bank: Washington DC.

World Bank. 2002. *Constructing Knowledge Societies: New Challenges for Tertiary Education*. May 7, 2002, draft version.

Corporate Universities: *historical development, conceptual analysis and relations with public-sector higher education*

Scott Taylor and Rob Paton

1 Introduction

"...so now we had a structure, we started going out to the workshops and talking to the employees. There is untapped potential in the blue-collar workforce as it exists at the moment – people that haven't gone to university because it wasn't the thing to do, or because the families couldn't afford it. What the men and women said to us was very interesting. They said, 'we missed a chance to go to university, we would like to do something like this, we would like to advance ourselves, we would like to be better, we would like to be part of what you do. Yes, we agree about using fancy words, we don't want jargon but don't look down your noses at us, we're just as capable of understanding what a university is all about as you are'. And then one morning I had an idea – I had to make a presentation to sell the Corporate University to the directors, so I trained a few employees in giving presentations. I kicked off the presentations, but I used these three workshop employees to do the presenting. Two results: number one, it stopped people like the chairman talking about how low level employees won't understand the corporate university, because it was them making the presentation; number two, it was the University in practice. It was actually taking people and giving them skills that they'd never dreamt that they would have – this for me was something way beyond the learning organization."

Director, Utility University[1]

This report offers an outline of the rapidly developing corporate university phenomenon. In recent years the number and visibility of training and development initiatives within multinational corporations that adopt the language, structure and practice of higher education has risen dramatically, yet empirical analyses of corporate universities remain rare. In this report, we bring together insights from previous descriptive accounts and present preliminary findings from our own research analysis. Through this, we locate the corporate university phenomenon in a number of ways. First, we trace the historical precedents for commercial companies taking primary responsibility for employee training and development. Second, we locate corporate university initiatives within the organisational world that has generated them, and in particular contextualise them within recent managerial discourses of learning and knowledge. We use interview data from directors of European corporate universities to suggest these initiatives are subject to a

---

[1] This is a quote from an interview with a senior manager at a British organization that operated a corporate university, part of an ongoing research project at the Open University Business School (www3.open.ac.uk/oubs). Names of organizations and individuals in the quotes have been changed to ensure anonymity.

range of intense pressures that should be taken into account in considering their significance and likely impact on existing educational providers. This enables us finally to discuss three potential futures for corporate universities within contemporary educational provision.

Throughout the report, we also explore how the notion of a corporate university has evolved out of a series of developments in technology, business organisation and education that are profoundly affecting how people work and learn. The increased temporal and spatial flexibility that information and communication technologies (ICTs) bring to training and education are enabling further advances in open and distance learning, providing a powerful driver for corporate university initiatives. At the same time, however, changes in managerial priorities and discourses in a globalising knowledge economy have put a premium on corporate learning processes of all sorts, and especially those that can contribute to organisational cohesion. We also note that strategic learning initiatives such as corporate universities are becoming increasingly common in the public sector, through initiatives such as the National Health Service University (NHS U)[2] in the UK and the Tennessee Valley Authority University in the USA. On this basis, we suggest that corporate universities have the potential to contribute towards the re-structuring of higher education, bringing higher education and work organisations even closer together through a re-definition of the nature of knowledge, learning and employability, supported by extensive use of ICT.

We suggest that there are three roles that corporate universities may take up in the evolving institutional field of higher education. First, we explore the possibility that they could become significant *competitors* in the market for vocationally oriented educational programmes. Second, we examine the idea that corporate universities may become *co-existing* hybrid institutions, providing

---

[2] For more information on this initiative see Department of Health. *Homepage*. Available at: www.doh.gov.uk. Last Accessed 22 April 2004.

skills training and socialisation to a parallel yet separate market within corporations. Third, we suggest that corporate universities may become important (and very demanding) *collaborators* with a small and selected number of existing educational institutions, with significant implications for how industry-university relations are managed and experienced. How far each of these possibilities is realised in different countries will depend on existing institutional arrangements and the responsiveness or engagement of existing universities to corporate universities.

This report is intended to enable readers to:

- recognise the historical and cultural contexts that have contributed to this development in the interface between the education and employment systems;
- appreciate the concerns that underpin the development of corporate universities, and engage with those responsible for running them;
- make informed contributions to debates about the nature of corporate universities and their potential significance for higher education and university-industry relations;
- anticipate whether and in what ways the further development of corporate universities may impact their own higher education institutions, and the strategic issues this may raise.

References to published papers from both business and educational perspectives can be found at the end of the paper, along with a list of website addresses for a selection of corporate universities.

2 Taking Hamburger U Seriously

2.1 Introduction: What's in a Name?

It seems that many who work in public or traditional universities find it difficult to take the idea of corporate university seriously. Perhaps the amalgamation of terminology from the context of high intellectual endeavour with the name of a corporation that makes hamburgers or cartoons contains an inherent potential for humor; perhaps the laughter indicates a discomfort with the idea that McDonald's or Disney could set up and run an institution to enable learning or knowledge production; perhaps treating corporate universities in this way masks fear of serious competition from the corporate sector. In any event, bringing corporate identity and terms such as university, academy or institute together seems to generate humour and anger in equal measure. This section presents some of the reasons why such reactions appear to us to be either condescending or shortsighted.

The term 'corporate university' first appeared in management and business literature in the early 1980s, referring to initiatives within corporations that are labeled university, academy, institute or school, and which often adopt the 'symbolic paraphernalia' of education (as one corporate university manager in our research put it). This usage is now widespread among both practicing managers and business school researchers, and should be clearly differentiated from similar, pejoratively employed expressions from Marxian analyses of education. Commentators in that tradition, such as Aronowitz,[3] have referred to 'corporate' and 'corporatised' universities to mean higher education institutions that have close research relations with industry or have adopted practices and values from the corporate sector. It is beyond the scope of this report to explore the extensive literature relating to university-industry relations; however, the use of the term corporatised university is indicative of continuing concern over the role of business within the educational sector. Doubts about the academic substance of business education,[4] reservations about 'massification', and concerns about the influences on universities of their industrial sponsors and collaborators, are significant in higher education in many countries. Hence, when global corporations are perceived to be usurping the terminology and symbols that denote

---

[3] Aronowitz, S. (2000) *The Knowledge Factory: Dismantling the corporate university and creating true higher learning*. Boston: Beacon Press.
[4] Tight, M. (1988) 'So what is academic freedom?', in Tight, M. (ed.) *Academic Freedom and Responsibility*, pp.114–132. Milton Keynes: Open University Press.

an educational institution of the highest level, to refer to initiatives that sometimes bear little resemblance to 'real' universities in activity, structure, or philosophy, incredulity and dismay are often the result. Academics both from business schools and from wider educational communities have protested vehemently that institutions such as McDonald's Hamburger U are debasing 'the idea of the university'.[5]

We have argued elsewhere that corporate universities are sometimes more 'university-like' than might be expected.[6] Much more importantly, we would suggest that assessing or testing corporate universities through comparison to a 19th century ideal of 'the university' is to fundamentally misunderstand the nature of the phenomenon. Corporate universities are not aspiring to compete with or replace existing educational providers – indeed, our research indicates that the managers involved in these initiatives do not see the symbolism or connotations of the university label as particularly attractive, and many seek to avoid the use of the term 'university' altogether. Nevertheless, language and symbolism are important dimensions of corporate universities, as in all managerial initiatives designed to motivate employees. For managers of corporate universities, as the three exhibits in the third section of the report demonstrate, the presentation of training and development in terms of a corporate university can be central to the initiative, with a view to increasing its credibility with internal and external stakeholders. It may even be that the notion of the 'corporate university' is a misnomer – it would be more accurate, if less attractive, to refer to them as 'strategic learning initiatives within large, complex organizations'. This would then enable us to

---

[5] Aronowitz, S. (2000) *The Knowledge Factory: Dismantling the corporate university and creating true higher learning.* Boston: Beacon Press, and Craig, R., Clarke, F and Amernic, J. (1999) 'Scholarship in University Business Schools: Cardinal Newman, creeping corporatism and farewell to the disturber of the peace?' *Accounting, Auditing and Accountabiulity Journal,* 12(5): 510–524.
[6] Paton, R. and Taylor, S. (2002) 'Corporate Universities: Between higher education and the workplace', in Williams, G. (ed) *The Enterprising University.* Buckingham: Society for Research in Higher Education and Open University Press.

examine the activities taking place under the corporate university umbrella with fewer presumptions and in a more empirically informed way. However, the 'corporate university' label is now well established within corporations and in research analyses, and it is this term that we use through the report. The next section briefly traces a number of precedents that contribute to the contemporary notion of the corporate university as we see it practiced today.

2.2 The Rise of the Corporate University

Although accurate numbers are difficult to come by, there can be little doubt that corporate university initiatives are increasingly numerous around the globe. There is a rise in visibility through the media, with the London *Financial Times* sponsoring an annual corporate university award; international conferences take place on a regular basis; corporate promotional literature often features a short section on the local corporate university initiative. Consultancy companies such as PriceWaterhouseCoopers, reliable indicators of current business trends, are also beginning to offer services to organizations that wish to set up or more effectively run corporate universities. Currently, the 'headline figure' supplied by the premier consultancy company in this area suggests that there are around 2000 such initiatives in the US alone, rising from 15 in the early 1980s and 400 in the mid-1990s (see www.corpu.com). Many of Europe's most prestigious corporations are either exploring the nature of corporate universities through peer groups facilitated by practitioner and professional organizations, or actively setting them up and running them. *Corporate University Xchange*, the leading consultancy company in this field, has even claimed that by 2010 there may be more corporate universities than public universities.

On their own, such figures invite, and warrant, some scepticism – future trend projection is an inexact science, and management and business initiatives are notorious for generating promotional hyperbole. More importantly, however, obvious questions relate to the difference made by corporate universities. How many initiatives, for example, constitute nothing more than a 're-badging' of existing training and development – 'changing the sign above the door and little else', as one manager in our study put it. Fashion is an important dynamic in the spread of ideas and practices among large corporations, and there are clearly some 'faddish' elements in the current high levels of interest. Some corporate universities have failed to find a secure niche in the ecology of corporate life, and been quietly closed down (as Exhibit 3 demonstrates). Nevertheless, there are several reasons for believing that corporate universities will become semi-permanent and embedded features in the corporate landscape, and as such public universities may need to engage with them, rather than simply seek distance through humour or disdain.

There are several bases for this contention. First, corporate universities have a significant pre-history. As Eurich pointed out in 1985, corporate dissatisfaction with educational 'products' (i.e., potential employees) and processes has existed since the earliest days of industrial production. 'Corporate classrooms' were set up by DuPont, General Electric and Edison in the 19th century to provide more suitably skilled employees than the US education system could at that time. We would also note here that the vision of the university as separate from business (and indeed as separate from any other societal institution) that led to the image of academics working in an 'ivory tower' is relatively recent. The roots and early development of universities in Europe located them in a messy and complex web of relationships within society, often with little regard to the notions of academic independence or freedom that are so central to our understanding of university work today. Corporate universities, then, are not generating interplay between education and business that has no precedents, and should not be demonized for 'poisoning' an ideal vision of the university.

Second, the extent of corporate education and training activity is economically enormous. Although reliable estimates of both the number of people and the amount of money in corporate training and development programmes are again lacking, estimates of spending levels sometimes reach as high as 10% of total corporate turnover. More importantly, as Eurich also noted, it is safe to speculate that the amount invested and the number of participants involved in corporate education and training is at least equal to levels in the 'traditional' higher education sector. In 2000, the 'Employment Policy Foundation' in Washington DC estimated that direct and indirect training and development costs totalled between 284 and 387 billion US dollars each year in the private sector alone, and they further claimed that the private sector is also the largest training provider in the US. While the proportions and total figures will vary from country to country, this gives an indication of the importance of the corporate education and training sector.

Third, and perhaps more important, is the cultural significance of large corporations. At the 'Academy of Management' meeting in Washington DC in 2001, Jeanne Meister of the *Corporate University Xchange* consultancy company, the closest that the corporate university phenomenon has to a guru figure, posed the following question to an audience of academics during a symposium on corporate universities – if your child were given the choice of attending a mediocre public university to study management, or a corporate university with the guarantee of a job at the end of a broadly similar degree course, which would you recommend to the child? The reaction was, predictably, on the side of the non-corporate institution, and there was some incredulity that the question could even be posed. However, the value of credentials from some public universities (when higher education participation rates approach 50% in the UK) may be less than the students (and academics) would wish. When the largest, most prestigious corporations routinely recruit from a very limited number of prestige universities that are increasingly difficult to access, and when a large consultancy company such as KPMG begins to recruit directly from schools through a 'cadetship' programme, Meister's scenario may not be far-fetched. It may constitute a serious dilemma for some universities. Of course, a degree from a prestige university will retain social value and cultural capital that cannot be replicated, but qualifications gained through a corporate university, and obtained while gaining considerable and prestigious industrial experience, may well acquire a currency that 'outperforms' credentials from less prestigious universities. Combining this with the increasingly active role that corporations can take on within societies around the globe, and it seems dangerous for public universities just to ignore or decry corporate universities.

This then is the background and context of the corporate university phenomenon. Historically, there are precedents for this kind of activity; corporate training and development is a huge market both economically and in terms of student numbers; and education as an institution in society is continually changing and reforming. In the next section, working from these bases, we seek to approach the corporate university phenomenon from the inside. We argue that in order to understand this development it is necessary to locate it within the discourses and dynamics of the corporate sector. We present the perspectives of three senior corporate university managers from our own ongoing research, and address some of the issues that they raise.

3   Understanding the Corporate Context

"The idea for having a corporate university you'd have to credit with the Chief Executive of the group. He started at the bottom in his first banking post many years ago, without any university qualifications or anything like that, and eventually worked his way up through the system – he got the books that MBAs were reading, but didn't do the MBA himself. He felt quite strongly that educating people was important, and that if the company aspired to attract and retain the people that we wanted, we had to do something else other than pay them more. I don't think you'd describe him as a liberal, you would just say that, actually, this makes good business sense. It was a set of ideals that we could see was a good idea – having corporate learning as part of the structure was good business sense."

Director, Financial Services University

3.1 Introduction

The essential question that we address in this section is *why* corporations want their own universities. There are many answers and, as we shall see, corporate universities can take very different forms. We suggest that the phenomenon is best understood by outlining three current managerial discourses, each of which readily accommodates the corporate university idea, and which together provide fertile ground for corporate university projects when a sponsor or champion of the idea emerges. These discourses centre on Human Resource Management (HRM), Knowledge Management (KM), and the Learning Organisation (LO). This means that corporate universities can be initiated and justified from several quite different perspectives – they need not be tied to the sponsorship of any single function or group, as most managerial initiatives are.

The rapidly changing vocabulary of business is often and understandably a target for criticism and merriment. It is important to remember that these discourses have gained wide currency because they help to express and address, at least aspirationally, important tangles of issues confronting businesses. In this context, the rapid development and deployment of new ICTs, the pace of industrial change and restructuring in Western economies, and the progressive integration of businesses across international frontiers have all been major drivers of change in corporate structures and processes, and provide the general context in which these discourses have become widespread and influential. This is not to suggest that they should be accepted uncritically, as unproblematic reflections of reality. However, they do provide a useful way of appreciating the business context of corporate universities, one aspect of which is unrelenting change. The section ends by highlighting the implications this has for the structure and functioning of corporate universities themselves.

3.2 Human Resource Management (HRM)

Although the term was used for many years, HRM came to have a clearly differentiated meaning in the early 1980s, as academics at the Universities of Michigan and Harvard put together new MBA modules under the title. The courses were in response to requests from senior managers and aspiring executives at those business schools for a course component that would enable them to understand 'people issues' (such as recruitment, appraisal, or training and development) at a strategic level – that is, to assess how these activities contributed to corporate goals and refine the ways in which they could be oriented towards competitive advantage. Thus, the building of a strong and distinctive corporate culture through 'people management' procedures became a concern within many large companies. This was in stark contrast to traditional personnel management courses, primarily concerned with the legal and administrative aspects of those same 'people issues'.

Differentiating HRM from personnel management and existing industrial relations practice was crucial to constructing it as a new discipline within the management and business area, and to convincing practicing managers that it could lead to competitive advantage. The notion of managing human resources to fulfil business strategy and aims dominated this endeavour, and is reflected in initiatives like the Investors in People (IiP) award in the UK. Companies that choose to be assessed for this award have to show that training and training assessment is consistently oriented towards the achievement of business goals. Similarly, recruitment and selection processes are often framed by the notion of competencies, as prospective employees are compared to a list of behavioural and attitudinal ideals that have been identified as business critical – helping to align a people management process and business aims.

The introduction of philosophies of HRM was supported by changing cultural understandings and structural conditions for many employees and managers. In the UK, legislation relating to work and the workplace diminished the role of collective representation and emphasised individualised contracts, as well as giving employers significantly more freedom to offer short-term contracts. The notion of 'employability' came to the fore, and the 'organisation man' [sic] transformed into the 'portfolio worker' or the 'knowledge worker'. In the US, this shift has been even more pronounced, as senior managers in large corporations redefined people as either 'core' (permanent and crucial) or 'periphery' (temporary and easily replaceable).

Popular representation of corporate university initiatives in the business press[7] and practitioner accounts emphasise the strategic HRM intent of corporate university practice and philosophy. In addition, corporate universities are sometimes credited with being a more active aspect of the re-definition of corporate responsibility towards employees. Companies may no longer be able to offer the security of a job for life or even a career, but corporate universities, it is often suggested, provide opportunities for individuals to ensure their own *employability* within and beyond the company. No longer will career development managers call people in once a year to remind them of the need to update or upgrade skills through training and development programmes – staff must be the masters of their own careers and they have access to the corporate university's programmes to achieve this. Our first exhibit, drawing on interviews within a British financial services company, shows how one organisation attempted to reconcile this 'hard' approach to people management with an existing structure of social responsibility.

Exhibit 1: Combining social values and commercial advantage

Setting up a corporate university is a public statement of the importance a company places on staff development and on professional standards. It is simultaneously a way of ensuring the company possesses the requisite know-how and of building a reputation for socially responsible employment. Thus, a corporate university is seen as one way of building employee commitment

---

[7] See, for example, accounts of the annual *Financial Times-Corporate University Xchange awards*, Available at: www.ft.com.

and making the company attractive to potential employees. It may also be used to develop relationships with customers. For example, in negotiating with an African government one oil company, highlighted (apparently to good effect) the way its corporate university would train local staff and ensure identical professional standards in its operations. The case presented here highlights the tensions between the twin strands of social values and commercial advantage that many corporate university are expected to integrate, in order to gain staff and customer commitment, and at the same time meet shareholder expectations – restructuring the HRM aspect of the company along the way.

> At an individual level, all of the senior personnel involved in the corporate university have strong social values, but I wouldn't want to overstate the case. We can see quite pragmatically that in a world where you have a commodity that looks similar to other commodities, you need to do something else to be able to create the differentiation – some of these differentiators could come from other areas. All that's fine as a kind of conceptual stuff, but of course you've got to pay for it – we are here to create value for the shareholders. Part of the very straightforward issue around creating value is that you've got to be able to get your cost base to a level where you can compete and create value and drive the share price up. One of the legacy costs that we're carrying is the costs in HR. In the past, the company has employed one member of HR staff for every 30 other staff, and a large part of the HR over-manning was in the training area. We had about one third of the HR staff employed in training in one way or other, designing, delivering or administering and running their own training functions. We had 26 training functions in the UK – 26 different training organisations or companies within the group.
>
> First of all, we created a brand and marketing around the corporate university – it's strong on principles, it's strong on values. When we set up the corporate university, we said that we're in the business of encouraging personal responsibility,

we will behave in a way that is adult, we wil challenge individuals around their learning, and we will be equally challenging of ourselves in the support. Structurally, as part of the establishment of the corporate university we created a number of faculties: on leadership, on customers, on technology, and on banking. They are our four faculties – we have deans of faculty, and in each case those people are members of the Group Executive Committee so they are significant players in their own right.

We need to have an infrastructure across the country, which means that the business case for learning development was to reduce the costs of training, and to facilitate a shift from classroom training to other forms of training. The corporate university laptops are part of the tangible manifestation of this... probably the greatest chunk of the investment has gone here. That and regional learning centres save hotel costs, so that's of benefit because we're spending less of the training budget on accommodation – the figure for this in our 2002 budget is many millions of pounds, so the corporate university is partly aimed at reducing that. The infrastructure obviously facilitates e-delivery, but that's quite a leap for people. The pressure for short-term results from the City [of London], particularly to reduce the cost base, creates huge pressures in the business for costs to be squeezed out, and yet things like the corporate university are longer term. To gain medium term benefits in a climate where you're trying to push the business cost as low as you can means that you've got to have quite a lot of resilience and quite a lot of patience, to believe that what you're doing is going to be the right thing in the long-term.

Director, Financial Services University

3.3 Knowledge Management

The second managerial discourse on which corporate university managers draw heavily is that of Knowledge Management (KM).

This has its origins in the claim that intellectual capital and other intangibles are critical assets of modern corporations.[8] KM has been especially well received in fast-moving science and technology based industries, where it is argued that success is achieved by companies that can draw on and integrate many different and often highly specialised or context-specific strands of expertise and experience to improve processes, tackle a new challenge, or avoid 're-inventing wheels'. Characteristically, however, such know-how or organisational knowledge is widely distributed, embedded in ways of working, and in important dimensions its significance may not even be recognised. KM, therefore, is a response to the perception that companies often have great difficulty in bringing to bear the knowledge they encompass, and that they need to do more to recognise it and make it an accessible resource. Hence the emergence of specialist KM consultancies, jobs with KM in their title, and postgraduate modules in business schools on KM concepts, approaches and issues.

As with HRM, there is doubt as to how much of what goes on in the name of KM is new, rather than a re-badging of familiar practices (such as information systems, libraries, professional networking, etc). Research indicates that much KM activity involves attempts to 'capture' and codify practice, or in other words to articulate explicitly knowledge that is more or less tacit, embedded and informal – a task that the first modern management movement, Scientific Management, sought to achieve in the early 20th century. Activities often involve the construction of databases where, for example, project documents are lodged, enabling employees to find out whether anyone else has faced similar problems. Less common but more sophisticated approaches recognise the social relations that are so important for processes of knowledge sharing and transfer, and try to foster 'communities of practice' across large companies.

---

[8] Scarbrough, H., Swan, J. and Preston, J. (1999) *Knowledge Management: A literature review*. London: Institute of Personnel and Development.

It is our belief that the knowledge production – research-oriented – activities of large companies may also be relevant in this context. In an influential analysis Michael Gibbons and colleagues[9] have argued that knowledge production has moved beyond the confines of the university and is now widespread in industry. A new form of knowledge creation has developed, 'Mode 2'. Traditional ('Mode 1') knowledge production, prominent in universities, is characterised by being largely discipline-based, separated from application, context-free and conducted and controlled through highly institutionalised processes. Mode 2 knowledge production has very different attributes:

- knowledge is produced in the context of application and is more contingent;
- research and the knowledge produced is transdisciplinary;
- research comes to conclusions more rapidly, is less institutionalised (i.e. it can take place on a range of sites), and is funded through diverse sources;
- quality control is achieved through diverse means, such as whether a solution to the driving problem is found, or whether the research and knowledge produced are cost effective.

As 'conventional' universities are based on the production, preservation and dissemination of knowledge, corporate universities would seem the natural location for the management or production of knowledge within work organisations. And indeed those involved often claim that knowledge management is a basic activity within their corporate universities. However, fewer refer to the production of new knowledge in the way that Gibbons and his colleagues write so persuasively about. Our research to date indicates that, with one possible exception in the business consultancy sector, formal research and development remains separate from corporate university operations, both physically (if the corporate university exists in a physical sense) and politically

---

[9] Gibbons, M. et al. (1994) *The New Production of Knowledge. The Dynamics of Science and Research*, London, Sage.

within the organisation. It remains to be seen whether this will continue to be the case, or whether in some industries at least, the corporate university will incorporate or be associated with certain R & D functions.

A secondary driver for investing in a corporate university is the rationalisation of relations with external suppliers and partners from the educational world – as one corporate university manager put it, training and development is the 'last great slush fund' through which just about anything could be funded. Senior directors perceive a need to manage the knowledge that comes into organisations through more formal relations with existing educational suppliers. The corporate university in one organisation studied was intended as a means of managing more than 100 individual contracts with educational suppliers and partners, many reliant on personal relations between individuals on both sides. We would suggest that this is potentially more significant for public universities than the production or management of knowledge – many large corporations have long established means of producing and managing knowledge, working in partnership with public universities. What may be changing is the nature of the client-supplier relationship that public universities have worked with since multinationals became significant customers. This dynamic is prominent in our second exhibit, an account from the director of a corporate university in the engineering sector in the UK.

Exhibit 2: The corporate university on the edge of the company: managing relevant learning

As strategic initiatives, corporate universities involve a degree of centralisation – their purpose is to ensure training and development are aligned with corporate goals and undertaken in ways that promote a common understanding between different business units. And yet standardisation and central control can easily be a recipe for local irrelevance. This case illustrates some of the challenges and tensions within a corporate university with a remit to examine and change practice within a corporation. The solution found by corporate university managers in this company rests on maintaining a distance from the corporate centre, while being careful not to become too marginal, and on being selective in their interventions.

The corporate university goes back to 1994 when the company was about to embark on a major corporate change program, and what really prompted that was poor perceptions in the market place and the City about our value and performance. We had a share crisis around that time and we were looking at the organization, recognizing its obvious strengths and recognizing its fragmentation. Best practice was unshared and remained where it resided. We had as many cultures and structures as we had business units, and there was a challenge to bring the organization together as a high performing company.

One of the principle actions in this change program was the establishment of a corporate university, charged with looking after the technology needs and the knowledge needs of the organization. It was launched in 1997 and comprised initially of a Benchmarking and Best Practice Faculty, an Engineering Faculty, a Learning and Development Faculty and a Business School to provide strategic level analysis. It's very much helping the organization, and as you can imagine the corporate university was devoted to the learning and development needs of the company, so we had a very tight relationship with where the company wanted to go from a strategy point of view. We were dealing with the strategy, the top level end of creating learning and developing opportunities for the business and the knowledge sharing, and other opportunities for the profits of the business. We were, and continue to be, a very small team, currently 19 people, facing off to 120,000 globally.

So, we work extensively through networks and preferred partners in the academic world. We do not manage or provide administration for people attending courses – we establish a framework of preferred partners, preferred courses, in keeping with our emphasis on engineering systems and managerial conferences, and the corporate university sets up the framework and partnerships, leaving the transactional side of learning provision to others. Our role is co-ordination more than anything.

We've invested heavily in applying knowledge management – how do you share best practice, a process that says, "I have a challenge in the business. How do I compare with world class or best of class companies? How do they achieve that performance? How might I adapt my practices to their practices in a way that's sensible to my business? And then how do I review the outcome? How do I share those lessons back into the organisation?" And we, I think, learnt the painful way about that process and what works and what doesn't work, because for many people sharing and learning should be the most natural thing in the world to do. We all do it as we grow from babies into adults, we learn continuously – those that nurture us teach us, but in organisations for some reason it doesn't work.

I think the corporate university has to be careful because we have finite resource – our first responsibility is to deliver value internal to the organisation. The second priority then is to our joint ventures, our customers and our suppliers. We find that we often talk to our joint venture partners about what we do, they find it very interesting, they like what we do, but for some reason they find it difficult politically to engage with us, because those that lead those businesses like to have their autonomy. To tie it too closely to us, in terms of infrastructure, strategy and methodology, would be uncomfortable.

The philosophy that we have is based on the idea that, although you need a building to physically locate people, we have always been a virtual concept, so if there are physical buildings that people need to go to have training, than it will be done remotely through third parties. The rationale – and it's probably obvious – is that we're not going to be good at everything. There are people that are well established, in traditional universities, or for example as Outward Bound trainers, in niches out there that are very specialised, who are very expert at what they do. The primary importance for us is to create a learning and development strategy that's right for the company and then we can deploy that strategy with our partners who do what they do.

Director, Engineering University

3.4 Learning Organisations

Finally, and perhaps most relevant to corporate university discourse, is the increased emphasis within management and business circles around the notion of learning. As long ago as the1950s, the founders of action learning claimed that for any organisation in a competitive environment to survive, the rate of learning within the corporation must exceed the rate of change in the environment. Learning took on a heightened, almost talismanic importance within the corporate context however with the publication of various theories of organisational learning and the Learning Organisation (LO) in the early 1990s.[10] Definitions of and recommendations to accomplish an LO are many and varied, but there are several recurring themes. First is the notion that LOs exist in a permanent state of transformation and change, in contrast to the fixed bureaucratic organisation of early 20th century accounts of organisation. Second comes the need for systems thinking, to see the interconnectedness of a 'bigger picture' and to avoid learning the wrong, parochial lessons. Finally,

---

[10] See especially Senge, P. (1993) *The Fifth Discipline: The art and practice of the learning organisation.* London: Century Business; Marquardt, M. and Reynolds, A. (1994) *The Global Learning Organisation* Irwin: Burr Ridge, Illinois.

LOs encourage learning by individuals and teams throughout an organisation.

This discourse, too, is open to criticism, particularly when we consider the power relations within large corporations and the idealistic nature of an LO as set out by its proponents (see Exhibit 2). The understanding of learning, and in particular the potential that a corporate university provides for employees to critically reflect within a transnational corporation (whether on the nature of current practices and procedures in the company or on a more personal level), appears to us to be circumscribed by the social and cultural location of the initiative. Nevertheless, the notion of the LO is pervasive and forms a backdrop for much managerial activity in training and development. Corporate university publicity has, unsurprisingly, adopted the discourse enthusiastically. The accounts in Exhibits 1 and 2 drew on a learning perspective in passing, and Exhibit 3, below, makes more explicit use of it.

3.5 The Precariousness of Corporate Universities

As noted above, being located within a profit-making organisation brings very particular pressures and tensions to learning, the management of learning, and the management of learning initiatives. Given also the pace of change in corporate structures and processes, it is unsurprising that the contribution and approach of corporate universities may be reviewed and adjusted every few years – and that some fail to secure a viable niche in the ecology of corporate life, as Exhibit 3 illustrates. The account indicates some of the tensions and issues that we believe are unique to corporate universities as educational initiatives. In order to piece together the life of 'Utility University', one of the best known British corporate universities, we have had to find and interview a number of managers who have left the company, retiring or moving on to new posts elsewhere. In addition, the university no longer exists in any sense within the organisation except 'in fragments, in people's heads', as one manager put it.

Hence those dealing with a corporate university from outside the corporation need to remember that such initiatives are an attempt on the part of senior managers to cope with rapid change, inside companies and in trading environments, and these initiatives are subject to those same changes and rates of change. Corporate university development can resemble time-lapse photography – it appears as if a flower is opening with incredible rapidity when a structure is set up within three years to manage training and development for more than 100,000 people. However, as the exhibit indicates, corporate universities can also wither and ultimately disappear equally rapidly. By comparison with public universities they are likely to resemble provisional arrangements lacking institutional qualities. This may not however be an accurate reflection of corporate university activity, as we shall argue in the final section of this report.

Exhibit 3: Virtual existence and real sponsors

In this exhibit, we follow the progress of a corporate university initiative from initial idea to disappearance, after the sponsor within the organisation leaves the company. For this corporate university head, it is clear that a corporate university needs a 'real' and tangible existence to become embedded in the organisation, and that reliance on language and representation is not enough to ensure corporate university life.

> Not long after privatisation we understood that we needed to be different – we'd become a well-organised company with a commercial view, but we knew that we were going to be under pressure. There was a view that we ought to be changing the very soul of the company, and we came up with the idea that we ought to have a university, a Corporate University. What could be better than a university, which was all about knowledge and learning and experience. The CEO went off to Harvard University and he came backfired up with the idea that we had to change the company, fired up with

the idea of a Corporate University. I was saying [to him] 'I've got a vision and I want you to sign up to the vision – just do it with your heart and we'll sort out the details afterwards', but now I think the trick is to just get enough detail sorted out up front to reassure the 'mechanics'. We knew it was a grand vision, but we were struggling with what the idea meant – we recognised that there was something important to do in terms of knowledge management, but there were people who were thought that it was all airy-fairy stuff that the employees wouldn't understand. In the end, we went ahead and organised the corporate university into four core capabilities, and had a very senior person in the organisation heading up each of the core faculties of the university. We had [Jim Smith] as the first faculty head – we gave him the mortarboard and gown and we had a celebration in the company!

We began to think of doing a variety of things, beginning to get more people involved – we went into this period and I really steamed ahead with all of it. I began to see things and introduced a whole variety of new ideas. There were issues around whether we could allow other people to share, would we allow other companies to share in it – we never got to the bottom of, and I still haven't made up my mind about it, as the corporate university was very much giving our company an advantage. It was also about being focused on our people, customers and employees, but at the end of the day it was about making a better company and it's a competitive world. We shared our ideas with everyone about what we were doing, but we didn't get to the point of allowing somebody from a competitor to join in with our master-classes. You'd have to think carefully about it – does BP allow Shell people to come into their classes? Why should you give away your intellectual advantage to other people?

Towards the end, there was no-one left to argue passionately in the organisation for all of this. We went from being a very high profile organisation globally because of the corporate university and it's just withered – they've regressed from the learning organisation back to conventional training programmes. People forgot that if you invest in all these wonderful ideas it enables the organisation to cut costs, cut people, improve and expand services and change. But you make all this investment in R&D and innovation and knowledge creation, then the investment is withdrawn because people can't see... the argument is always 'show me what benefit it's going to be next year', and you can't. You can't connect the success of downsizing with a corporate university – there isn't an 'a leads to b'.

Did we have any problems? Yes, of course. First of all, we said initially that we wanted everyone to be a student of the corporate university, and that everyone had to do something, but the first problem we had was the director of finance, who refused to participate. Second, if we could have produced the structure of the corporate university much earlier, senior people would have been engaged earlier, so that when I left it would have been harder for it to fail. We took so long – it took five years to get all the structures, mechanisms and models worked out, the way in which the open learning centres would link in and the best practice teams migrating knowledge throughout the organization, all of this stuff, the development of the intranet. But a corporate university depends so much on the personalities of individuals.

Director, Utility University

4 Corporate Universities – The Variety of Strategic Intent and Practice

Finally, there is a dilemma in that we need to stand slightly outside the company to take a view of it and understand what it needs – but we can't become too distant or detached, because our ability then to deliver operational related value will diminish. Our ability then to differentiate ourselves from any other third party, or learning and development supplier, will diminish, so there is a fine balance to be struck. Although we stand slightly outside of the business, it's imperative to move with the business.

Director, Engineering University

4.1 Introduction

It is becoming clear, through description and analysis of corporate university initiatives, that a corporate university can take a wide variety of forms, some more relevant to higher education than others. This section tries to map that variety and to identify the main trends in the practice of corporate university management. We suggest that it is useful to think of corporate universities as varying on two key dimensions. The first concerns the nature of the learning: this axis ranges from a narrow training focus (imparting information, developing specific vocational skills), through broader forms of education and professional development (including a socialisation into organisational values and practices), and finally on to those that encompass forms of research as well as advanced teaching and learning.

The second dimension concerns the spatial organisation of the corporate university – whether it is focussed on a specific facility or network of learning centres (the campus model), or whether it is primarily 'virtual', delivering training and learning through electronic media. We are able to combine these two dimensions (see Figure 1 below), and to highlight four different types of corporate university. In reading this diagram, it should be borne in mind that such 'types' are of course simplifications – real organisations are messier and more dynamic than this.

The most familiar type represented here is the classic company training school or college. Many of these have been upgraded recently in various ways to raise the status and profile of training

Figure 1 A Tentative Typology of Corporate Universities Along Two Axes

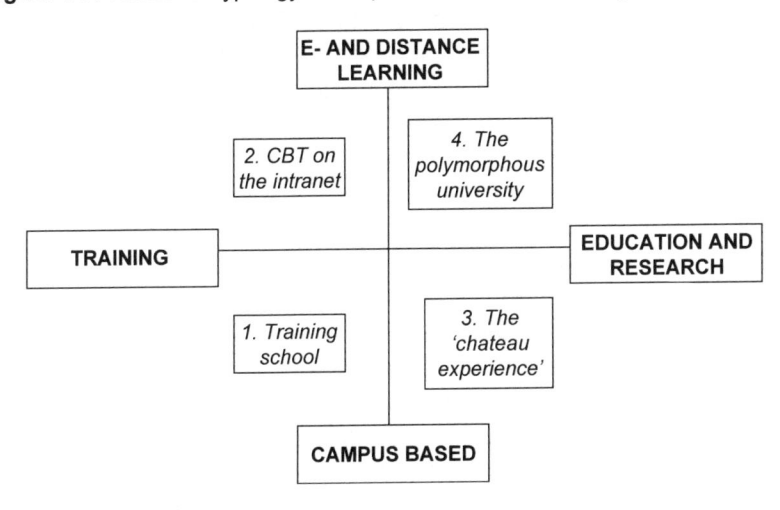

```
                    E- AND DISTANCE
                       LEARNING
                           |
           ┌───────────┐   |   ┌──────────────┐
           │  2. CBT on│   |   │   4. The     │
           │the intranet│  |   │ polymorphous │
           └───────────┘   |   │  university  │
                           |   └──────────────┘
  ┌──────────┐             |             ┌──────────────┐
  │ TRAINING │─────────────┼─────────────│ EDUCATION AND│
  └──────────┘             |             │   RESEARCH   │
                           |             └──────────────┘
           ┌───────────┐   |   ┌──────────────┐
           │1. Training│   |   │   3. The     │
           │  school   │   |   │  'chateau    │
           └───────────┘   |   │  experience' │
                           |   └──────────────┘
                           |
                    ┌──────────────┐
                    │ CAMPUS BASED │
                    └──────────────┘
```

both inside and outside the organisation – McDonalds Hamburger U can be seen as an exemplar of this type of corporate university. They focus on delivering the skills needed for consistency, quality and efficiency in core operations. Such initiatives are often represented as compensating for the shortcomings of secondary educational systems, as at one of the original corporate universities, Motorola U.

The second type of corporate university – best described as 'Computer-Based Training (CBT) on the Intranet' – is much more recent, but has been the focus for very considerable investment in particular industries and contexts, and provides the basis for much popular press coverage of corporate university initiatives. The reason for investment in this type of corporate university is obvious: whenever large numbers of staff have to be regularly re-trained (to use new software tools, for example, or to comply with new legislation), or updated (for example, on the features and terms of the latest products they sell), the costs of providing such training on a face-to-face basis have been considerable.

Hence, by switching to electronically delivered training companies may save enormously on staff travel and accommodation costs, particularly when they are internationally distributed. Managers have also found it easier to provide the training consistently, in a timely manner, and with less disruption to work schedules (sometimes because training takes place outside work time). Debate may continue over the scope for this method of delivery in the longer term – whether and how far it can be used for 'softer' topics less amenable to right and wrong answers; how far it can develop beyond its pedagogic origins in programmed learning. Nevertheless, that there are important contexts in which it can be highly cost-effective is no longer in question. The Shell Open University is an example both of reducing training spend and of a highly distributed organisation that needs to pass on information quickly, as a manager involved in our research has outlined; a second is Unipart, where (it is said) you can learn in the morning and apply it in the afternoon – not least because there is a dedicated PC on every shopfloor that links to the Unipart U.[11]

The third type of corporate university – designated the 'chateau' or 'country house' experience – was also a familiar feature of the corporate landscape before corporate universities became common. Management, leadership and executive development has traditionally taken place in well-appointed rural locations away from the headquarters, but in recent years such initiatives have had a renaissance. They are now seen as one way of addressing a major corporate challenge – how to promote cohesion across highly differentiated international businesses, especially those that have often grown through acquisition and merger. The importance, and the difficulty, of building a common understanding and effective management teams out of diverse national and corporate cultures cannot be over-stated. The reinvention of the management college

---

[11] For details see Unipart Group of Companies, *The Learning Organisation*. Available at: www.ugc.co.uk/learning/lea_0100.htm. Last Accessed 22 April 2004.

as the incubator of a shared corporate culture, through intense face-to-face development activities and the creation of cross-organisational networks, may then be a result of the increased frequency of multinational mergers. Being semi-detached from the pace and pressure of mainstream corporate life, such facilities may also provide a social space where the normal codes are, to a degree, relaxed, and assumptions can be questioned. To this extent they may also have a role as corporate 'think tanks', where senior figures or rising stars can take time out to analyse, debate and think through emerging challenges, in relation both to internal issues faced by the organisation, and wider concerns over, for example, the natural environment or the location of production. Examples of this sort of corporate university are the Rüschlikon facility in Switzerland owned by Swiss Re and Boeing's Leadership Development Center[12] in the US.

Finally, there is what we call the polymorphous corporate university. This may embrace a wide range of learning (that is, technical and professional as well as business management), supported in diverse ways (combining e-learning with face-to-face elements, mentoring, action learning, placements, and so on). However, it is also polymorphous in the sense that the form and focus are likely to change quite frequently, in response to shifting perceptions of strategic priorities (re-structuring being a normal rather than an exceptional occurrence in corporate life). The corporate university of Cap Gemini Ernst & Young has several of these features, having played different roles at different points in the twelve years of its existence. While the chateau campus near Paris remains the heart of the corporate university, the corporate university staff is distributed around the world. Increasing use is made of e- and blended learning, and professional updating in a very fast-moving industry is provided through an on-line magazine. Great emphasis is also given to fostering communities and

---

[12] See Boeing, *Boeing Leadership Center Website*. Available at: www.boeing.com/companyoffices/aboutus/leadershipcenter. Last Accessed 22 April 2004.

networks among the different sorts of professionals that work in the company.

4.2 Trends in Corporate University Development

We end this section by offering some observations on the future of corporate universities – even if, for all the reasons already discussed, confident claims would be foolhardy. We would not be surprised if in a few years the upsurge in use of academic labels, such as university, subsides, perhaps being superseded by a different organising aspiration. We *would* be surprised, however, if corporations ceased to be concerned with the underlying issues of corporate university activity, and no longer promoted strategic learning initiatives of different sorts to address them. Cultivating and combining diverse, specialised expertise looks set to remain a fundamental challenge for business. To be economically productive, such expertise cannot be detached and abstracted; it must be or quickly become highly contextualised, both as regards specific features of the situations in which it is applied, and in terms of the social codes and priorities of the organisational setting. Hence, the drive by large corporations to exercise a far higher degree of influence over learning processes is about seeking the greatest value for money in relation to their particular operating circumstances and strategies. How consistently, with what priority, and in what ways particular companies address this concern will doubtless continue to vary, but it is a concern that is unlikely to fade to any great extent – if only because the sums involved are so considerable.

Moreover, these challenges also arise in the public sector. In the UK, initiatives such as the National Health Service University, alongside the revision of longer established colleges for police forces and the military, indicate that corporate universities already exist beyond the corporate sector, and are expanding. Indeed, a corporate university approach may offer particular attractions to governments that are impatient with the slow pace of change in reforming professional education, or are keen to develop new styles of management and leadership in the highly institutionalised settings of public service.

Further, if there is an underlying trend in the shape of such initiatives, it may be from the 'classical' to the 'polymorphous'. This suggestion rests largely on expectations about the development of ICT applications for learning. Corporate universities that focus largely on 'CBT on the Intranet' or 'the chateau experience' may well be transitional forms as ICT applications evolve to provide richer media for the support of virtual communities and pedagogically more sophisticated forms of e-learning. Further, these may then be blended with other modes of professional development (under the banner of 'technology-enhanced learning').

This brief treatment of the potential futures for corporate university development leads us to the final section of this report, where we deal in more depth with three aspects of corporate university-public education interaction-coexistence, competition and collaboration.

5 Competition, Co-existence and Collaboration[13]

Notwithstanding the many differences between corporate universities and public universities that we have set out in this report, there still appears to be significant resistance from within academic communities to the idea of a corporate university, and fear as to whether these new initiatives will threaten established educational institutions. This section considers the impact of corporate universities on the wider institutional field of higher education in terms of three ways in which they may relate to public universities – as self-contained, co-existent entities, as competitors, and as collaborators.

---

[13] This section draws on and seeks to extend the work of Eddie Blass at Derbyshire Business School (University of Derby). Details of her work can be found in the references at the end of the report.

5.1 Coexistence

Public universities are uniquely differentiated in many ways: often operating in protected markets with limited competition, providing a service or product that cannot be replicated either in terms of content or outcome, valued societally for the provision of critical thought and independence to individuals both in terms of teaching and learning. Socially, they provide formative experiences and rites of passage in the transition to adulthood for many young people, and furnish them with social networks that are often important thereafter. Clearly, these contributions are not about to be swept away by corporate universities. Pre-vocational and liberal arts higher education, in particular, may feel little impact from the development of the corporate university phenomena, especially in countries where degree awarding powers are tightly controlled.

5.2 Competition

Where universities are engaged in various forms of professional development and already count corporate-sponsored students among their customers, there is clearly scope for competition. Some corporate universities (such as ABN-Amro in the Netherlands and the Tennessee Valley Authority in the USA) are extending their offerings to stakeholders such as customers and suppliers, and in the US some have been 'spun off' as subsidiary companies. For example, the Arthur D. Little School of Management in the USA began life in 1964 as the training arm of the Arthur D. Little consulting firm, became an independent not-for-profit organisation in 1997 with an open recruitment policy, but maintained close ties with the parent company. The School is the only corporate university known to have regional accreditation in the United States. Arthur D. Little itself is currently in Chapter 11 bankruptcy protection and in the midst of being split up and sold, but the School is affected only insofar as its associated companies will be under new ownership. In other countries, such as India and Canada, consortia of private companies have sponsored the creation of private higher education initiatives in order to obtain more of the skilled personnel they require; these may not be corporate universities in a precise sense, but they are another form of hybrid institution. A further form competition could take is the effective relocation of areas of higher education from public universities to newly formed corporate universities serving industries like health, education and welfare in the public sector. At this point it is impossible to anticipate how such rivalries will unfold — not least because much depends on the responsiveness of public universities, and their willingness to engage with corporate customers and to provide contextualized programs. This brings us to the third possibility, collaboration.

5.3 Collaboration

Collaboration in this context will primarily be a matter of working with corporate customers. We noted earlier that attempts to rationalize the sourcing of services from universities and other educational providers is a common feature of corporate university initiatives. Characteristically, decisions that had been made independently at lower levels within separate business units are dealt with at corporate level in order to achieve a notion of improved quality or return on investment (e.g., strategic fit, a common vocabulary across the organization, economies of scale). At the same time, many corporate universities have built up their own capacities for the in-house provision of management and leadership development, often buying in the best available expertise from universities and consultancies on an ad-hoc basis. In consequence, these training and development activities have become increasingly sophisticated. The training manager of yore may have been easily impressed by academic staff, but the head of a corporate university, often an academic by training, will run a much more critical eye over who and what is proposed (and may anyway only be interested in cherry-picking academic stars as occasional contributors to the corporate university's programs). The implications of these two trends do seem fairly clear: corporate universities are likely to be more informed and demanding customers of university programs.

Patterns of collaboration are also likely to reflect the trend towards distance learning in its various forms. Consistent messages and vocabularies are important in developing common understandings across nationally and internationally dispersed companies, and distance learning offers cost-effective ways of working towards such standardisation. Hence, some corporate universities choose to collaborate with universities having expertise in e- and distance learning, and when they do so, the size of the contracts involved are correspondingly great. The experience of the Open University with the COROUS initiative (www.corous.com) and the number of e-learning suppliers around the world (such as Cardean University-www.cardean.com) indicates that large corporations are willing to work with credible collaborators, if the universities can engage with client needs.

This brings us to the final point that this report seeks to make. Co-operation between public universities and other societal institutions is a difficult and complex process, as the many accounts of research funded by commercial companies emphasise.[14] Negotiation of, for example, publication rights for scientific knowledge produced, or curriculum content in management courses, can be problematic, and may even result in the quiet death of a project if there is no consensus. However, if corporate universities are *not* to become competitors, and if collaboration is not to be forced on the educational sector by state regulation, it may be that some voluntary co-operation on the part of public universities can provide a middle ground. Universities have rarely been isolated from the

---

[14] Aronowitz, S. (2000) *The Knowledge Factory: Dismantling the corporate university and creating true higher learning.* Boston: Beacon Press; Buchbinder, H. (1993) 'The market-oriented university and the changing role of knowledge'. *Higher Education*, 26: 331–347; Marginson, S. and Considine, M. (2000) *The Enterprise University: Power, governance and reinvention in Australia.* Cambridge: Cambridge University Press.

societies that they reflect, serve, and are protected by;[15] corporate universities are becoming an established part of these societies. To deny this, and to refuse to engage with them and the people running them, would be at best short-sighted, and at worst potentially damaging.

6 Conclusion

For at least a century centres of higher learning in Europe have been subject to one cultural expectation that is stronger than any other – a degree of distance from other societal institutions. This has been conceptualized in a number of ways: sometimes through the notion of academic freedom, sometimes by reference to the 'ivory tower' cliché of working life in universities, and sometimes, indeed, by universities themselves seeking limited 'engagement'. However, the constant underlying these various perspectives is that universities are a milieu apart, whether spatially, structurally, or culturally. We would suggest that corporate universities have the potential to change this understanding, and also the practice of how public universities and multinationals interact.

As we outlined in the first two sections, the corporate sector and publicly owned work organizations are much more than just key clients for business schools-infrastructure support, research funding, sponsorship for chairs, and research access are all aspects of the industry – university dynamic. Corporate universities, by blurring the boundaries between education and business further than before (and in new ways), have the potential to impact on all of these areas of interaction. It appears at the time of writing that corporate universities may provide impetus towards the re-definition of institutional conditions that universities work within.

However, the processes of structural change can be seen, when looking at corporate universities conceptually, as part of a dynamic

---

[15] Derrida, J. (1983) 'The principle of reason: The university in the eyes of its pupils'. *Diacritics*, 13(3): 3–21.

historical tradition, rather than as a temporally isolated initiative. Thus, we can trace the development of corporate schools and universities through distinct periods of focus since the earliest initiatives. As Eurich demonstrates, the first corporate educational initiatives of the 19th century concentrated on providing job-related skills training as the state was too slow to develop appropriate learning opportunities. This phase can be seen as providing an alternative (almost in opposition) to state provision, in which corporate aims were the primary goal.

The second phase is defined by a complimentarity in the two systems. Wiggenhorn, for example, emphasizes how Motorola U (founded in the 1970s) focused on providing skills that had not been fully assimilated during compulsory state education, such as basic literacy or numeracy. In this phase, nascent corporate university and schools operated in a way that emphasized adding to state education, rather than providing an alternative. The third phase may be seen in the development of training and enculturation 'boot camps', as initiatives such as GE's Crotonville establishment have been termed.[16] These institutions – what we have referred to as the chateau experience – are best seen primarily as a means of bringing the individual employee into close contact with the corporate practices and value systems of organizations with very strong 'cultures of control'. They bear little relation to the public education system, and can operate in isolation from it.

The fourth and present phase, we would suggest, is the current one. Contemporary corporate universities, and particularly those that have appeared in the last five years, emphasize two aspects of managing people. First, much of the promotional discourse revolves around the need for large companies to aspire to become learning organizations in order to achieve and maintain competitive advantage. Second, and related to this first area, many accounts of managing corporate universities refer to a perceived need to

---

[16] For an account of this initiative from an academic seconded to a corporate university see Tichy, N. (2001) 'No Ordinary Boot Camp', *Harvard Business Review*, April: 63–70.

manage knowledge. The close relations with existing educational providers, the focus on theories of individual and organizational learning, and the potential to operate as centres of Mode 2 knowledge production, all indicate that contemporary corporate universities are a significant innovation in organizational practice within a wider societal context.

Further Reading

Selection of Corporate University Websites (some within the body of the report):

McDonald's Hamburger U: www.mcdonalds.com/corporate/careers/hambuniv/index.html
The Disney Institute: http://disney.go.com/vacations/websites/disneyinstitute/
Barclays University: www.barclays-university.com/
Motorola U: http://mu.motorola.com/
The BT Academy: www.groupbt.com/society/education/btacademy/index.htm
BAe Systems Virtual University: www.baesystems.com/virtualuniversity/virtualuniversity.htm
Cap Gemini Ernst & Young University: www.cgey.com/U/index.shtml
Tennessee Valley Authority University: www.tva.gov/tvau/index.htm
Clearly, there are many others; on this short list are some of the better known and longer established with websites that are either open or informative.

Management and Business Oriented Analyses of Corporate Universities:

Blass, E. (2001) 'What's in a Name? A comparative study of the traditional public university and the corporate university' *Human Resource Development International*, 4(2): 153–173.

Blass, E. (2002) 'Corporate and Conventional Universities: Competition or collaboration?' in Williams, G. (ed) *The Enterprising University*. Buckingham: Society for Research in Higher Education and Open University Press.

Craig, R., Clarke, F. and Amernic, J. (1999) 'Scholarship in University Business Schools: Cardinal Newman, creeping corporatism and farewell to the disturber of the peace?' *Accounting, Auditing and Accountabiulity Journal*, 12(5): 510–524.

Prince, C. and Beaver, G. (2001) 'The Rise and Rise of the Corporate University: The emerging corporate learning agenda' *The International Journal of Management Education* 1(3): 17–26.

Taylor, S and T. Phillips (2002) *The Corporate University Challenge: Corporate Competitiveness, Learning and Knowledge,* Brussels: The European Foundation for Management Development and Milton Keynes: The Open University Business School

Educational Analyses of Corporate University:

Aronowitz, S. (2000) *The Knowledge Factory: Dismantling the corporate university and creating true higher learning.* Boston: Beacon Press.

Davies, C. (2002) 'The Potential of the NHS University: Tracing the emergence of an idea' *Paper presented to the Lifelong Learning in the NHS Conference, London.*

Eurich, N. (1985) *Corporate Classrooms: The learning business.* Princeton, NJ: The Carnegie Foundation for the Advancement of Teaching.

Hawthorne, E., Libby, P. and Nash, N. (1983) 'The Emergence of Corporate Colleges' *Journal of Continuing Higher Education,* Fall: 2–9.

MacFarlane, B. (2000) 'Inside the Corporate Classroom' *Teaching in Higher Education* 5(1): 51–60.

Paton, R. and Taylor, S. (2002) 'Corporate Universities: Between higher education and the workplace', in Williams, G. (ed) *The Enterprising University.* Buckingham: Society for Research in Higher Education and Open University Press.

Pietrykowski, B. (2001) 'Information Technology and Commercialization of Knowledge: Corporate universities and class dynamics in an era of technological restructuring' *Journal of Economic Issues* 35(2): 299–306.

Selected Practitioner Accounts of Corporate University Practice:

Bruch, H. and Sattelberger, T. (2001) 'Lufthansa's Transformation Marathon: Process of liberating and focusing change energy' *Human Resource Management* 40(3): 249–259.

Ellis, S. (1998) 'Buckman Laboratories Learning Center' *Journal of Knowledge Management* 1(3): 189–196.

Galagan, P. (2001) 'Mission e-possible: The Cisco e-learning story' *Training and Development* February: 46–56.

Matthews, P. (1997) 'Aqua Universitas' *Journal of Knowledge Management* 1(2): 105–112.

Meister, J. (1994/1998) *Corporate Universities: Lessons in building a world class workforce.* New York: McGraw Hill. See also www.corpu.com. An informed review of the 1998 edition of Meister's book can be available at www.educause.edu/ir/library/html/erm9857.html.

Miller, R., Stewart, J. and Walton, J. (1999) 'Opened University' *People Management* 17th June: 42–46.

Moore, T. (1997) 'The Corporate University: Transforming management education' *Accounting Horizons* 11(1): 77–85.
Tichy, N. (2001) 'No Ordinary Boot Camp', *Harvard Business Review*, April: 63–70.
Wiggenhorn, W. (1990) 'Motorola U: When training becomes an education'. *Harvard Business Review*, July–August: 71–83.

Additional References

Buchbinder, H. (1993) 'The market-oriented university and the changing role of knowledge'. *Higher Education*, 26: 331–347.
Calas, M. and Smircich, L. (2001) 'Introduction: Does the house of knowledge have a future?'. *Organisation*, 8(2): 147–148.
Derrida, J. (1983) 'The principle of reason: The university in the eyes of its pupils'. *Diacritics*, 13(3): 3–21.
Gibbons, M. et al. (1994) The New Production of Knowledge. The Dynamics of Science and Research, London, Sage.
Marginson, S. and Considine, M. (2000) *The Enterprise University: Power, governance and reinvention in Australia*. Cambridge: Cambridge University Press.
Marquardt, M. and Reynolds, A. (1994) *The Global Learning Organisation* Irwin: Burr Ridge, Illinois.
Scarbrough, H., Swan, J. and Preston, J. (1999) *Knowledge Management: A literature review*. London: Institute of Personnel and Development.
Senge, P. (1993) *The Fifth Discipline: The art and practice of the learning organisation*. London: Century Business.
Tight, M. (1988) 'So what is academic freedom?', in Tight, M. (ed.) *Academic Freedom and Responsibility*, pp.114-132. Milton Keynes: Open University Press.

In addition, a number of US doctoral dissertations have examined individual programmes and relations between corporations and universities in partnership, providing detailed accounts of the potential dangers and rewards of collaboration:

Bober, C. (2000) *Utilization of Corporate University Training Program Evaluation*. University of Illinois at Urbana-Champaign.
Colgan, A. (1989) *Continuing Professional Education: A study of collaborative relationships in engineering between universities and corporations*. University of Illinois at Urbana-Champaign.

Del Monico, K. (1993) *Report of an Academic Partnership with GE Capital and Sacred Heart University.* Columbia University Teachers College.

Patterson, T. (1998) *Corporate Education and Training for Adult Learners: A comparative study of two corporate education models.* University of California, Davis.

Vernon, T. (1999) *The Techno-MBA: One alternative for knowledge workers.* University of Pennsylvania.

Mapping the Education Industry, Part 1: *public companies – share price and financial results*

Richard Garrett

Abstract: The Observatory has brought together a unique collection of international share price and financial data on public companies with interests in the broad area of postsecondary education. The main finding is the relative success of 'bricks and mortar' firms compared to collapsed share prices and widespread losses among e-learning and related companies. However, the data also suggests that on average e-learning and related firms are edging closer to profitability. The methodology reported in this paper will be used by the Observatory to support future trend analysis.

1 Introduction

An important feature of borderless higher education is the rise of commercial companies that either offer higher education programmes directly to students, or provide a range of teaching and learning-related services to 'conventional' universities and colleges and/or other organisations. To date, the characteristics of these firms have been poorly documented, particularly outside the United States. This briefing note is the first in a series that will work toward creating a more clearly defined map of this 'education industry', collating information on the activities and financial position of selected firms, and exploring their relationships with 'conventional' universities and colleges. This data will enable a more informed assessment of the stability and viability of these companies, and improve understanding of shifting roles and responsibilities between the public and private sectors for the delivery of higher education in the 21st century. The Observatory aims to collect this data on an ongoing basis to provide a unique longitudinal picture of developments.

The present text, part one in the series, concentrates on selected public education companies, that is, companies traded on stock markets around the world. The initial focus is analysis of stock price and financial results. Part two will discuss emerging relationships with 'conventional' universities and colleges.

2 Methodology

It is not straightforward to identify public education companies internationally. 'Education' rarely features in the industry classification models employed by national exchanges. Companies operating in the broad area of 'education and training' are typically scattered across standard industry categories such as 'Support Services', 'Diversified Services', 'Computer Software & Services' and 'Media'. The problem is particularly acute outside the United States. Companies with diverse portfolios that include education as a minority interest, may be found in such unexpected places as 'Motion Picture Producers and Distributors' and 'Diversified Textiles'.

For initial analysis, the Observatory identified fifty publicly-traded education companies, quoted on eleven exchanges and with headquarters in ten countries. About half (26) are from United States, reflecting the concentration of activity in that country, and the remainder (24) are from other countries, including Canada, India, Singapore and the UK. The companies range from firms operating for-profit universities (e.g. Apollo Group, DeVry), companies that run multi-campus colleges internationally (e.g. INTI Universal Holdings, Raffles La Salle International), IT training companies entering the higher education arena (e.g. Informatics, NIIT), e-learning firms (e.g. SkillSoft, Epic Group) and multinational publishing houses (e.g. Thomson, Pearson). The selection was designed to encompass the broad range of borderless higher education (e.g. e-learning, for-profit universities, corporate development, transnational delivery), and while acknowledging the concentration of activities in the United States, also recognising developments elsewhere. The selection encompasses a continuum between very large and very small firms. Given identification difficulties noted above, the selection is also pragmatic. The Observatory is not aware of any comprehensive directory of public education companies worldwide. The selection consists of companies well-known to the Observatory, plus others identified through initial research. The list may be added to/ revised as and when other relevant companies come to light. Annex A contains a list of the fifty companies. The Observatory would be very interested to receive information on additional companies, particularly those operating in continental Europe, South America and China. The next sections contain analysis of share price and financial results.

3 Share Price

In terms of third party analysis, pubic companies offer certain advantages. Share price offers an indication of perceived commercial viability, success and prospects. As a condition of public status, companies are obliged to regularly disclose detailed financial results. Using historical share price data, the Observatory created a 'Global Education Index' (GEI) to chart the progress of selected companies over time. (Financial results are detailed in the next section). An index provides a statistical measure of changes in the value of a portfolio of stocks that represent a portion of a particular market. The Dow Jones Industrial Average (DJIA) and the Standard & Poor's 500 are two well-known examples.

With the DJIA the most notable exception, most contemporary indices track market capitalisation (obtained by multiplying share price and shares outstanding). This is to avoid stock split distortion- that is, where a company increases or decreases the number of shares per shareholder in order to artificially decrease or increase their stock price. However, for the present at least, the Observatory has chosen to use stock price alone for the GEI. This is partly because it is not generally possible to obtain detailed historical market capitalisation data, but also because the purpose of the GEI is different from the majority of its counterparts. The aim is not to guide investors in education companies, but rather to offer a more broadly-based indication of perceived value over time. This study has a more diverse audience, and thus information on shares outstanding and market capitalisation is of less interest. To avoid distortion, every effort has been made to use share price data adjusted for stock splits.

The GEI tracks share prices from January 1993, providing a ten year perspective on the companies concerned. It was important to begin the Index prior to the so-called 'e-education bubble' of 1997 to early 2000.[1] This period saw greatly inflated stock prices across many companies in the GEI as part of the 'dotcom bubble'. Indeed, many GEI companies went public during this period. Analysis of pre-1997 prices as well as the situation after the dotcom crash provided a

---

[1] Ryan, Y. (2002) *Emerging Indicators of Success & Failure in Borderless Higher Education,* Observatory on Borderless Higher Education, February, p2. Available to subscribers at: www.obhe.ac.uk.

more rounded view. The GEI is not a measure of absolute share price, but of relative movement from the base period (January 1993). Closing prices were tracked on a weekly basis, beginning 4th January 1993. All non-US prices were converted to US dollars. In rare cases where share price information was not available for particular companies for certain periods of time, the immediate subsequent available price was used as a proxy. Given that many companies went public since January 1993, the index divisor was recalculated upon the entry of each company to neutralise the addition of the opening price. Thus it must be emphasised that the figures below concern relative movement not absolute share price. Three South African public education companies were identified, but the absence of historical share price data meant they could not be included in the Index. The companies will be added to the Index following this analysis.

Chart 1 compares the ten year trajectory of the GEI with the Standard & Poor's 500 (an index of 500 large US companies across a range of industries) and the NASDAQ Composite Index (an index of primarily new technology stocks). Many of the US firms in the GEI are traded on the NASDAQ.

Chart 1 GEI, S & P 500 and NASDAQ Composite 1993–2002

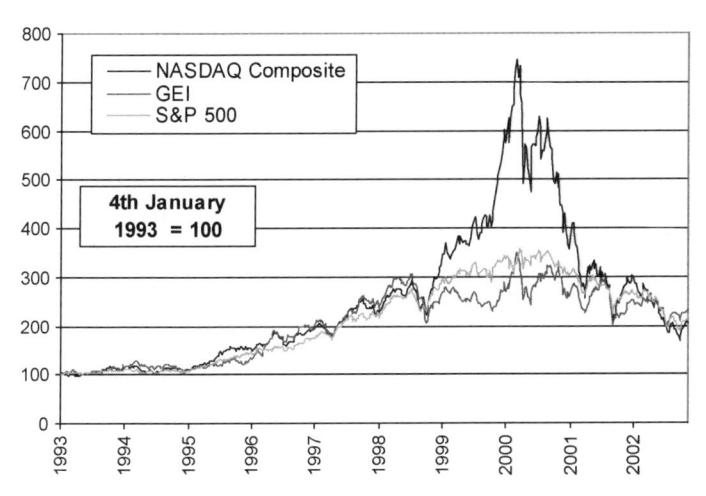

Chart 1 shows that the relative stock price growth of the education companies surveyed here kept pace with the comparator indices between 1993 and 1998 but then lost ground, particularly against the NASDAQ composite, during 1999 and 2000. The three coincided once more in 2001, with the GEI edging ahead towards the end of 2002. Overall, following wider trends, the relative stock price of the education companies more than tripled between 1993 and early 2000, before slipping back following the dotcom crash of April 2000. When the education companies are split by country (US and non-US) and by type (e.g. e-learning, bricks and mortar, IT training companies), different patterns emerge. US firms were categorised as those with headquarters in the United States, and excluded non-US firms traded on US exchanges.

Chart 2 reveals significant differences in relative stock price movement between US and non-US education firms. While US firms almost tripled in value during the dotcom boom of 1997 to

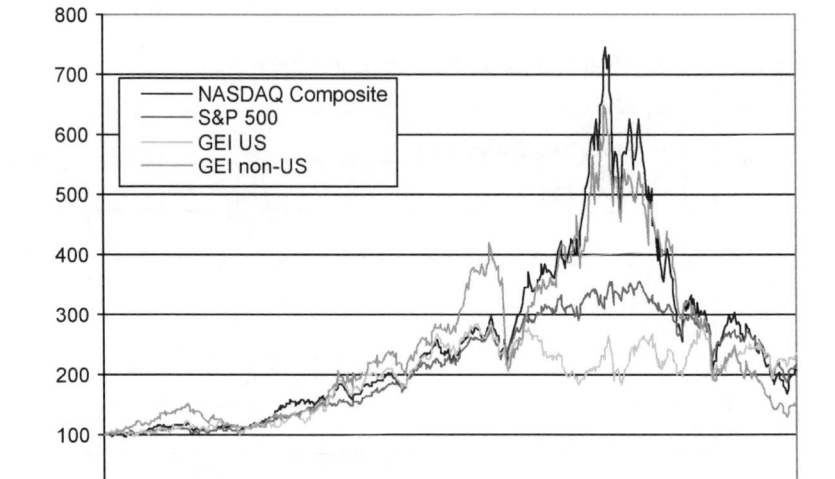

Chart 2 Education Companies: US and non-US

early 2000, non-US companies exhibited a six fold increase, almost matching the heights of the NASDAQ Composite during this period. This in part reflects the relatively weaker state of non-US education stocks at the base period (January 1993). Total stock price for non-US companies listed at that point was 17.37, compared to 70.46 for US firms (all figures in US dollars), despite the number of quoted companies in each case being all but identical – six and seven respectively. However, towards the close of 2002, non-US education stocks have sunk back to close to 1993 figures, while non-US firms have held a steadier position at about 2.5 times their 1993 value. Of course, these figures mask disparate movement by individual stocks. Such differences become clearer in Chart 3, which shows relative price movement by category.

Some companies do not fit neatly into any category. For example, the Indian firm NIIT and the Singapore firm Horizon Education & Technologies both specialise in IT training and IT software and consultancy, while a number of bricks and mortar institutions

Chart 3 Education Companies by Type

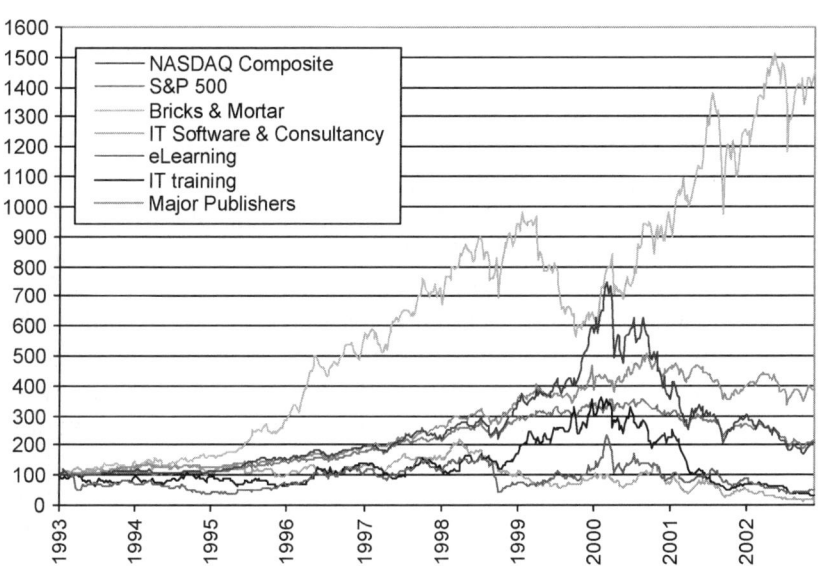

(e.g. Strayer Education) are developing e-learning capacity. (Annex A gives details of category assignment for all companies).

The most striking feature of Chart 3 is the relative progress of 'bricks and mortar' education companies. These are firms that operate physical college or university operations (e.g. Apollo Group and Corinthian Colleges in the United States, INTI Universal Holdings in Malaysia and CDI Education in Canada). These firms dwarfed NASDAQ growth and are the only category to have made significant positive progress following the dotcom crash. Some firms in this category performed significantly below average. By contrast, the e-learning firms profiled managed only a brief two fold increase in early 2000 (due to short lived enthusiasm for the IPOs of Centra and DigitalThink), and are currently languishing at about half their 1993 value. The main reason for this poor performance is excessively high initial valuations for IPOs during the dotcom boom (VCampus, eCollege and Healthstream, as well as Centra and DigitalThink, are the prime examples). By November 2002, Centra had dropped to less than 4% of its initial valuation, and the figure was less than 5% for Digital Think.

The picture is very similar for 'IT Software & Consultancy' firms, consisting of three companies quoted from the base period, and two IPOs during the dotcom boom. Four out of five exhibit late 2002 prices far below initial figures/IPO valuation. Only People-Soft achieved a price significantly higher than its starting point, although well-below the highs achieved during 2000 and 2001. Saba and Docent, with sky-high IPOs during 2000, were reduced to 10% and less than 5% of their initial value respectively by mid-November 2002. 'IT training' companies suffered the same fate- ProSoft Training from the US, Horizon Education & Technologies from Singapore and Boston Education & Software Technologies from India failed to live up to high IPO valuations. India's NIIT soared during the dotcom boom but has since dropped back significantly. Singapore's Informatics has maintained significant growth, but prices are modest when converted to US dollars.

The three large publishers in the Index, McGraw-Hill, Pearson and Thomson, are the only other current success story, sustaining a four fold increase at mid-November 2002. An individual success story, not well reflected by the above categories, is the University of Phoenix Online, which achieved in excess of a three fold increase by mid-November 2002 relative to its initial valuation in October 2000.

Overall, this data suggests that current investor confidence is confined to bricks and mortar education companies and publishing giants. The dotcom excitement over e-learning, support software and IT training has waned significantly – with some exceptions (e.g. University of Phoenix Online, PeopleSoft and Informatics). This view of the market is supported by financial results, discussed below. In general, bricks and mortar firms are longer established, operate proven business models and did not fall victim to dotcom enthusiasm. Only four out of nineteen bricks and mortar firms profiled (21%) issued IPOs during the so-called 'e-education bubble' of 1997 to early 2000, compared to 10 out of 18 e-learning and support software companies (55%). Investor confidence in bricks and mortar businesses has been allowed to develop gradually, supported by positive financial results, premised on unproven assumptions about the potential of the Internet. Indeed, it is notable that many bricks and mortar firms are beginning to experiment with e-learning (e.g. DeVry and Career Education Corporation), but as a supplement to the core business and in light of the experience of early e-learning firms. Similarly, the three publishing giants, while experiencing mixed fortunes in terms of e-learning ventures, have continued to develop the core business and have sufficient capital to sustain initially unsuccessful ventures long-term.

4 Financial Results

Stock performance is only part of the evidence for the current and long-term viability of a public company. To provide additional detail, revenue and net profit data was collected for all fifty education companies – including the three South African firms yet to be included in the GEI. Data was obtained from company websites, national exchange websites and aggregators such as Hoover's and Yahoo Finance. Figures were sought for at least three years, starting with 1999. Most companies do not make earlier data readily available.

4.1 Note on Methodology

Different companies operate a range of reporting cycles. To provide some consistency, annual results posted prior to the end of June in each year were classified as results for the previous calendar year. This meant that for a few firms, results posted as, say, 2002, were classified here as 2001. In some cases it was not possible to obtain full data for three years. As a tracking stock, no data was available for the University of Phoenix Online. All figures were converted to US dollars.

Many of the companies profiled have the broad area of post-secondary education as only part of their operations. In some cases, the distinction is clear cut, but in many instances it is difficult to make an unambiguous judgement about relevance. Many firms serve the corporate market, a market that is of growing importance to conventional universities and colleges, but some firms provide a range of services beyond the scope of most 'conventional' universities and colleges, e.g. IT consultancy and support, as well as training and e-learning software. Indeed, financial statements often do not break down revenue into categories suitable for the current analysis. For the purposes of this briefing note, company revenue is given in its entirety. Future analysis may attempt to distinguish 'relevant' income (i.e. relating to activity in direct competition or of direct interest to higher education institutions).

Table 1 sets out average revenue over three years and indicates a modest positive revenue trend over the period, rising about 12% between 1999 and 2001 (14% if publishers are excluded). All categories exhibited growth, with the exception of IT training,

Table 1 Average Revenue by Category & Country 1999–2001 (US dollars, millions)

Category/Country	2001	2000	1999
Bricks & Mortar	214.3	168.4	158.2
eLearning & related	168.2	165.3	143.9
IT training	68.6	73.8	63.2
Publishers	6287.1	5652.9	5015.3
Non-US	52.2	56.6	57.5
US	279.8	228	198.4
ALL	545.4	501.3	488.8
ALL (excluding publishers)	170.9	150.1	149.3

(Average figures were used to overcome the problem of missing data and unequal sized categories. The three publishers were excluded from the US and non-US averages to avoid outlier distortion).

which lost 7% between 2000 and 2001. The figures for 'Bricks & Mortar' companies help explain the substantial stock price growth discussed in Section 3. Revenue for these companies grew over 35% over the period, compared to 16% growth for e-learning and related firms. The standard deviation for all categories also grew over the period, rising 27% for e-learning and related companies, and 42% for bricks and mortar firms, reflecting the increasing strength of a handful of businesses (e.g. Apollo Group, PeopleSoft) compared to the average. Indeed, if PeopleSoft is removed, average revenue for 'eLearning & related' for 2001 drops to US$ 56.2 million – a drop of almost 67%. By contrast, the removal of Apollo Group, the company with by far the largest revenue among 'Bricks & Mortar' firms for 2001, results in a reduction of average revenue to US$185.1 million – only a 14% drop. Again, this reflects greater maturity and stability across the 'Bricks & Mortar' category. Table 2 considers net income.

This data cautions that while revenue has increased over the three year period, 2001 saw a sharp decline in net profits. The only exception was 'eLearning & related' which continued to reduce the size of an average loss, moving closer to mean profitability. The

Table 2 Average Net Income by Category & Country 1999–2001 (US dollars, millions)

Category/Country	2001	2000	1999
Bricks & Mortar	14.7	26.8	13.9
eLearning & related	−3.2	−8.6	−20.9
IT training	3.4	10.8	11.4
Publishers	179.7	645.3	482.6
Non-US	−0.6	1.5	7.9
US	11.6	18.9	−6.2
ALL	16.4	51.5	35.7
ALL (excluding publishers)	5.8	11	−0.49

figures may reflect the worsening economic climate post-dotcom bust, a more competitive marketplace where margins are squeezed and the obligation on many newer firms to begin to repay venture capital and other investments. Results are also affected by more localised problems. For example, Advtech from South Africa has been beset by a number of complex legal actions. Again, if PeopleSoft are removed, average net income for 2001 among 'eLearning & related' companies drops to US$ − 14.6 million, and US$ − 18.9 million for 2000. Nonetheless, the positive trend remains, if on a flatter curve. To a lesser extent, the situation is mirrored among 'Bricks & Mortar' firms. Apollo Group accounted for about a third of total average net income for 'Bricks & Mortar' firms in 2001.

Taking profitable companies only, average profit margins dropped from 10.5% in 2000 to 9.3% in 2001. Of 49 firms with data, thirty-five were profitable in 2000 (71%), compared to 29 in 2001 (59%). Looking at the latest quarterly data (where available), one firm moved out of the red, but two others made a loss following annual profits for 2001. The significant reduction in the profits of the three publishers reflects a major loss by Pearson in 2001, partly due to a number of weak Internet ventures. Current announcements from SkillSoft about the need to restate the balance sheet of recently

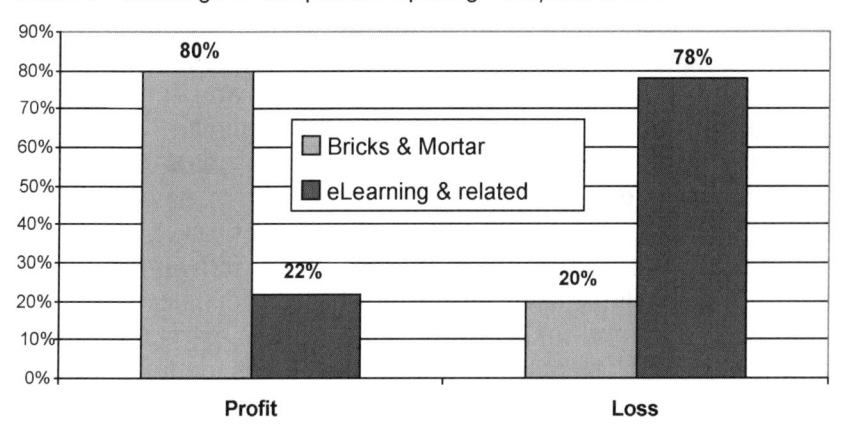

Chart 4 Percentage of Companies Reporting Profit/Loss in 2001

- Bricks & Mortar
- eLearning & related

	Profit	Loss
Bricks & Mortar	80%	20%
eLearning & related	22%	78%

merged SmartForce may impact previously stated revenue and net income figures for the company.

Chart 4 highlights the two categories of most interest to 'conventional' universities and colleges. It shows that in 2001, sixteen 'bricks and mortar' firms were in profit (80%), with four in the red (20%), compared to only four 'e-learning and related' firms in profit (22%) and fourteen in the red (78%). The figures were only slightly different for 2000. However, the general trend suggests that the losses among e-learning firms are getting smaller over time.

5 Conclusion

This analysis offers a unique international perspective on the financial position of public companies with postsecondary education interests. The main finding is confirmation that the claims made for the market impact and financial viability of e-learning and related companies during the 'e-education bubble' of 1997 to early 2000 were generally over-stated. Few such firms are currently in profit and share prices have suffered accordingly. The success story among firms generally are the bricks and mortar companies, exhibiting widespread profitability, growing revenue and share prices seemingly impervious to the economic downturn. These firms are generally older and have built up a more secure asset and revenue base. Proven business models won through after the dotcom bubble burst. Nonetheless, e-learning losses are shrinking year on year, suggesting that 3–5 years of product development and operational reality may begin to pay dividends. There is also a notable blurring of categories, such as bricks and mortar firms embarking on e-learning (e.g. Strayer Education) and IT training firms diversifying into higher education provision (e.g. NIIT, Informatics). Backed by a proven parent company (Apollo Group), University of Phoenix Online has made impressive progress as an e-learning specialist (although financial results are not available).

The financial data outlined here provides a basis on which to track future developments of these companies. Additional companies may be added to the Index as they come to light. The next chapter will discuss emerging relationships between these firms and 'conventional' universities and colleges.

Annex – Company Details

This annex provides a list of the fifty companies profiled in the briefing note. Additional detail will be given in the next Observatory briefing that will discuss emerging relationships between these firms and 'conventional' universities and colleges. Presentation here is confined to company name, country of headquarters, exchange and category assigned for the purpose of the above analysis. Companies are ordered by country.

Company	Country	Exchange	Category
1) Entertainment World	Australia	ASX	e-learning & related
2) Garratt's Limited	Australia	ASX	Bricks & Mortar
3) CDI Corporation	Canada	TSX	Bricks & Mortar
4) Serebra Learning Corporation	Canada	TSX	e-learning & related
5) Thomson Corporation	Canada	TSX	Publishers
6) Aptech	India	NSE	IT Training
7) Boston Education & Software Technologies	India	Bombay	IT Training
8) NIIT	India	NSE	IT Training
9) SkillSoft Corporation	Ireland (planned)	NASDAQ	e-learning & related
10) Mentergy	Israel	NASDAQ	e-learning & related
11) Boustead Holdings	Malaysia	KLSE	Bricks & Mortar
12) INTI Universal Holdings	Malaysia	KLSE	Bricks & Mortar
13) Stamford College Holdings	Malaysia	KLSE	Bricks & Mortar
14) SEG International	Malaysia	KLSE	Bricks & Mortar
15) Horizon Education & Technologies	Singapore	SGX	IT Training
16) Informatics	Singapore	SGX	IT Training
17) Raffles La Salle International	Singapore	SGX	Bricks & Mortar
18) Advtech	South Africa	JSE	Bricks & Mortar
19) Nova Education & Technology Holdings	South Africa	JSE	e-learning & related
20) Primeserv Group	South Africa	JSE	IT Training
21) BPP Holdings	UK	LSE	Bricks & Mortar
22) Epic Group	UK	LSE	e-learning & related
23) Futuremedia	UK	NASDAQ	e-learning & related
24) Pearson	UK	LSE	Publishers
25) Apollo Group	USA	NASDAQ	Bricks & Mortar

(*Continued*)

Annex *(Continued)*

Company	Country	Exchange	Category
26) Canterbury Consulting Group	USA	NASDAQ	e-learning & related
27) Career Education Corporation	USA	NASDAQ	Bricks & Mortar
28) Centra Software	USA	NASDAQ	e-learning & related
29) Concorde Career Colleges	USA	NASDAQ	Bricks & Mortar
30) Corinthian Colleges	USA	NASDAQ	Bricks & Mortar
31) DeVry	USA	NYSE	Bricks & Mortar
32) DigitalThink	USA	NASDAQ	e-learning & related
33) Docent	USA	NASDAQ	e-learning & related
34) eCollege	USA	NASDAQ	e-learning & related
35) Education Management Corporation	USA	NASDAQ	Bricks & Mortar
36) EVCI Career Colleges	USA	NASDAQ	Bricks & Mortar
37) Franklin Covey	USA	NYSE	e-learning & related
38) HealthStream	USA	NASDAQ	e-learning & related
39) ITT Educational Services	USA	NYSE	Bricks & Mortar
40) McGraw Hill Companies	USA	NYSE	Publishers
41) New Horizons Worldwide	USA	NASDAQ	IT Training
42) PeopleSoft	USA	NASDAQ	e-learning & related
43) PLATO Learning	USA	NASDAQ	e-learning & related
44) Prosoft Training	USA	NASDAQ	IT Training
45) Strayer Education	USA	NASDAQ	Bricks & Mortar
46) Sylvan Learning Systems	USA	NASDAQ	Bricks & Mortar
47) Saba	USA	NASDAQ	e-learning & related
48) University of Phoenix Online	USA	NASDAQ	e-learning & related
49) VCampus Corporation	USA	NASDAQ	e-learning & related
50) Whitman Education Group	USA	AMEX	Bricks & Mortar

Mapping the Education Industry, Part 2: *public companies – relationships with higher education*

Richard Garrett

1 Introduction

This is the second in a series of reports on companies involved in the broad area of postsecondary education. Part one, published by the Observatory in January 2003, introduced the 'Global Education Index' (GEI). The GEI is based on share price analysis from January 1993 for fifty companies from ten countries. The first briefing also included company financial results for 1999–2001. An important aspect of 'borderless' higher education is the growing role of commercial entities in aspects of teaching and learning. The present briefing note positions these companies in relation to non-profit higher education, and explores emerging relationships between the two sectors. The extent to which education companies pose a threat to non-profit higher education is a matter of considerable hype and speculation. This review of company activities and relationships seeks to marshal the available evidence.

Within these parameters, companies generally fall into one of three types:

1. **Direct Competitors** with little or no other relationship with the non-profit sector
2. **Indirect Competitors**, serving markets of generally minor or potential interest to the non-profit sector
3. **Service Providers and Clients**, offering a range of services to non-profit higher education and/or benefiting from particular services from non-profit higher education.

Type 1 is exemplified by the independent for-profit university or college networks in the United States. These institutions offer their own degree provision, have standard regional/specialist accreditation and specialise in market segments that are important to many non-profit higher education institutions. Examples include the Apollo Group, Sylvan Learning Systems, Career Education and Corinthian Colleges. Type 2 concerns the various e-learning and human capital development firms focused on the corporate and government sectors. These companies offer specialist software, courses and related services, with a strong emphasis on business and technology development. This territory overlap with the remit of many business schools in higher education, but would generally not be regarded as the latter's core business (particularly the emphasis on software development and delivery). Example companies include DigitalThink, SkillSoft, Saba and Centra.

Type 3 is more complex. Companies of this type provide a range of services to non-profit higher education including provision of learning management software, marketing online course material, creation of online portals to promote the awards of particular universities overseas, development of outsourced course design and delivery for specialised areas of the curriculum, and funding for new ventures. Non-profit higher education institutions also provide services to these companies, particularly franchised degree-awarding powers and academic credit for company courses. Example companies include Thomson Learning, INTI Universal Holdings, NIIT and Informatics.

Some companies do not fit neatly into a single type. Some offer services to the non-profit sector but also operate forms of indirect or even direct competition. Examples are discussed below. It is helpful to think of relationships between companies and non-profit higher education on a two dimensional axis. The first axis is a scale between direct competition and no competition, and the second between major service provision and no service provision to the non-profit sector. See Section 4 for an illustration.

Following a discussion of methodology, Section 3 sets out additional detail of Type 1 and 2 companies. Examples of the range of relationships between relevant companies and non-profit higher education are given in the discussion of Type 3. Section 4 provides an illustration in grid-form of the range of relationships between the two sectors, which is followed by the conclusion. Annex A gives an indication of the spread and significance of different relationships by company. Additional detail on all GEI companies will shortly be available on the 'Key Resources' page of the Observatory website.

2 Methodology

The report is based on analysis of public information on fifty quoted companies operating in the broad area of postsecondary education. The fifty are almost identical to those listed in the Observatory's first report in this series. For details of company selection, see the methodology section in the first report. As stated in that report, the composition of the GEI will change over time as companies shift priorities or fold and new companies appear or are judged appropriate for inclusion. Four changes have been made since the publication of the first briefing. Canturbury Consulting Group and Franklin Covey from the United States have been replaced by Click2Learn and SCT, also both with headquarters in the United States. The two additions were judged to be more significant players in postsecondary education. Boston Education & Software Technologies from India and Nova Education & Technology Holdings from South Africa have been replaced by MXL and Amtech from Australia. Boston and Nova were removed on the grounds that there is presently insufficient information in the public domain about company activities (e.g. inaccessible/non-existent company website).

The present study is based on detailed analysis of company websites and other information where available. What follows is not an exhaustive account of relations between individual companies and individual non-profit higher education institutions, but rather a discussion of types of known relationship. The Observatory would be pleased to hear of additional relationship types, sub-types and examples.

3 Relationship Types

For the purposes of this analysis, all GEI companies were allocated to one of the three relationship types outlined above – Direct Competitors, Indirect Competitors and Service Providers & Clients. As noted, some companies do not fit neatly into a single type. Section 4 provides a more detailed illustration of the range of relationships and where companies cross type boundaries. In Section 3, ambiguities are discussed but each company is listed under a single type.

3.1 Direct Competitors

The current GEI contains 17 companies best described as direct competitors with non-profit higher education:

Advtech, South Africa
Amnet, Australia
Apollo Group, USA
Career Education Corporation, USA
CDI Education, Canada
Concorde Career Colleges, USA
Corinthian Colleges, USA
DeVry, USA
Education Management Corp, USA

EVCI Career Colleges, USA
Garratt's Limited, Australia
ITT Educational Services, USA
Primeserv, South Africa
Strayer Education, USA
Sylvan Learning Systems, USA
University of Phoenix Online, USA
Whitman Education Group, USA

The majority of Type 1 firms are for-profit college/university networks from the United States, plus similar institutions in Australia (Garratt's), Canada (CDI Education Corporation) and South Africa (Advtech and Primeserv). As an example, Sylvan International Universities, part of Sylvan Learning Systems, is profiled below. The remaining company is Amnet, an Australian IT firm that recently embarked on a programme of private university acquisition in China. For an account of Amnet, see the Observatory's Breaking News archive for January 2003.

Companies in this category tend not to have significant non-competitive relationships with non-profit higher education. This is due to a combination of similarity and difference between the two sectors. In many ways, the majority of these firms closely resemble conventional universities and colleges. In both sectors, a central part of the core business is offering postsecondary programmes of study. But there are important ideological and emphasis differences. The for-profit sector focus on the commercial potential of postsecondary education, and many companies of this type entered the postsecondary market to fill a perceived gap in the offerings of the non-profit sector. This might constitute offering different subject areas, flexible contact time, improved location convenience, focusing on a particular student type, enhanced student support or workplace relevance.

It would be a mistake to over-state ideological and emphasis differences. Over the past generation, pushed by expansion pressures and government policy, the non-profit sector has also moved into non-traditional markets and sought greater income diversification and independence. Equally it is generally misleading to characterise the for-profit sector as motivated solely by profit. Driven by a customer service ethos, many providers have developed impressive models of teaching and learning, student support and workplace relevance. Nonetheless, in terms of non-profit versus for-profit status and general versus specialised provision, the two sectors remain distinct.

Example 1: Sylvan International Universities

Sylvan International Universities (SIU) was created by Sylvan Learning Systems (SLS) in 1999. SLS, founded in 1979, is a school tutoring and assessment firm that has recently added higher education to its portfolio. SIU has grown through acquisitions of existing private universities and other higher education institutions in Europe, Central and South America, and now boasts about 60,000 students worldwide (almost two-thirds at the Universidad del Valle de Mexico). The company's first purpose-built institution, the South Asia International Institute in India, will open in 2003. Study is concentrated in business, IT, healthcare and hospitality management. Unlike the University of Phoenix and other leading for-profit providers in the USA, SIU targets both full-time traditional age students and part-time working adults, and some campuses offer a range of conventional facilities (e.g. accommodation, sports, leisure).

SLS view higher education as a massive growth market in the coming decades. This is premised on predictions of substantial under-supply as emerging economies begin to send ever-greater proportions of school leavers to higher study and continuing professional development becomes the norm. All SIU institutions are run on the 'Sylvan Signature' approach, constituting "relevant, career oriented fields of study at affordable tuitions, English language proficiency and on-campus use of technology".[1] Aside from SIU, Sylvan also owns outright or a majority share of National Technological University (an engineering distance learning institution first formed by a number of US non-profit universities), Walden University (a US private distance learning institution) and Canter & Associates (a US professional development firm for school teachers).

Sylvan's share price, long buoyant, has suffered recently following poor financial results. Third quarter 2002 results showed a net loss, due largely to losses associated with the investments of Sylvan Ventures, the company's venture capital arm. However, SIU was one of the highlights of the quarter, exhibiting a 29% year-on-year enrolment increase and revenue growth of 22% (to almost US$61 million).[2]

The relationship between the for-profit and non-profit sectors is sufficiently close to constitute competition but sufficiently different to impede significant collaboration. This difference forms a key part of the ongoing competitive advantage of the direct competitors – their relative nimbleness in the marketplace. These firms do not undertake many activities of central importance to the majority of institutions in the non-profit sector, e.g. basic research, student accommodation, sports and leisure facilities. They thus have a narrower brief than the vast majority in the non-profit sector, and are less tied to particular locations and facilities. The larger firms in North America lease rather than own many of their numerous teaching sites. Companies also target a more specialist market – employed mature students who wish to study part-time while they continue working and who seek a qualification relevant to

---

[1] Sylvan International Universities (2003) *What is the approach of 'Sylvan Signature? And what is the hallmark of it?* Available at: www.sylvanu.com/company/company_faqs.asp#4. Last Accessed 22 April 2004.
[2] Sylvan Learning Systems (2002) *Sylvan Learning Systems, Inc. Reports Third Quarter 2002 Financial Results; Sylvan International Universities Reports 29% New Student Enrollment Growth.* Available at: www.sylvan.net. Last Accessed 22 April 2004.

their current or future employment; and who are less interested in traditional academic research and campus facilities. Other examples of relative nimbleness and competitive advantage include a more standardised curriculum and teaching approach, limited subject range, considerable use of contract and part-time staff and a preference for faculty who also work in their field of instruction. Standardisation and centralisation allow many companies to operate more easily and effectively on a corporate level than their non-profit counterparts.

The majority of firms in this category operate nationally or subnationally. Limited exceptions are DeVry that also operates in Canada, Career Education, which also operates in the United Arab Emirates and the United Kingdom, and Amnet, which is expanding in China. The two South African firms have some operations in neighbouring countries (Advtech also owns three non-education businesses in Australia). The two major exceptions are Apollo Group and Sylvan. Sylvan is profiled separately above, while Apollo has outposts in Canada, Germany, the Netherlands, Brazil, Mexico and India, plus plans in China. Some of this activity is through Apollo International, a related company started by the founder of Apollo Group in which the Group has minority ownership. Details of the national/international reach of all current GEI companies will soon be available on the Observatory's 'Key Resources' page. Many firms are developing significant online offerings, extending their scope for recruitment.

Four firms use the university title directly- Apollo Group (University of Phoenix, Western International University), DeVry (DeVry University), Education Management Corporation (Argosy University) and Strayer Education (Strayer University). Four others have either acquired pre-existing institutions with that title (Amnet, Sylvan and Career Education, which acquired American International University), or formed an association with a non-profit university (Advtech and Bond University).

It is not possible to gauge the market presence of the for-profit postsecondary sector in precise terms. Data is generally inadequate and the lines between higher, further and continuing education, and professional development are blurred and shifting. Yet even in countries, such as the USA, where the sector is relatively strong, for-profit institutions constitute only a small proportion of total enrolments. For example, in the USA in 1999 (the latest year for which figures are available), for-profit degree and non-degree granting institutions eligible for federal financial aid made up only 4.1% of all enrolments.[3] But the market is growing. The number of degree-granting for-profit institutions in the United States grew by over 300% between 1980 and 1999 (from 165 to 721), exhibiting much faster growth than the public or private non-profit sectors (although, of course, from a much lower base).[4] Substantial enrolment growth in many of the leading for-profit networks, such as Apollo, Career Education and DeVry, suggests that the market share of the for-profit sector in terms of student numbers has grown since 1999. The for-profit sector may become increasingly significant as a source (both imported and indigenous) of higher education capacity in the developing world, and a source of competition as developed countries begin charge, raise and deregulate tuition fees in the public sector.

Advtech in South Africa is a good example of a firm with a more ambiguous relationship with the non-profit sector. Advtech is the South African partner for Bond South Africa, Australia's Bond University South Africa campus. Bond South Africa operates as part of Advtech's 'Global School of Business' chain. Thomson Learning, included under Type 3, also exhibits elements of Type 1. The company operates *Education Direct,* an online education site offering programmes up to associate degree. The operation is accredited by the Distance Education & Training Council (DETC), the leading distance education accrediting body in the United States. The company also owns the California College for Health Sciences, a for-profit institution that offers programmes up to masters level and is also accredited by the DETC. Informatics, also

---

[3] Educause (2002) *The Pocket Guide to US Higher Education 2002,* Educause, Washington, p2.
[4] Ibid, p3.

included under Type 3, owns Salem International University in the USA (regionally accredited by the North Central Association in the USA); and Horizon majority owns the United Institute of International Education in Hong Kong SAR (which offers franchised degrees from foreign universities – see below).

3.2 Indirect Competitors

The current GEI exhibits 12 companies best described as indirect competitors in relation to the non-profit sector:

Centra Software, USA	Mentergy, Israel
Click2Learn, USA	New Horizons Worldwide, USA
DigitalThink, USA	Prosoft Training, USA
Docent, USA	Saba, USA
Epic Group, UK	Serebra Learning Corp, Canada
Futuremedia, UK	SkillSoft, Ireland/ USA

Companies allocated to this type are either general e-learning software and courseware providers focused on the corporate and government sectors (e.g. SkillSoft, DigitalThink) or specialist training firms (New Horizons Worldwide and ProSoft Training, both IT training companies). These companies are grouped as indirect competitors insofar as they offer products and provision of tangential interest to the majority of non-profit higher education.

The confluence of human capital theory, continuing professional development, knowledge management and new technology has energised workforce training in recent years. The majority of the above firms (IT trainers excluded) were either formed in the heat of the dotcom boom (e.g. Saba, Docent and SkillSoft- pre-merger with SmartForce) or re-engineered their business during that period to take advantage of new technology and the new enthusiasm for learning. What is interesting about these firms is that many have appropriated elements of the nomenclature of higher education (e.g. knowledge, learning, campus, and less so university), and are taking advantage of a new corporate interest in workforce development that the non-profit sector might also wish to benefit from. Indeed, many Type 2 firms support corporate university initiatives.

Example 2: Click2Learn

Click2Learn, founded in 1984, is a typical example of a Type 2 firm. The company's headline product is the Aspen platform, an integrated learning and content management system, including live virtual classroom functionality. "Click2learn's customers recognize learning and knowledge management as mission critical, and they use the Aspen Platform across the entire business value chain to educate employees, suppliers, distributors, partners and customers."[5] The company is a form of business consultancy, but with specific products to sell as solutions. Click2Learn examine client needs and ways of working, and implement customised versions of Aspen to enable cost savings, efficiency gains, new customers etc.

Click2Learn Alliance Partners brings together a selection of third party technology, content and services for customised integration into an Aspen package. Content partners include SkillSoft, Element K and Netg (part of Thomson Learning), offering clients a range of business and IT course options. Other partners include Centra and NIIT. Click2Learn claims almost 400 platform customers, including a majority of the Fortune 100. Outside the USA, the company has offices in the UK, India and Japan.

The company has yet to make a profit and the share price is depressed. However, 4th quarter results for 2002 showed a greatly reduced loss of less than US$1 million compared to the same period in 2001,[6] suggesting that like a number of other e-learning firms, profitability may soon be realised.

Some Type 2 firms also provide various kinds of service to non-profit higher education institutions, but relationships appear to not

---
[5] Click2Learn (2003) *Product Overview*. Click2Learn has now merged with Docent to form SunTotal Systems.
[6] Click2Learn (2003) *Click2learn Announces Fourth Quarter And Year-End 2002 Results*, 6 February 2003.

be sufficiently extensive or significant for either party for placement under Type 3. Examples include:

- SkillSoft, an online professional development and courseware company, has a small higher education client base for some of its IT and business skills courses. Universities and colleges tend to deploy this provision as part of general staff development. In 1999, the company partnered with Wharton Business School at the University of Pennsylvania in the United States to develop online provision in finance. The project is still listed on the company website, but its current status is unclear.
- The Epic Group has done some work for the UK eUniversities Worldwide, the UK national eUniversity, and has a three year contract to quality assure learning software for the UK University for Industry (Ufi), a government initiative to improve learning opportunities for the workforce and general population.
- Learndirect, the operational arm of Ufi, is a Saba client. (Some UK higher education institutions are part of the Ufi network).
- DigitalThink has a small number of higher education clients in the United States – including Stanford, Ohio State and Arizona universities. Online content delivered by Harvard Business School Publishing utilises the Docent platform, and a number of universities (e.g. Columbia, New York and Texas A&M universities) have purchased Centra's 'live e-learning' product. For an account of the London Business School's adoption of the Centra platform, see the Observatory's Breaking News archive for July 2002.
- Serebra Learning Corporation recently announced an e-learning development partnership with the Pakistan Virtual University (see the Observatory Breaking News archive for December 2002) and has sold courses to the University of Waterloo in Canada.

There are also a smaller number of cases where higher education institutions provide services to Type 2 companies. SkillSoft has secured academic credit for its courses through agreements with American Military University and two companies under Type 1 – Strayer University and the University of Phoenix (part of Apollo Group). INSEAD, the French business school, and Cardean University (featuring content form Columbia, Chicago, Stanford and Carnegie Mellon universities and the London School of Economics) are Docent 'content' partners. The only known example of use of the university title by a Type 2 company is Docent University, the company's in-house corporate university initiative.

IT training firms (e.g. New Horizons Worldwide and ProSoft Training) are of interest as potential partners to non-profit higher education institutions with a view to boosting the marketability of university and college IT awards. Many universities and colleges have become accredited centres for courses from major hardware and software companies such as Microsoft and Cisco Systems. Non-specific training companies, like New Horizons and ProSoft, offer the advantage of multiple vendor certification. New Horizons, which is currently the largest IT training company in the world in terms of revenue,[7] appears to have no substantive relationships with higher education. By contrast, ProSoft Training includes a number of higher education institutions among its 'authorised training partners' (e.g. Syracuse and California universities in the USA, Monash and Swinburne universities in Australia and Strathclyde University in the UK). The company also markets provision through content partnerships with the leading learning platform providers to higher education, Blackboard and WebCT. The Indian IT firms Aptech and NIIT, discussed under Type 3, are examples of IT training companies going beyond the franchise model to offer universities a completely

---

[7] New Horizons (2002) *New Horizons Announces Third Quarter Results*, 23 October. Available at: www.corporate-ir.net/ireye/ir_site.zhtml?ticker=NEWH&-script=410&layout=-6&item_id=348501&sstring=largest. Last Accessed 22 April 2004.

outsourced IT training solution and co-development of university IT awards.

It is not straightforward to gauge the international reach of Type 2 firms. It is difficult to draw a line between international sales, offices, franchises and distributors. Most of the US firms have at least one European and one Asian office, while the two UK firms operate solely from the UK. Mentergy's US arm was recently subject to a management buyout. Ongoing financial difficulties, and the sale of other parts of the business, have left the direction of the company uncertain.

To summarise, Type 2 firms use terminology akin to that common in non-profit higher education, and target recent enthusiasm for workforce and specialist (particularly IT) training, development and certification. These firms generally do not view higher education as a major market, nor as a direct competitor, and vice versa. However, there are examples of mutually beneficial relationships. In terms of products and services supplied to non-profit higher education there are examples of specialist e-learning software, IT vendor certification, courseware for staff development and one case of joint development of an academic programme. In terms of products and services supplied by higher education, there are examples of academic credit for company provision and higher education content integrated into company e-learning platforms targeted at third parties. Given this range of collaborative possibilities, but limited interaction between the two sectors to date, the scope for future partnerships may be significant.

3.3 Service Providers and Clients

There are 21 GEI companies that are best allocated to Type 3 – companies that offer services to and benefit from services from non-profit higher education:

Aptech, India
Boustead Holdings, Malaysia
BPP Holdings, UK
eCollege, USA
Entertainment World, Australia
HealthStream, USA
Horizon Ed. & Tech., Singapore
Informatics Holdings, Singapore
INTI Universal Holdings, Malaysia
MXL, Australia
NIIT, India

Pearson, UK
PeopleSoft, USA
PLATO Learning, USA
Raffles LaSalle Int., Malaysia
SCT, USA
SEG International, Malaysia
Stamford College Hldgs, Malaysia
The McGraw-Hill Companies, USA
Thomson Corporation, Canada
VCampus Corporation

This category captures the sheer diversity of emerging relationships between commercial entities and non-profit higher education. Relationships are discussed below under eight headings: software sales & services, materials sales, non-core course sales, franchising/marketing, funding, accreditation, joint content development and core course sales. Annex A gives an overview of the activities of all GEI companies in relation to these headings. Of course, there is often a blurred line between different headings (e.g. between software, materials and courses).

Software sales and services
With the growth of academic computing, accelerated by Internet technology, universities and colleges have become increasingly dependent on commercial software vendors. Learning and content management systems, portals and a variety of administrative applications have become essential features at many campuses worldwide. The current GEI includes companies that view this field as core business, a potential area of expansion or a relatively minor activity.

SCT (administrative software firm and systems integrator) and PeopleSoft (pioneering enterprise resource planning and customer relationship firm, with a range of education-specific applications) view higher education as a major market. SCT has over 1300 higher education clients, including a growing number outside the United States. PeopleSoft does not give a detailed client figures for higher education, but also operates internationally. MXL offers similar software to SCT and People-Soft and is beginning to target the tertiary market in Europe and Asia.

eCollege and VCampus were established just prior to the e-education boom of 1997 to early 2000 as e-learning development firms, with higher education as a major market. Both operate on a number of levels, including consultancy to determine development needs, learning management and related software, hosting services, third party content delivery and local content creation. Both firms seek to offer a more comprehensive service than leading platform specialists Blackboard and WebCT. eCollege claims to have more than 100 higher education clients, while VCampus does not give a figure. eCollege is beginning to market internationally (e.g. the partnership with the 'Dubai Internet City' project[8]), but at present both firms are essentially confined to the USA. Neither company is yet profitable.

The three multinational publishers – McGraw-Hill, Pearson and Thomson – offer a range of software and related services to higher education. All three market a form of learning platform for academics to create online course content based on company texts. Pearson's *Course Compass* was developed in partnership with Blackboard, the second largest platform provider to higher

---

[8] ECollege (2002) *eCollege and Dubai Internet City Form 'Knowledge Access' to Make Education More Accessible to the Gulf Region and Surrounding Areas,* June 17. Available at: www.ecollege.com/stories/press_06_17_02.html. Last Accessed 22 April 2004.

education in the world in terms of client numbers.[9] McGraw-Hill offers *PageOut* and Thomson *MyCourse*. These tools are free for instructors to use, but student access tends to require textbook purchase. McGraw-Hill also markets *GradeSummit,* an online tool to help instructors gauge student learning styles and progress; and a custom e-book service to combine chapters from different company titles into a bespoke volume. *Knowledge Gateway* (in partnership with US CollegisEduprise, a higher education technology consulting firm), is a guide website for instructors using McGraw-Hill online content, including through third party platforms. Pearson also offers a custom e-book service – *Pearson Custom Publishing*.

It is interesting to contrast the above activities of multinational publishing firms with the years prior to the dotcom crash. In 1998 and 1999, both McGraw-Hill and Harcourt General (now part owned by Thomson) both began to offer online courses direct to the public. In 1998, McGraw-Hill formed the 'McGraw-Hill Lifetime Learning Unit', offering courses based on company textbooks. Courses were supervised by authors or other academic/ industry experts. In January 2002, citing changing market conditions, it was announced that the unit was to close. Harcourt had more ambitious plans. In 1999, the company created 'Harcourt Higher Education' and planned to offer a range of arts and sciences courses to working adults. Harcourt proposed 'Harcourt University', approaching the New England Association of Schools and Colleges for regional accreditation. Harcourt as a whole was sold to fellow publisher Reed Elsevier in 2001, and then Reed sold parts of the business (including Harcourt Higher Education) to Thomson. In view of poor recruitment figures, Thomson closed down Harcourt Higher Education.

FT Knowledge, the Pearson subsidiary offering business and finance provision, formed a string of partnerships with UK and US

---

[9] Observatory on Borderless Higher Education (2002) *Leading Learning Platforms: international market presence*.

universities up to 2000, but the current position is unclear. The 1999 annual report mentions Wharton Business School at the University of Pennsylvania, University of Michigan Business School and Excelsior College,[10] but neither more recent annual reports, nor the current FT Knowledge website, mention these initiatives. Websites exist for both the Wharton and Michigan partnerships but their current status is ambiguous. Partnerships reported in 1999/ 2000[11] with Cambridge, Heriot-Watt, Nottingham Trent and Leeds Metropolitan universities in the UK are also not mentioned in Pearson annual reports or on the current FTK website. According to the latest half-yearly figures from Pearson, FT Knowledge continues to make a loss.[12]

The fate of McGraw-Hill's and Harcourt's direct course provision, and the ambiguities over FT Knowledge, placed alongside the current higher education activities of Pearson and McGraw-Hill, suggest a move away from direct engagement in higher education provision. Instead the firms have focused on redefining the core business of providing supplementary materials (whether physical or online), but continue to experiment with additional features such as course platforms, assessment tools and non-degree corporate development. The main exception is Thomson's *EducationDirect* – see above. See below for other activities of Thomson Learning.

Aside from IT training (see below), NIIT is a technology systems developer and integrator. The company is expanding into learning technology, targeting both corporate and higher education clients. For example, in 2001 NIIT won a major contract from Singapore's

---

[10] Pearson (1999) *Annual Report 1999*, p23–24. Available at: www.pearson.com/investor/reports.htm. Last Accessed 22 April 2004.
[11] CVCP (2000) *The Business of Borderless Education: case studies & annxes*, London, Committee of Vice-Chancellors & Principals/Higher Education Funding Council for England, p25.
[12] Pearson (2002) *Pearson Interim Results for the Half Year to June 30 2002*, p5. Available at: www.pearson.com/investor/reports.htm. Last Accessed 22 April 2004.

Institute of Technical Education to customise, implement, integrate and maintain a suite of learning and administrative platforms across the institution's 13 campuses. NIIT has also developed its own *CLiKS*learning platform. [See the Observatory's Breaking News archive for November 2002 for an account of the University of Wisconsin's decision to adopt *CLiKS*]. NIIT recently purchased Cognitive Arts, a US corporate development firm with its origins at Northwestern University.[13] Entertainment World sell licensing and conversion services for educational material at postsecondary level, while HealthStream offer a bespoke learning platform aimed at healthcare facilities, including university-run hospitals.

Materials sales

Textbooks, study guides and course packs produced by private sector publishers play an accepted part in teaching and learning in higher education, and have done for many years. New technology has expanded format possibilities. The Internet suggests a quantum leap, integrating text, images, sound and interaction. The three multinational publishers in the GEI have all made substantial investments in online companion material for textbooks. Associated learning platforms – mentioned above – are an attempt to position the material at the heart of the teaching and learning process. In an attempt to add value to its learning platform, eCollege offers users third party content from the likes of Delmar Learning (a Thomson company specialising in professional and vocational consultancy and materials) and Harvard Business School Publishing. HealthStream operate a similar service. Part of Entertainment World's core business is production and sales of postsecondary education materials in video, video streaming and CD formats. The company markets third party material from the UK's Open University.

---

[13] NIIT (2003) *NIIT acquires US based CognitiveArts*. Available at: www.niit.com//niit/ContentAdmin/NWS/NWSPR/NWSPR1/pr-120203-tech.htm. Last Accessed 22 April 2004.

Example 3: Aptech

Aptech is one of the largest IT training companies in the world. Founded in India in 1986, the firm operates a vast international franchise network of almost 2500 centres in 52 countries (260 outside India), and claims to have trained more than 2.5 million students. Aptech has also branched out into multimedia training, general business skills, management development and e-learning consultancy. The company's 'Online Varsity' site offers a range of online provision. Aptech has devoted considerable energies to pedagogy. The AMEDA (Aptech Multimodal Education Delivery and Architecture) model for learning, combining face-to-face and online instruction, is said to be based on in-depth instructional design research.[14]

The company has a rather complex relationship with higher education. The company website states that "Aptech's Global Education focuses on being the preferred alternative to University IT education in developing countries".[15] This means offering fully outsourced IT training solutions to universities and colleges rather than direct competition. Aptech has also formed alliances with three universities – Southern Cross in Australia, Excelsior College from the USA and Sikkim Manipal University from India – offering Aptech students credit towards a degree. Another initiative is the 'India Windows Programme', where university students from the developing world come to India for training in the latest technologies and an internship with an Indian IT firm. Aptech recently extended the IPW to Bangladesh. Finally, the company is building academic research links, particularly in the field of multimedia, establishing a special interest group and holding a conference to bring together the work of practitioners and academics.

Following unprecedented revenue growth in 2000 (annual revenue of about US$97 million), the company's fortunes were

---

[14] Aptech (2003) *Corporate Profile: unique hybrid methodology of learning*. Available at: www.aptech-worldwide.com/aptech/corporate.htm. Last Accessed 22 April 2004.
[15] Ibid.

> less favourable in 2001 (annual revenue down to about US$23 million). However, quarterly results from 2002 show positive growth.[16] Aptech went public in September 2002.

Non-core course sales
'Non-core' programmes of study are those that are not standard provision towards a mainstream higher education qualification. Examples include staff development provision and student remedial work. Some firms offer courses from a wide range of third parties to add value to their core learning platform or other services (e.g. VCampus and HealthStream). Other companies specialise in such courses. Plato Learning, for example, markets online and standalone remedial reading, writing and mathematics courses to higher education institutions, plus life skills and English as a second language provision. Similar to alliances with SkillSoft outlined above, courseware from Netg, part of Thomson Learning, has been adopted by some universities as a source of online business and IT development for staff and students. Comat Training Services, a Horizon Education & Technologies company, and NIIT's *NetVarsity* offer the same sort of provision, targeted at individuals, higher education and the private sector. PeopleSoft offers 'academic use' licenses for its latest products, plus associated materials and courses, in a bid to increase the number of IT graduates familiar with its offerings.

Franchising/marketing
One of the most common types of relationship between GEI companies and higher education is franchising/marketing. A typical arrangement is for a university to franchise one or more degree programmes to another higher education institution that lacks degree-awarding powers. SEG, INTI, Stamford and Horizon have arrangements of this kind. For example, INTI offers degrees from the universities of Hertfordshire, Hull, Leeds, Liverpool and

---

[16] All figures derived from Aptech press releases and annual reports, plus online information from the India National Stock Exchange – Available at: www.nse-india.com/homepage.htm.

Northumbria in the UK, and Adelaide in Australia. An alternative is for the company to simply market a university programme to a particular constituency or region. BPP, Entertainment World and Informatics fall under this sub-heading. Entertainment World markets the MBA from Heriot-Watt University in the UK, while BPP offers an accountancy-related BSc and MBA from Oxford Brookes University, also in the UK. A third sub-type is characterised by Thomson Learning's relationship with Cardean University (described above) and Universitas 21 Global (an international university consortium developing remote online provision). While Thomson plays a more diverse role in the case of Universitas 21 Global (see below), in both cases the company is central to marketing efforts.

Funding
This is less common than many of the other relationship types. Two examples are Thomson's contribution of US$25 million to Universitas 21 Global and Boustead Holdings financial backing of the University of Nottingham's Malaysia campus. [For details of University of Nottingham in Malaysia see the case study in the Observatory briefing note on 'International Branch Campuses' from June 2002]. Another example is Informatics' investment in PurpleTrain, the company's online education portal that markets degrees from universities such as Portsmouth and Wales in the United Kingdom, and Capella in the USA.

Accreditation
This is the clearest instance of higher education providing a service to GEI companies, whereby a higher education institution awards academic credit for company provision. For example, Aptech, Informatics and NIIT have credit arrangements to allow their diploma graduates to obtain advanced standing towards a degree. NIIT has won general credit approval from the American Council on Education (a status recognised by hundreds of US universities). Raffles La Salle International has agreements with Curtin University in Australia and Middlesex University in the UK. Netg, part of Thomson Learning, has a credit agreement with Fort Hays State University in the USA.

Example 4: Informatics

Informatics began in 1983 with a single computer training school in Singapore. The company now runs over 450 centres in 42 countries, and operates across pre-school, K-12, higher education and corporate training. Informatics' mission is to be "a global leader in providing quality online learning services",[17] and the company has expanded beyond the initial emphasis on IT.

Development of the higher education business was achieved through acquisition and alliances with existing players, plus selected new initiatives. Higher education services are divided into three 'schools' (Information & Communication, Business, Engineering), plus a distance learning arm. Sub-degree, bachelors and postgraduate programmes are available. Sub-degree qualifications are awarded by Informatics itself or through a partner (e.g. University of Cambridge Local Examinations Syndicate), subsidiary (e.g. Thames Business School in New Zealand) or acquisition (e.g. NCC, the former UK government IT training organisation). Bachelors and postgraduate awards are the fruit of alliances with universities in Australia (e.g. Murdoch, Southern Queensland), Canada (e.g. Ottawa), UK (e.g. Lincoln, Thames Valley) and USA (e.g. Hawaii Pacific). Informatics bought an accredited private liberal arts college in the US – Salem International University – in 2001. The company has credit transfer arrangements with over fifty universities worldwide.

Informatics' distance learning arm consists of two very similar operations – Informatics Virtual Campus (www.informaticsgroup.com/ivc) and PurpleTrain (www.purpletrain.com/index.htm). Both are online portals offering direct access to fully online programmes from selected partner universities. Students are mailed hard copies of key textbooks and have access to other materials online.

---

[17] Informatics (2003) *Welcome to Informatics*. Available at: www.informaticsgroup.com. Last Accessed 22 April 2004.

> Examinations are conducted in person at Informatics centres and partner centres worldwide.
>
> Beyond headline claims that the Informatics Group as a whole teaches over 600,000 students a year, and has an "online learning community" of over 67,000,[18] there is little data on higher education enrolments. The company share price has suffered in a generally weaker economic climate, but remains significantly above its IPO price in 1993. Financial results are encouraging - the latest results for the six months to October 2002 show a 3.5% rise in revenue to about US$58 million, and post-tax profits up over 21% to over US$6.6 million.[19]

Joint content development
There are two main forms of this relationship. The first is exemplified by Aptech and NIIT who offer joint IT degree programme development with universities as part of a wider outsourced IT training package. The second relates to the role of Thomson in Universitas Global. It appears that Thomson plays a role in course content development (alongside more clearly defined funding, marketing and support materials/ software roles), but precise details are not available.

Core course sales
This heading encompasses provision excluded from the non-core course sales heading above – that is, provision leading to a standard higher education qualification. This relationship is perhaps rarest of all at present. The only clear examples are, again, efforts by Aptech and NIIT to integrate their IT provision into higher education IT degree programmes. The alliance between SkillSoft and Wharton noted under Type 2 would be another example.

---

[18] Both figures taken from the Informatics website, as footnote 17.
[19] Informatics (2002) *Informatics' profit after tax up 21% to s$11.6 million in 1hfy03*. Available at: www.informaticsgroup.com. Last Accessed 22 April 2004.

4 Grid Analysis

In an attempt to show the spread of relationships between GEI companies and non-profit higher education, all companies were given two scores:

1. **Competition** – a score between 0 and 5 where zero equals no competition and five equals a major competitor.
2. **Service** – a score between 0 and 5 where zero equals no service and five equals a major service provider.

Scores were arrived at by means of a judgement about the relative importance of the higher education market to a company, competitive stance and relative market penetration (based on company data where available, and financial results). Scores are not, of course, precise measures but rather indicative of the main thrust of company activities. This approach enables comparison between firms and allows relationships to be tracked over time. Figure 1 shows the position of each company on the two axes. Company codes are given in Annex A.

Figure 1 shows a significant spread of relationships – across 20 of 36 possible co-ordinates. What is the balance between competitive and service relationships? Seventeen companies (34%) were judged to have a significant competitive relationship with non-profit higher education (i.e. placed in a lower quadrant). Of these, 11 (22%) had no additional service relationship. The remaining six (12%) combined significant competitive and service relationships. However, all but four companies (8%) were judged to have at least a minor competitive relationship with non-profit higher education. Seventeen firms (34%) were judged to have no service relationship, and only nine firms (18%) were positioned in a right quadrant (indicating a significant service relationship).

Figure 1 Competitive and Service Relationships Between GEI Companies and Non-Profit Higher Education

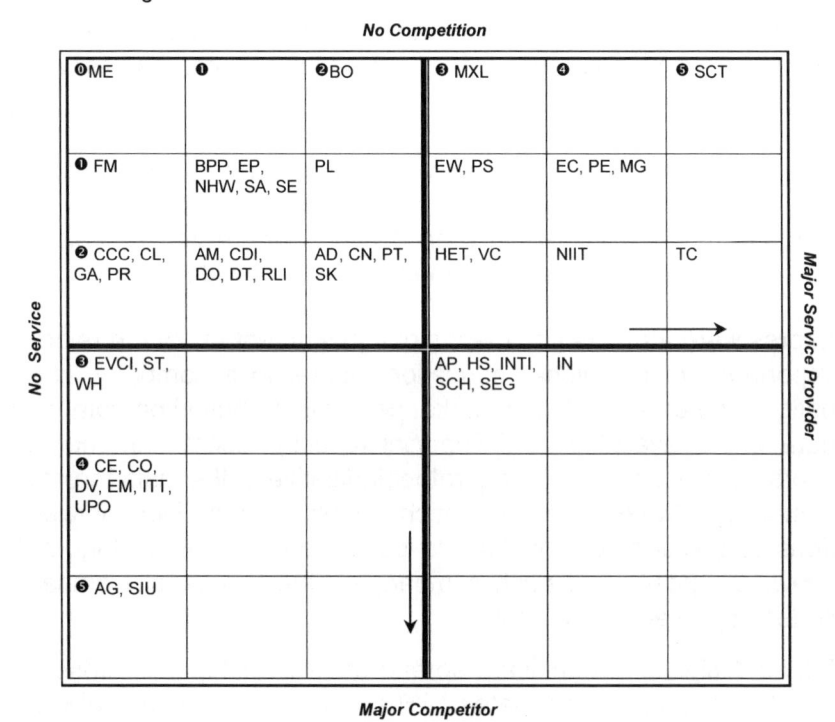

No Competition

	⓪	❷ BO	❸ MXL	❹	❺ SCT
⓪ ME					
❶ FM	BPP, EP, NHW, SA, SE	PL	EW, PS	EC, PE, MG	
❷ CCC, CL, GA, PR	AM, CDI, DO, DT, RLI	AD, CN, PT, SK	HET, VC	NIIT	TC
❸ EVCI, ST, WH			AP, HS, INTI, SCH, SEG	IN	
❹ CE, CO, DV, EM, ITT, UPO					
❺ AG, SIU					

No Service (left axis) → *Major Service Provider* (right axis)

Major Competitor (bottom axis)

5 Conclusion

This briefing has attempted to provide evidence of the balance of competitive and service relationships between postsecondary education companies and non-profit higher education. Companies in the GEI fall into one of three types: Direct Competitors, Indirect Competitors and Service Providers/Clients. In fact, many firms exhibit characteristics of more than one type. Only 17 firms (34%) were judged to have a significant competitive relationship with the non-profit sector. These included US for-profit college and university networks (e.g. Apollo, Sylvan), similar institutions in Malaysia (e.g. INTI, SEG), and two leading IT training firms

(Informatics and Aptech). A number of these firms also presented forms of service relationship with higher education. Overall, among GEI companies, competitive relationships are more common than service relationships, but in many cases the competitive threat is minor, tangential or latent. By contrast, the competitive position of multinational publishers has weakened compared to 1998–2000.

What is the potential for movement of position over time? The two possible shifts of most significance were thought to be a more competitive stance from the Malaysian college networks and an improved service relationship with corporate e-learning firms. In most respects, the Malaysian college networks resemble the for-profit universities and colleges of the United States, but with one crucial difference. Government regulation currently bars private colleges in Malaysia from seeking their own degree-awarding powers.[20] This restriction spurred alliances with universities from Australia, the UK and elsewhere, and is the key determinant of the companies' current mixed competitive/service position in Figure 1. Without this restriction, the current service rationale might weaken and the colleges might begin to compete with the non-profit sector without the present ambiguity. In the case of corporate e-learning firms, it was noted above that non-profit higher education might seek a more significant service relationship in terms of provision of online content.

To summarise, this analysis suggests that the competitive threat to non-profit higher education remains relatively minor in absolute terms, but recent years have witnessed significant recruitment growth among certain companies, international expansion, and ambitious plans by new entrants. New technology and new markets have prompted a range of innovative service relationships between companies and higher education. The rise of borderless higher education is characterised by deeper and more complex relationships between commercial entities and non-profit higher education. The unknown is the extent to which these relationships will develop

---

[20] See the descriptions at *Study Malaysia website*. Available at: www.study malaysia.com/is/education12.shtml. Last Accessed 22 April 2004.

further, what will remain the province of the non-profit sector and what services and activities will become viable commercial propositions.

Annex A – Service and Competition Scores by Company

Section 4 used a grid representation of the range of competitive and service relationships between GEI companies and non-profit higher education. This annex gives company codes used in the grid, plus overall service and competition scores that served as grid coordinates. Individual company scores are also given for the eight headings discussed in Section 3. The eight headings cover the range of current relationships between companies and non-profit higher education. There is an indirect link between a company's scores under the eight headings and its overall service score. The overall score is not an average, but rather a judgement about both company priorities and market penetration. The overall competition score was derived from a broad assessment of company activities and market presence. The higher the score in each case, the more significant the service relationship/competitive position. The scale used is 0–5.

Company	Code	Country	Relationship Type	Software Sales & Services	Materials Sales	Non-Core Course Sales	Franchise/Marketing	Funding	Accreditation	Joint Course Development	Core Course Sales	Overall Service Score	Overall Competition Score
Advtech	AD	South Africa	DC*			2	2					2	2
Amnet	AM	Australia	DC	1			1	1		1		1	2
Aptech	AT	India	SC		2				2	2	2	3	3
Apollo Group	AG	USA	DC									0	5
Boustead Holdings	BO	Malaysia	SC					2				2	0

(*Continued*)

Mapping the Education Industry, Part 2　　　　　　　　　　　　　　　　315

Annex A (*Continued*)

Company	Code	Country	Relationship Type	Software Sales & Services	Materials Sales	Non-Core Course Sales	Franchise/Marketing	Funding	Accreditation	Joint Course Development	Core Course Sales	Overall Service Score	Overall Competition Score
BPP Holdings	BPP	UK	SC					1				1	1
Concorde Career Colleges	CCC	USA	DC									0	2
CDI Education Corporation	CDI	Canada	DC			1				1		1	2
Career Education Corporation	CE	USA	DC									0	4
Click2Learn	CL	USA	IC									0	2
Centra Software	CN	USA	IC	2								2	2
Corinthian Colleges	CO	USA	DC									0	4
Docent	DO	USA	IC	1	1							1	2
DigitalThink	DT	USA	IC	1	1							1	2
DeVry	DV	USA	DC									0	4
eCollege	EC	USA	SC	4	2	1						4	1
Education Management Corporation	EM	USA	DC									0	4
Epic Group	EP	UK	IC	1								1	1
EVCI Career Colleges	EVCI	USA	DC									0	3
Entertainment World	EW	Australia	SC	1	3		1					3	1
Futuremedia	FM	UK	IC									0	1
Garratt's Limited	GA	Australia	DC									0	2
Horizon Education & Technologies	HET	Singapore	SC			2	2					3	2
HealthStream	HS	USA	SC	2	1	1						3	3
Informatics Holdings	IN	Singapore	SC			3	2	1				4	3
Inti Universal Holdings	INTI	Malaysia	SC			3						3	3
ITT Educational Services	ITT	USA	DC									0	4
Mentergy	ME	Israel	IC									0	0

(*Continued*)

Annex A (*Continued*)

Company	Code	Country	Relationship Type	Software Sales & Services	Materials Sales	Non-Core Course Sales	Franchise/Marketing	Funding	Accreditation	Joint Course Development	Core Course Sales	Overall Service Score	Overall Competition Score
McGraw-Hill	MG	USA	SC	2	4							4	1
MXL	MXL	Australia	SC	2								3	0
New Horizons Worldwide	NHW	USA	IC			1						1	1
NIIT	NIIT	India	SC	2		2			2	2	2	4	2
Pearson	PE	UK	SC	2	4							4	1
PLATO Learning	PL	USA	SC			3						2	1
Prosoft Training	PT	USA	IC	1	2	2						2	2
Primeserv	PR	South Africa	DC									0	2
PeopleSoft	PS	USA	SC	3	1	1						3	1
Raffles LaSalle International	RLI	Singapore	SC							1		1	2
Saba	SA	USA	IC	1								1	2
Stamford College Holdings	SCH	Malaysia	SC				3					3	3
SCT	SCT	USA	SC	5								5	0
Serebra Learning Corporation	SE	Canada	IC	1		1						1	1
Strayer Education	ST	USA	DC									0	3
SEG International	SEG	Malaysia	SC				3					3	3
Sylvan Learning Systems	SIU	USA	DC									0	5
SkillSoft Corporation	SK	Ireland	IC			1			2	1		2	2
Thomson Corporation	TC	Canada	SC	2	4	2	3	3	1	2		5	2
University of Phoenix Online	UPO	USA	DC									0	4
VCampus Corporation	VC	USA	SC	3		3						3	2
Whitman Education Group	WH	USA	DC									0	3

* DC = Direct Competitor, IC = Indirect Competitor, SC = Service/Client relationship.

Section III: Market Analysis

Transnational Higher Education: *major markets and emerging trends*

Richard Garrett and Line Verbik

Abstract: The scale of in-country transnational higher education has grown markedly in recent years. Hong Kong and Singapore are two of the most significant sites of activity. This report offers an analysis of which foreign institutions are involved, which countries are represented and which programmes offered, plus an overview of enrolments. There is also a discussion of data inaccuracies and discrepancies and examination of the activities of one of the main exporters (Australia). Data suggests that the range and scale of Australia's export activity has grown markedly over the past decade. The 'traditional' markets of Hong Kong SAR, Malaysia and Singapore remain dominant, but delivery in other countries is increasingly significant. Exploration of data from five (majority) importer nations indicates the widespread dominance of the main English-speaking exporter countries (Australia, UK, USA). A conceptual model is put forward, setting out the factors that influence import/export potential at the national level.

1 Introduction

The conventional form of transnational higher education is for students to travel abroad to study. Rising costs for the student, and government concern over brain drain and lost revenue prompted an alternative model, whereby the provision travels to the student. Transnational higher education is a global phenomenon, with ever more countries involved as importers and exporters, and often as both. The conventional flow is from developed countries to emerging economies, but other relationships exist. The scale of transnational provision has increased dramatically in recent years. For example, transnational programmes from Australian universities grew from less than 50 in 1992 to about 1500 in 2002, with almost all the country's universities involved.[1]

This report attempts to map current knowledge of transnational higher education worldwide. By 'transnational higher education' is meant higher education provision from one country offered in another (and excludes provision where solely the student travels abroad). By 'mapping' is meant specifically charting which higher education institutions and other organisations are involved in transnational delivery, which countries are represented and which programmes are offered. There is brief discussion of the nature of transnational provision, its regulation and the global/national drivers that propel it, but these are not the main focus of the report.

2 Methodology

Mapping transnational provision is not straightforward, not least because few countries keep adequate records of either imported provision, or programmes exported by their own higher education

---

[1] Australian Vice-Chancellors' Committee (2003) *Offshore Programmes of Australian Universities*, May, p.4. Available at: www.avcc.edu.au/policies_activities/international_relations/internationalisation_initiatives/OffshorePrograms_AustralianUnis.pdf. Last Accessed 22 April 2004.

institutions. For this reason, any mapping must remain partial at this juncture. That said, as the scale of transnational provision has increased and governments begin to view it as an important component of domestic capacity (import perspective) or source of diversified income (export perspective), regulation of activity is evermore common. A typical aspect of regulation is that host governments require transnational providers to register in some form, and often use a list of registered institutions to guide consumers towards 'legitimate' providers. Such lists – and other data – form the basis for this study.

The report begins by looking at data from two of the largest markets for transnational higher education – Hong Kong and Singapore. These two city states host over 1000 transnational postsecondary programmes between them, and official lists give details of providers, source countries, local partners, disciplines and awards. Along with Malaysia, Hong Kong and Singapore currently constitute the most significant markets for transnational provision in the world. For example, taking perhaps the most active source nation, the three territories account for more than 70 percent of Australia's transnational provision.[2] Only one major source country publishes details of the transnational activities of its universities – Australia. This data gives a sense of the global spread of Australian university provision, plus details of enrolments by country and mode of study (e.g. distance learning, period of study in Australia, entirely offshore). There is also analysis of other known national data on transnational provision (e.g. in Malaysia, Thailand and South Africa). This data is either incomplete or suggests a relatively low level of activity. The report concludes with a discussion of a theoretical model of the development of transnational higher education worldwide, revealing the complexities of national positions and offering an explanation of how those positions change over time.

---

[2] Australian Vice-Chancellors' Committee (2003) *Offshore Programmes of Australian Universities*, May, p.4. Available at: www.avcc.edu.au/policies_ activities/international_relations/internationalisation_initiatives/OffshorePrograms_ AustralianUnis.pdf. Last Accessed 22 April 2004.

The Observatory is grateful to all the national agencies that have provided the data used in this series, and would encourage equivalent bodies in other countries to consider collecting and publishing similar information. Analysis of such data may help host/source countries regulate imported/exported provision to their best advantage. The availability of import and export data from independent sources also allows comparison, revealing sometimes significant discrepancies. Comment on any aspect of this work will be gratefully received.

The Observatory is not in a position to comment on the official status or quality of any transnational provision.

3 Hong Kong and Singapore – Context and Regulation

Imported transnational provision has been an important feature of higher education in both Hong Kong and Singapore since the 1980s, and has played a role in transforming their respective economies. As two of the four original Asian Tigers, both city states experienced rapid industrialisation after World War II as centres of manufacturing. But by the early 1980s, competition from other lower-cost industrialising Asian nations forced a re-think. Both economies committed to moving up the value chain, developing knowledge industries (finance, chemicals, design, technology). With few natural assets, Hong Kong and Singapore opted to court multinational companies to set up operations in their territories and invest in their own human resources. Both required massive expansion of postsecondary education.

In the mid-1980s, Singapore experienced its first recession since independence in 1965. The government undertook a comprehensive review of the economy, resulting in the report *The Singapore Economy: New Directions* in 1986. The report recommended an expansion of postsecondary education, with the effect that school-leaver participation almost doubled from 8% in 1985 to 15% in 1990. Spurred by the rapidly approaching handover from British to Chinese rule in 1997, and smarting from a sharp rise in professional emigration in the wake of the Tianaman Square massacre of 1989, Hong Kong followed Singapore's lead. From a participation rate of 8% of school-leavers in 1989, the government set a target of 15% by 1994/5.[3]

The two national strategies had much in common but also exhibited important differences. Both encouraged a more entrepreneurial culture in their universities, increasing local autonomy but at the same time instituting a range of audit measures to oversee quality and promote efficiency. Both instituted tuition fees alongside massive increases in overall public funding (recently cut back in Hong Kong). Singapore has attempted to diversify university income through the creation of endowments, and is committed to matching any funds raised by the universities themselves. Hong Kong proposed a similar matched-funding arrangement in March 2003. Hong Kong opted to convert a number of pre-existing higher education institutions into universities during the 1990s, while Singapore has stuck with two public universities plus a more stable complementary system of polytechnics, university colleges etc. Both countries fostered private provision but not at university level[4] and without degree awarding powers. Hong Kong has considered the possibility of privatising some or all of its universities.[5]

Overseas study became an increasingly popular option for middle-class parents, but involved considerable expense and the risk of brain drain. Moreover, the practice did little to develop domestic capacity on a broad scale. Initially occurring outside government influence, examples of in-country transnational provision, notably

---

[3] For all these figures, see Lee, M. & Gopinathan, S. (2003) 'Reforming University Education in Hong Kong and Singapore', *Higher Education Research & Development*, Vol.22, No.2, pp167–182.
[4] A partial exception is Singapore Management University founded in 1999, an unusual combination of private status and substantial public funding.
[5] See the discussion in Lee, M. & Gopinathan, S. (2003) 'Reforming University Education in Hong Kong and Singapore', *Higher Education Research & Development*, Vol.22, No.2, pp167–182.

franchising and twinning programmes, sprung up from the mid-1980s. The decision by the UK in 1980 to charge full cost fees to Commonwealth citizens, such as those of Hong Kong and Singapore, was a particularly significant driver. This model was a useful foil for the expansion ambitions of local private providers, offered students a lower cost route to a foreign degree, and provided universities from (primarily) the UK and Australia (then and now the dominant providers) with a competitive edge in the rapidly growing Asian market.

Transnational provision grew quickly in both countries and remained free of specific local regulation for some time. The Hong Kong Education Commission expressed concern over the growth of foreign programmes as early as 1986, but it was not until 1997 that the *Non-Local Higher and Professional Education (Regulation) ordinance* was enacted. Foreign providers partnering with one of Hong Kong's eleven publicly-funded universities and other higher education institutions must apply for 'exemption from registration', while all other foreign providers must apply for registration. Distance learning providers are also exempt from registration but are encouraged to register to demonstrate quality. The application process is per programme and is similar in both cases – the foreign institution must provide details of course content, delivery methods, admission requirements, staffing, in-country facilities and quality assurance processes. Evidence must be provided that the foreign institution is legitimate and recognised in its own country. Applicants must also make clear those tasks to be carried out by the local partner. Applications for exemption where a recognised local institution has endorsed the application tend to be less closely examined than applications for registration.[6] However, there is no attempt to directly gauge the quality of foreign provision through institutional visits or ongoing scrutiny (beyond annual updates to the above information). Successful applicants (there are currently over

---

[6] For an account of the 1997 ordinance, see McBurnie, G. & Ziguras, C. (2001) 'The regulation of transnational higher education in Southeast Asia: case studies of Hong Kong, Malaysia and Australia', *Higher Education*, Vol.42, pp85–101.

Transnational Higher Education

800 approved foreign programmes in Hong Kong) must simply display their registration/exemption number on all promotional material. An important emphasis is evidence that transnational provision is of the same quality as comparable provision in the source country. It is important to note that the registration process does not confer official recognition on non-local provision.

In 2001, as part of wider quality assurance reforms, Hong Kong introduced a voluntary accreditation scheme for self-financing postsecondary programmes (many of which involve foreign providers). Following cases of alleged misleading advertising by some foreign providers, the government now encourages foreign institutions to seek accreditation for their provision.[7] The process involves programme validation and institutional review. As an incentive, the government has set aside HK$30 million (US$2.2 million) to cover the entire institutional cost of validation and 50 percent of the cost of review (payable upon successful accreditation). On the 2003/04 list of accredited provision, only two transnational providers are mentioned – Southern Cross University and Victoria University of Technology (one programme each), accredited through the Hong Kong Institute of Technology.[8]

In Singapore, transnational provision must be registered, again by programme, with the Ministry of Education. The requirements for registration are similar to those in Hong Kong, although there is no distinction between exempt and registered provision, and no system of accreditation.[9] The Ministry is keen to emphasise that registration does not imply official recognition. Singapore recently introduced the 'Singapore Quality Class', a voluntary accreditation

---

[7] Observatory on Borderless Higher Education, 'Spate of Bogus Advertising Prompts Hong Kong Authorities to Recommend Foreign Universities Seek Local Accreditation', *Breaking News*, 26 September 2002.

[8] Education and Manpower Bureau, Government of the Hong Kong Special Administrative Region, *List of Full-time Accredited Self-financing Post-secondary Programmes for 2003/04*, Available at: www.emb.gov.hk/index.aspx?nodeid=2110&langno=1#citsd. Last Accessed 22 April 2004.

[9] Ministry of Education, Singapore, *Registration of Distance Learning Programmes*. Available at: www1.moe.edu.sg/privatesch. Last Accessed 22 April 2004.

process for local private providers (many of whom work with foreign universities), but it does not target foreign organisations directly. The Spring Singapore website (the organisation that runs the scheme) lists only accredited institutions, not the programmes they offer. Thus it is not clear how many transnational programmes are now associated with accredited local providers. The absence of the registered/exempt distinction may mean that distance-only provision (i.e. with no local support) may opt to avoid registration – but this is not clear. Unlike Malaysia, neither Hong Kong nor Singapore have attempted to stipulate aspects of curriculum content from transnational providers.

Foreign universities play a dual role in Singapore. Aside from 'unofficial' transnational provision, a select number of foreign institutions have been invited to establish operations in the country. The original target of ten has been met, and includes MIT, Wharton, Chicago Graduate School of Business and Georgia Institute of Technology from the United States, INSEAD from France, Technische Universiteit Eindhoven from the Netherlands and Technische Universität München from Germany. These institutions are not included in the registration process for transnational providers.

Looking forward, Singapore's ambition to become a regional education hub cites an ongoing role for foreign universities – both a selected elite and mass market provision.[10] Struggling with system reform and budget cuts, Hong Kong does not appear to have formulated a comparable strategy. That said, data below on the significance of transnational provision in the territory suggests an ongoing role, not least in helping meet the current national target of 60% school-leaver participation in higher education by 2010. In Singapore, there is also an emerging trend to gradually roll out degree-awarding powers to domestic institutions, thus perhaps undermining the rationale of transnational provision.

---

[10] Ministry for Trade & Industry, Singapore, *Developing Singapore's Education Industry*. Available at: www.mti.gov.sg/public/ERC/frm_ERC_Default.asp?sid=124. Last Accessed 22 April 2004.

4 Analysis of Transnational Activity in Hong Kong

Hong Kong's Education and Manpower Bureau provides a list of registered 'Non-local Higher and Professional Education Programmes', which is updated monthly.[11] The data analysed below relates to June 2003. The most recent list (from October 2003) shows that another 37 programmes have been added since the summer. This increase of about four percent over four months indicates slight but not dramatic change. The lists provide information on foreign institution, title of degree programme, operator and local agency (where applicable). They do not provide information about country of origin (this has been added by the Observatory), mode of delivery, how long the programmes have been running or enrolment figures. Where possible the data provided by the Bureau is supplemented with and compared to other sources such as the Australian Vice-Chancellors' Committee and the University Grants Committee in Hong Kong.

In June 2003, 858 higher education programmes from foreign institutions were registered/exempt in Hong Kong. The current regulations in the Special Administrative Region (SAR) state that foreign providers of higher education must obtain registration for the programmes offered unless they can prove exemption – see Section 3. Of the total number of foreign higher education programmes offered in Hong Kong, 385 were registered and 473 were exempted. It is not possible to ascertain from the data provided by the Bureau whether a course is exempted from registration because it is taught in co-operation with a selected local higher education institution or because it is taught entirely at a distance.

This section will examine the providers (which countries and universities are involved, who operates the programmes locally) and programmes offered (level, discipline). As trends in the two

---

[11] Government of the Hong Kong Special Administrative Region, Education and Manpower Bureau, *Non-Local Higher and Professional Education Programmes*. Available at: www.emb.gov.hk/index.aspx?nodeID=226&langno=1. Last Accessed 22 April 2004.

categories, registered and exempted programmes, vary, the two groups will be described individually and compared where appropriate. It has not been possible to ascertain full details for approximately 4 percent of the registered programmes and 7 percent of the exempted (due to missing data on the official lists).

According to the June list, institutions and organisations from eleven different countries were offering registered/exempt higher education provision in Hong Kong. Identifying the exact number of institutions involved is complicated by inaccuracies in the lists. These mainly occur where institutions have changed names and are listed both under their new and old name, or where the same institution is listed under two different names, e.g. University of Ottawa is also listed as Ottawa University. Allowing for these inaccuracies, a total of 168 different institutions and organisations were listed as offering registered/exempt programmes in Hong Kong. As many institutions are offering programmes both in the registered and the exempt category, this figure (of 168) is less than the total number of institutions in the registered plus exempted categories. The number of institutions active in Hong Kong and the number of programmes offered are set out in Table 1 (in descending order by number of institutions per country):

Table 1 Programmes by Institution

Country	Registered Programmes				Exempted Programmes			
	Programmes	% of Total	Institutions	% of Total	Programmes	% of Total	Institutions	% of Total
UK	173	45	54	43	279	59	35	46
Australia	141	37	35	28	126	27	21	27
USA	38	10	23	19	20	4	12	16
Canada	9	2	7	6	3	0.6	3	4
China	2	0.5	1	0.8	6	1.2	2	3
New Zealand	–	–	–	–	2	0.4	2	3
Ireland	2	0.5	1	0.8	–	–	–	–

(Continued)

Table 1 (*Continued*)

Country	Registered Programmes				Exempted Programmes			
	Programmes	% of Total	Institutions	% of Total	Programmes	% of Total	Institutions	% of Total
Singapore	1	0.2	1	0.8	–	–	–	–
India	–	–	–	–	4	0.8	1	1
Macau	6	1.5	1	0.8	–	–	–	–
Philippines	1	0.2	1	0.8	–	–	–	–
Unknown	12	3.1	–	–	33	7	–	–
Total	385	100	124	100	473	100	76	100

The UK and Australia together accounted for 314 of the 385 registered programmes (more than 80 percent) and 405 of the 473 (just over 85 percent) of the exempted programmes. Institutions from the United Kingdom (this includes a small number of professional bodies and other non-university institutions) accounted for the largest number of programmes, with almost 45 percent of the registered programmes and approximately 59 percent of the exempted. Australian institutions were the second largest provider in both categories with just under 37 percent of the registered programmes and 27 percent of the exempted programmes. The US came third with a significant lower share of the total – approximately 10 percent of the registered programmes and only about 4 percent of the exempted programmes. Canada, Macau (China), Mainland China, New Zealand, India, Ireland, Philippines and Singapore all accounted for 2 percent or less of registered and exempted programmes. The absence in both categories of programmes from any non-English speaking European institutions is noteworthy.

The country with the highest number of institutions represented both in the registered and exempted categories was the UK followed by Australia, the US and Canada. The rest of the countries with a presence in Hong Kong had between one and five institutions represented in one or both categories. The number of institutions represented was significantly lower in the exempted category compared to the registered category, although the total number of programmes was higher. UK institutions were, for example, offering an average of 3.2 programmes in the registered category and an average of 7.9 in the exempted. Australian institutions also offered more programmes per institution in the exempted category than in the registered. The nature of the programmes in the exempted category, particularly those taught entirely at a distance, might explain why institutions are able to offer a higher number of exempted than registered programmes.

Table 1 also indicates the relative intensity of transnational activity by Australian and UK institutions. For example, under registered provision, Australia exhibited an average of four programmes per institution, compared to only 3.2 for the UK. So despite lower overall activity, Australia outpaced the UK in intensity. Using membership of the two national inter-university bodies (Australian Vice-Chancellors' Committee and Universities UK), 87 percent of Australian universities had a presence in Hong Kong compared to 45 percent of British universities.[12] While the UK's former polytechnics were particularly prominent, older, more 'traditional' universities also featured.

As noted above, Australia is thought to be the only major source country to publish detailed information on the transnational activities of its universities. Earlier this year, the Australian Vice-Chancellors' Committee (AVCC) published a list of transnational activity by its members (relating to May 2003). According to the AVCC data, Australian universities offered 223 programmes in Hong Kong, whereas according to the list provided by the Hong Kong government the figure was 254. While the discrepancy is not as marked as is the case for Singapore (see below), in many instances there were differences between the lists concerning the number of programmes offered by particular institutions. For example, Charles Sturt University offered 28 programmes in Hong

---

[12] In the case of both AVCC and UUK, only university or equivalent members have been counted.

Kong according to AVCC data (May 2003), and 18 according to the lists available from Hong Kong (June 2003). Even when the number of programmes do correspond, programmes titles do not necessarily conform.

More than two-thirds (67 percent) of institutions offering registered provision were offering only one or two programmes. In the exempted category over half (55 percent) of institutions offered one or two programmes. As shown in Table 2, a small number of institutions dominate foreign provision in Hong Kong. Ten institutions (8 percent of the total) accounted for over 30 percent of the registered programmes. In the exempted category, 10 institutions (13 percent of the total) accounted for 56 percent of the programmes.

Table 2 Dominant Institutions

Registered Programmes			Exempted Programmes		
Institution	Country	Number of Programmes	Institution	Country	Number of Programmes
1. University of Leicester	UK	16	1. University of London[13]	UK	122
2 = Sheffield Hallam University	UK	13	2. Middlesex University	UK	18
2 = University of Southern Queensland	Australia	13	3. Curtin University of Technology	Australia	17
2 = Charles Sturt University	Australia	13	4 = Monash University	Australia	15
5. Macquarie University	Australia	12	4 = University of New England	Australia	15
6 = NCC Education Limited	UK	10	6 = University of Warwick	UK	14
6 = RMIT	Australia	10	6 = University of Western Australia	Australia	14
8. University of Ballarat	Australia	9	6 = University of Leicester	UK	14

(*Continued*)

---

[13] It should be noted that the institution offering the highest number of programmes in the exempted category is the UK's University of London, a federation of 30 London-based colleges and institutes (there are virtually no instances where a member institution is listed separately). While it is not made clear, it is likely that most provision comes under the University of London External Programme (distance learning).

Table 2 (Continued)

Registered Programmes			Exempted Programmes		
Institution	Country	Number of Programmes	Institution	Country	Number of Programmes
9 = Upper Iowa University	USA	8	8. Victoria University	Australia	13
9 = Deakin University	Australia	8	9 = University of Wollongong	Australia	12
9 = Victoria University	Australia	8	9 = University of Ulster	UK	12

As shown in Table 3 below, masters programmes formed the largest group in both categories, followed by bachelors programmes in the registered category and other postgraduate programmes in the exempted. Compared to registered provision, there were less programmes leading to a first or second degree qualification amongst the exempted programmes, suggesting that the delivery form of some of the exempted programmes (i.e. distance learning) might be more suitable for non-degree programmes, particularly at postgraduate level.

Table 3 Programmes by Level

Registered Programmes			Exempted Programmes		
Programme	Number of Programmes	% of Total	Programme	Number of Programmes	% of Total
Bachelor	114	30	Bachelor	118	25
Masters	156	40	Masters	141	30
Other Undergraduate	72	19	Other Undergraduate	54	11
Other Postgraduate	35	9	Other Postgraduate	126	27
Unknown	8	2	Unknown	34	7
Total	385	100	Total	473	100

For the purpose of this report the programmes were grouped in subject areas: Business (including Finance, Accountancy, Management, Marketing), Social Science, Humanities, the Sciences (including the Natural, Physical, Biological, Life and Health Sciences), IT, engineering and miscellaneous. Some programmes (approximately 5 percent of the registered programmes and 13 percent of the exempted) covered more than one discipline, e.g. a degree in Management and Law. In those cases both disciplines were counted and as a result the total number of disciplines is higher than the total number of programmes. This is naturally also reflected in the accompanying percentages. Where programmes cover two different areas within the same discipline, e.g. a degree programme in Business and Finance, the subject area 'Business' was counted only once.

As Table 4 shows, the most common subject amongst registered and exempted programmes was business. However, in the exempted category business accounted for only 37 percent of programmes, compared to 64 percent of registered programmes. There was significant variation by subject between the two categories.

Table 4 Programmes by Discipline

Discipline	Registered Programmes		Exempted Programmes	
	Number of Programmes	% of Total	Number of Programmes	% of Total
Business	245	64	177	37
IT	42	11	39	8
Humanities	40	10	85	18
Sciences	32	8	115	24
Engineering	17	4	18	4
Social Science	6	2	47	10
Miscellaneous[14]	23	6	12	3

There was a significant difference (of approximately 26 percent) between registered and exempted programmes in terms of the scale of business provision. Programmes in the sciences and humanities accounted for a substantially larger proportion of the exempted programmes than the registered. The same was the case

---
[14] Includes general studies, architecture, law and unknown subject areas.

for social science programmes. IT and engineering programmes were nearly equally represented in the two categories. Greater instance of science and humanities provision in exempted programmes might be explained in terms of the involvement of Hong Kong universities – reflecting their broader interests and resources. By contrast, the striking dominance of business provision in the registered sector may reflect the niche markets pursued by local private partners.

The foreign institutions have chosen a number of different operational models. Some appear to be operating their programmes themselves, some have chosen to operate some of their programmes themselves and make franchise arrangements for the rest and some are offering all their programmes through another, usually local, institution. Approximately 25 percent of the registered programmes were offered and operated by the same organisation or institution. It is not clear from the data available from the Bureau how those foreign institutions that are operating their programmes themselves are conducting their operations, e.g. from which premises. As mentioned above, all the exempted programmes are either offered entirely at a distance or with a specified local higher education institution.

Some of the local partners were operating programmes for more than one foreign institution. The Hong Kong Management Association was operating 34 foreign programmes for 11 different institutions and organisations, and two of the local colleges (Caritas Francis Hsu College and Hong Kong College of Technology International Ltd) were running 13 programmes for five different institutions and 8 programmes for three different institutions respectively.

Information from the Education and Manpower Bureau[15] and the University Grants Committee[16] gives an indication of student

---

[15] Information from correspondence with the Registrar of Non-local Higher and Professional Education Courses, Education and Manpower Bureau.
[16] University Grants Committee, India, *Website Statistics Menu*. Available at: www.ugc.edu.hk/english/statistics/index_nf.html. Last Accessed 22 April 2004.

enrolment in foreign and local institutions. The UGC only provides information about enrolment in programmes funded by the Committee (at eight institutions in total). The table below does therefore not include enrolment in local private institutions other than that offered in connection with a foreign institution.

Table 5 Enrolment by Programme Type

Year	Enrolment – Programmes Offered by Foreign Providers	Enrolment – UGC-funded Programmes
2002–03	34,949	78,731

Table 5 indicates the significance of transnational education in Hong Kong. Taking the students enrolled in private local institutions of higher education into account, it seems reasonable to suggest that at least a quarter of students in higher education in Hong Kong are enrolled in foreign programmes (and the figure would be significantly higher if only degree programmes were considered).

5 Analysis of Transnational Activity in Singapore

Singapore's Ministry of Education updates its public directory of registered foreign postsecondary programmes once a month.[17] The data analysed below relates to June 2003. Where relevant, the contents of the most recent list (31 October 2003) are also discussed. The lists give details of foreign institution, country of origin, programme title and level, and local partner. There are no details of how long each programme has been running, how long each partnership has been in place, mode of delivery, enrolments or attainment. Other evidence (e.g. from the Australian Vice-Chancellors' Committee and Singapore's Department of Statistics) help fill in some of the gaps.

---

[17] Ministry of Education, Singapore, *Private Schools in Singapore*. Available at: www1.moe.edu.sg/privatesch. Last Accessed 22 April 2004.

The June 2003 directory lists 522 programmes. Identifying the exact number of foreign institutions involved in offering these programmes is not straightforward. The list contains a number of ambiguities. For example, State University of New York and State University of New York, Buffalo are listed separately, but it is unclear whether this reflects genuinely distinct provision or confusion over correct nomenclature. University of Lincoln in the UK is listed under its former name, University of Lincolnshire & Humberside and as University of Humberside; while both University of East London and Sheffield Hallam University in the UK are also listed under their former polytechnic names. Central Queensland University is also listed as University of Central Queensland. Allowing for what appear to be duplicate entries, foreign programmes were offered by a total of 127 foreign institutions. Foreign institutions by country were as follows:

Table 6 Representation by Country

Country	Programmes	% of Total	Institutions	% of Total
Australia	279	53%	35	28%
UK	172	33%	54	43%
USA	36	7%	22	17%
China	12	2%	7	6%
New Zealand	6	1%	1	0.8%
Switzerland	5	1%	3	2.3%
Ireland	4	0.75%	1	0.8%
Netherlands	3	0.5%	1	0.8%
Canada	2	0.4%	1	0.8%
Australia/UK	1	0.2%	N/A	N/A
Finland	1	0.2%	1	0.8%
Philippines	1	0.2%	1	0.8%
Total	522	100%	127	100%

Table 6 shows the dominance of Australia and UK in this market – constituting 86% of programmes and 71% of institutions. The UK had 43% of institutions but only 33% of programmes, whereas Australia had only 28% of institutions but 53% of programmes.

While some institutions are far more active than others (see below), the overall 'intensity' of Australian activity was 7.97 programmes per institution, compared to only 3.18 for the UK. What proportion of Australian and UK universities offer provision in Singapore? Using membership of the two national university bodies (Australian Vice-Chancellors' Committee and Universities UK), 33 (87%) of AVCC members are active in Singapore, compared to only 54 (40%) of UUK members.[18] Again, this emphasises the intensity and scope of Australian activity. As in Hong Kong, a range of UK universities are involved, but the former polytechnics particularly so.

The presence of China and the Philippines, as well as a number of continental European countries, is a reminder of the market value of non-English language provision, and the trend for institutions from non-English speaking countries to deliver in English. Only one cross-national programme was recorded on the list (involving one Australian and one UK university), emphasising that transnational provision in Singapore is characterised by national delivery rather than international partnership (i.e. between two countries, aside from Singapore itself). Only three programmes were said to involve partnerships of any kind between source institutions.

It is notable that in the October update, the directory lists 643 registered programmes, an increase of 23%. The difference is partly due to an increase in the number of institutions involved (up 15, or 12%), but primarily due to increased activity by selected established players (but see below for a possible third explanation). The new institutions broadly reflect the pattern by country seen in the June data, but with more than a third of new entrants (6) from the United States. The University of La Rochelle marks France's first appearance on the list. Another interesting addition is Universitas Global (registered as a company in

---

[18] In the case of both AVCC and UUK, only university or equivalent members have been counted.

Singapore), the international consortia of universities offering online programmes.

It is interesting to compare the June 2003 data from the Ministry of Education in Singapore with the information on offshore provision collected by the Australian Vice-Chancellors' Committee (AVCC) concerning May 2003. While the Singapore list contains 279 entries for Australia, the AVCC list contains 375 entries. At least one Australian university was listed in the Singapore directory and not in the AVCC directory, and vice versa. Some universities are said to be far more active on the AVCC list than on the Singapore list. For example, in the Singapore list, Charles Sturt University was reported as running seven programmes in Singapore, compared to 35 on the AVCC list. Given that the two directories often list different local partners for Australian provision, it does not appear to simply be a matter of the AVCC directory including distance-only programmes that have opted not to register in Singapore. It also seems unlikely that the difference of one month could account for such significant discrepancies between the two directories.

Some of the discrepancies can be resolved in terms of fuller disclosure of degree specialisms, but much cannot be so easily explained. It may not be a question of any university deliberately misleading either the Ministry of Education in Singapore or the AVCC, but rather that the discrepancies may have arisen due to different data collection methods, different respondents within the institution and incomplete institutional data. A problem may be that given that students wishing to access foreign in-country provision will rely on the Singapore data, any institution/programme not on that list (for whatever reason) might be disadvantaged. Of course, the apparent discrepancy on the Australian data raises the possibility of under-reporting across the board, undermining not only the accuracy of the Ministry's directory but also the attempt to improve consumer information.

On the June list, 39 percent of institutions are listed as operating only one programme in Singapore, and 70% have three programmes or less. A small number of institutions dominate. Table 7 lists the eleven most active institutions.

Table 7 Most Active Institutions

Institution	Country	Programmes
1. Curtin University of Technology	Australia	36
2. Open University	UK	22
3. RMIT University	Australia	17
4. Monash University	Australia	16
5. University of South Australia	Australia	14
6. University of Wales[19]	UK	13
7 = Southern Cross University	Australia	12
7 = University of New South Wales	Australia	12
8 = Edith Cowan University	Australia	10
8 = La Trobe University	Australia	10
8 = University of Wollongong	Australia	10

These eleven institutions made up less than 9% of all foreign institutions active in Singapore, but accounted for 33% of programmes. Over 83% of institutions use a university title, and a number of others are known to be part of a university (although the identity of the university is not listed or not listed clearly). Non-university institutions include university colleges, polytechnics, colleges, institutes etc. There is only limited overlap between the most active institutions in Hong Kong and Singapore. The lack of a specific injunction for distance-only programmes to register in Singapore, may explain the absence of University of London (External Programme) and University of Leicester (a UK university with significant distance learning) from the top ten.

Fifty seven percent of programmes were at masters level, and 28% at bachelors level. The remainder constituted undergraduate certificates/diplomas (6%), postgraduate certificates/diplomas (5%)

---

[19] The University of Wales is a federal institution but all but one entry for the institution is listed simply as 'University of Wales'. It is not clear whether this reflects a genuinely central initiative, a branding strategy adopted by the constituent members, or imprecise reporting on the list.

and doctoral programmes (4%). Given Singapore's emphasis on capacity building through transnational provision, it is perhaps surprising that only about a third of programmes were at undergraduate level (but see below). This suggests that the remainder are being accessed by existing graduates, whether from Singapore or elsewhere. There were no significant differences by level in terms of provision offered by Australia and the UK.

As might be expected, business subjects were by far the most common – prominent in 62% of the total number of programmes. Other relatively popular disciplines included IT (8%) and education (6%). Many other subjects featured to some extent – including law, engineering, English language, Chinese literature, religious studies, media studies, communications, economics, psychology, sociology and health sciences. Of course, many programmes featured elements from more than one discipline (typically business and something else), meaning that non-business subjects were present in somewhat higher numbers that the above figures suggest (although not independently). There were no differences in the dominance of business provision between Australia and the UK, but it is interesting that for most of the countries with only a minor presence (Canada, Finland, Netherlands, Philippines, Switzerland) business programmes were the sole focus. This suggests that business provision is viewed as the most robust market, although the experience of Australia, UK and USA suggests that rising participation leads to subject diversification.

The June directory lists 122 local partners in Singapore, almost as many as the total number of foreign institutions. Just ten account for 40% of programmes, and just one (Singapore Institute of Management) for 12%. An important difference compared to Hong Kong is that Singapore's public higher education institutions do not feature as local partners. All Singapore partners are private sector, non-university bodies, both non-profit and for-profit. A handful have non-Singapore origins (e.g. British Council). While some local partners are reported as working with only one foreign institution, some have multiple alliances. For example, as of June 2003, the Asia Pacific Management Centre worked with eleven foreign universities, from Australia, Ireland, UK and USA; covering a range of disciplines (e.g. business, education, law, communication, social science) and levels (undergraduate diplomas, masters, doctorate). Similarly, some foreign institutions work with only one Singapore operation, but others have forged a number of partnerships. For example, Australia's Edith Cowan University is listed as working with six local organisations.

Overall enrolment data is available from the Singapore Department of Statistics. The Singapore Department of Statistics began to publish data on enrolments in "external degree programmes" in 1997. Two key reports offer an analysis of enrolment and graduation data.[20] Figures for 1997–2002 for bachelors provision are presented below:

Table 8 Foreign Enrolment and Graduates

Year	Local Universities- Enrolment	Foreign Universities- Enrolment	% Foreign	Local Universities- Graduation	Foreign Universities- Graduation	% Foreign
1997	31,730	13,990	31%	8,680	2,600	23%
2000	37,650	21,010	36%	9,410	5,350	36%
2002[21]	–	–	–	10,200	7,994	44%

Table 8 shows that foreign provision constituted more than one third of bachelors enrolments in Singapore in 2001 (probably higher in 2002 – data not available, see footnote 21) and 44% of bachelor graduates in 2002. Foreign enrolments and graduates appear to be increasing faster than those from local universities. This reinforces how central in-country foreign provision has become to higher

---

[20] See Yeo Soek Lee (2001) 'Educational Upgrading through External Degree Programmes', *Singapore Department of Statistics*, pp2–8. Available at: www.singstat. gov.sg/ssn/feat/4Q2001/pg2-8.pdf. See Wu Wei Lin (2003) 'Educational Upgrading through Private Educational Institutions', *Singapore Statistics Newsletter*, September, pp5–9.

[21] Figures for local and foreign university enrolment in 2002 do not appear to be available. The *Ministry of Education, Singapore: Educational Fact Sheet 2003* gives enrolments for full-time students only.

education in Singapore. The data also indicates that while the majority of foreign programmes in Singapore are at masters level (see above), the majority of enrolments and graduates are at bachelors level. For example, in 2001, 73% of enrolments at degree level were in bachelors programmes, compared to 25% in masters programmes.[22]

Masters level enrolments and graduation present a contrasting picture. Full data does not appear to be available, but after rising to almost 50% of total masters graduates in 1999,[23] graduate numbers from foreign masters programmes actually fell by 976 (to stand at 2,594, only slightly above the 1999 figure of 2,154).[24] It is clear that the drop is partly due to an increased emphasis on graduate provision in local universities. Given the apparent under-reporting on Australian provision on the Ministry of Education's list of foreign programmes (see above), the impressive performance of foreign institutions may in fact be underestimated.

6 Australia

The Australian Vice-Chancellors' Committee (AVCC) publishes information on its 38 member institutions' transnational activities (described as 'offshore programmes').[25] 'Offshore' is defined for the purposes of the AVCC survey as higher education award-bearing

---

[22] See Statistics Singapore Newsletter (2002) *Educational Upgrading through Private Diploma & Degree Programmes, 2001*, p2. Available at: www.singstat.gov.sg/ssn/feat/oct2002/pg18-20.pdf. Last Accessed 22 April 2004.
[23] See Yeo Soek Lee (2001) 'Educational Upgrading through External Degree Programmes', *Singapore Department of Statistics*. p5. Available at: www.singstat.gov.sg/ssn/feat/4Q2001/pg2-8.pdf. Last Accessed 22 April 2004.
[24] Wu Wei Lin (2003) 'Educational Upgrading through Private Educational Institutions', *Singapore Statistics Newsletter*, September, p9.
[25] The AVCC has 38 members. According to the Committee, the only Australian university not a member of the AVCC is the private University of Notre Dame. See Australian Vice Chancellors' Committee (2003) *Offshore Programmes of Australian Universities*, May, p4. Available at: www.avcc.edu.au/policies_activities/international_relations/internationalisation_initiatives/OffshorePrograms_AustralianUnis.pdf. Last Accessed 22 April 2004.

programmes offered outside Australia (including distance learning) and delivered in partnership with a local organisation. Credit articulation and other advanced standing agreements are excluded, as is distance learning without local partnership. The AVCC list is updated every other year and the data in this briefing note relates to May 2003. The AVCC list provides information on Australian institutions operating offshore programmes, countries in which they are operating, partner institutions, the qualifications offered, mode of delivery, duration of programmes and when the courses were established. In what follows, the terms 'offshore' and 'transnational' are used interchangeably.

As pointed out above, some discrepancies were found when the AVCC data was compared to government statistics in Hong Kong and Singapore. Allowing for some inaccuracies, occurring either on the AVCC list or on those from Hong Kong and Singapore (and it is not possible to judge which account is most accurate), the AVCC data is a very valuable source of information. According to this data, with the exception of the University of Melbourne,[26] all members of the AVCC are involved in some form of transnational provision. Australian universities are offering almost 1,600 programmes in a total of 42 countries. As shown in Table 9, most activity is concentrated in a few countries in Asia with a relatively high or

---

[26] Data from the Ministry of Education in Singapore includes four programmes in the city-state from the University of Melbourne, in co-operation with the Singapore Institute of Management. Furthermore, the Education and Manpower Bureau lists two courses offered by the University of Melbourne in Hong Kong. In the latter case, these courses are on the 'exempt' list, meaning that they are either distance learning or offered in partnership with a local university or other public higher education provider (see Section 4 for more information about Hong Kong's 'registered' and 'exempt' categories). Both Melbourne courses list a local partner. The AVCC definition of offshore provision includes programmes "conducted in accordance with a formal agreement between the Australian university and an overseas institution or organisation" (p3). This would suggest that the four Melbourne programmes in Singapore and the two in Hong Kong would in fact fall under the AVCC definition. The list from the Ministry of Education in Singapore is available at: www1.moe.edu.sg/privatesch/. The list produced by Hong Kong's Education and Manpower Bureau can be found at: www.ncr.edu.hk/eng/index.asp.

Table 9 Top Ten Countries for Australian Offshore Programmes

Country	Number of Programmes	% of Total
Singapore	375	24
Malaysia	319	20
Hong Kong (SAR)	227	14
China	201	13
Thailand	48	3
India	41	3
South Africa	36	2
Vietnam	36	2
Canada	27	2
United Kingdom	17	1
Total for Top 10	1325	84
Total for all Programmes	1571	100

rising GDP and an increasing demand for higher education that domestic provision has been unable to meet.

Seventy-one percent of Australian transnational programmes are offered in Singapore, Malaysia, Hong Kong and Mainland China. No other country accounts for more than about three percent of the total. Interestingly, the UK, one of the other major transnational exporters alongside Australia, is found in the top ten countries (although it accounts for a mere one percent of the total). This point is analysed further below. Table 10 sets out Australian activity by region.

Table 10 Australian Offshore Programmes by Region

Region	Number of Programmes	% of Total
Asia	1356	86
Australasia	63	4
Africa	48	3
Europe	41	3
North America	37	2
Middle East	24	2
Unknown	2	0
Total	1571	100

The vast majority of programmes are offered in Asia, with no other region accounting for more than four percent of the total. There is no reported activity in the Caribbean or Central and South America. The Australian activities in Europe are primarily concentrated in English speaking countries (more than 65 percent of programmes are offered in the UK and Ireland). Australian institutions are present in four African countries, but 73 percent of programmes are concerned with South Africa. In the Middle East, Australian institutions are offering programmes in six countries, but again there is obvious concentration (the United Arab Emirates accounts for 38 percent of programmes, and Oman for 33 percent). The total for North America includes 10 programmes in the USA.

Aside from region, is there any other pattern to the spread of activity? As discussed later in this paper, it might be argued that significant transnational education is most likely to be found in countries that have experienced rapid economic growth and a dramatic increase in demand for higher education. Very often domestic provision has been unable to meet this demand, and governments have turned to foreign institutions in some form to close the gap. The argument might continue that once a country reaches a certain level of economic development, it would have sufficient funds to support an adequate domestic higher education sector, and the rationale for imported provision would weaken. Is this borne out by the Australian data? The Human Development Index (HDI) offers a way of categorising countries by stages of development. The HDI is a composite indicator of relative development (broadly defined) by country (covering 173 countries in total), and was created by the United Nations Development Programme. The HDI measures progress towards the 'Millennium Development Goals'. This briefing uses the indicators from 2002, based on 2000 data. Countries are split into three categories: 1) High Human Development (53 countries), 2) Medium Human Development (84 countries), and 3) Low Human Development (36 countries).

Following the argument made above, one would expect most Australian transnational activities to be concentrated in countries in category 2. However, the evidence is not that straightforward.

When the AVCC data is analysed in relation to the HDI, 43 percent of the countries in which Australian universities offer programmes are placed in category 1,[27] 50 percent in category 2[28] and 7 percent in category 3. In programme terms, the figures are very similar – 47 percent of the total number of programmes are offered in countries belonging to the first category, 52 percent are in the second category and only 1 percent belong in the third category.[29] It is clear that not all of Australia's major markets for transnational education fit the above description of transitional countries with rapidly developing economies and inadequate resources to develop domestic provision. While Hong Kong and Singapore once fitted the definition of transitional economies, they now rank amongst the most developed territories in the world. However, as noted above, both continue to heavily rely on imported higher education. Australian activity in other highly developed countries, such as Canada, Denmark, Germany, Ireland, New Zealand, Norway, UK and USA, is of a different scale and character. Imported provision appears to fill perceived small gaps in otherwise well-developed higher education sectors. Provision tends to involve low-profile local higher education institutions or other organisations that desire additional validation/accreditation arrangements. The background and contacts of certain individuals in the local organisation may explain the selection of an Australian, rather than local institution. In a few cases, the partnership is between an Australian and a domestic university. For example, the University of Tennessee in the USA offers a number of engineering programmes (including a masters degree) from Monash University. It is difficult to comment on the rationale in specific cases, but it is clear that imported

---

[27] Taiwan, which is not listed as a separate country in the UN index, has for the purpose of this report been included as a country in category 1.
[28] The Kingdom of Tonga was not included on the UN index and has been added as a country in category 2.
[29] If the four biggest markets (i.e. Hong Kong, Singapore, Malaysia and China) for transnational Australian education are taken out of the equation, 30 percent of programmes are offered in countries placed in category 1, 65 percent in category 2, 4 percent in category 3 and one percent is unknown.

Australian provision in these countries could in no way be characterised as meeting mainstream demand, and is unlikely to grow significantly.

Other category 1 countries, such as Bahrain, Kuwait and United Arab Emirates, arguably do fit the 'rapidly transforming economy' model. In contrast to Hong Kong and Singapore, these countries have grow rich through a natural resource (oil) rather than human capacity development. Only now, as part of a desire for economic diversification, have these countries opted to utilise transnational provision as part of substantive upgrading of domestic higher education. Japan, Taiwan and South Korea are examples of category 1 countries that combine relatively little imported transnational activity, mature domestic sectors and quite punitive regulation of foreign providers. (Both South Korea and Taiwan have recently moved to encourage or at least more readily permit foreign provision, and Japan is under pressure to do so[30]). All category 2 countries where Australia is active do broadly conform to the 'rapidly transforming economy' model, to a greater or less extent. Indeed, the three countries in category 3 (Bangladesh, Nepal, Pakistan) all feature near the top end of that category, and could be plotted on a transitional continuum with category 2. Of course, economic and associated development is only one factor determining where Australian institutions choose to operate. Language barriers and regulation of foreign higher education are also important. The former helps explain why Central and South America are not target markets, while both partly illuminate the reasons for the relative lack of activity in Japan, South Korea and Taiwan. Section 8 attempts to build a conceptual model of transnational provision, taking these and other factors into account.

According to the AVCC data, the first relevant Australian presence overseas was established in 1985. It is important to note that the AVCC data lists current programmes only, and that year of

---

[30] For further details of these developments, see Observatory *Breaking News* stories for 14th March 2003 (South Korea), 20th June 2003 (Taiwan) and 2nd December 2003 (Japan).

commencement was not available for some 20 percent of entries. Fifty-seven percent of current programmes with this information were established in 2000 or more recently. It is clear that the overall level of activity has increased, but in view of the lack of data on discontinued provision it is not possible to arrive at a precise picture of levels of growth over time. For ten years from 1985, activities were almost solely focused on the 'traditional' markets of Singapore, Hong Kong and Malaysia. Until 1995, only six current programmes (less than eight percent of the total) were operating outside these territories. Since 1995 the number of programmes in 'new' countries has increased dramatically, particularly given development in China. From six percent of total current programmes in 1994, 'new' countries grew to 34 percent in 2000, and 42 percent in 2003. However, given overall growth in transnational activity, the 'traditional' markets show no sign of weakening. In 2003 more than twice as many new programmes were established in Singapore, Hong Kong and Malaysia compared to the 'new' countries, and no 'new' country (aside from China) has achieved anything close in terms of scale. Section 8 explores these issues in more detail.

While most Australian universities (73 percent) offer more than ten programmes, Table 11 indicates that a few institutions dominate. Three universities (8 percent of AVCC members), University of Southern Queensland, Charles Sturt University and Curtin University of Technology, together account for 42 percent of programmes. These three institutions are all relatively new universities (given university title between 1986 and 1990), but all have roots as other kinds of higher education institution. University of Southern Queensland is operating in 28 countries, whereas Charles Sturt has programmes in 16. Curtin University of Technology has concentrated its 127 programmes in only six countries and is operating solely in Asia.

As shown in Table 12, the most common programme offered is the bachelor's degree, followed by master's programmes. This concentration on protected titles (protected in some form in most countries) reflects the relative lack of domestic provision of this kind in host nations.

Table 11 Australian Offshore Programmes by Institution (ten most active)

Institution	Number of Programmes	% of Total
1. University of Southern Queensland	307	20
2. Charles Sturt University	226	14
3. Curtin University of Technology	127	8
4. Edith Cowan University	95	6
5. Victoria University	76	5
6. RMIT University	59	4
7. University of Newcastle	56	4
8. Monash University	53	3
9. Central Queensland University	50	3
10. La Trobe University	43	3
Total	1092	70

Table 12 Australian Offshore Programmes by Qualification

Qualification	Number of Programmes	% of Total
Bachelors	669	43
Masters	534	34
Other Postgraduate	203	13
Other Undergraduate	158	10
Unknown	7	–
Total	1571	100

For the purpose of this report, programmes were grouped into broad subject areas: Business (including Finance, Accountancy, Management, Marketing), the Sciences (including the Natural, Physical, Biological, Life and Health Sciences), Humanities (languages, arts subjects, education, teacher training etc), IT, Social Science, General Studies (such as foundation programmes and other preparatory courses), Engineering and Miscellaneous (including Law, Journalism, Architecture). As set out in Table 13, a small number of programmes (just under 1 percent) could not be identified according to discipline. Some programmes (just under 6 percent of the total) covered more than one discipline, e.g. a degree in

Table 13 Australian Offshore Programmes by Discipline

Discipline	Number of Programmes	% of Total
Business	768	49
Humanities	231	15
Sciences	219	14
IT	189	12
Engineering	104	7
Social Science	82	5
General Studies[31]	33	2
Law, Journalism, Architecture and unknown	23	1

Construction Engineering and Management. In those cases both disciplines have been counted and as a result the total number of disciplines is higher than the total number of programmes. This is naturally also reflected in the accompanying percentages. Where programmes cover two different areas judged to be within the same discipline, e.g. a Business degree in Accounting and Finance, the subject area 'Business' has only been counted once.

Not surprisingly, and similar to the findings in Hong Kong and Singapore, business was the most common subject area. Other common disciplines were the sciences, humanities and IT. There were no significant differences by level.

Current Australian offshore programmes are operated in partnership with more than 400 different institutions.[32] Seven Australian institutions are operating programmes themselves through what are described as branch campuses (such as Swinburne Sarawak

---

[31] This discipline is only found among 'other undergraduate' courses preparing students for university studies.
[32] The exact number of partner institutions is difficult to ascertain. Many institutions on the AVCC list have very similar names and it is not absolutely clear whether they are one or two organisations. Examples include the Sumbershire Education Consultants and Sumbershire Educational Consultants; SEG International, 'SEG International, PRIME College, IBMS College, MSC International College' and SEGI; Asia Pacific Management Centre and Asia Pacific Management Institute.

Institute of Technology in Malaysia and Bond University – South Africa Campus). The remaining programmes are operated by local partner institutions/companies. In a very few cases, the named operator is an individual. More than two-thirds of local partners are operating three programmes or less each. However, some local institutions are operating numerous programmes for different institutions. For example, the Hong Kong Management Association is operating 24 programmes in partnership with 5 Australian universities. Some local partners are operating programmes for a single Australian university in more than one country. An example is Singapore's AEC Group, which is running 43 programmes for University of Southern Queensland in nine different countries.

The AVCC data also indicates mode of instruction. As shown in Table 14, the vast majority of programmes have only one delivery mode and more than half are provided entirely offshore. Programmes taught solely at a distance or by a combination of offshore and distance learning account for approximately 17 and 16 percent of the total number of programmes respectively. There are very few programmes combining all three delivery-modes and very few taught partly at a distance and partly at an Australian institution's

Table 14 Australian Offshore Programmes by Mode of Delivery

Mode of Delivery	Number of Programmes	% of Total
Solely offshore	888	56.5
Solely by Distance Learning	261	16.6
Offshore as well as by Distance Learning	250	15.9
Offshore and on Campus in Australia	151	9.6
Offshore as well as by Distance Learning and on Campus in Australia	12	0.8
By Distance Learning and on Campus in Australia	9	0.6
Total	1571	100

home campus. It should be noted that reference to distance learning provision reflects the definition of 'offshore' used by the AVCC (i.e. including distance learning but only if a local partner is involved).

The Australian Department of Education, Science and Training (DEST) publishes data on students enrolled on Australian university and other higher education programmes inside and outside the country.[33] In 2002, 24,197 overseas students were enrolled on "external" programmes, an increase of 11.3 percent from the previous year.[34] (Changes in data collection mean it is not possible to directly compare 2002 enrolment with data prior to 2001). An 'external' programme is defined as provision where "all units of study for which the student is enrolled involve special arrangement whereby lesson materials, assignments etc. are delivered to the student, and any associated attendance at the institution is of an incidental, special or voluntary nature".[35] Importantly, enrolments on offshore campuses of Australian universities are regarded as 'internal'.[36] Not surprisingly, just over 70 percent of total 'external' students were residents of countries constituting the main markets for Australian transnational education – Malaysia, Singapore, Hong Kong and Mainland China.

As shown previously, other significant importers of Australian programmes include Thailand, India, South Africa and Vietnam. In each of these four countries external student enrolment in 2002

---

[33] See Department for Education, Science & Training (2002) *Students 2002 – selected higher education statistics*, p170. Available at: www.dest.gov.au/highered/statistics/students/02/student_table/students2002.pdf. Last Accessed 22 April 2004.
[34] The DEST data includes a third category: students studying in 'mixed modal'. This is defined as provision where "at least one unit of study is undertaken on an internal mode of attendance and at least one unit of study is undertaken on an external mode of attendance" (Ibid, DEST (2002), p170). The number of students in this category is very low (for Singapore for example, this category accounts for a mere 1 percent of the total number of students enrolled on Australian programmes in 2002), and this mode of study has therefore not been further discussed in this report.
[35] Ibid, DEST (2002), p170.
[36] Private email communication with Geoff Izzard, University Statistics Section, Department of Education, Science & Training, 17 November 2003.

accounted for less than two percent of the total number of students enrolled on Australian programmes externally. Furthermore, the share of the total number of external students was lower in these countries compared to their share of offshore Australian programmes (see Table 9). In South Africa and Vietnam this may be because branch campuses account for a significant proportion of Australian activity (as noted above, enrolments at overseas branch campuses are not counted as 'external'). This may also affect the Malaysian figures (there are three branch campuses of Australian universities in Malaysia). The vast majority of students from the four main importer countries are enrolled on internal programmes. Ninety-two percent of students from Mainland China enrolled in Australian higher education institutions are enrolled internally. The figures are 88 percent for Hong Kong, 80 percent for Singapore and 73 percent for Malaysia. Only in the United Kingdom do external enrolments (slightly) outnumber internal. The overall growth in external enrolment between 2001 and 2002 (11.3 percent) was lower than the growth in internal enrolment (18.9 percent) over the same period. In 2002, external enrolments made up just over 14 percent of all overseas enrolments in Australian higher education. This emphasises that while external enrolment is significant in a few countries, internal provision remains dominant. That said, evidence that the number of offshore programmes and host countries is increasing, plus demand for lower-cost alternatives to overseas study, suggests that this is a growing market.

It is interesting that South Africa is recorded as having one of the most balanced enrolments between external and internal entry (389 and 425 enrolments respectively). It is well known that in recent years South Africa has clamped down on offshore provision without a local presence by the foreign operator. According to official data, only two Australian universities are registered in South Africa as private providers.[37] Both operate branch campuses and thus their enrolment would count as internal. The AVCC data does

---

[37] See Registrar for Private Higher Education Institutions (2003) *Registration Status Report, 4th December.* Available at: www.saqa.org.za. Last Accessed December 2003.

list other South African activity by Australian universities, but it is unclear whether this is offshore franchising (arguably illegal under current regulations) or 100 percent distance learning (that arguably should not have been included on the AVCC list in the first place). The DEST figures may perhaps refer to non-university Australian activity, but the question of strict legality would remain. Another explanation may be that branch campus enrolments may in fact have been counted as external.

7 Other National Data

Sections 4 and 5 above analysed data from two of the leading importers of transnational provision – Hong Kong SAR and Singapore. This section pulls together other national import data known to the Observatory – covering Jamaica, Malaysia, Pakistan, South Africa and Thailand. The rationale for this selection is that these countries, against the prevailing trend of lack of data collection, publish official lists of imported provision. The authors would be pleased to hear of additional lists. There is no space here to analyse the data in detail. What follows offers a sense of scale, origins and types of providers, subjects and local partners. In two cases, comparison with Australian data allows an assessment of whether particular official lists encompass all apparent activity. The online locations of the lists are given in the footnote below.[38]

---

[38] For Jamaica see: University Council of Jamaica, *Accreditation Webpage*. Available at: www.ucjamaica.com/credit/index.htm (list updated January 2002), Last Accessed 22 April 2004. For Malaysia see: Study Malaysia, *International Students Webpage*. Available at: www.studymalaysia.com/is/education12.shtml (not stated when list was updated). Last Accessed 22 April 2004. For Pakistan see: Higher Education Commission, Pakistan, *About Affiliated/Recognized Institutions Webpage*. Available at: http://hec.gov.pk/colluni/foreign%20University%20-Institutes.htm (list updated 1 August 2003), Last Accessed 22 April 2004. For South Africa see: Registrar for Private Higher Education Institutions, part of the South African Qualifications Authority www.saqa.org.za (list updated 30 March 2004), Last Accessed 22 April 2004. For Thailand see: Commission on Higher Education, Thailand, *Homepage*. Available at: www.inter.mua.go.th/links/index.html (not stated when list was updated). Last Accessed 22 April 2004.

The five lists are not identical in terms of coverage – see Table 15. The Jamaica, Malaysia and Pakistan lists concern institutions only, while the remainder concern institutions and programmes. The Jamaica, Pakistan and South African lists refer to processes of approval and claim to be comprehensive. The Malaysia list is officially approved but covers only so-called 3+0 bachelors programmes (i.e. programmes where the student undertakes the entire programme in-country). Thus the majority of in-country activity (e.g. 1+2, 2+1 etc) is excluded. The Thailand list makes no explicit reference to approval, is concerned only with Thai universities (public and private), and it is not clear whether the 'international programmes' described cover forms of co-operation aside from in-country delivery of foreign programmes. Some lists do not give adequate details of subjects and levels.

Data from these countries closely matches that for Hong Kong and Singapore, in terms of countries involved, subjects and local partners. The two dominant source countries in Hong Kong and Singapore – Australia and UK – are also most prominent here in most cases. The obvious exception of Jamaica (no Australian activity) can be explained in terms of geographical distance, which also explains the dominance of US institutions. The handful of providers from other countries (e.g. Canada, France, Ireland) also mirrors the situation found in Hong Kong and Singapore, as does the appearance of major importers as exporters (Malaysia and Singapore in Pakistan). Business, IT, English and education were again the most popular subject areas. As with Hong Kong, when local universities are involved, the subject range tends to be wider (see Thailand).

It should be noted that it was only possible to compare host data with AVCC information for three of the five countries, and only possible to make a judgement on discrepancies in two cases. No Australian universities are currently active in Jamaica, and the focus of the Malaysian data (3+0 provision) was not clearly distinguished in the AVCC information. Thus only data from Pakistan, South Africa and Thailand was compared.

Table 15 Transnational Provision in Jamaica, Malaysia, Pakistan, South Africa and Thailand

Host Country	Number of Foreign Institutions (programmes)	Source Countries (by programme)	Subjects (in order of significance)	Levels	Local Partners
Jamaica	4 institutions (programmes not listed)	6 USA, 2 UK (joint programme), 1 Canada,	Unclear	unclear	Four in collaboration with local private colleges; four independent
Malaysia	33 institutions (45 programmes)	26 UK, 15 Australia, 2 New Zealand, 1 France, 1 Ireland	Unclear	unclear	Wide range of private colleges
Pakistan	5 institutions (programmes not listed)	2 UK, one each for Australia Ireland, Malaysia, Singapore and USA (some joint programmes)	Unclear	unclear	Local private colleges and companies
South Africa	4 institutions (14 programmes)	2 Australia, 1 Netherlands, 1 UK	Business, IT, communications, arts	Bachelors, masters	Independent (with some local company assistance)
Thailand	14 institutions (17 programmes)	9 UK, 5 Australia, 2 USA, 1 Canada	Business, education, engineering, English as a foreign language, IT, pharmacy, statistics	Bachelors, masters	Thai public and private universities

Transnational Higher Education 357

In Pakistan, the local list includes an unstated number of programmes from five foreign institutions, including one Australian university. The AVCC list records seven programmes offered by three Australian universities. AVCC data on Australian activities in South Africa features four universities offering 36 programmes, whereas the information provided by South Africa lists 14 programmes from only two Australian universities. When the two lists are examined, only two of the five programmes are identical in terms of subject area and Australian or local provider. The Thai list records five Australian programmes from five universities offered in co-operation with local public or private universities. According to the AVCC data, eight Australian universities match this profile and offer one programme each.

The Thai list's lack of precision makes direct comparison problematic, but it is difficult to explain the Pakistan and South Africa discrepancies. In both cases, the local and Australian data relates to 2003 (AVCC is May 2003, the Pakistan list is August 2003, and the South African list is December 2003). Both the Pakistan and South Africa lists are explicit in stating that only listed institutions are permitted to operate. It was also not possible to explain the discrepancies in terms of mode of delivery. Residents of Pakistan or South Africa are free to sign up for non-targeted distance learning provision from Australian universities (e.g. to online programmes available to anyone), but the AVCC list includes only those distance learning programmes that feature some form of in-country partnership. Further analysis would be needed to determine definitively whether the additional programmes might be judged to be operating illegally, but what is certainly clear is that forms of unofficial provision appear to exist.

8 A Conceptual Model of Transnational Higher Education

While data on the extent, regulation and impact of transnational higher education is far from comprehensive, there would appear to be sufficient commonality of rationale and circumstance to attempt a conceptual model of development at the national level. Figure 1

Figure 1 Conditions for the development of transnational higher education at national level

IMPORT	EXPORT
Mainstream	
a. Domestic public higher education capacity gap (institutional type/ number/ size/ culture)	a. Public higher education under pressure to diversify income; desire to enhance international reputation; capacity surplus; part of broader strategic alliances
b. Domestic private higher education cannot fill any public sector capacity gap alone	b. Private higher education under pressure to diversity income; desire to enhance international reputation; capacity surplus; part of broader strategic alliances
c. Sufficiently high 'Human Development Index' value to ensure a critical mass able to pay for imported provision	c. Sufficiently high 'Human Development Index' value commensurate with a mature and stable higher education system and the ability to export
d. Domestic tuition fees (if any) perceived as high/ poor value for money	d. In-country pricing perceived as good value for money
e. Overseas study too expensive for majority (but sufficiently large population willing and able to afford in-country fees)	e. In-country delivery offers significant recruitment potential
f. Value particular foreign higher education	f. Domestic higher education is valued in other countries
g. Speak or desire to learn 'premium' language	g. Teach in 'premium' language (or willingness/ ability to do so)
h. Regulatory environment encourages, or at least allows import	h. Regulatory environment encourages, or at least allows export
Niche	
i. Desire for specific cultural provision not available locally	i. Acknowledged source of specific cultural provision

sets out a range of conditions that determine the extent to which a country is an attractive location for transnational delivery, and the extent to which a country can embark on an export strategy. While concerned with the national perspective, the various conditions also reflect student and institutional concerns. The term 'transnational higher education' is used here to refer to taught programmes of study offered by an institution in one country in another country. It excludes provision aimed at students from the source country (e.g. study abroad schemes). It is acknowledged that some arrangements combine relevant taught provision with other activities (e.g. research, staff and student exchange and industry links).

Transnational provision is divided into 'mainstream' and 'niche'. This is an attempt to distinguish between provision targeted at the general population and provision targeted at specific populations. For example, the former would include a general MBA from an Australian university marketed in Singapore, while the latter would include an Indian university offering provision on Tamil culture to a Diaspora community in California. Mainstream transnational delivery reflects national circumstances at the macro level, whereas niche provision responds to very particular conditions pertaining to certain sub-groups that may bear no resemblance to those which affect the general population. For these reasons, mainstream and niche provision must be modelled separately.

Some of the conditions above warrant additional explanation. Conditions a and b in the right hand column are an attempt to capture the sometimes multi-layered rationale for export (e.g. encompassing some or all of the items listed).[39] The term 'premium' language refers to the handful of languages that are widely regarded by non-native speakers as desirable to learn. English, and to a lesser extent Spanish and French, currently fall into this category. Russian might be an example of a language formerly in this category (during the Soviet era). The vast majority of mainstream transnational higher education is delivered at least partly in a premium language. This is not to ignore the fact that some imported transnational provision is delivered in a local language, but what data there is suggests sole local language delivery is uncommon. There are also cases that blur the line between mainstream and niche provision. An example would be

---

[39] For a discussion on this point see Knight, J. (2003) 'New rationales driving internationalisation', *International Higher Education*, Number 34, Winter 2004, p3–4.

Dutch or Portuguese language programmes in mainstream subjects marketed to a very restricted range of former colonial outposts. It should also be recognised that as translation software improves and online delivery plays a more important role, local language in-country delivery may become more widespread. This will reduce the importance of 'premium' language capacity, and will allow a wider range of providers/countries to compete (i.e. language of source country will be less significant). However, in many cases, provision delivered in a 'premium' language will continue to offer market advantage. The use of 'in-country' in conditions d and e refers to delivery in the host country (not the source country). The Human Development Index was introduced in Section 6 of this report.

It is suggested here that if any of the conditions a–h are not met, imported mainstream transnational provision is unlikely to develop on any scale. (Condition d may not apply where the state sector is very dominant and does not charge tuition fees). For example, if a government does not perceive a capacity gap between its domestic provision and socio-economic ambitions, and there is no separate demand from students, imported transnational provision is unlikely. Or if, despite disquiet about capacity, government continues to take the view that imported provision should be illegal or subject to punitive sanction, significant transnational activity will not materialise. A tight connection between national culture and domestic higher education might undermine the perceived value of foreign provision. Figure 2 sets out this hypothesis in more detail, giving different scenarios for least developed, transition and developed economies. By contrast, with the possible exception of condition h (regulation), niche provision can occur if condition i alone is satisfied.

Similarly in terms of export, it is argued that if any of the conditions a–h are not met, export of provision is unlikely on any scale. (The exception may be condition b if private education is minimal or does not exist). For example, if a country does not have a higher education capacity surplus, or bars its institutions from operating abroad, exported transnational provision will not develop.

Transnational Higher Education 361

Distance learning is included in the above account of transnational delivery. Forms of distance learning are simply alternative ways of accessing foreign provision, and rationales for import/export would conform to conditions *a–h* above (with only minor modification of wording). Provision may be entirely at a distance or may overlap with in-country delivery where remote activities are matched with in-country support. As discussed below, a 'regional hub' model may form an intermediate stage between majority import and majority export, and helps explain the transition process.

Figure 2 is an attempt to model the range of factors that determine the suitability of a country for imported transnational higher education.

Figure 2 A model for the development of imported transnational higher education at national level

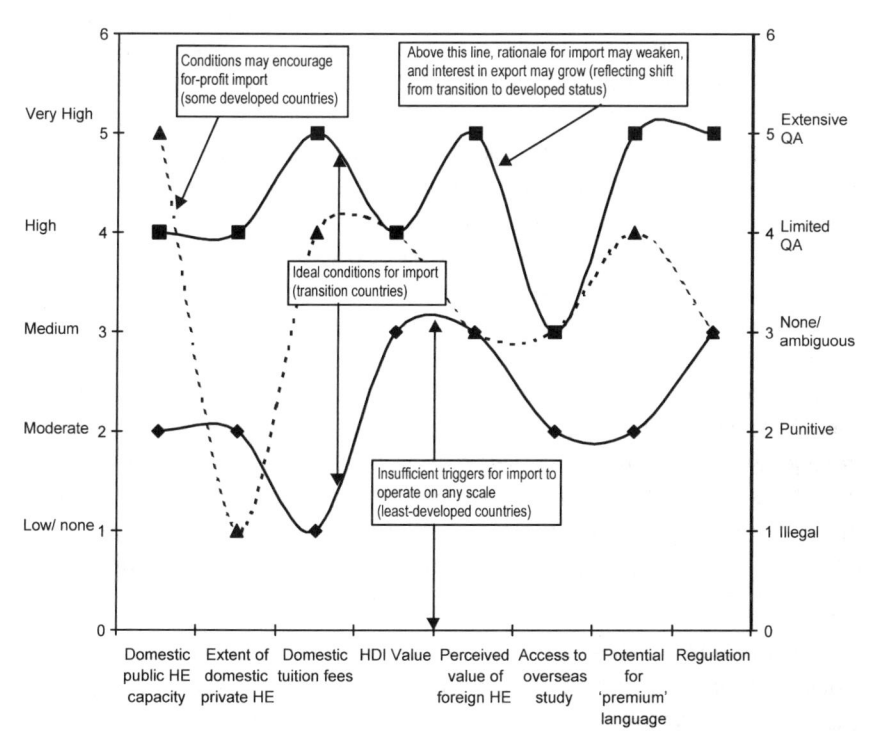

The left y axis refers to all items on the x axis save regulation (which is covered by the right y axis). The space between the two solid lines is judged to represent 'ideal' conditions for import, while the space below the lower of the two solid lines is judged to represent less than ideal conditions. Broadly speaking, the former space reflects the situation in many transition economies, while the latter pertains to least developed countries. The positioning of some points was relatively flexible. For example, the distinction between public and private domestic capacity works differently in particular countries, depending on whether one or other sector is dominant. One or both at least at 'moderate' level are judged to be sufficient to encourage imported transnational provision (it was not possible to show this clearly on the chart).

The dashed line represents the situation in some developed countries (e.g. UK) where the public sector is dominant, there is little private capacity, tuition fees are rising, and regulation of foreign providers is relatively liberal. Foreign provision, notably for-profit institutions from the United States, might view such countries as potentially attractive markets. Equally, diversified/incentivised domestic public provision might be judged sufficiently robust to weaken the case for market entry. Not shown is the situation in some other developed countries, where imported provision has occurred in response to a perceived capacity gap in the domestic public sector. For example, in pre-Bologna continental Europe, in the absence of internationally marketable short postgraduate provision, many countries imported masters provision from UK universities. In these instances, the dashed line might drop to 'high' for 'Domestic public HE capacity' and the 'Domestic tuition fees' category would refer to specific postgraduate study (many countries in continental Europe do not charge significant tuition fees to undergraduates). Also not shown is any niche provision which, it is argued, can occur regardless of the various conditions in Figure 2 (with the possible exception of regulation).

The distinctions between the three main categories (least developed, transition and developed) are not hard and fast. As discussed in Section 6, some very active importer nations (e.g. Hong Kong SAR and Singapore) have attained developed country status, but while this shift has included significant investments in domestic higher education, the scale of imported provision has not diminished, and arguably has increased. That said, there is evidence from Singapore, for example, of a policy to gradually extend degree-awarding powers to local private colleges, which would have the effect of reducing dependence on imported degrees. However, as shown above, both territories now depend on transnational provision for a large minority of higher education enrolments. This may suggest that some countries may choose heavy dependence on transnational provision during transition economy status and beyond as an almost permanent arrangement. Figure 3 offers a model of export at the national level.

Figure 3 is an attempt to model the range of factors that determine the suitability of a country to export higher education internationally. The left y axis refers to all items on the x axis save regulation (which

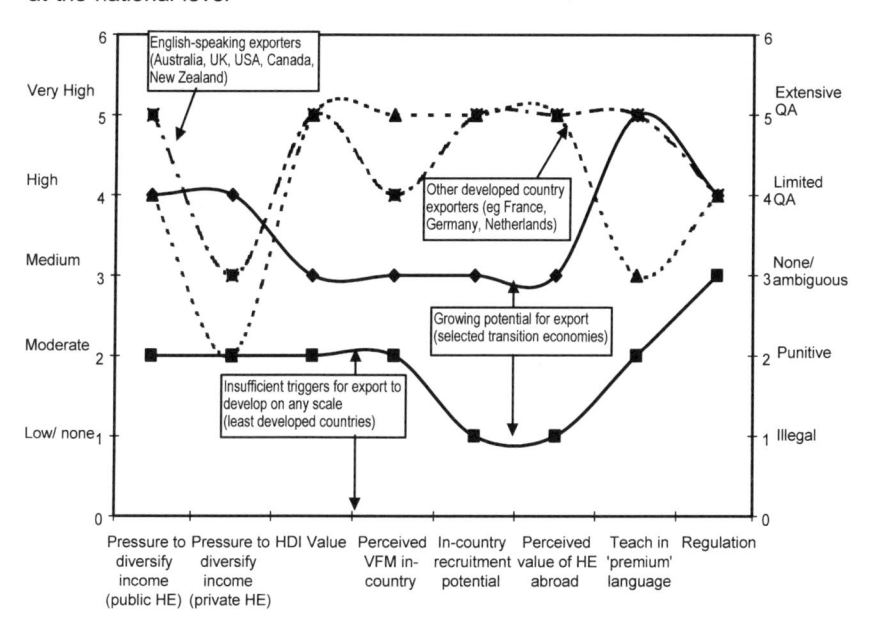

Figure 3 A model for the development of exported transnational higher education at the national level

is covered by the right y axis). The two broken lines represent the majority of the main exporting economies, split into two categories – category 1 encompasses the main English-speaking exporters,[40] and category 2 other exporters. This distinction captures broad differences in terms of pressure to diversify income and ability to teach in a 'premium' language (both judged to be generally higher for category 1 countries); and perceived value for money (many category 2 countries do not charge student fees at levels seen in category 1). There is a certain amount of intra-category diversity not shown on the chart. For example, the figure for 'pressure to diversify income' might be higher for private higher education in the USA than in the other countries in that category (where private provision is much less prominent).

The space between the two solid lines is judged to represent 'emerging' conditions for export (e.g. India, Malaysia, Singapore), while the space below the lower of the two solid lines is judged to represent unsuitable conditions (e.g. least developed countries). Chart 1 positions 35 countries on two axes – extent of import and export of transnational provision.

Chart 1 focuses on those countries known to be among the world's most active importers and exporters, those where import/export is under development and those that have made or are considering regulatory change in this area. Positioning on the chart reflects both absolute levels of import/export and proportion given size of the host/source country. As noted throughout these briefings on transnational provision, national data is often inadequate. Country

---

[40] Spain might also fit into category 1 (offering provision in the other 'premium' language). A report for the Confederation of European Union Rectors' Conferences on transnational provision in and from western Europe pointed to Spain as a significant source of provision to Latin America (and parts of the United States) but stated that any detailed assessment of scale was impeded by lack of data collection at the national level. See Adam, S. (2001) *Transnational Education Project: report & recommendations*, Confederation of European Union Rectors' Conferences. Available at: www.crue.org/espaeuro/transnational_education_ project.pdf. Last Accessed 22 April 2004. The Observatory is currently researching developments in Latin America and will report in 2004.

Chart 1 Transnational Higher Education: import and export activity by country

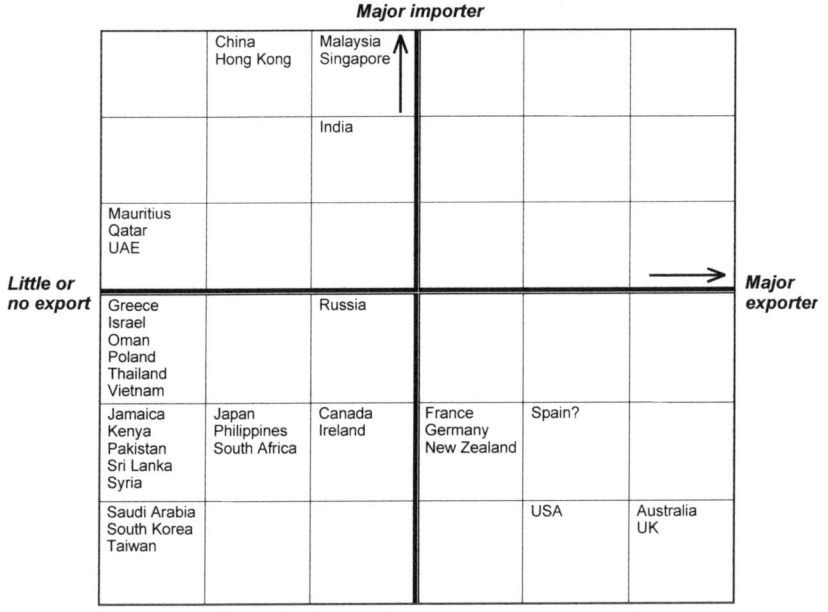

	Major importer					
	China Hong Kong	Malaysia Singapore ↑				
		India				
Mauritius Qatar UAE						
Greece Israel Oman Poland Thailand Vietnam		Russia				
Jamaica Kenya Pakistan Sri Lanka Syria	Japan Philippines South Africa	Canada Ireland	France Germany New Zealand	Spain?		
Saudi Arabia South Korea Taiwan			USA	Australia UK		

Little or no export ←——————→ *Major exporter*

Little or no import

positioning is based on the best evidence available to the Observatory, and uses official sources where possible. The authors would be pleased to receive views on the positioning of particular countries. Of the 35 countries discussed here, 20 (57%) exhibit only import or export activity (or neither on any scale), while the remainder (43%) exhibit both import and export activity. Almost all countries present unequal import and export activity. Only one country (Russia) is judged to exhibit import and export activity in roughly equal measure. Four countries (India, Malaysia, Russia and Singapore) are characterised by both significant import and export activity, although for all but Russia import remains dominant. India, Malaysia and Singapore have developed explicit export strategies, and a number of institutions are already active. No country presented both major import and export activity, although on current projections Malaysia and Singapore may achieve this in the coming years (at least temporarily).

Not shown in Chart 1 is intelligence on how national positions may change over time. For example, countries such as Taiwan, South Korea, Saudi Arabia and Japan have either recently moved to encourage forms of imported provision or are under pressure to do so. Others (e.g. Oman, Vietnam) are stepping up their import activities. These trends, if matched by foreign interest, would see these countries move up the vertical axis. New regulations may act to reduce import levels in some countries. Both China and India have recently introduced much stricter requirements for in-country providers that, if enforced, might consolidate what has arguably been uncoordinated and under-regulated growth in recent years. This has already transpired in South Africa (see Section 7), where the effective outlawing of import by franchising led to the exit of the vast majority of foreign providers, leaving only those willing to invest in a branch campus (the only import model currently permitted).

Some active importer countries (e.g. Malaysia, Singapore, UAE, Mauritius) are pursuing 'regional hub' status, utilising both domestic and imported provision to attract students from the region. This encourages a version of the conventional form of transnational provision, where the student, rather than the institution, moves across borders. While this is not export as such, only a slightly modified version of export criteria a–h would apply. However, 'domestic' provision would encompass both local and foreign providers, making 'export' fundamentally dependent upon import. This notion of a regional hub partly based on imported provision may form an intermediate stage between majority import and majority export, raising a country's profile but maintaining foreign associations. As is beginning to happen in Malaysia and Singapore, gradual rolling out of degree-awarding powers to domestic institutions may prove the catalyst for progression, whereby those institutions begin to jettison their foreign partnerships and attract foreign students in their own right. Despite a similar history as a major importer, Hong Kong has yet to embark on a comparable hub strategy. To date, its geographical and political position has led to an export focus on Mainland China.

Canada and Ireland are examples of English-speaking countries that exhibit some export activity but not on the scale of market leaders such as Australia and the UK. Both may have potential for growth if wider pressures dictate (e.g. on public funding) and each country can carve out a suitably competitive marketing strategy. New Zealand is an aggressive importer on the Australian model, but its size will inhibit significant expansion. Russia, despite an official policy to expand exports, may in fact suffer decline in the coming years. Loss of regional status following the fall of communism has weakened the appeal of the Russian language and Russian higher education in the former heartlands of Eastern Europe and Central Asia.

Among the major exporters, France and Germany have both stepped up their export strategies, partly in response to growing pressure to diversity income at home, and also to counter the dominance of English-language exporters. While evidence is inadequate, it appears that Spain is a major source of transnational provision in Latin America, and one might expect this to develop over time. As the Bologna Process makes headway (e.g. by instituting a bachelors/masters structure across member countries), France, Germany and Spain may be subject to reduced imported provision (that typically exploited the absence of internationally understood short postgraduate awards). The United States is relatively active as an exporter in absolute terms, but much less so by proportion. It is estimated that fewer than 50 of the USA's 4,000 or so postsecondary institutions operate abroad (about 1 percent),[41] but ongoing tracking by the Observatory suggests that the number of institutions involved is steadily increasing.

The two countries judged to be the most active exporters – Australia and the UK – are expected to maintain and probably increase their export activities, focusing on both 'traditional' and new markets.

---

[41] *Foreign students get a U.S. education at home*, South Florida Sun-Sentinel, 29 Nov 2003. The article cites the view of Allan Goodman, President of the US Institute for International Education.

As discussed above, various factors in the UK (rising tuition fees, insignificant private sector, high HDI value, liberal regulation of foreign universities) might push the country up the import axis. Many of the same factors apply in Australia, with the possible exception of liberal regulation of foreign universities. While not as prescriptive on foreign institutions as on domestic applicants for university title, the MCEETYA protocols,[42] instituted in 2000, are nonetheless more demanding than current arrangements in the UK. The most important criteria is that foreign applicants must demonstrate comparability with Australian provision in terms of "requirements and learning outcomes" (not defined). It is not known whether the protocols have been tested against an application from an established/accredited foreign university, or whether the criteria might inhibit the prospects for, say, one of the large US for-profit institutions.

Chart 1 offers a model to track national developments over time, and allows additional countries to be added. One can surmise that almost all least developed countries would fall into the far left corner of the lower left quadrant, and many transition economies that failed to meet one or more of conditions a–h above (see Figure 1) would be similarly placed. Ongoing work by the Observatory will enable the position of additional countries to be plotted in the future.

9 Conclusion

This analysis of transnational activity in Hong Kong and Singapore indicates the scale of the phenomenon, and its significance as a component of national higher education capacity. Transnational provision currently accounts for a large minority of degree-level

---

[42] See *National Protocols for Higher Education Approval Processes* (MCEETYA Protocols), Protocol 2: National Tertiary Education Union, *Overseas Higher Education Institutions Seeking to Operate in Australia*. Available at: www.nteu. org.au/freestyler/gui/files/file3bf9e6dd10a4b.pdf. Last Accessed 22 April 2004.

enrolments and graduates in both territories. The trend is set to continue. Both Hong Kong and Singapore have now attained school-leaver participation of around 20 percent,[43] but are committed to further expansion. Whether or not explicitly framed in policy terms, transnational provision is regarded as an important resource in achieving these goals. While conventional overseas students still significantly outnumber those offshore, transnational provision represents an increasingly important source of enrolments and revenue for source country institutions.

Both Hong Kong and Singapore have attempted to oversee transnational provision through forms of registration, and this has been a helpful development in enhancing quality and consumer information. However, both public directories of programmes contain duplicate entries for the same institution under different names, missing information, and neither agrees entirely with data published elsewhere, notably by the AVCC. The differences between the Singapore and AVCC data are particularly marked, suggesting that the true picture of transnational activity remains beyond the scope of official information at present. The significant rise in the number of programmes on the Singapore list between June and October 2003 might suggest improved coverage of extant phenomenon as much as increased activity. Enhanced co-ordination between host and source countries might improve the robustness and consistency of data collection. Of course, the lack of adequate data collection in most source countries makes it impossible to undertake such comparisons in the first place.

This report was an attempt to enhance understanding of the place and character of transnational higher education in both importer and exporter nations, and to hypothesise on how and why national positions might change over time. Given the significant gap between current higher education capacity in emerging economies and projected participation to achieve socio-economic goals,

---

[43] Lee, M. & Gopithan, S. (2003) 'Hong Kong & Singapore's Reform Agendas', *International Higher Education*, Summer.

the scale of transnational provision in Hong Kong and Singapore may be indicative of what will become a genuinely global phenomenon. Data from one of the leading exporters, Australia, revealed an increasingly diverse range of target countries but ongoing concentration in 'traditional' markets. Similarly, while almost all Australian universities are involved in transnational delivery, a handful account for a majority of programmes. While offshore students from some countries make up a large minority of total enrolments, 'internal' recruitment remains dominant. All these findings suggest that transnational provision is a relatively minor feature of international enrolment for most host countries and source institutions. That said, growth trends are undeniably positive. As discussed in relation to Hong Kong and Singapore, a comparison between 'official' lists of imported programmes in Pakistan and South Africa, and Australia's list of exported provision highlighted discrepancies, pointing to the need for enhanced co-operation between the relevant agencies in host and source countries.

Section 8 sets out a conceptual model of the development of transnational higher education at the national level. Recent years have seen many transition economies pursue transnational imports as part of wider economic reform and development, and a desire on the part of some longstanding importers to leverage their experience in support of their own export strategy. The coming years will determine whether net importers such as Malaysia and Singapore decide to significantly reduce their foreign dependency as part of 'regional hub' ambitions, or whether imported provision will remain a key element of their competitive advantage. One historical parallel is validation arrangements between the University of London and a number of fledgling institutions in the former British Empire (e.g. University of South Africa, University of the West Indies). As part of wider independence movements, these institutions gradually emerged as self-standing universities. It could be argued that this transnational replication of elite higher education is now being repeated as evermore countries attempt to move to mass participation. However, the range of countries and institutions involved, and different partnership models employed, suggest that progression will prove more complex than a simple linear movement from dependence to independence. The methodologies developed in Section 8 will allow the Observatory to plot shifting national positions, and assess the importance of particular factors as catalysts of change.

Higher Education in China: *context, scale and regulation of foreign activity*

Richard Garrett

Abstract: China is of considerable interest as an emerging economy developing a mass higher education system, and as a site for transnational delivery. This report describes the main features of Chinese higher education, including online learning capacity, plus regulation of foreign activity. In general terms, foreign higher education involvement is encouraged, but a recent decree adds to the compliance burden in important respects. Data on the scale of foreign higher education activity in China is inadequate but the evidence suggests rapid development. There are tensions between official statistics and local practice and ambiguities over approved and non-approved status, as well as a flexible approach to legislation. The examples of foreign activity discussed are indicative of the range of rationales, countries, delivery models and partnerships involved.

1 Introduction

China is perhaps the world's most over-hyped, under-analysed and complex market for transnational higher education. A combination of size, transition from a command to a pseudo-market economy and potential as a superpower has prompted many higher education institutions in the developed world to explore the possibilities for market entry. The recent accession of China to the World Trade Organisation and the increasingly favourable official view taken of in-country activity by foreign education institutions (new regulations came into force in September 2003), suggest a genuine opening up of the market. Foreign providers are becoming increasingly knowledgeable- numerous universities and colleges already operate in China, and many institutional leaders have visited the country. At this time of change, the Observatory sees value in bringing together information on the Chinese higher education system itself, with an overview of the relevant regulations, and data on a sample of foreign higher education institutions operating in the country. This paper is not a detailed 'marketing guide', but rather pools a range of contextual intelligence that may prove helpful to institutional strategy development.

Data on Chinese higher education and transnational activity is scattered across books, academic journals, newspapers, institutional publicity and websites, with few attempts at synthesis.[1] This paper is an attempt to pull together a range of sources and offer some analysis.

2 Higher Education in China

This section outlines the size and shape of higher education in China, private provision and use of information of

---

[1] For an earlier overview of the Chinese market from a UK perspective, see British Council (2001) *The International Market for UK Distance Learning: China.*

technology/ e-learning. The section concludes with an assessment of the potential for foreign involvement.

2.1 Size and Shape of Provision

Chinese higher education has experienced dramatic change over the past decade. In 1990, the system was characterised by a large number of relatively small, youth-oriented, specialist universities and colleges enrolling a tiny proportion of the 18–22 age group (about 2%[2]). There were also numerous adult education institutions and large distance learning institutions such as the China Central Radio & TV University. Different institutions were controlled by national/municipal government departments and had limited autonomy. As the country began to embrace aspects of capitalism, evidence of inefficiency and over-specialisation became a cause for concern. In recent years, the government has promoted education as critical to national economic success[3] and has pursued a policy of institutional mergers and massive expansion of student numbers.

From a 1997 total of approximately 3.2 million students[4] in regular higher education (about 4% of the 18–22 age group), numbers reached a staggering almost 7 million by 2000 (about 10% of the cohort).[5] The Ministry's target, including adult and distance enrolments, was 16 million enrolments by 2010. Given success to date, the new target is 2005. The 18–22 component of the 16 million target would represent about 15% of the cohort. Enrolments were further boosted by population growth, the removal of the requirement for final examinees to be single and under 25,

---

[2] China Education & Research Network, *Number of Student Enrolment By Level And Type Of School*. Available at: www.edu.cn/20010101/22286.shtml. Last Accessed 22 April, 2004.
[3] Weifang, M. (2001) 'Current Trends in Higher Education Development in China', *International Higher Education*, Winter.
[4] China Education & Research Network, *Number of Student Enrolment By Level And Type Of School*. Available at: www.edu.cn/20010101/22286.shtml. Last Accessed 22 April, 2004.
[5] Weifang, M. (2001) 'Current Trends in Higher Education Development in China', *International Higher Education*, Winter.

and by recent attainment gains in primary and secondary education. The loosening of state-determined structures of job determination, and evidence of improving rate of return for graduates, have also contributed to growth. Since 2000 expansion has continued but at an ever-slower pace. Hundreds of institutions were merged during the 1990s, both small institutions merging with larger ones, and the combination of equally-sized institutions. According to Chen, by 2000, 612 institutions out of China's 1000+ universities and colleges had been merged into 250.[6]

Expansion and rationalisation were accompanied by devolved authority. Many institutions have moved from central to local authority control, and work with block rather than line budgets. A small number of flagship universities remain under the direct authority of the Ministry of Education (and have been fostered as potentially world-class research institutions), but have greater local power than was previously the case. An important aspect of greater autonomy is the part deregulation of tuition fees. Fees were first widely introduced in China in 1996,[7] and are determined by a complex mix of national, municipal and institutional policy, varying by location and institution. Fees are also often differentiated by subject. Many colleges and universities used to charge higher fees to some students with below average entry grades, but this was outlawed by the government.[8]

Average fees have risen quite steeply in recent years and represent a significant proportion of institutional income. In 2000, to combat fee hikes perceived as excessive, the government decreed that annual tuition should be no more than around 5000 yuan (about US$600) and tuition income should not exceed 25% of an institution's operating budget. This has kept fee rises under control,

---

[6] Chen, D. (2001) 'Restructuring through Amalgamation in China', *International Higher Education*, Fall.
[7] Wang, C. (2000) 'From Manpower Supply to Economic Revival: Governance and Financing of Chinese Higher Education', *Education Policy Archives*.
[8] Dongping, Y. (2001) *2000 Educational Evolution in China II: justice & corruption*. China Education & Research Network. Available at: www.edu.cn/20010101/22291.shtml. Last Accessed 22 April 2004.

but the guidance is not universally followed. Some local governments have also acted. The Beijing municipal government recently restricted fees to between US$525 and US$750 a year. With the average income of urbanites around 6,860 yuan per capita in 2001, and for rural dwellers 2,366 yuan, even capped fee levels represent considerable outlay for many citizens. In some cities, such as Beijing where disposable income alone averaged 12,000 yuan, the problem is less acute.[9] Government loans have been available since 1998, but are targeted at the poorest students.

2.2 Private Provision

Another striking feature of Chinese higher education over the past decade is the rise in private, or 'non-government funded' provision. Of course, private enterprise in China more generally has suffered considerable legal ambiguity for many years. Private ownership (on a par with public ownership) and the rule of law were only formally incorporated into the Chinese constitution as recently as 1999.[10] The 1982 constitution gave private education official sanction for the first time in 30 years but, until 2002, the sector operated in the "absence of a clear legal framework".[11] Crucial matters of status (for-profit, non-profit), parity with the public sector and tax and property arrangements remained unclear. Nonetheless, the sector has flourished at tertiary level, with over 1,300 institutions in operation by 2002.[12] Aside from a handful of private universities, only four private colleges have the right to award degrees, and a further 129 are licensed to offer sub-degree programmes. The remainder offer unofficial awards or non-award provision (e.g. university entrance preparation). In December 2002, after lengthy

---

[9] Xinhua News Agency (2003) *Per Capita Dispensable Income for Beijingers Exceeds 12,000 Yuan in 2002*. Available at: http://test.china.org.cn/english/BAT/ 53072.htm. Last Accessed 22 April 2004.
[10] Story, J. (2003) *China: the race to market*, Edinburgh, FT/ Prentice Hall, p71 & p128.
[11] Yan, F. & Levy, D. (2003) 'China's New Private Education Law', *International Higher Education*, Spring.
[12] Ibid.

debate, China put forward the first national legislation on private education. This clarifies a number of legal issues (e.g. private institutions are now permitted to make a "reasonable return", although that term itself is ambiguous) and reduces legal inequalities between public and private institutions. However, by legitimising the private sector, the law also pulls it into a wider framework of national education policy, raising the possibility of additional regulation and manipulation over time.[13]

2.3 Information Technology and Online Learning

One of the first ever surveys of use of information technology in Chinese higher education was undertaken in 2002 under the auspices of the Asian Campus Computing Survey Project (ACCS).[14] The ACCS is the first international extension of the well-established Campus Computing Project in the United States. The survey was carried out by the Educational Technology Department, Graduate School of Education, Peking University.[15] With Ministry of Education support, the researchers contacted 836 higher education institution presidents and received usable responses from 384 (46% response rate).

The survey analysis argues that the relatively recent adoption of information technology in Chinese higher education is reflected in a dominance of spending on hardware and networking, rather than utilising well-established infrastructure to develop online learning or e-commerce. In general terms, Chinese higher education lags

---

[13] The Observatory would like to thank Professor Daniel Levy, Programme for Research on Private Higher Education, University of Albany, New York, and Professor Fengqiao Yan at Peking University for additional information on the 2002 law on private education.
[14] For more details see Asian Campus Computing Survey Project, *Asian Campus Computing Survey Project homepage*. Available at: www.accsonline.net. Last Accessed 22 April 2004.
[15] Guodong, W. (2002) From *'Hardware'* to *'Software'*, *From Digital resources to On-line Instruction: Introduction to Information Technology Use in China Higher Education*. Available at: www.accsonline.net/research/index.htm. Last Accessed 22 April 2004.

behind the USA in terms of information technology and online learning development, but in some instances the Chinese would appear to in a similar position. In the following analysis, comparative USA data is given from the 2002 Campus Computing Survey.[16]

According to the ACCS survey, facilities such as "faculty/student e-mail" (78%; 98% USA) and online "library/card catalogue" (73%; 88% USA) were widely available, but "online courses " (33%; 63% USA) and online "course registration" (39%; 71% USA) were less common. The proportion of academic units and departments with their own web page was quite low (13% on average, rising to 27% for ministry-funded universities). The figure was 35% in the USA.

China's academic network, the China Education and Research Network (CERNET) was built in 1994 and use is now widespread. Currently, CERNET has nearly 900 institutional users and 7.47 million individual users. Over 80% of China's higher education institutions have constructed a campus network linked to CERNET (the majority since 1999). The proportion of campus networks capable of transmitting high-speed video was 44% in China and 47% in the USA, but a further 49% of Chinese institutions pointed to planned capacity by 2004, compared to only 23% in the USA. This may reflect the comparative advantage of Chinese institutions embracing this information technology later than their US counterparts, thus avoiding problems associated with antiquated infrastructure. Another factor may be widespread experience of TV-based distance learning at regular Chinese universities, often in partnership with the Central China Radio & TV University network. Six percent of Chinese respondents reported local or campus-wide wireless networks, compared to 68% in the USA. Despite official sanction to replace computer hardware at least every five years, the survey found large numbers of institutions did not have a replacement strategy for lab (47%) or faculty (50%) computers (all USA respondents pointed to replacement cycles of between one and five years for labs and two and five years for faculty).

---

[16] Green, K. (2002) *Campus Computing 2002: the 13th national survey of computing and information technology in American higher education*, Encino, CA.

On average, about a quarter of students at Chinese institutions owned a computer (rising to just over 30% in ministry-funded institutions), compared to over 75% in the USA.

None of this is to say that Chinese institutions do not have ambitions for online learning. On a scale of 1–7 (where 1 = poor and 7 = excellent), Chinese respondents scored "web resources to support instruction" available on their campus as 3.81, compared to 5.10 in the USA. However, in terms of perceived importance of this area of development, Chinese respondents scored an average of 5.74 compared to 6.00 in the USA. Almost 55% of respondents pointed to a formal plan for online learning, and an average of 41% of classrooms and 36% of dormitories had Internet access. This suggests rapidly developing strategy and infrastructure, but is some way off US figures of 82% for classrooms and 81% for dormitory beds (i.e. access in each *room* rather than just the dormitory as a whole).

Distance learning has long been a mainstay of participation in China, with many conventional universities operating forms of remote provision.[17] Extending this tradition, China has witnessed a series of national funding efforts for online learning development- notably the 1999 'Modern Distance Learning Project' and the 10th five year 'National Technology Plan' in 2000. Both distributed funds to a number of universities to develop both synchronous and asynchronous provision, and support work on platforms, metadata and standards. Some of the most prominent universities involved include Tsinghua University, Peking University, Beijing Normal University, China People's University and Chongqing University. In all, sixty-seven institutions (out of over 1200 regular higher education institutions) have been funded to develop online learning, known as 'network-education colleges' (NECs). The remainder, if developing online learning, are doing so within existing budgets. NECs were granted considerable autonomy over curriculum development and recruitment. (It is important to note that in June

---

[17] Zhang, W, Niu, J. & Jiang, G. (2002) 'Web-based education at conventional universities in China', *International Review of Research in Open & Distance Learning*, January.

2002, the Ministry of Education decreed that network-education colleges could only admit part-time students. This obviously excludes full-time students, but includes the important post-experience market. In fact the change was in line with recruitment. According to a survey of 13 NECs in 2001, full-time students represented a mere 3% of enrolments[18]).

Predictions for growth are bullish. In a report by CCID, a Chinese IT research firm, investments in online university education in China reached US$360 million in 2001. IDA of Singapore predicts that the academic e-learning market in China will reach US$876 million by 2005.[19] According to Zhang, these colleges enrolled 240,000 students in 2001.[20] Ru gives a cumulative figure of 800,000 students by the end of 2002.[21] While ostensibly online initiatives, poor student infrastructure led many NECs to utilise face-to-face instruction and posted CD-ROMs.[22]

While the government has granted the 'network-education colleges' considerable autonomy over future development, the growth of online provision to date has been tightly state controlled. According to Ming, after a period of relatively unregulated growth and development in the late 1990s, in April 2000 the Ministry of Education announced that all online schools and universities had to gain ministry approval prior to domain name registration and enrolment.[23] No foreign partnerships are evident in these flagship

---

[18] Zhao, G. & Wang, Q. (2002) *Network Education Colleges in Chinese Universities: A Survey Report.*
[19] Both figures cited in Ru, J. (2002) 'A Look at Online University Education in China', *Singapore's e-learning house*, November.
[20] Zhang, S. (2002) *Distance Learning in China.* Available at: www.apan.net/home/organization/wgs/education/documents/phuket1.ppt. Last Accessed 22 April 2004.
[21] Ru, J. (2002) 'A Look at Online University Education in China', *Singapore's e-learning house*, November.
[22] Zhao, G. & Wang, Q. (2002) *Network Education Colleges in Chinese Universities: A Survey Report*, p3.
[23] Ming, S. (2002) 'Distance Education: new initiatives in China' in Jantan, A. *et al.* (eds) *Integrated Approaches to Lifelong Learning*, papers presented at the ASEM International Conference on Lifelong Learning, Kuala Lumpar, Malaysia, May 13–15, p287.

initiatives (although some domestic private companies are involved[24]). The emphasis has been on utilising existing resources and expertise, not least the national network of support centres under the Radio & TV University network. A recent review of the network-education colleges reported a range of issues familiar to practitioners in the west- shortage of online instructional resources, user access issues, duplication of effort and staff development.[25]

Other interesting online developments:

- an example of ICT fundamentally changing a core higher education process is the recent shift to online admissions. Replacing the old system where university admissions staff would travel to major provincial centres to select students, national examination and other information is now increasingly available online. According to Tan and Ouyang, this has improved efficiency and accountability.[26]
- Some prominent Chinese universities have been permitted[27] to establish private arms with online interests. For example, Tsinghua University developed Tsinghua Tongfang, listed on Shanghai Stock Exchange in 1997. The subsidiary seeks to leverage university-based technology research into marketable products, including in the areas of e-commerce and e-learning.
- A handful of leading Chinese universities are represented in some of the prominent international online learning initiatives. For example, one Chinese university (Fudan) is a member of

---

[24] Zhang, W, Niu, J. & Jiang, G. (2002) 'Web-based education at conventional universities in China', *International Review of Research in Open & Distance Learning*, January.
[25] Ibid.
[26] Tan, Z. & Ouyang, W. (2002) *Global & National Factors Affecting e-Commerce Diffusion in China*, Irvine, Centre for Research on Information Technology & Organisations, p30.
[27] For legislative encouragement of technology transfer see Ministry of Education (24 December, 1998) *Action Scheme for Invigorating Education Towards the 21st Century*. Available at: www.edu.cn/20010101/21883.shtml. Last Accessed 22 April 2004.

- Universitas 21 Global, and two (Nanjing and Zhejiang) are members of the Worldwide Universities Network.
- A rare foreign partnership in this area- as part of wider Chinese-Japanese co-operation, Fudan University and North East University were funded under the 'China & Japan Distance Learning Model Project' to develop online provision with Japan's Aoyama University.
- In 2002, Peking University installed the first wireless campus in China.

More generally, the data on IT and e-commerce in China is mixed. In sheer numbers, China boasts one of the largest online populations in the world (about 60 million[28]) and the largest market for mobile phones, but by proportion, access remains very limited. That said, the proliferation of Internet cafes is a reminder that access and ownership are not the same thing. In 2001, Internet users in China reached 33.7 million, compared to only 12.5 million computers with Internet connections.[29] By January 2002, 31% of Chinese Internet users had made at least one purchase online.[30] Telephone line density per capita remains low nationally at 20% in 2000, but is much higher in major cities. Gradual deregulation of domestic telecommunications provision will lower prices and speed adoption (post-WTO membership, this sector is only now being opened to foreign involvement). The recent SARS outbreak had the effect of increasing ICT usage. According to BDA China, an e-commerce research firm, Internet traffic was up by 40%.

---

[28] This figure is taken from the January 2003 survey by the China Internet Network Information Centre (CNNIC). The figure of 59.1 million counts all Internet users by mode of access, and double counts users with more than mode of access (e.g. with both dial-up and broadband). The extent of double-counting is thought to be small. See China Internet Network Information Centre, *11th Survey Report on on the Internet Development in China*. Available at: www4.cnnic.net.cn/download/manual/en-reports/11.pdf. Last Accessed 22 April 2004.
[29] Tan, Z. & Ouyang, W. (2002) *Global & National Factors Affecting e-Commerce Diffusion in China*, Irvine, Centre for Research on Information Technology & Organisations, p13.
[30] Ibid, p16.

In addition, many transactions went virtual, such as online banking, and offices continued work via messaging and e-mail.[31]

While it is true that the Chinese authorities are making huge steps to expand telecommunications access, pushing adoption growth rates of 100% a year on some technologies (e.g. mobile phones), the scale of China is such that only a relatively small proportion of the total population need have access to ICT to create a large market for foreign provision. There are admittedly few examples of foreign higher education institutions offering online provision in China, but the growth of face-to-face partnerships may prove a valuable base for future development. Despite China's extraordinary efforts to expand the higher education participation rate, higher education remains a relatively elite preserve, encompassing a population more likely than average to have ICT access. Foreign higher education institutions targeting the large corporate market will be similarly advantaged. The government '2000 – year for enterprises online' programme pushed adoption of e-commerce and e-learning in major companies – but various foreign firms are already well-advanced in this market, such as News Corporation's Worldwide Learning and CIBT under Canada's Capital Alliance Group.

Other issues remain, namely intellectual property and censorship. In joining the WTO and to support the growing domestic software industry, the Chinese government is committed to protecting both conventional and online intellectual property. In 1997, China agreed to implement fully the WTO's TRIPS agreement (Trade-Related Aspects of Intellectual Property Rights) upon WTO accession. Nonetheless low incomes, ease of copying and under-developed legal protection in this area point to ongoing problems. Building on a culture of communist censorship, the government has been quite successful at restricting domestic access to what are regarded as undesirable foreign websites. China has divided its Internet service

---

[31] Cited by Wani, A. (2003) *BDA: SARS a boost for telecommunications in China*, June 2nd. Available at: www.onlinejournalism.com/ojc/topics/index.php?tID = 52. Last Accessed 22 April 2004.

operators into two categories – interconnecting networks and access networks. Only the former, of which there are a mere eight (tied to government agencies or state telecommunications firms), are connected to the international Internet. All access networks must connect users through the interconnecting networks. This structure, plus use of firewalls and filtering software, gives the government the capability to block domestic access to any foreign content. This has implications for remote online learning, but the extent to which any such provision has been blocked is unknown.

2.4 Potential for Foreign Involvement

As discussed below, many foreign higher education institutions are already in the Chinese market, and recent legislation has emphasised government interest in imported provision (see below). From the Chinese perspective, the major benefits of foreign involvement are capacity, status and innovation. China is rapidly becoming the most significant source of students studying abroad (sending over 63,000 students to the US alone in 2002[32]), but, like some other major source countries such as Malaysia and Singapore, China may come to view foreign-sourced in-country provision as more cost-effective (in terms of reducing travel costs and stemming brain drain). That said, China boasts the best national savings record in the world – 43% of national income on the latest figures, with future education costs a central rationale[33] – suggesting relatively robust ability-to-pay at consumer level in segments of the population.

Recent rapid domestic expansion of student numbers had led to disquiet in some quarters. A number of China's leading universities (e.g. Peking and Tsinghua) have announced a halt to on-campus expansion in the interests of quality. While the government has

---

[32] Institute of International Education (2002), *Open Doors 2002: International Students in the U.S.* Available at: http://opendoors.iienetwork.org/?p=25083. Last Accessed 22 April 2004.

[33] Story, J. (2003) *China: the race to market*, Edinburgh, FT/ Prentice Hall, p71.

accompanied expansion with additional investment (US$843 million over the past three years), a recent survey by the 'Beijing Municipal Education Committee' covering 50 colleges and universities in the capital found that 86% reported inadequate teachers and accommodation, 65% said they could no longer afford to expand and only 15% indicated potential for further expansion. Foreign investment offers additional capacity towards the national 16 million student target, and any subsequent targets. Private higher education institutions in China, the majority of which lack degree-awarding powers, may value a validation relationship with a foreign university (although there is little evidence of this occurring).

While foreign online provision appears minimal to date, rapid consumer ICT adoption, a strong Chinese tradition of distance learning and government recognition that distance learning must play a major role in further expansion, all point to growth in this market. An ageing population, urbanisation, and rapid transition to a market economy demand that China develop its human capital more generally over the next generation. According to one estimate, China faces the task of "creating an economy that supports between 400 and 700 million additional jobs within the next fifteen years,"[34] an increasing proportion of which will demand forms of higher education and continuing professional development. Meeting this need may prove lucrative, but in many areas will put universities and colleges in competition with the private sector.

3 Legislation on Foreign Education Activity in China

Prior to 1995, the few instances of Sino-foreign education co-operation existed outside any specific legal framework. In that year, based on the country's Education Act of 1995 which offered encouraged co-operative provision with foreign partners, the State Education Commission (SEC) produced the first official guidance

---

[34] Ibid, p117.

on foreign education activity – the 'Contemporary Regulation on Operation of Higher Education Institutions in Co-operation with Foreign Partners'.[35] The key points of the legislation, which characterise transnational provision in China to date, were as follows:

- no transnational provision can be provided absolutely and solely by a foreign institution (article 40). All activity must be in partnership with recognised Chinese higher education institutions. All foreign partners must be 'accredited' in their home country in a manner acceptable to the Chinese authorities, and partnerships must be approved by the SEC. Municipal and other local authorities have supervisory oversight of partnerships in their localities. Non-award provision is not covered and, judging by current activity, is free to operate without special permission. Twinning programmes where students complete their award at the home campus of the foreign university also operate outside this framework.
- not less than half the members of the governing body of the institution must be Chinese citizens and the post of president or equivalent must be a Chinese citizen resident in China. The governing body has "full autonomy" (article 26 – within the relevant legal frameworks) over budgets, teaching, planning and operations. Partnerships wishing to offer foreign degrees must obtain additional approval, but no such approval is required in the case of foreign "vocational" awards (article 27).
- partnerships "shall not seek profits as the objective" (article 5); and tuition income "shall be used solely for the expenditure and development of the institution" (article 28).
- partnerships seeking approval must submit detailed documentation outlining provision and objectives. The 1995 regulations list requirements such as a "qualified faculty" and a "fund

---

[35] The full text of the 1995 provision is available at China Education & Research Network, *Contemporary Regulation on Operation of Higher Education Institutions in Co-operation with Foreign Partners*. Available at: www.edu.cn/HomePage/english/education/laws/index.shtml. Last Accessed 22 April 2004.

needed for starting the educational undertaking" but do not prescribe specific qualifications or amounts of money (article 8).
- the "basic language used in a co-operative educational institution is Chinese, but certain courses may be taught in foreign languages" (article 26)
- fines and closure will be meted out to partnerships that fail to comply.

In 1997 the 'Degree-Granting Commission of the State Council promulgated the 'Notice of Strengthening Degree-Granting Management in Activities concerning the Operation of Institutions in Co-operation with Foreign Partners'.[36] This document affirms the 1995 provisions, but adds the important proviso that approval for transnational partnerships will only be given on evidence of demand that cannot be met solely by Chinese institutions; and that foreign partners must enjoy a high international reputation in the fields they wish to offer in China. There are no published criteria for either stipulation and it is unclear how these provisions have been interpreted.

After months of delay and speculation, the third and most recent piece of legislation on transnational provision was released in March 2003. 'Chinese-Foreign Co-operation in running Schools' offers clarification on the 1995 regulations and will come into effect on September 1st 2003. The decree states that it provides additional legal protection to Sino-foreign education institutions and their students, and is cognisant of WTO guidance on market access. It is important to note that the term 'schools' applies to any educational institution/ operation, with an emphasis on higher and vocational provision. An official English translation of the 1995 regulations is publicly available,[37] but there is currently no official

---

[36] The account of this document is based on the treatment in Huang, F. (2003) 'Transnational higher education: a perspective from China', *Higher Education Research & Development*, Vol.22, No.2, pp193–203.
[37] See China Education & Research Network, *Contemporary Regulation on Operation of Higher Education Institutions in Co-operation with Foreign Partners*. Available at www.edu.cn/HomePage/english/education/laws/index.shtml. Last Accessed 22 April 2004.

translation of the 2003 decree.[38] The Observatory has obtained an unofficial translation.[39]

The main clauses additional to the 1995 provisions are:

- degree provision must be approved by the Ministry of Education; sub-degree provision must be approved by the relevant provincial/ municipal authorities.
- partnerships must first seek approval, and then undertake preparatory work. Only once the preparatory work has itself been approved can the institution enrol students. (This clarifies the wording of the 1995 provisions).
- all foreign teaching and managerial staff must have a bachelors degree, any relevant professional qualifications and at least two years teaching experience. At least some teaching staff must be from the foreign institution.
- jointly-run operations must include programmes required at Chinese institutions at the same level (examples given are moral studies, Chinese constitution and current affairs). Curricula and teaching methods are part of the approval process.
- tuition fees shall not be raised without approval; the co-operative must publish annual financial accounts.
- foreign institutions may bring intellectual property (i.e. expertise, reputation, rather than financial or other resources) as their principal contribution to a partnership. Except for foreign institutions expressly invited to operate in China (see below for examples), foreign-sourced intellectual property should not amount to more than the equivalent of one third of total investment in a joint venture.

---

[38] In October 2003, after this report was published in its original form, an official English translation was released. See Ministry of Education PRC, (2003) *Regulations of the People's Republic of China on Chinese-Foreign Cooperation in Running Schools*. Available at: www.moe.edu.cn/guoji/wsfagui/hzbanxue/hzbxtl_e.htm. Last Accessed 22 April 2004.

[39] The Observatory would like to thank Min Li at the University of Leeds for her assistance with the translation of Decree 372; and for the advice of Professor Levy and Professor Yan, as above. The Observatory is confident that the translation is accurate but neither the Observatory nor its sources may be held liable for any errors or omissions.

Arguably, the decree increases the compliance burden on Sino-foreign partnerships. The requirements that students be taught generic subjects compulsory elsewhere, that tuition fees may only be raised on approval, and that curricula and teaching methods are subject to approval, are the main examples. The other stipulations concerning faculty/ management qualifications and experience and use of some faculty from the home campus of the foreign institution might be expected to be standard features of the majority of existing provision. All existing Sino-foreign partnerships are required to comply with the recent decree within two years (i.e prior to 1st September 2005).

To summarise, Chinese legislation on incoming transnational provision is characterised by Sino-foreign partnership. This accords with wider legislation on foreign business activity. In most business areas, foreign firms are able to establish wholly-owned businesses in China, but are not generally permitted to sell directly and primarily to the domestic market.[40] The aim rather is to boost Chinese exports. Some firms get around this by exporting and re-importing but have to shoulder import duties. Firms that establish joint ventures with local companies are permitted to sell to the domestic market. By definition, transnational education in China is 'selling' to the domestic market, hence the stipulation for partnership. At least in some respects, rather than a barrier to foreign involvement, the partnership stipulation offers incoming institutions valuable local knowledge. It is important to note that additional regulation, expanding on the March 2003 decree, is said to be forthcoming.

The sustained proscription on foreign education institutions making a profit in China is in contrast to the aforementioned 2002 law on domestic private higher education which permits a "reasonable return". According to Huang, no Chinese private higher education institution has yet won approval to offer programmes leading to

---

[40] For an overview of forms of incorporation in China, see China Unique, *Forms of Incorporation*. Available at: http://chinaunique.com/business/incorp.htm. Last Accessed 22 April 2004.

foreign degrees,[41] so the combination of a for-profit domestic provider and a foreign provider has yet to arise, at least at degree level. Indeed, the Observatory is not aware of any foreign for-profit higher education institution currently operating in China at bachelors degree level or above.[42] Known examples of other foreign for-profit education activity include IT education firms, such as NITT, and brokers such as CIBT.

None of the regulation on foreign education activity appears to mention online learning or distance learning of any kind. According to Huang, there are no officially approved examples of Sino-foreign online provision,[43] suggesting that approval would be required (see below for some recent examples). While online provision is not directly mentioned in the regulation of Sino-foreign partnerships, any such activity would constitute offering foreign provision in China and would thus appear to fall under the scope of the decree.[44] China has yet to clarify the matter by publishing its offer in terms of 'educational services' under the General Agreement on Trade in Services (GATS – which includes mode 1 – cross-border supply, encompassing distance learning).

In general, and in the case of China in particular, legislation, practice and compliance do not always go hand-in-hand. China is in transition from autocracy to rule of law, and the shift towards a market economy has added to a climate of special privileges and official discretion. The PricewaterhouseCoopers 'Opacity Index 2001'

---

[41] Huang, F. (2003) 'Transnational higher education: a perspective from China', *Higher Education Research & Development*, Vol.22, No.2, p197.

[42] In February 2004, after this report was published in its original form, Western International University and ITT Educational Services (for-profit institutions from the United States) announced that they had both secured 'approved' status from the municipal authorities in Beijing. For a discussion on this development, see Observatory on Borderless Higher Education, 'First foreign for-profit providers to secure 'approved' status in China – but what sort of approval?' *Breaking News*, 20 February 2004.

[43] Huang, F. (2003) 'Transnational higher education: a perspective from China', *Higher Education Research & Development*, Vol.22, No.2, p202–203.

[44] This is also the view of a 2001 British Council report on China referred to above. See British Council (2001) *The International Market for UK Distance Learning: China*, p6.

(designed to identify the incremental borrowing costs of "lack of clear, accurate, formal and widely accepted practices" in terms of regulation and legal protection for business) ranked China bottom out of 35 countries.[45] Regional/municipal/local devolved authority, including special economic zones, also complicates matters. Examples of Sino-foreign partnerships suggest a broad interpretation of the law, rather than point-by-point compliance. The Observatory has anecdotal evidence that some foreign programmes that do not match up to official specifications have secured 'approval' through behind-the-scenes influence of their Chinese associates.

4 Scale of Sino-foreign Cooperation

According to the 2003 decree concerning foreign education activity in China, there are currently 712 "approved" jointly-run education institutions in China, scattered across 28 provinces, municipalities and autonomous regions. 'Jointly-run education institutions' encompass activities ranging from co-developed new institutions, to a foreign degree franchised to an existing Chinese university, and much sub-degree and non-degree provision at various levels of education. (Non-degree provision would include sub-degree qualifications, international schools, language training, IT training and corporate development). The decree states that the USA is the source of the highest number of partnerships, followed by Australia, Canada, Japan, Singapore, UK, France and Germany. The Observatory is not aware of any comprehensive published list of these partnerships. As discussed in the first part of this reports, China's size, devolved authority and ambivalent practice of the rule of law,[46] have led to a situation of both officially approved and

---

[45] See PricewaterhouseCoopers (2001) *PwC Launches First Global Index that Measures The Impact of Business, Economic, Legal and Ethical Opacity On the Cost of Capital Around the World*. Available at: www.pwcglobal.com/extweb/ncpressrelease.nsf/DocID/7AA10B8E3BC832FE852569DE0054519E. Last Accessed 22 April 2004.

[46] For a discussion of this issue across the Chinese economy, see Story, J. (2003) *China: the race to market*, Edinburgh, FT Prentice Hall.

non-approved foreign provision, and various types of approval. For example, the national Ministry of Education regularly publishes a list of "approved higher education joint programmes in China leading to the award of overseas degrees or degrees of the Hong Kong Special Administrative Region". In 2002, this list contained 67 partnerships covering 72 joint programmes, roughly a tenth of 712 total mentioned above. Huang states that the number of ministry-approved degree-level partnerships has risen rapidly, up more than 300% from around 20 in 2001.[47] Comparing the 2002 figures with 2001 data from the British Council suggests a more modest rise of about 50%.

According to Huang, aside from these 72 approved joint programmes, the "remainder ... are only authorised to offer certificates and diplomas".[48] Other data suggests that there are in fact many non-approved joint programmes in China leading to the award of a foreign degree, or such provision 'approved' in other ways. Very few countries collect or publish detailed data on the offshore activities of their universities. The main exception is Australia. Data published by the Australian Vice-Chancellor's Committee in May 2003[49] lists 200 current offshore programmes in China undertaken by Australian universities, 157 (79%) of which involve either Australian bachelors or masters programmes. If one assumes that American, UK and other major source countries are also offering non-approved degree provision on a similar scale, it is clear that the 'real' extent of foreign degree activity is far in excess of that reported on the official ministry list. Indeed, it is unclear what the figure of 712 joint programmes is based on. Given the apparent scale of non-approved activity, the variety of sources of non-ministry approval (e.g. municipal, provincial, local governments)

---

[47] Huang, F. (2003) 'Transnational Higher Education: a perspective from China', *Higher Education Research & Development*, Vol.22, No.2, p199.
[48] Ibid, p198.
[49] Australian Vice-Chancellor's Committee, (2003) *Offshore programs conducted under formal agreements between Australian universities and overseas higher education institutions or organisations*, Canberra. Available at: www.avcc.edu.au/policies_activities/international_relations/internationalisation_initiatives/offshor.htm. Last Accessed 22 April 2004.

and the possibility that some programmes lack any form of government approval at all, the figure may be only an approximation of a phenomenon beyond the scope of official statistics.

The official list from the Chinese Ministry of Education[50] (July 2002) shows the breakdown of approved joint programmes leading to a foreign degree by country:

USA	24
Australia	16
Hong Kong[51]	11
Canada	5
France	5
Netherlands	3
UK	3
Belgium	1
EU	1
Singapore	1

Almost 50% of these officially approved joint degree programmes lead to an MBA, with economics, IT and English language the other major areas. All Chinese partners are universities or equivalent, with some universities (e.g. Fudan) having more than one official foreign alliance. The first ministry-approved degree partnership began in 1994 (La Trobe University from Australia with Yunna Normal University offering an MA in English Language).

As noted above, the AVCC is the only detailed source of information on both approved and non-approved degree programmes from a major exporter to China. Taking the AVCC data as a whole (i.e. covering all countries with reported franchise activity involving Australian universities), all AVCC members report some level of offshore activity. The only exception is the University of Melbourne that has a longstanding policy not to enter into offshore franchising

---

[50] Cited in Huang, F. (2003) 'Transnational Higher Education: a perspective from China', *Higher Education Research & Development*, Vol.22, No.2, p200.
[51] For the purposes of the 1995 regulations, Hong Kong institutions are classified as foreign.

arrangements. The data shows that 27 Australian universities have current offshore programmes in China (excluding Hong Kong SAR). This represents 71% of AVCC's 38 university members, suggesting China as a major site of offshore activity for a large majority of Australia's universities. Offshore programmes in China represent 13% of all reported current offshore activity by AVCC members. Using current data only, China represented less than 2% of offshore activity in 1995, rising to 3.6% in 1998 and 9.3% in 2001, emphasising the growing importance of this market.

While most Australian universities are involved in offshore degree provision in China, some institutions are much more heavily involved than others. Fifty-three percent of joint programmes are offered by only three universities – Charles Sturt, Southern Queensland and Victoria. By level, 50% of programmes are at masters level, 29% at bachelors level, with the remainder a mixture of postgraduate/undergraduate certificates, diplomas, foundation courses and English language provision. By subject, approximately 60% of provision is in the broad area of business and management, with IT, law and education the other prominent disciplines. Approximately 75% of listed Chinese partners are universities or equivalent, with the remainder featuring education service companies, professional associations, government departments and schools. In some cases a partnership listed both a university and another Chinese entity.

The AVCC data also includes valuable information on mode of delivery. For example, the data shows that less than 17% of Australian offshore programmes in China included a period of study in Australia. Just over 25% include at least some study by distance learning, while only 15% are offered wholly at a distance. Overall, this data suggests that the majority of Australian offshore provision in China is offered entirely in China with no study period in Australia, and only a relatively small minority feature distance learning of any kind. There were no obvious patterns suggesting greater or reduced resort to in-Australia study and/ or distance learning over time (although some lack of data on year of first intake inhibited analysis). The AVCC data gives no details of enrollments.

5 Examples of Foreign Activity

Both official Chinese data and information from AVCC suggest the increasing significance of China as a site for transnational higher education. Willis[52] has developed a useful four level typology of Sino-foreign education cooperation.

Level of Alliance	Type of Activities
Level 1	Relatively unstructured alliance; informal programme delivery; staff/student exchange
Level 2	More formalised and strategic; teaching using foreign staff
Level 3	Formal Sino-foreign centre on an existing Chinese campus
Level 4	Joint venture to establish semi-independent/independent campus or institution

Sino-foreign co-operation for provision of foreign degrees would fall under levels 2, 3 or 4. In 2000, Willis commented that level 1 was most common but declining in favour of the higher levels – a trend borne in this paper.

As already noted, there would appear to be no comprehensive list of foreign higher education activity in China. For the purposes of this paper, 20 Sino-foreign education partnerships were selected for analysis (see Table 1). All are at levels 2–4, or do not fit neatly into the Willis typology. The majority involve a foreign university/ college and a Chinese university/ college, but a few involve a foreign company and a Chinese university/ college, or a foreign university and a Chinese company. All operate at least in part at associate degree level and above. The selection is designed to be broadly representative in terms of source countries, focus, level and subject, but should not be taken to imply particular status or standing. As discussed above, not all Sino-foreign education

---

[52] Willis, M. (2000) 'How Chinese State Universities and Foreign Universities Co-operate in an International Education Market: the development and application of a four tiered Sino-Foreign higher education Cupertino model" *ANZMAC 2000– Visionary Marketing for the 21st century: facing the challenge.*

Table 1 Twenty Examples of Sino-foreign Higher Education Partnerships in China (Ordered by Date of Foundation)

Main Foreign Partner	Country	Chinese Partners	Category	Founded
John Hopkins University	USA	Nanjing University	Joint centre/ special programme	1986
China-Europe International Business School	EU	Shanghai Jiaotong University	New institution	1994
Capital Alliance Group (CIBT)	Canada	Beijing Polytechnic University	Foreign-owned	1995
Webster University	USA	Shanghai University of Economics & Finance; University of Electronic Science & Technology in China	Joint centre	1997
Lambton College and others – see below	Canada	Jilin University and Southern Yangtze University	Joint centre	1998
NIIT	India	Various	Foreign-owned	1998
University of New England	Australia	Wuxi South Ocean College	Joint centre	1999
University of Dundee	UK	Zhejiang Wanli University	Quality assurance	1999
University of Waikato	New Zealand	Peking University	Joint centre	2000
University of Southern Queensland	Australia	Kangda College, branch of South China Normal University	Joint centre	2001

(*Continued*)

Table 1 (Continued)

Main Foreign Partner	Country	Chinese Partners	Category	Founded
National University of Singapore	Singapore	Peking University and others	Joint centre; special programme; branch campus	2001
University of Cambridge	UK	Tsinghua University	R&D; e-learning	2001
University of the Incarnate Word	USA	Kangda College, branch of South China Normal University	Joint centre	2002
Amnet	Australia	Chongqing Hailan University	Foreign-owned	2002
University of Liverpool	UK	China Education Service Centre	e-learning	2002
Olin School of Business, Washington University in St Louis	USA	Fudan University	Joint centre	2002
SEG International	Malaysia	CUU Education Development Corporation	Joint centre	2003
Cass Business School, City University	UK	Shanghai University of Finance & Economics	e-learning/ joint centre	2003
Oklahoma City University	USA	part of the Oriental City of Universities, a consortium of public universities in Langfang, China, south of Beijing	Branch campus	2003 (to open)
University of Nottingham	UK	Zhejiang Wanli Education Group	Branch campus	2003 (letter of intent)

partnerships operate within the letter of the law, approval is ambiguous and multi-level, and not all partnerships clarify their legal status publicly. The Observatory is not in a position to comment on the approved status or otherwise of particular partnerships. All twenty examples are listed in Table 1, and some are then discussed in more detail (in some cases data draws on Observatory breaking news stories from the past eighteen months).

Covering nine countries and six categories, Table 1 gives a sense of the range of providers and activities featured in contemporary transnational higher education in China. As would be expected, almost all activity began following the 1995 regulations, and there is evidence over time of more ambition and greater commitment on the part of joint ventures – moving from joint centres/ programmes to branch campuses. Both Nottingham and Oklahoma City were expressly invited by the national authorities to set up operations in China, marking the first official push in this direction. (Both initiatives are yet to open and little detail is in the public domain). Indeed, various so-called 'university towns' are under construction in China (e.g. Suzhou Graduate Town, Xianlin University Town and Guangzhou University Town) hoping to attract provision from foreign universities in some form, and suggesting a shift towards the branch campus model.

The three foreign-owned examples are all private companies, none of which have degree-awarding powers in their own right, but all of which offer degrees through some form of partnership with at least one Chinese university. NIIT, the multinational Indian IT software and training firm, works with ten Chinese universities on joint curriculum development up to bachelors level. Its foreign-owned status would appear to derive from its software business, onto which it has grafted its education arm (which on a general reading of the law would not by itself be permitted to be wholly foreign-owned). Amnet is an Australian IT networking firm that purchased private Chongqing Hailan University in 2002. To comply with the relevant legislation, the firm made the previous head of the university chief executive of the acquisition and allocated him company stock. To this extent, the arrangement was a joint venture under Chinese law, but in effect Amnet bought the university outright. Two Australian public universities are to offer provision at the institution – an interesting combination of a private Chinese university, a foreign company with no previous involvement in higher education delivery, and two foreign public universities.

CIBT (part of Canada's Capital Alliance Group – a large multinational with interests in investments, training and marketing) works with a number of US higher education institutions to offer degrees as part of its corporate development portfolio. Describing itself as a "prestigious institution of higher learning", CIBT focuses solely on China through its subsidiary, CIBT School of Business that has three campuses in Beijing and joint operations in Shanghai, Jinan, Weihai and Zhengzhou. CIBT's main Chinese partner is Beijing Polytechnic University – joint venture partner in CIBT School of Business. Foreign university partners include City University from the United States (a multinational for-profit university) offering an MBA, California State University Sacramento offering certificate programmes in management and ITT Educational Services (the US for-profit college network) offering an IT diploma. The company also mentions credit agreements with other foreign universities (e.g. Portsmouth in the UK, La Trobe in Australia and Assumption in Thailand). CIBT targets the multinational business community, providing western management and technology training to the in-country employees of firms such as Cisco Systems, KPMG and Motorola. This is another example of a complex configuration of public and private universities, both Chinese and foreign, working with a foreign company to deliver higher education.

While still a minority delivery mode, e-learning is an increasingly common feature of transnational higher education in China, as well as domestic provision (see above). The University of Liverpool from the UK claimed to launch the first fully online MBA from a foreign institution in China in 2002, and City University's Cass Business School is an example of another UK institution that has followed suit. The distributed nature of fully online provision reduces the practical value of a local university partner in a particular location.

Promotional work can be undertaken by a specialist (in Liverpool's case, the China Education Service Centre, a government organisation authorised by the Ministry of Education to provide consulting and develop international links). This suggests that greater foreign provision online may disrupt the partnership structures envisaged in current legislation. Liverpool's launch in China is essentially simply extending the marketing of its extant online masters provision, with Chinese students enrolling alongside recruits from many other countries. Indeed, this is an example of a foreign university offering a degree in China without a Chinese university partner (but with clear official approval – Madam Lin Wenyi, Deputy Mayor of Beijing, officiated at the programme's launch in Beijing in February 2002, and a ministry – approved Chinese company is involved in delivery). University of Liverpool offers its online masters provision in partnership with KIT e-learning, a Dutch e-learning specialist.

Alongside the rise of e-learning, face-to-face provision continues to be championed. The Olin Business School at Washington University St Louis flies faculty in from the United States and team teaches with academics from one of China's leading universities (Fudan). Olin explicitly cites this arrangement as indicative of a high quality student experience. As part of the Executive MBA, students are required to complete a two-week residency in St Louis. Face-to-face contact is supplemented with classroom-based online simulations and online distance learning. Taking all twenty examples of transnational provision, face-to-face delivery remains the dominant delivery model (this is supported by the AVCC data- see above).

While the majority of transnational higher education activity in China involves foreign universities, colleges are also vying for market share. An example is Lambton College from Canada. Lambton College, based in Ontario, is a small undergraduate institution with international and business activities that belie its size. In 1999, Lambton established a joint centre with Changchun Institute of Post and Telecommunications (CIPT) and a private company, the True North Group, in northern China; and a second centre in 2001 with Wuxi University of Light Industry in southern China. Lambton offers programmes in business and IT, leading to a diploma (plus English language provision). To enable students to pursue a bachelors degree, the college has partnered with fellow Canadian institutions Memorial University Newfoundland, University of New Brunswick and College of the North Atlantic, plus Northwood University from the United States. Students may either complete their studies in North America or remain in China. As part of the Chinese government's attempt to consolidate public higher education through mergers, Lambton's Chinese partners recently became part of much large entities – Jilin University and Southern Yangtze University respectively. Lambton has remained a key partner, with the joint ventures being named Jilin University – Lambton College and Southern Yangtze University – Lambton College. Lambton has carved out a role as broker between Chinese and foreign universities.

The twenty examples of foreign activity include a number of Asian universities and colleges (India's NIIT was dealt with above). This is a reminder that increasingly it is not only western higher education institutions that see potential in China. The cultural and geographical proximities of Malaysian and Singaporean institutions are particularly noteworthy. Building on a joint MBA with Peking University, National University of Singapore, the country's flagship university, is embarking on the creation of a graduate school in China with Fudan University. The new graduate school will be situated in Suzhou Graduate Town, a large-scale project within the Suzhou Industrial Park (launched in 1994 with the backing of the Chinese and Singapore governments), northwest of Shanghai. The Graduate Town project, which is still under development, aims to attract between 10 and 20 foreign universities to the area to work with Chinese institutions, and to accommodate 50,000 students. The only other foreign university known to already be involved is University of Dayton from the United States. The Suzhou Industrial Park will bear the costs of building the new NUS-Fudan Graduate School and the two universities will be responsible for provision. A number of Malaysia's large for-profit college networks have expanded into China. INTI College in Beijing was established as early as 1993, while SEG International recently announced a joint venture with JPI, a Chinese investment and development firm, to offer MBAs. Both Malaysian institutions boast a range of franchise arrangements with western universities, offering those universities access to the Chinese market but further complicating the quality assurance of franchised provision.

There are a number of atypical examples in the list above. John Hopkins University has run a joint US/ China cultural centre for US and Chinese students with Nanjing University since 1986 – indicative of the characteristics of most Sino-foreign partnerships prior to the current boom in transnational delivery. Provision is short, focusing on cultural exchange for existing students rather than recruitment of new students. University of Dundee in the UK offers quality assurance services to what is now Zhejiang Wanli University, once a private college that sought Dundee's help to attain university status. Dundee has secured preferential progression articulation from its partner, fostering a steady stream of students for overseas study in Scotland. University of Cambridge, as part of its work with MIT, is exploring learning management system functionality under the auspices of the Open Knowledge Initiative (an open source/ open standards co-operative building higher education-led learning platforms and tools). Since 2001, a professor at Tsinghua University has collaborated on the work – including spending time in Cambridge. Building on this initial contact and the resultant platform, Cambridge now aims to offer online English language training to Tsinghua faculty, and perhaps more widely. As well as its local recruitment initiatives described above, National University of Singapore recently established its third 'overseas college' in Shanghai. Mirroring similar arrangements NUS has fostered in the United States, the college is designed to offer select NUS students the opportunity to study and gain work experience in China.

Despite official objection to education institutions with a religious affiliation operating in China (reinforced in the 2003 decree on foreign education activity), two example institutions, University of the Incarnate Word and Oklahoma City University, have strong

Catholic/ Methodist allegiances respectively. Although neither institution is adopting a strongly religious stance in China, this is yet another example of the ambiguous relationship between official Chinese policy and local practice.

Taking all twenty example programmes, and reinforcing AVCC data, almost all provision is in business studies, accountancy, IT, English or law; and most programmes are taught using a mix of local and foreign faculty (although some pride themselves on 100% foreign teaching). Joint centres/ programmes tend to have between about 30 and a few hundred students, with the three corporate players said to be enrolling thousands (precise enrollment figures are rarely available). Against the current regulations, many programmes are taught entirely in English.

6 Conclusion

Demand and supply for higher education in China have expanded markedly in recent years and this is expected to continue. On the domestic front, the government has demanded extraordinary expansion in student numbers and rationalisation of institutions. A large private sector has grown up and is now officially encouraged and protected. Higher education investment in IT and online provision is behind many western nations in some respects, but rapid consumer take-up, a tradition of mass distance learning and state-backed online learning in selected universities suggests this as a growth area.

Partnerships with foreign institutions have been officially encouraged for nearly ten years and can bring valuable additional capacity, status and expertise. Detailed regulation of Sino-foreign collaboration is in place, and the number and sophistication of partnerships are growing. The recent decree on collaboration essentially clarifies existing 1995 legislation, but does add to it in important respects. Time will tell how particular aspects of the law – and any accompanying regulation – will be interpreted and applied in practice.

While few importer countries publish detailed information on the activities of their higher education institutions, evidence from Australia indicates that the total number of ventures involving degree programmes from foreign institutions greatly exceeds the number reported on the official ministry list. There are clear ambiguities over approved and non-approved status, with approval operating at various 'official' levels. The range of known partnerships suggests a flexible relationship between government regulation and local practice. What is indisputable is that transnational activity in China has expanded rapidly in scale in recent years, the extent of foreign commitment is growing and the types of providers involved are becoming increasingly diverse.

It is clear based on the AVCC data that while traditional offshore markets such as Hong Kong, Malaysia and Singapore continue to host the majority of franchise activity, China is increasingly significant and, given its size, has the potential to dwarf all others. Key questions for the future include: how the roles of Chinese regulation, enforcement and local practice will develop; the extent to which official statistics and practice will be aligned; and whether exporter nations will follow Australia's lead and collect better data on the activities of their institutions (not least in the interests of quality assurance). Finally, and related to the last point, as China becomes an increasingly significant site for higher education delivery from all over the world (perhaps the most significant site within a decade), and as delivery involves an ever-more complex mix of public and private partners, what might be a legitimate (and feasible) role for national quality agencies in overseeing activity?

Both Chinese higher education, and foreign higher education partners, are embarking on a period of unprecedented expansion and innovation. The development of mass higher education and transnational provision in emerging economies will play out on no bigger stage than China.